Towards a New Map of Africa

Towards a New Map of Africa

Edited by

Ben Wisner, Camilla Toulmin
and Rutendo Chitiga

London • Sterling, VA

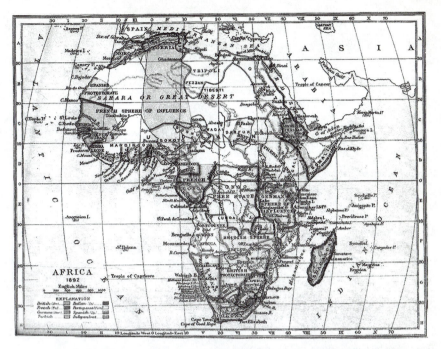

Map of Africa drawn in 1892 by F S Weller for A School Atlas of English History,
edited by Samuel Rawson Gardiner, published by Longmans, Green, and Co., London

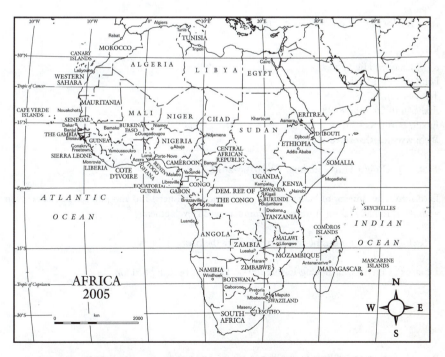

Map of Africa drawn in 2005 by MapSet Ltd of Gateshead, UK, for this book

First published by Earthscan in the UK and USA in 2005

ISBN-10: 1-84407-093-X   paperback
          1-84407-092-1   hardback

ISBN-13: 978-1-84407-093-0   paperback
          978-1-84407-092-3   hardback

Typesetting by Composition and Design Services
Printed and bound in the UK by CPI Bath
Cover design by Susanne Harris

For a full list of publications please contact:

Earthscan
8–12 Camden High Street
London, NW1 0JH, UK
Tel: +44 (0)20 7387 8558
Fax: +44 (0)20 7387 8998
Email: earthinfo@earthscan.co.uk
Web: **www.earthscan.co.uk**

22883 Quicksilver Drive, Sterling, VA 20166-2012, USA

Earthscan is an imprint of James and James (Science Publishers) Ltd and publishes in association
with the International Institute for Environment and Development

A catalogue record for this book is available from the British Library

Library of Congress Cataloging-in-Publication Data has been applied for

Printed on elemental chlorine-free paper

Contents

List of Boxes, Figures and Tables

Boxes

Figures

Tables

List of Acronyms and Abbreviations

ABN	Autorité du Bassin du Niger (Niger river basin agency)
AFFORD	Africa Foundation For Development
AIDS	Acquired Immune Deficiency Syndrome
ANC	African National Congress
ARED	Associates in Research and Education for Development
ART	anti-retroviral treatment
AU	African Union
BARA	Bureau of Applied Research in Anthropology
BBC	British Broadcasting Cooperation
BDP	Botswana Democratic Party
BOAG	British Overseas Aid Group
BWI	Bretton Woods Institution
CAMPFIRE	Communal Areas Management Programme for Indigenous Resources
CARE	CARE International
CCG	Centre for Common Ground (Angola)
CCR	Centre for Conflict Resolution
CDD	Centre for Democracy and Development
CEDA	Centre pour l'Environnement et le Développement en Afrique (centre for the environment and development in Africa)
CEEAC	Communauté Economique des Etats de l'Afrique Centrale (economic community of central African states)
CFA	Communauté Financière Africaine (African financial community)
CFU	Commercial Farmers Union
CGIAR	Consultative Group on International Agricultural Research
CIFOR	Center for International Forestry Research
CNPS	Senegalese national fishermen's association
CNSHB	Centre National des Sciences Halieutiques de Boussoura (centre of fisheries sciences, Boussara)
CODESRIA	Council for the Development of Social Science Research in Africa
COMESA	Common Market of Eastern and Southern Africa
COSATU	Congress of South African Trade Unions
CPPR	Centre for Public Policy and Research
CSKSL	Kayar/St Louis Solidarity Committee
CSO	civil society organization
DAC	Development Assistance Committee
DESTIN	Development Studies Institute
DFID	Department for International Development (UK)
DR Congo	Democratic Republic of Congo
EAC	East African Community

ECA	Economic Commission for Africa
ECC	Economic Committee of the Cabinet
ECOWAS	Economic Community Of West African States
EITI	Extractive Industries Transparency Initiative
EU	European Union
FANTA	Food And Nutrition Technical Assistance
FAO	Food and Agriculture Organization
FCFA	Franc de la Communauté Financière Africaine (African financial community franc)
FDI	foreign direct investment
FEWS	Famine Early Warning System
GDP	gross domestic product
GIEWS	Global Information and Early Warning System
GMO	genetically modified organism
HIPC	Heavily Indebted Poor Countries
HIV	Human Immunodeficiency Virus
HMSO	Her Majesty's Stationery Office (former name for The Stationery Office (TSO))
HPTN	AIDS/HIV Prevention Trials Network
ICASA	International Conference on AIDS and Sexually Transmitted Infections in Africa
ICCAF	Inter-Church Coalition on Africa
ICIHI	Independent Commission on International Humanitarian Issues
ICLAD	International Consortium on Law and Development
ICLARM	International Center for Living Aquatic Resources Management (former name for WorldFish Center)
ICRC	International Committee of the Red Cross
ICRISAT	International Crops Research Institute for the Semi-Arid Tropics
IDEA	International Institute for Democracy and Electoral Assistance
IDS	Institute for Development Studies
IFI	international financial institution
IFREMER	Institut français de recherche pour l'exploitation de la mer (French research institute for exploitation of the sea)
IGAD	Intergovernmental Authority on Development
IIED	International Institute for Environment and Development
ILO	International Labour Organization
IMF	International Monetary Fund
IPCC	Intergovernmental Panel on Climate Change
IRD	Institut de recherche pour le développement (French research institute for development)
IRIN	United Nations Integrated Regional Information Networks
IS	import substitution
KPP	keynote policy paper
LDC	less developed country
LEA	adult life expectancy
LEB	life expectancy at birth
LSE	London School of Economics

MAP	Millennium Partnership for the African Recovery Programme
MDC	Maputo Development Corridor
MDG	Millennium Development Goal
MEMBOT	Macroeconomic Model for Botswana
MFDP	Ministry of Finance and Development Planning
MITI	Ministry of International Trade and Industry
MMSD	Mining, Minerals and Sustainable Development
MNC	multinational corporation
MP	Member of Parliament
MVA	manufacturing value added
NAFTA	North American Free Trade Agreement
NEMIC	National Employment, Manpower and Income Council
NEPAD	New Partnership for Africa's Development
NGO	non-governmental organization
NIH	National Institutes of Health
NRA	National Resistance Army
NRI	Natural Resource Institute
OCHA	United Nations Office for the Coordination of Humanitarian Affairs
ODA	Overseas Development Administration
ODI	Overseas Development Institute
OECD	Organisation for Economic Co-operation and Development
OMVS	Organisation pour la mise en valeur du fleuve Sénégal (river valley development office, Sénégal)
OSTROM	French institute of research for development (now known as IRD)
PDM	Programme de développement municipal
PPF	Peace Parks Foundation
PRSP	Poverty Reduction Strategy Papers
PVO	Private Voluntary Organization
QUNO	Quaker United Nations Office
RCA	revealed comparative advantage
ROCCIP	rule, opportunity, capacity, communication, interest, process and ideology p193
SADC	Southern African Development Community
SADCC	Southern African Development Coordination Conference
SANCO	South African National Civic Organisation
SAP	structural adjustment programme
SCF(UK)	Save the Children Fund, UK
SDI	Spatial Development Initiative
SFLP	Sustainable Fisheries Livelihoods Programme (West Africa)
SIDS	Small Island Developing States
SMCP	Société Mauritanienne de Commercialisation du Poisson (Mauritanian fish marketing board)
SPLA	Sudanese People's Liberation Army
SSA	sub-Saharan Africa
SUNY	State University of New York

TFCA	Trans-frontier Conservation Area
TFP	total factor productivity
TGLP	Tribal Grazing Land Policy
TI	Transparency International
TRC	Truth and Reconciliation Commission
UBLS	University of Botswana, Lesotho and Swaziland
UK	United Kingdom
UN	United Nations
UNAIDS	Joint United Nations Programme on HIV/AIDS
UNCDF	United Nations Capital Development Fund
UNCTAD	United Nations Conference on Trade and Development
UNDP	United Nations Development Programme
UNECA	United Nations Economic Commission for Africa
UNEP	United Nations Environment Programme
UNESCO	United Nations Educational, Scientific and Cultural Organization
UNFPA	United Nations Population Fund
UN-Habitat	United Nations Human Settlements Programme
UNHCR	United Nations High Commissioner for Refugees
UNICEF	United Nations Children's Fund
UNIDO	United Nations Industrial Development Organization
UNOCHA	United Nations Office for the Coordination of Humanitarian Affairs
UNRISD	United Nations Research Institute for Social Development
US	United States
USAID	United States Agency for International Development
USIP	United States Institute for Peace
USSR	Union of Soviet Socialist Republics
VAM	Vulnerability Analysis and Mapping
VCT	voluntary counselling and testing
WAILDSC	West Africa Institute for Legislative Drafting for Democratic Social Change
WCSDG	World Commission on the Social Dimension of Globalization
WEHAB	Water, Energy, Health, Agriculture and Biodiversity
WFP	World Food Programme
WHO	World Health Organization
WTO	World Trade Organization
ZALA	Zimbabwe Adult Learners Association
ZANU-PF	Zimbabwe African National Union Patriotic Front

Acknowledgements

We would like to acknowledge the following for their invaluable help: the International Institute for Environment and Development, London; Oberlin College, Ohio; the London School of Economics; the MARDOS Memorial Library; and Michigan State University map library, for their many and various forms of support.

Thanks are also due to our original list of advisers:

Dr Kassahun Chekole, Publisher, Africa World Press/Red Sea Press
Dr Calestous Juma, Harvard University
Professor Mahmoud Mamdani, Colombia University
Dr Firoze Manji, Oxford University
Dr Thandika Mkandawire, Director, UN Research Institute for Social Development
Professor Roch Mongbo, Université de Benin
Professor Abdi Samatar, University of Minnesota
Professor Ann Seidman, Clark University
Dr Zene Tadesse, University of Addis Ababa
Dr Anthony Zwi, London School of Hygiene and Tropical Medicine

In addition Ben would like to thank Harold and Annette Miller, Bernardo Kilonzo, Germano Mwabu, Ken Westgate, Henry Bernstein, Marja-Liisa Swantz, Chris Wood, Paul Richards and Malcolm Segall none of whom commented on ongoing work but all of whom were inspirations to him in the past as he worked in Africa. Ben would also like to thank James Putzel, Teddy Brett, John Harriss, Tim Forysth and other colleagues at the Development Studies Institute (DESTIN), LSE. Finally, thanks to Phil O'Keefe and John Kirby, who provided comments on the AA.

Camilla would like to thank many colleagues and partners of IIED who have provided much material and feedback on the issues raised in this book. In particular she would like to thank those who have helped with editing and preparation of this book over the last couple of years, including Su Fei Tan, Nicole Kenton, Kate Copeland and Diana Biggs. Jonathan Sinclair Wilson, Ruth Mayo and Victoria Brown at Earthscan have been astonishingly patient editors, for which we are extremely grateful. Additional thanks go to Dzodzi Tsikata and Anne Whitehead for their work on gender and land rights, included in the Introduction.

Notes on Contributors

Mamadou Baro is a Mauritanian anthropologist working on livelihood security issues and rural development in several African and Caribbean countries. He is associate professor at the Bureau of Applied Research in Anthropology (BARA) and in the Department of Anthropology at the University of Arizona.

Simon Batterbury grew up in London and now teaches geography and environmental studies at the University of Melbourne. He has researched rural development and the political ecology of natural resource management and rural development in West Africa (particularly in Burkina Faso and Niger) since 1992.

Jo Beall is a Reader in Development Studies at the Development Studies Institute (DESTIN) at the London School of Economics (LSE). She is a specialist on urban social development and urban governance, and has researched these issues in South Asia and South Africa. She is co-author of *Uniting a Divided City: Governance and Social Exclusion in Johannesburg* (Earthscan, 2002) and editor of *A City for All: Valuing Difference and Working with Diversity* (Zed Books, 1997).

Christophe Breuil works in West Africa for the DFID/FAO Sustainable Fisheries Livelihoods Programme (SFLP). He is based in Cotonou, Benin.

Rutendo Chitiga has just completed her MSc in Environment and Development at the London School of Economics and Political Science. She has worked for the International Institute for Environment and Development (IIED) on the UNEP/GRID-Arendal EarthWire website and is pursuing a career as a freelance writer. Her research interests include youth and development, land issues in Southern Africa and the African Diaspora. She works with African youths in her local community in London.

B. Ikubolajeh Logan is originally from Sierra Leone, where he obtained a degree in geography. He has a doctorate in geography from UCLA and is currently Professor of African Studies and Geography at Pennsylvania State University. His teaching and research areas include sustainable development, household livelihood and coping strategies, and policies for poverty alleviation in Africa. He has written several articles and edited three volumes on these subjects.

Mahmood Mamdani is the Herbert Lehman Professor of Government at Columbia University and Director of the Institute of African Studies. An expert in African history, politics and international relations, Professor Mamdani has an important voice in contemporary debates about the changing role of Africa in a global context. His book *Citizen and Subject: Contemporary Africa and the Legacy of Late Colonialism* (Princeton University Press, 1996) has been hailed as one of the best scholarly works on Africa published in English and won the prestigious Herskovits Award of the African Studies Association of the USA (1998). He is the founding Director of the Centre for Basic Research in Kampala, Uganda, and former President (1999–2002) of the Council for the Development of Social Science Research in Africa (CODESRIA). Professor Mamdani's current work focuses on internal conflict and civil war in Africa, with particular attention given to the political and social restructuring that such conflict elicits.

Firoze Manji is a Kenyan with more than 30 years' experience in international development, health and human rights. He is Director of Fahamu, an organization committed to using new technologies for supporting progressive social change in Africa. He has previously worked for Health Sciences in Eastern and Southern Africa, the Canadian International Development Research Centre in Nairobi, the Aga Khan Foundation (UK) and Amnesty International. He is currently Visiting Fellow in International Human Rights at Kellogg College, University of Oxford. He is also senior editor for the Adilisha series of interactive training materials for African human rights organizations, produced by Fahamu in association with the Department for Continuing Education, University of Oxford.

Thandika Mkandawire is Director of the United Nations Research Institute for Social Development (UNRISD). He is an economist with long experience in the promotion of comparative research on development issues. From 1986 to 1996 he was Executive Secretary of the Council for the Development of Social Science Research in Africa (CODESRIA), based in Dakar. Dr Mkandawire has published extensively on structural adjustment, democratization and social sciences in Africa.

Pierre Morand is a researcher at the Institut de recherche pour le développement (IRD), Mediterranean and Tropical Fisheries Research Centre, Sète, France.

William G Moseley is an Assistant Professor of Geography and coordinator of the African Studies Program at Macalester College in St Paul, Minnesota. He is a human environment and development geographer with research interests in political ecology, tropical agriculture, environment and development policy, and livelihood security. He is the editor of *Taking Sides: Clashing Views on Controversial African Issues* (McGraw Hill/Dushkin, 2004) and co-editor of *African Environment and Development: Rhetoric, Programs, Realities* (Ashgate, 2004). His research and work experience have led to extended stays in Mali, Zimbabwe, Malawi, Niger, South Africa and Lesotho.

Phil René Oyono is a rural sociologist at the Center for International Forestry Research (CIFOR) in Cameroon. He is currently leading a joint WRI (World Resources Institute)/CIFOR research on forest policy change, environmental decentralization, and local democracy in community-based forest management. He has published several articles on local governance of forests in Cameroon and in Central Africa.

Michelle Parlevliet has been the Manager of the Human Rights and Conflict Management Programme at the Centre for Conflict Resolution in South Africa since its inception in 1999. She has designed training workshops for a variety of audiences in southern Africa and now undertakes facilitation and other interventions, and conducts research. She has worked with groups and organizations in Kenya, Malawi, Zimbabwe, South Africa, Lesotho, Northern Ireland, Denmark and Norway, and is also a lead facilitator for a UN System Staff College capacity-building project on early warning and preventive measures. Much of her current work focuses on human rights in conflict interventions and peace-building processes.

Edward Ramsamy is Assistant Professor in Africana Studies and a member of the graduate faculties of geography and urban planning policy development at Rutgers University. His book, *From Projects to Policy: The World Bank and Urban Development,* will be published by Routledge in 2005. In addition to his research in international development planning, Dr Ramsamy's interests include the Black experience in America, comparative race relations and the political economy of transition in post-colonial societies. He has published several articles on regional integration and nation-building in southern Africa and is currently writing a new book on the politics of reconstruction in South Africa. He has also served as editor of *Common Purposes*, a Rutgers University publication exploring pluralism and cross-cultural understanding.

Jesse C Ribot is a Fellow at the Woodrow Wilson Center for International Scholars in Washington, on leave from the World Resources Institute. He has taught rural political economy and environmental policy at MIT, was a research associate at Harvard Center for Population and Development and was a Fellow in Agrarian Studies at Yale. Ribot has published on social vulnerability in the face of climate change, concepts of property and access, natural resource commodity chains, and democratic decentralization of natural resources. His work concentrates on West Africa with comparative material drawn from around the world.

Abdi Samatar is Professor of Geography and Global Studies at the University of Minnesota. Recent publications include: 'Ethiopian federalism: Autonomy versus control in the Somali region' in *Third World Quarterly* (2004) and, co-edited with Ahmed Samatar, *The African State: Reconsiderations* (Heinemann, 2002). He recently served as the Chairman of the Harmonization Committee in the Somali Peace Conference in Kenya.

Ann Seidman, an institutional economist, has taught economics in the Universities of Ghana (1962–66) and Tanzania (1966–6), and served as Chair of the economics departments of the Universities of Zambia (1972–74) and Zimbabwe (1980–83). For several years, she served on the board of directors of the African Studies Association and, in 1990, became President of the association. She has written, co-authored and edited some 20 books and over 80 articles. In 2004, together with colleagues from 20 countries, she and her husband established the International Consortium on Law and Development. ICLAD aims to facilitate international research to deepen legislative drafting theory and methodology, and to exchange information and coordinate programmes to strengthen country-based drafting capacity and law-making institutions.

Robert B Seidman graduated from Harvard University and practised law for 14 years in New York City, and later in Norwalk, Connecticut, before becoming Senior Lecturer in Law (later Presidential Professor of Law), University of Ghana, in 1962. In 1966 he took up a post as Professor of Law at the University of Wisconsin in Madison. He has also served as Visiting Senior Lecturer in Law, University of Lagos; Visiting Professor of Law at the Universities of Dar es Salaam, Zambia, and Zimbabwe; and Visiting Distinguished Professor of Law, University of Witswatersrand (South Africa). Since 1974 he has been Professor of Law and Political Science at Boston University School of Law, becoming Emeritus in 1993.

Thomas A Smucker is an Assistant Professor at the University of South Florida, St Petersburg and Visiting Scientist at the International Livestock Research Institute in Nairobi, Kenya. His research examines land tenure change and its implications for rural development, resource management, and coping with drought in East Africa. He holds a PhD in Geography from Michigan State University.

Oumar Ibrahima Sy works at the Cellule d'Étude et de Planification (Research and Planning Unit) of the Ministère des Pêches (Ministry of Fisheries) in Dakar, Senegal.

Camilla Toulmin, an economist by training, has worked mainly in West Africa, on agricultural, pastoral and tenure issues. She joined the International Institute for Environment and Development (IIED) in 1987, having formerly worked for the International Livestock Research Institute (ILRI) and the Overseas Development Institute (ODI). She wrote her doctorate on livestock–crop relations in central Mali (*Cattle, Women and Wells – Managing Household Survival in the Sahel*, COUP, 1992). She was a member of the International Expert Panel for the Convention to Combat Desertification. Current work includes research on land tenure, livelihoods and poverty in West Africa. Since 2004 she has been Director of IIED.

Alex de Waal is former director of Justice Africa, London, and a fellow of the Global Equity Initiative, Harvard. In his 20-year career as a writer and activist on Africa, he has studied the social, political and health dimensions of famine, war and genocide in the Sudan, and the HIV/AIDS epidemic, especially in the Horn of Africa and the Great Lakes.

Edna Wangui is an Assistant Professor at San Francisco State University, California. She holds a PhD in geography from Michigan State University. She has carried out research on land use and land cover change in several countries in eastern and southern Africa. Her most recent research focuses on the evolution of gender roles and relations in the context of the changing livelihoods of Ilkisongo Maasai of Kajiado District, Kenya.

Ben Wisner began work in Tanzania in 1966, living for two years in a Tanzanian *ujamaa* village. From 1966 to 1995 he worked mostly in Africa on questions concerning wood fuel and rural energy, water and sanitation, drought, flood, community health and food security, summarizing much of this work in *Power and Need in Africa* (Earthscan, 1988). He has taught in the medical school of Dar es Salaam University and taught geography at Eduardo Mondlane University. Wisner was lead author of *At Risk* (2nd edition, Routledge, 2004) and is research fellow at the Development Studies Institute (DESTIN), London School of Economics (LSE) and Benfield Hazard Research Centre, University College London. He is also Visiting Professor of Environmental Studies, Oberlin College, Ohio.

Foreword

New Promise, New Challenges

The year 2005 has seen Africa take centre stage on the global political agenda. The Blair Commission on Africa report was launched in March and was the focus of attention at the meeting of G8 heads of government in Scotland in July. The review of the Millennium Declaration in September at the UN General Assembly will highlight the particular difficulties faced by many African countries in making progress towards achievement of the Millennium Development Goals. In November, the 13th Conference of the Parties to the Climate Change Convention will be hosted in Montreal, which will provide yet clearer evidence for the damaging and escalating impacts of climate change on the security and livelihoods of people around the world. Foremost among those affected are communities in the least developing countries, mainly in Africa. And, in December, in Hong Kong we hope the World Trade Organization will agree a timetable for phasing out by rich country governments of subsidies on farm production and export of foodstuffs.

For many people lobbying for change in global policy, 2005 constitutes a year when we must achieve a radical shift in relations between rich and poor nations. Part of this involves educating the citizens of rich nations about the impacts for good or ill of their actions on people the other side of the planet, whether through the effects of global warming on rainfall patterns, recruitment of scarce nursing staff from Ghana, Malawi and South Africa, or the dumping of cheap farm products on market prospects for Africa's smallholder farmers.

But much of this global debate skates over the huge diversity of experience, perspectives and practice within the continent. 'Africa' is often spoken of as though it is a single country with a single set of problems – universally beset by conflict, hunger, disease and misgovernment. And despite the huge wealth of talent and experience in many parts of the continent, too much pontificating about Africa is carried out by European or North American researchers, consultants and politicians. Too little is heard of multiple voices and visions –particularly women's voices and visions – expressed by those from this enormous and varied land.

Hence, this collection of papers in *Towards a New Map of Africa* provides a very welcome body of evidence of how changes in economy, environment and politics have panned out in diverse settings across the continent. Originally conceived to follow-up Lloyd Timberlake's landmark book – *Africa in Crisis*, published in 1985 – this selection of papers takes a long-term perspective on many of the changes underway. This helps to avoid the snapshot approach so common with much writing on Africa. History has left only too many heavy imprints on the lives and landscapes of today, in the form of institutions, power structures and distribution of wealth. Many of the hardest challenges now being faced involve the righting of past historic wrongs, as we see with the urgent need for land reform in southern Africa. The book also represents a collaboration between a range of actors in Africa, Europe and the US, and builds on networks linking friends and colleagues of many years' standing.

The book rightly argues that there are many positive initiatives underway throughout the continent, which need higher profile and which act as a source of inspiration. Often against the odds, African farmers and entrepreneurs demonstrate great energy and ingenuity in improving their living conditions. Governments need to find much better ways of supporting such dynamism, recognizing the value of a vibrant entrepreneurial culture in which the state provides credible and predictable systems of regulation and administration. We must also acknowledge that there are great challenges to be faced in areas of conflict, where social and political structures have broken down, and the horrifying consequences for families, communities, even whole societies of the continued advance of HIV/AIDS. Global support for the African Union is vital to help them check the causes of conflict, strengthen capacity for peace-keeping and bring to justice the violent warlords who slaughter, rape and pillage with impunity. Thankfully, making serious inroads into diseases like malaria has now become a global project, after decades of neglect.

At the core of development in all parts of the world, a new compact is needed between citizens and the state to restate the principles of accountability and the mutual rights and responsibilities that tie people and government. But non-state structures also count. These play a hugely important role in spiritual, social and economic life in many parts of Africa. They provide in many places the major share of health, education and caring services where government provision is woefully inadequate. They are also of vital importance in providing some kind of check and balance on governments that too often enjoy the fruits of power with little reference to their constituents.

Like so many, I hoped that the 21st century would usher in an era of greater peace and prosperity, in which through collective global action we could take in hand problems of climate change and huge inequities in life chances. The fall of the Berlin Wall could have provided a dividend to invest in development and peace. But the last ten years have shown us a harsher face. The new security agenda and the focus on the war against terrorism have worsened divisions around the world, divisions which we must bridge if we are to uphold the rule of law at all levels – whether local, national or global. We need to press for a global alliance which has security at its heart, but a security borne of justice, equity and respect.

Mary Robinson
President, Ethical Globalization Initiative
New York, July 2005

Introduction

Camilla Toulmin and Ben Wisner

Need for a Replacement for *Africa in Crisis*

When it was first published in 1985, *Africa in Crisis* (Timberlake, 1985) provided a fresh, powerful analysis of the droughts and famine then scourging much of the continent. It forced people to take a new look at why the livelihoods of many millions of people were under threat and the need to move beyond immediate causes – the failure of the rains – to longer-established underlying problems. In his book Timberlake managed to combine a heartfelt disgust at the waste and suffering experienced by so many with a clear description of how power, greed and ignorance had led to environmental bankruptcy. Sixteen years after the second edition of *Africa in Crisis* was published in 1988, many of the same problems confront ordinary Africans and their leaders. Chronic hunger and disease (malaria, tuberculosis, AIDS), war, abuse of power and poor governance still affect large parts of the continent. World market prices for many of Africa's raw materials are at an all time low,[1] and most countries remain highly dependent on foreign aid. However, many of the underlying causes and processes that might lead to more sustainable development are much better understood at the beginning of the 21st century.

Furthermore, in the international movements for millennial debt cancellation, human rights and peacemaking, some of the problems are taking on a higher international profile, generating hopes for more focused attention, if not resolution. Importantly, in the spring of 2004 the presidents of Tanzania and Finland launched the report of the World Commission on Social Dimensions of Globalization. This and other major statements (such as the British prime minister's Commission for Africa) emphasize the need for 'fair' as well as 'free' trade in the global economy. Their insistence on an ethical framework for globalization introduces (correctly in our view) the key question of justice into sterile, technical debates about the situation in Africa. In doing so they recall earlier, similar work (too soon pushed aside and nearly forgotten) by leaders such as Julius Nyerere (the South Commission) and Willy Brandt (the North–South Commission).

Despite these positive trends, the popular image of Africa remains that of 'The hopeless continent' (*The Economist*, 13 May 2000), the entire land mass condemned because of its inability to follow the Western model of economic and political change. The press continues to analyse 'Africa's elusive dawn' (*The Economist*, 24 February 2001), as though the continent has no history and still waits to be 'awoken'. Africa is commonly viewed as being different from the rest of the world, as typified in the US Central Intelligence Agency's report, *Global Trends 2015*. In their picture of the future, Africa is the only continent represented exclusively in terms of hunger, disease and war. It is considered to be moving backwards, and many of its nations are considered to be 'failed states'. Such pessimistic perceptions of Africa remain very hard to dispel. Commenting on the lyrics of Band Aid 20's Christmas 2004 pop song, 'Do They Know It's Christmas?', Mark Curtis, the director of the World Development Movement, says: '[T]he song perpetuates the myth that Africa's poverty can be blamed on natural causes … is it too much to ask for lyrics that inspire people to take action and explain the real reasons why Africa remains poor?' (Curtis, 2004, p31). The lyrics that offend him include reference to an Africa 'underneath a burning sun', where 'nothing ever grows' and 'no rain nor river flows'.

For these and other reasons discussed below, we felt that a replacement for *Africa in Crisis* was needed. This new book reviews similar issues, but from the perspective of a continent now with a free South Africa, peaceful nations, recovering from destabilization and civil war (Mozambique, Angola, Sierra Leone, Liberia), and a Nigeria again with civilian government and a wide regional peacekeeping role. *Africa in Crisis* was written before the genocide in Rwanda, now thought to have claimed 937,000 (UNOCHA, 2004). Its publication also pre-dated the self-destruction of Somalia, the long and costly war between Ethiopia and Eritrea, the frightening disorder in Zaire/Congo that for a time threatened to pull in many surrounding countries, and the appalling genocide in Darfur, western Sudan. Also, of course, AIDS had not yet exploded in eastern, central and southern Africa. A new book must face these tragedies and challenges squarely. Written during the drought and famines that hit the Sahel and Horn of Africa in the mid-1980s, *Africa in Crisis* was able to look back at an earlier Sahel famine (1967–73) and the war in Biafra (1968–70) in order to demonstrate Africa's capacity for recovery and transformation. We now have an opportunity to document how Africa is still moving on, after two decades in which many countries have suffered devastating economic decline and civil war.

But, these past two decades have also generated many successes in citizen-based resource management, locally controlled peacemaking, rehabilitation of child soldiers and recovery of whole communities following brutal war and calamities such as drought, flood and cyclone. New initiatives and models of urban governance and rural development exist in African countries that have failed to grab the headlines; that have instead highlighted 'blood diamonds' and famine. Stories of promise and progress very rarely get into the press, yet they constitute a growing body of experience and enormous promise throughout the continent, on which to build further.

Promise can be found at both local and national levels. Evidence stemming from small-scale projects at community level shows what can be done when conditions are favourable. Research at micro-level also demonstrates clearly the enormous ingenuity and energy that Africa's farmers, traders and migrants put into managing and developing their activities (Toulmin and Guèye, 2003). At national level, Botswana and Mozambique have both achieved much progress against the odds, and are offered as examples of good governance to other parts of the continent (Ferraz and Munslow, 1999; Samatar, 1999). Ghana, Senegal and Mali are similarly often held up as exemplars of democratic process, each experiencing a government and president going quietly, having been voted out of office by the electorate in favour of the opposition.

Homogenizing Complexity

Africa more than most continents has been subject to extensive comment and analysis, mainly by outsiders, who alternate between the following:

- breast-beating anguish, recognizing some responsibility stemming from the colonial legacy and current barriers to trade and migration set up by Western nations;
- condemnation of brutality, conflict, corruption and unaccountable regimes deaf to the needs of their impoverished peoples;
- treating Africa as a laboratory for the latest theories: whether testing the effect of 'fee for service' on the 'demand' for health care and water, the viability of ecotourism, injections of Depo-Provera as contraception, militarized 'peacekeeping' or handing over major areas of government responsibility to NGOs;
- using Africa as the 'control' case or null hypothesis in comparisons with other parts of the world: for example, why the 'green revolution' in agriculture has not taken place in the same fashion as in Asia.

Africa more than most continents is spoken of in aggregate, its enormous size (bigger than the United States and Europe combined in land mass) and huge diversity (more than 1000 languages spoken) condensed into simplistic assessments and generalities.

The African continent spans great diversity within its 7000km breadth and 8000km length, whether in ecological terms, cultural and religious beliefs and practices, histories or social and political systems (Reader, 1997). This tendency to lump together such diversity means that anyone can find support for their particular viewpoint. Thus Western observers establish a false homogeneity and lack of distinction between the very different countries and peoples, their paths and options, often ignoring historical depth or understanding the whys and wherefores of current situations.

This assumption of homogeneity is not limited to the Afro-pessimists. A variation on the theme is the discovery by one researcher or NGO of 'the special project, village, community' that is the model answer to Africa's woes. Much recent writing about Africa focuses narrowly on such 'success stories', identifying the key factors that have enabled such a fragile flower to bloom and lamenting the fact that such plants do not find such fertile ground in which to grow elsewhere.

History is taken selectively, rewritten and dished up to suit particular settings and palates. Most Westerners have had only a very brief acquaintance with African history, having learnt about the most celebrated Victorian explorers – Burton, Speke and Livingston – who 'discovered' Africa's great unmapped interior. Thus, many outsiders are ill-prepared to comprehend the ever-changing mosaic of social and political forces that have lain and overlain the continent from the earliest times. In this matter Africa is simply a more extreme example of the general lack of historical knowledge, the low esteem in which it is held, and reluctance to accept that history matters in helping us understand where we are today (Godlewska and Smith, 1994).

History matters for many reasons, not least as can be seen from the shameful traffic established by the Atlantic slave trade, which has left clear traces on patterns of settlement and social structures throughout the continent. For those areas most affected, it led to a prolonged period of insecurity and disruption, during which people were extremely vulnerable to warfare and capture led by rival polities, as well as rogue raiding parties seeking plunder. The two centuries of havoc wrought upon Africa led not only to a massive outflow of young men and women but also to concentration of energies on military strength and protection rather than trade and productive activity (Rodney, 1981; Davidson, 2004). Thus weakened, colonial penetration was all the easier and devastating in its impact on local livelihood systems (Kjekshus, 1976; Davis, 2001).

Some have argued that one must not ignore the widespread and extensive use of domestic slavery in many African societies from very early times, as if to excuse the West of blame. But this is to confuse two forms of 'slavery' which were radically different in nature and degree. In most African settings, the master–slave relationship was deeply embedded in social relations and structures, and one involving responsibility on the part of the master, so that the slave had some assurance of basic rights to food and shelter. The Atlantic slave trade established slaves as being stripped of all social attributes, to be bought, sold and disposed of solely as a commodity.

History shows its ever-present grip on today's events in southern Africa, where the land is scarred by the invisible wounds of land seizures, people dumped on barren and infertile soils, and patterns of settlement which can only be understood through the lens of conquest. White settlement and seizure of the best lands remain emotive issues of enormous historical charge, given continued dependence for so many on land and cropping, even in marginal areas. Rural settlement still provides the definition of person and identity, despite a century of displacement and a semi-urban existence.

Twenty Years on from *Africa in Crisis*

The world in 1985

When Timberlake drafted and first published his book, the world was in many ways a very different place. Let's take 1985, the date of the first edition, and see what was happening in different parts of the world.

The USSR was still an apparently mighty world power, with Gorbachev not yet in place, and *perestroika* still to come. The Soviet Union played an active role in regional politics and conflicts around the world, providing a check on 'Western imperialism' in the developing world, just as the US devoted itself to stopping the 'spread of Communism' (Kalb and Kalb, 1982; Oyebade and Alao, 1998; Huband, 2001). Examples include the struggles between states in the Horn of Africa, in which Soviet–US patronage shifted between different players according to the rulers in power and alliances with neighbours, and the Portuguese colonial wars in Angola, Mozambique and Guinea-Bissau in which both superpowers took sides indirectly. Now, Russia plays little role in global diplomacy and power games, being too preoccupied by the risks of collapse and insurgency within her own borders.

There was some organized violence, but this was a period before the rise of warlords and most of the civil wars that have affected Africa since the late 1980s and early 1990s. There was conflict in Africa, but it was largely a continuation of colonial wars (Eritrea's struggle to be free from Ethiopia, to which it had been appended by colonial fiat; strife in the former Portuguese colonies) or encouraged by great power Cold War disputes and interests (Ethiopia vs Somalia). Nigeria's civil war in the late 1960s is the exception to this generalization.

Africa in Crisis was written before the impunity of dictators and mass murderers was firmly contested. The war crime tribunals in Arusha and The Hague had not been created, nor the International Court of Justice. The indictment of high-profile individuals such as Augustin Bizimungu (head of the army in Rwanda during the genocide), Augusto Pinochet and Slobodan Milosovic was yet to come. Many of the great despots among Africa's first generation of leaders were still firmly in power: Bokassa, Doe, Habré, Mobutu, Mengistu, Obote (Roberts, 2003).

In 1985, the Asian 'tiger economies' were still growing. Their meltdown lay still in the future. Latin America was struggling with mounting debt but many of its economies were still protected from foreign competition and there was more employment. In the post-NAFTA era, there is much more openness to the global economy, and several countries have adopted the US dollar as a second currency (Cuba, El Salvador, Ecuador, Argentina).

Africa in Crisis was written during and after the 1984 droughts of East and West Africa – the era of Band Aid and massive famine relief efforts. This spurred recognition of the huge, continued vulnerability to drought and disaster and the West's partial responsibility for this disaster and obligation to help. The wholesale shift of development aid for Africa into famine relief during this earlier crisis was still thought to be an aberration and temporary measure. The rise of the 'aid-dependent state', African countries that had effectively become 'wards of the international community', was yet to come. Equally, at that time, while NGOs were starting to become important, especially in delivering the famine relief activities, they had yet to mushroom into their current numbers. Commenting on the massive growth in the numbers and importance of development NGOs in the past two decades, Bergen University's Centre for Development studies observes:

In 1994 ... $8 billion of public development aid was channelled through NGOs, surpassing the volume of the combined UN system ($6 billion). The EU for *instance does not intervene directly on the ground, but rather channels its assistance through a great number of NGOs. In 2003, Norway as a donor country, channels more of its total aid through NGOs than its main cooperating partner countries in the South.* (Centre for Development Studies, 2003)

Moreover, *Africa in Crisis* was written during the first few years of a new ideology or world-view, neo-liberalism, which was adopted by Ronald Reagan, Margaret Thatcher and Helmut Kohl in the early 1980s, to become nearly hegemonic by the start of the 21st century. This ideology promoted free trade, privatization of government functions and assets, the shrinking of public budgets and the civil service, and above all the primacy of the marketplace and market values as the final and most important measure of value in human affairs. Mrs Thatcher's own dictum – there is no such thing as 'society', only individuals – neatly encapsulates the spirit of this thinking, and its scorn for collective action and responsibility.[2]

When *Africa in Crisis* was published, offices were still equipped with telex machines and the rare fax machine was of little value to anyone because so few other offices had one. The explosion in global communications, information technology, financial transactions and capital flows has carved new pathways of interdependence and tighter bonds between those parts of the world so connected. But those without ready access to such systems have found themselves unable to connect, as though operating in a parallel universe. This globalization of networks and communications has brought great mobility of capital, trade and information flows, and generated yet greater levels of wealth for those able to harness these processes. However, with tight controls maintained on migration from poorer to richer nations, disparities depending on chances of birth are becoming ever more extreme.

Finally, *Africa in Crisis* was prescient in the links it made between environment and development, the first edition being written before the Brundtland Commission report on environment and development (Brundtland Commission, 1987), and both editions preceded the Rio Earth Summit of 1992. Yet Timberlake describes very clearly the enormous importance of setting environmental debates within the interplay of economic, social and political forces, and the need to demonstrate the linkages between local and global levels.

What's Happened to the Crisis since *Africa in Crisis* was Published?

Africa's economic global position

The continent's economic position and opportunities have worsened in relative terms.

In 1999 Africa generated 2 per cent of world exports, in comparison with more than 3 per cent (even when excluding South Africa) in 1985 and 3.5 per cent in 1970.[3] Many African countries were poorer in 2000 than they were a decade earlier (UNDP, 2003a). FAO (Food and Agriculture Organization) lists 21 African countries as highly dependent on a single export commodity, more than for any other region of the world.[4] When one excludes South Africa and Nigeria, the rest of Africa received only 3 per cent of worldwide foreign direct investment in 2001, a proportion that had declined from a similar level in 1982–87 to as low as 0.9 per cent in 1996. Indeed, Africa seems still to be suffering from net capital flight (Mkandawire in this volume).

Over the last 20 years, many countries have experienced low and even negative levels of economic growth per capita. A 7 per cent growth rate in GDP has been calculated to be the level required if African governments are to meet the Millennium Development Goals by 2015 (UNECA, 2002b). During the 1980s and most of the 1990s few African nation came anywhere near that rate of growth. In the late 1990s a number of countries began to grow more vigorously – although the continent's average growth did not exceed the 3–4 per cent range. In 1998, when the IMF declared Africa to be the fastest growing region in the world, the average rate was only 3.7 per cent (Africa Recovery, 1998). Nevertheless, the UN Economic Commission for Africa (UNECA) writes encouragingly:

> *In a clear departure from the past, no African country experienced negative GDP growth in 1999, and only one posted growth of less than 1 per cent. In that year 19 countries had growth rates between zero and 2.9 per cent, another 17 were clustered between 3 per cent and 4.9 per cent, and 12 had growth rates between 5 per cent and 6.9 per cent. Equatorial Guinea and Mozambique recorded the highest growth rate: 10 per cent. The number of countries with growth rates above the 7 per cent required to reduce poverty by half by 2015 rose to five, up from two in 1998.* (UNECA, 2002a, p4)

Petroleum has had a controversial role in Africa (Manby, 1999; Manby, 2003). Oil wealth has been partly responsible for civil wars in Nigeria (as early as 1969) and Sudan, and it has often been the focus of corruption and human rights abuses (as in Equatorial Guinea and southeastern Nigeria, where protests lead to the execution by government officials of activist writer Ken Sarowiwa). So glaring has been the theft of government oil revenues that the World Bank stipulated, as a condition for its loan financing the new Chad–Cameroon oil pipeline, the creation of a separate, offshore account for a percentage of oil income to be used, under the scrutiny of an independent international board of trustees, for education and health in Chad. As the US, in particular, looks for non-Middle Eastern sources of oil, Africa will likely see greatly increased oil exports.

Oil will continue to be a major African export. Gary reminds us that:

> *Africa accounts for 14 per cent of U.S. oil imports. A report issued last year by the National Intelligence Council predicted that by 2015, that figure would grow to 25 per cent. Some have started to call the Gulf of Guinea – the arc of oil-rich countries including Nigeria, Equatorial Guinea, Chad, Cameroon, Gabon, the Republic of Congo and Angola – the 'new Persian Gulf'.* (Gary, 2001)

Regional trading blocks might be a means towards the further strengthening of the division of labour and specialization in larger economic groupings. In the past few years the East African Community has been relaunched (potentially combining the internal markets of Kenya, Uganda and Tanzania), and trade within the

Southern African Development Community (SADC) continues to grow (see Ramsamy in this volume). However, West African integration has progressed more slowly (through ECOWAS). Concerning intra-regional trade among the 15 ECOWAS countries, its Executive Secretary, Dr Mohamed Ibn Chambas, recently noted that 'Trade ... amounts to about 10 per cent of the 15 countries' total trade – far lower than the comparable level in other regional trade blocs' (World Bank, 2004). Despite the proliferation of nominal 'blocks' – such as the creation in 2000 of COMESA[5] – most have had limited effectiveness to date (World Bank, 2003).[6] In Chapter 11, Ramsamy takes up an example of such regional economic cooperation and linkage.

Export earnings and access to Western markets have shown little evolution for the better, although there are a few products for European markets where great advances have been made. These include cut flowers, exotic fruit and vegetables, from Kenya (where air freight allows for such perishables to be grown close to the capital, Nairobi). Subsidies to agricultural production in Western countries are estimated by the OECD to have exceeded US$330,000 million in the year 2000 (larger than the combined Gross Domestic Product (GDP) of all sub-Saharan Africa; also larger than the total sum of debt relief accorded to African countries). Meanwhile agricultural support measures in Africa have been comprehensively dismantled. Although there is agreement in principle to move towards tariff-free access for poorer African countries to EU markets, the current subsidy regime is reckoned to cost African economies some US$20,000 million a year, a sum substantially bigger than the total aid flow. Other non-tariff barriers add further constraints on opportunities for African producers seeking to gain better incomes through trade.

The way that African nations and their economies mesh with the rest of the world and a critique of foreign-aid policies have been themes of much recent scholarship. Considerable attention has been given to the impact of World Bank structural adjustment and its more recent poverty reduction strategy programmes on African economies and people (Cheru, 1989; Mengisteab and Logan, 1995; Simon et al, 1995; Hanlon, 1996; Mlawa and Green, 1998; Mkandawire and Soludo, 1999; Albugre, 2000; Bourne, 2003).

Livelihoods and well-being

UNDP's *Human Development Report 1999* ranked 174 nations according to their score on an index that measures a combination of poverty, gender equality, longevity, literacy and economic growth. The 22 lowest ranked are African countries. Likewise, of the 44 Highly Indebted Poor Countries (HIPCs) recognized by the World Bank, 31 are in Africa. In individual human terms, 52 per cent of Africans live on less than the equivalent one US dollar a day (UNECA, 2002a, p2). Africa also has the most inequitable income distribution of any region in the world, with a Gini coefficient of 51 per cent (UNECA, 2002a, p2). Raychaudhuri (1999) observed that 'only 0.1 per cent of the population of sub-Saharan Africa uses the internet, whereas more than 35 per cent of Icelanders use it'.

These statistics are the consequence of the economic trends just discussed. They are also misleading because they fail to capture the ingenuity that ordinary

Africans show in pursuing their urban and rural livelihoods under conditions of great uncertainty, often with little or no assistance from the state. A balance needs to be struck. One must not romanticize the poor and their 'local knowledge' and creativity – because, after all, as we will show below, such 'bootstrapping' still leaves very many people vulnerable to hunger, disease, dangerous urban slum conditions and violence. One must also not fall prey to pessimism and cynicism.

Peopling the landscape

Africa's population grew from 221 million in 1950 to 785 million in 2000, but still remains less densely settled than most other parts of the world. The rate of population growth has decreased since the mid-1980s, due in part to female education and employment, family planning and, from the 1990s, the tragic impact of HIV/AIDS. However, Africa remains the world's fastest growing region, at an estimated 2.4 per cent per annum, and overall numbers may reach 1406 million by the year 2030 (UNEP, 2002a).

Rapid urbanization is underway in much of Africa, as people seek alternative patterns of income and activity and as rural people, who have been displaced by violent conflict,[7] dispossession and collapse of rural livelihoods, seek shelter. This process of rural–urban transformation is sometimes referred to as 'de-peasantization' (Bryceson et al, 2000). Urbanization has both positive and negative aspects. On the positive side, urbanization can make it easier to provide cheap, efficient health care and educational opportunities as well as improvements in water supply and sanitation. Some have also argued that cities act as sites of accelerated social transformation (Mabogunje, undated). On the negative side, the unplanned influx of many hundreds of thousands to cities that are poorly governed and have few formal sector jobs to offer has produced 'mega slums' (Davis, 2004). Urbanization in Africa is sometimes called 'perverse' because high rates of urban migration continue despite low national economic growth or even economic contraction (Davis, 2004, citing Simon, 1997, p95). Growth of what is known as the 'informal' economy has been spectacular in many African cities, and quite dwarfs growth in formal sector employment. Chapter 3 in this volume explores the way in which urban livelihoods are thus cobbled together from diverse opportunities.

Major corridors of urbanization now exist such as the swathe inhabited by 70 million people that runs from Abidjan to Ibadan (Davis, 2004). Lagos alone has an estimated 14 million. South Africa also has a true megacity (larger than 10 million): greater Johannesburg (now more or less coincident with Gauteng Province) runs from Pretoria south through the Midrand and Johannesburg itself and on to Vereeniging and Sasolburg, a gritty refinery town (Wisner, 1995a). Currently, Africa has 40 cities with populations of more than a million and could have as many as 70 such cities by 2015. In 2001 some 297 million Africans lived in urban areas, 38 per cent of the total population. By 2030, the number of urban dwellers could reach 703 million, or 54 per cent (UNEP, 2002b). Shortage of employment and lack of public money for infrastructure mean that many of Africa's urban dwellers must provide their own shelter and make do with minimal services (water, sanitation, drainage, electricity). UN Habitat's report, *The Challenge of Slums* (2003a) finds that 72 per cent of Africa's urban population live in

Box 0.1 *Contested land in urban and peri-urban areas of Ghana*

In Ghana, three major studies have been carried out on how land is managed and transacted in urban and peri-urban areas of Accra and Kumasi, the two largest urban centres in Ghana (Kasanga et al, 1995; Kasanga, 1998; KNRMP, various literature, 1997–2001). Other work by Kotey (2001) and Abudulai (2001) confirms the impacts of land transactions on those with weak claims to land. There is a very active land market around urban centres transforming agricultural land to roads, housing, commercial and industrial buildings, schools and clinics, which some see as 'vibrant' and others as 'ill-disciplined and chaotic'. Building often precedes the formal planning process, and it is common to see notices declaring 'Stop Work', 'If permit not produced by [date] this building will be demolished, by order KMA (Kumasi Metropolitan Authority) (Kasanga, 1998). Great tensions arise from the gains and losses made in Ghana's urban areas, as can readily be seen in Ghana's press. Communities and their traditional leaders are taking the government to court over compulsory acquisition for which there has been no compensation, or when the acquired land has subsequently been sold by the state for commercial purposes (Larbi, 2000; Kotey, 2001). The Land Valuation Board-estimated that outstanding compensation claims had reached US$110 million by the end of 1999.

Villagers argue that their chiefs are selling off village land to 'strangers' – builders and speculators (often civil servants, and other 'urban' elites) without consultation or compensation (Abudulai, 2001; Agbenyega et al, 2001). Poorer people (women, widows and young people) claim that their family heads are benefiting from such transactions while they lose their farmlands and hence their livelihoods (see Box 0.3, below). Buyers are also at loggerheads with sellers over double-dealing, a common topic for Ghana's television soap operas. 'This is a volatile sector where many would-be house owners and tenants have had their fingers burned. In the absence of any legislative control over estate agencies, a number of self-styled estate agents has emerged, many of whom have succeeded in landing their unsuspecting clients in protracted land disputes and expensive litigation' (CDD, 2000). In many cases, there are protracted land disputes between different clans within peri-urban settlements (Kasanga, 1998; Agbenyega et al, 2001). In Kumasi, this issue has been seen as so problematic by the new Asantehene that he has directed that all land and chieftaincy disputes should be removed from the judicial courts and heard by traditional councils. According to Kasanga, this has greatly reduced outstanding cases.

Source: Kasanga and Kotey (2001)

slums.[8] It is no wonder that one of the Johannesburg Earth Summit targets (now added to the Millennium Development Goals)[9] is 'to achieve a significant improvement in the lives of at least 100 million slum dwellers' by 2020.[10]

Thus the majority of recent migrants live in very poor housing and sanitary conditions, whether in the capital city or secondary towns. The 'backwash' effects of urban growth on the rural hinterland are significant. The urban 'footprint' is increasingly indenting the livelihoods and assets of neighbouring rural areas and their people. For instance, wood fuel and charcoal for growing cities are harvested in large areas increasingly far from the urban centres. Such pressures are by no means universally negative, since urban demand provides a valuable chance for farmers to intensify and gain cash through sales of grain, fruit and vegetables. Thus it is common to find a much denser pattern of agriculture in the nearer hinterland of major cities and towns across the continent.

The study of West Africa over the last forty years has shown clearly the enormous importance of urban growth for generating employment, incomes and wealth in their surroundings (Cour and Snrech, 1998; IIED, 1999). As the peri-urban fringe extends, land becomes increasingly valuable and an asset of speculative value. In many places, land has become a commodity to be bought, sold, rented and mortgaged, with all the consequences for poorer groups who cannot raise the necessary funds. At the same time, groups who found it difficult to access land through customary channels, such as women, may find their situation improved, so long as they can find the necessary money to enter the land market. Historically, African cities and the countryside have had a rather fluid interdependence. Cities have often been the refuge during times of rural stress (drought, war); while urban populations often return to their rural origins seasonally, according to stages in the family life cycle, or when urban stress (political oppression, unemployment) become too much (Guyer, 1987).

The resilience and adaptability of the urban poor in Africa is the focus of such authors as Tripp (1997), who recounts the history of urban livelihood strategies in Tanzania. Jones and Nelson (1999) have edited a collection dealing with the ways that urban Africans make ends meet in a number of the continent's growing cities. The dynamism of the informal urban economy in Kenya is made evident in the book, *Jua Kali*, by King (1996) and the regular bulletins of the journal, *Environment and Urbanization*, published by IIED's Human Settlements Programme. Contributor Jo Beall takes up the subject of African urban livelihoods in Chapter 3.

What evidence for a healthier people?

Sadly, the answer has to be, very little. The *World Health Report 2003* describes the situation starkly:

> *Global health is a study in contrasts. While a baby girl born in Japan today can expect to live for about 85 years, a girl born at the same moment in Sierra Leone has a life expectancy of 36 years. The Japanese child will receive vaccinations, adequate nutrition and good schooling. If she becomes a mother she will benefit from high-quality maternity care. Growing older, she may eventually develop chronic diseases, but excellent treatment and rehabilitation services will be available. She can expect to receive, on average, medications worth about US$550 per year and much more if needed.* (WHO, 2003, p5)

Meanwhile, the girl in Sierra Leone has little chance of receiving immunizations and a high probability of being underweight throughout childhood. She will probably marry in adolescence and go on to give birth to six or more children without the assistance of a trained birth attendant. One or more of her babies will die in infancy, and she herself will be at high risk of death in childbirth. If she falls ill, she can expect, on average, medicines worth about US$3 per year. If she survives middle age she, too, will develop chronic diseases but, without access to adequate treatment, she will die prematurely.

Six kinds of disease in Africa accounted for 84 per cent of deaths in 2002 (WHO, 2003, Statistical annex 2). All of these are preventable at low cost. In most cases, the prevalence of this cause of death was greater in 2002 than it was 10 to 15 years earlier.

The list leads off with HIV/AIDS, which killed more than 2.2 million Africans in 2002, totalling 35 per cent of all deaths that year.[11] During the 1990s the regional focus of the epidemic has moved southward from eastern and central Africa, and now affects many people in southern Africa (Wisner et al, 2004, Chapter 4). HIV prevalence in women attending antenatal clinics in South Africa increased rapidly from 0.7 per cent in 1990 to 10.5 per cent in 1995, and then 22.8 per cent in 1998, 22.4 per cent in 1999 and 24.5 per cent in 2000. HIV prevalence rises as high as 36.5 per cent (2000) in KwaZulu-Natal, Mpumulaga and Gauteng provinces and is still exhibiting an upward trend in these parts of South Africa (OCHA, 2004). Death rates among 15–60 year olds more than doubled in some African countries in the late 1980s and early 1990s. In Zimbabwe, which had relatively low adult death rates before the HIV/AIDS epidemic, adult mortality among men nearly tripled between 1988 (when the second edition of *Africa in Crisis* was published) and 1998. Among women in Zimbabwe, the probability of dying between ages 15 and 60 more than doubled over the same period. In Zambia, during that period, mortality among men nearly doubled, and among women it increased by two-thirds (UNAIDS/WHO, 1998). One must remember, of course, that the year when *Africa in Crisis* was first published, 1985, was the year the first ever antibody test for HIV was licensed and the year of the first international conference on HIV/AIDS (HPTN AIDS Timeline, 2001). In combination with violent conflict, population displacement, malnutrition and other diseases, the progress of HIV/AIDS in Africa has been astoundingly rapid and catastrophic. The problem of HIV/AIDS in Africa is so severe and has so many ramifications (production, governance, social structure) that we devote the whole of Chapter 4 to this topic.

Next comes malaria, preventable via insecticide-treated bed nets, environmental management (management of watery breeding sites of the mosquito) and preventive drugs for pregnant women and young children. It killed over a million, accounting for 17 per cent of deaths in Africa in 2002. This is a terrible scourge of Africa. In the words of Dr Wen Kilama, Tanzanian parasitologist who is chair of the Malaria Foundation International, '[t]he Malaria epidemic is like loading up seven Boeing 747 airliners each day, then deliberately crashing them into Mt. Kilimanjaro' (Kilama, 2004). One bright spot on the horizon was the report in late 2004 of a successful trial in Mozambique of a possible malaria vaccine (Boseley, 2004). In the trial that involved 2000 children, vaccinated children were 58 per cent less likely to develop severe, life-threatening malaria.

Diarrhoeal diseases (11 per cent) and childhood diseases (12 per cent) are jointly in third place. These deaths are in some ways the most shameful as there have been international and national commitments to providing safe domestic water supplies and childhood immunization for several decades. Here, too, Africa seems to be slipping backwards. The incidence of cholera, the most deadly of the diarrhoeal diseases, is increasing. During the first six weeks of 2004 alone, the WHO registered epidemic outbreaks of cholera in Burundi, Cameroon, Mali, Mozambique, South Africa and Zambia (WHO, 2004). The most dramatic threat to international efforts to maintain childhood immunization status concerns polio. During 2004 new cases appeared in northern Nigeria, where several state governments refused to allow polio vaccination because of rumours of corrupted vaccines. In war-ravaged countries, immunization has also been disrupted. The measles vaccine, for example, requires a 'cold chain' that is impossible to maintain in situations of violent conflict. Thus in 2002 half of all deaths in the category 'childhood diseases' were from measles (probably interacting with malnutrition).

Tuberculosis (5 per cent) and 'maternal conditions' (death related to pregnancy and childbirth) (4 per cent) account for more than half a million more African lives wasted. Because of problems with health care delivery, much tuberculosis is untreated or insufficiently treated, so that antibiotic resistant strains have developed. In the case of maternal mortality, the contrasts with the rest of the world remain a testament to the lack of status, power and access enjoyed by African women. In 1995, Africa accounted for approximately 30 per cent of all maternal deaths in the world, and in that year 21 countries in Africa had maternal mortality rates above 1000 per 100,000 (equivalent to 1 per cent). In rank order, the highest (rate of 1.3 per cent or more) were Rwanda, Sierra Leone, Burundi, Ethiopia, Somalia, Chad, the Sudan, Côte d'Ivoire, Equatorial Guinea, Burkina Faso, Angola and Kenya (UNICEF, 2003). These rates should be compared with ratios of 8 per 100,000 live births in Japan, 7 in Italy, 6 in Australia, and 4 in Sweden (1990–94 data) (Government of Australia, undated). This persistent gap is equivalent to maternal death rates being 100–250 times higher in most African countries when compared to rich countries. And it becomes all the more poignant in the light of the decision by the US in July 2002 to cut US$34 million from its support for the UN Fund for Population Activities, one of whose principal functions is to assure safe motherhood (UNFPA, undated). Women bear a very heavy disease burden in Africa, with those aged 15–24 constituting the majority of new HIV/AIDS infections, more than twice the rate for young men (Fleshman, 2004).

During the years since publication of *Africa in Crisis*, African nations have cut back funding for public health care, privatized some or all of it under the rubric of 'cost sharing', and relied increasingly on overseas donor budget support and NGOs for routine health care provision. In the early 1990s NGOs provided anything from 30 per cent to 60 per cent of health services in a sample of 12 African countries (Turshen, 1999, pp86–91). The trend towards African state abandonment of its public health mandate (pushed by the financial pressure of structural adjustment programmes) had been evident and discussed from the late 1980s (Wisner, 1992). What makes the situation even worse today is that the remaining health care capacity is swamped with the needs of patients living with HIV/AIDS and its opportunistic infections.

The international debate about the cost and accessibility of pharmaceutical products to poor people is highly significant to Africa. A landmark court case in South Africa in December 2001 saw 32 international drug firms suing to block production or import of inexpensive, generic medications for HIV/AIDS. Owing to local and global protest and extremely negative publicity, the pharmaceutical companies withdrew their suit. This case could provide a forerunner of major changes in other fields in which adherence to private intellectual property rights and return on capital can be shown to bring unacceptable levels of misery at global level. However, despite the availability of much cheaper generic anti-retroviral treatment (ART), in 2003 only 50,000 of the 4 million people living with AIDS in sub-Saharan Africa have access to it (WHO, 2003, Overview, p3). As recently as March 2004, the Bush administration resisted purchase of generic ART through its consolidated programme for global AIDS (based in the US State Department).[12]

Also important is the question of why 90 per cent of the research on new drugs is focused on diseases that affect the 10 per cent of world population who live in the rich world. There needs to be more work on a vaccine for malaria. There have been some recent signs that more investment is finally going in this direction. The UN Secretary General's global initiative to raise funds to address HIV/AIDS, malaria and tuberculosis is an inspiring example of what can be done when the energies and strengths of collective action are reaffirmed. Another is the work, supported by the Gates Foundation,[13] that reported some moderate early success with a malaria vaccine in October 2004 (Boseley, 2004).

What can be said of educational progress?

Primary education, especially for girls, has also been a major national focus and international donor commitment. Education is given prominence among the Millennium Development Goals and shares a place with reduced child mortality, addressing hunger, and improvements in water and sanitation. Worldwide from 2000 there has been an effort to get some 100 million children, who are of school age but who do not attend school, to enrol and attend. Many of them are girl-children (Colclough, 2004). A UNESCO progress report on Education for All published in 2004 found that:

> Sub-Saharan Africa has low enrolments rates and strong gender disparities and inequalities. A third of the countries have GPIs [Gender Parity Index] of under 0.76 – Chad, Burkina Faso, Mali, Ethiopia, Guinea, Guinea-Bissau, Côte d'Ivoire, Benin, the Central African Republic, Mozambique and Liberia. (UNESCO, 2004)

This international effort includes abolishing primary school fees which act as a major impediment to enrolling all Africa's 42 million primary-school-aged children (Machipisa, 2000). Having missed the international goal of achieving universal primary schooling by the year 2000, the Millennium Declaration has revived this target and has given the world, including Africa, until 2015 to reach it. Of the regions of the world, Africa has the biggest challenge: to get from 51 per cent enrolment in 2000 to 100 per cent by 2015. South Asia only needed to climb from 74 per cent of that age group in school, and North Africa and the Middle East began with a baseline enrolment in 2000 of 83 per cent (Millennium Development Goals, 2000).

Current analysis of progress towards this education goal shows little advance during the first three years (2000–03), with only a 'slight increase' in sub-Saharan

Africa (UN, 2004). The report notes that there are a number of African countries where only one in three children of school age goes to primary school. At the same time, HIV/AIDS has produced many orphans who face many other challenges in addition to finding the wherewithal to attend school. School systems are also stressed because of teacher deaths from HIV/AIDS.

The other, and far darker and more troubling, side of the coin is continued trafficking of possibly as many as 100,000 African children a year, a problem that persists despite reports by UNICEF and human rights organizations (*Guardian*, 2001; Gillan, 2004; UNICEF, 2004b).

Establishing new political systems

In 1985, Nigeria was ruled by an unelected military leader, Muhammadu Buhari. South Africa, of course, was still under the yoke of the apartheid system. That year saw Daniel Arap Moi at the height of his dictatorial power in Kenya (while 1986 saw the publication of his curious book that defined politics as *Nyayo*, literally, following in Moi's footsteps). Since the publication of *Africa in Crisis*, the African continent has had a mixed experience with democracy, although overall the balance has shifted in favour of more accountable structures of governance. By 2004 Nigeria, South Africa, Kenya, Senegal, Mali and Ghana all had successful multi-party elections. In 2002 alone, 19 African countries held presidential elections (of varying degrees of fairness). However, there are also plenty of other examples, such as Zimbabwe, Uganda, Eritrea and Burkina Faso, where presidents are keen to ensure that they stay in power and show themselves willing to change the constitution to achieve this goal.

The move towards more democratic systems has been accompanied by an improvement in human rights and greater checks on corrupt behaviour, through an active and open press in many places. However, the record is far from unblemished, even in those countries that profess to follow democratic principles. Investigative journalists cannot be assured an easy time, and may find their lives threatened for delving too deep into the business deals of highly placed people and their family members. In 1999 Human Rights Watch Africa listed countries where the 'political landscape [has] historically been dominated by single-party structures, de jure and de facto', and where they believe it is still difficult for people to participate in political life: Angola, Burkina Faso, Cameroon, Chad, Côte d'Ivoire, Equatorial Guinea, Gabon, Gambia, Guinea-Bissau, Kenya, Niger, Tanzania, Togo, Zambia and Zimbabwe (Human Rights Watch Africa, 1999).

Of these, by 2004 only Kenya had witnessed an internationally accepted multiparty election. In its report on human rights in Africa for 2002, Human Rights Watch adds Eritrea, Sudan and Swaziland to this list of countries that 'continued to undermine progress towards respect for human rights and the rule of law across the continent' (Human Rights Watch, 2003).

There has been a significant shift towards decentralization, with many countries across the continent establishing new or revived systems of elected local government. The explicit objectives of such processes to decentralize power have been to bring government closer to the people and ensure that local decision-making is better informed by knowledge of local circumstance. The less overt agenda

---

Box 0.2 *Women's relations with the state*

Women in Africa have particular reasons to be disillusioned with the state, which in many cases has had a history of resisting women's demands. There is a poor record of women's participation in government and in politics at national and local levels. The main holders of power nationally do not even need to use the language of custom to undermine gender justice and women's claims. Recent manoeuvring around Uganda's new land legislation is instructive in this regard. Highly effective lobbying and alliance-building strategies by Ugandan women's groups and lawyers resulted in a clause on spousal co-ownership being included in the draft land legislation. Yet despite assurances that this clause would be passed, the final late night parliamentary sittings passed the new land law without this provision. This clause has not been reinstated to this day.

The main problem in achieving greater democratization is that women have too little political voice in decision-making bodies, whether in local level management systems, within the formal law, or within government and civil society itself. Use of indigenous structures is also open to abuses of power, since the operation of new or modified local institutions does not take place in a vacuum, but depends on the way in which local and national power relations feed into the new structures established.

Source: Tsikata and Whitehead (2004)

---

has often involved the desire by central governments to establish elected local bodies that are dependent on central power and patronage and displace customary structures of authority. But traditional chiefs have shown they will not go without a fight, as seen in South Africa over contested authority regarding local government roles and powers. Equally, traditional chiefs are fighting to maintain their prerogatives regarding the management of land rights in Burkina Faso, Niger and Ghana.

An additional question about decentralization is whether, and under what circumstances, it actually benefits ordinary people as opposed to a local elite. Chapters 9 and 10 are devoted to questions concerning local government and decentralization.

'Good government' and 'democracy' are the subject of much recent work, which explores the relationship between democracy and development. Ake (1996) and Abrahamsen (2001) believe that the governmental reforms required by the World Bank and IMF have little to do with the establishment of deeply rooted democratic institutions. The widespread poverty produced by this economic conditionality is not an environment in which democracy is likely to flourish. Some argue that development must come first, and then democracy can become rooted among ordinary people. Those who have looked at the subject from the point of view of civil society and the aspirations of the masses (Bayart, 1993, in a book subtitled, appropriately, *The Politics of the Belly*; and Kasfir, 1998), come to similar conclusions. Others are more concerned with formal methods of institution building (Hyden et al, 1999; Mengisteab and Daddieh, 1999). Still others emphasize the failures of governance, for example de Waal in *Famine Crimes* (de Waal,

1997). Salih (2001) has argued that Western-style democracy is simply incompatible with the social relations in ethnically diverse and tribal situations, and that uniquely African systems can utilize customary institutions in ways that are, in fact, participatory and fair (in contrast to Mamdani in this volume). In Chapter 7, the focus is the basic legal framework that underlies 'good governance', while Chapters 10 and 11 delve deeper into its details at national level.

Spiralling conflict and disorder

Processes of positive political change and decentralization are by no means universal in Africa. During the 1990s the number of violent conflicts in Africa doubled from 11 to 22 (USIP, 2001). Areas of civil disorder and conflict have grown and spread, spilling over from one nation to another as neighbours become sucked into another's war. Thus has developed a vortex of violence, plunder and anarchy sweeping Sierra Leone, Liberia and patches of Guinea, occasionally whipping up trouble in bordering Côte d'Ivoire. This appears to have mirrored the larger scale events in the Congo and Great Lakes area where, at one point, seven African nations fought on one side or the other of the complex civil war that tore Zaire/ DR Congo apart. The chaos of civil disorder can also cloak an increase in the flow of commodities such as diamonds and ivory through illegal channels. Lack of effective government has also led to international plundering of ocean fishery resources within the territorial waters of Somalia, where there has been no government to protest or try to stop it, and a large but unknown amount of trafficking in children as cheap labour throughout West Africa, as domestic servants and farm labour.

There has been a dramatic increase in the number and scale of violent conflicts since the publication of *Africa in Crisis*: major conflicts in Somalia, Ethiopia, Eritrea, Sudan, Rwanda, Burundi, Liberia, Sierra Leone, Côte d'Ivoire, Chad, Mozambique, Angola, Congo, Zimbabwe and Uganda; minor ones in Lesotho, Malagasy Republic and Guinea-Bissau. As a result, Africa is awash with a large number of small arms, and many countries are heavily mined. Angola has the highest number of amputees injured by landmines in the world.[14] The human cost in lives and displacement has been staggering: 2.5 million people may have died quietly and invisibly (to the international observer) in the forest in eastern Congo since 1998, according to one estimate (IRIN, 2002). The WHO estimated in September 2004 that 6000 to 10,000 displaced persons in Darfur region of western Sudan were dying each month of disease and hunger, having been among the 1.2 million driven from their homes by the Janjawid militia supported by the Sudanese state (IRIN, 2004). By October 2004 a WHO report estimated that 70,000 had succumbed to hunger and disease in the camps over the previous year and a half (Reuters, 2004), confirming the mortality rate of 10,000 per month.

On the positive side, some long-standing conflicts have ended (Ethiopia vs Eritrea) or seem to be in the process of being resolved (DR Congo, southern Sudan). Also, in 2004, African defence ministers met in Libya and drew up a plan for an All Africa Rapid Deployment Force in order to intervene in such conflicts. Already there had been intra-African peacemaking and peacekeeping operations that involved Nigeria and other ECOWAS members in West Africa (in Sierra

Leone) and South Africa with Botswana in the Kingdom of Lesotho. Very positive has also been the rise in the large number of local, national and regional civil society institutions in Africa dedicated to conflict management, monitoring, early warning and peace-building. Some are very localized, such as the Wajir (a small town in the north of Kenya) Peace and Development Committee. Some work in a single zone within a nation, such as the Acholi Religious Leaders' Peace Initiative in Uganda or Kenya's Mombasa-based Coast Interfaith Clerics' Peace Initiative. Still others are national or regional in scope: the West African Network for Peace Building (headquartered in Accra, Ghana), Uganda's Centre for Conflict Resolution, Kenya's Women's Peace Forum and Nairobi Peace Initiative-Africa (Nairobi Peace Initiative, 2003). Chapter 12 is devoted to the question of human rights and conflict resolution in Africa.

However, the volatility of the 'peace' in a number of areas was underscored in October and November 2004 when violence again erupted in Liberia, Côte d'Ivoire and in Somalia, where the armies of two of the three 'administrative regions' of this disintegrated state – Puntland and Somaliland – fought on their border.

Several recent works shed light on the difficulties but also the successes in providing the peace and stability necessary for any kind of development (Chabal and Daloz, 1999; Mekendamp et al, 1999; Ouédraogo, 1996). Richards (1996) provides a unique perspective of survival during civil disorder through the eyes of young combatants in Sierra Leone. Others, especially those involved with faith communities, have attempted the shift in viewpoint practised by Richards, eyeing the world from the standpoint of different parties in conflict, for example, in a series of consultations reported by the Quaker United Nations Office (2001, 2002). Møller (2001, pp3–4) analyses the economic aspects of violent conflict – pillage, privatization of security and illegal trade – an important perspective also developed by Duffield (2001, 2002).

Overseas development assistance

Levels of overseas development assistance have declined during the 1990s (Inter-Works Europe, 1998). Some countries have been largely abandoned by Western donors, as pariah states (Sudan), insufficiently important for Western interests (Chad, Niger), or not strongly enough committed to the precepts of the Washington consensus which now dominates world economic and political policy-making. With debt, there has been significant movement due to concerted lobbying by an alliance of civil society groups. This has helped affirm G8 commitment to debt relief, and got the Highly Indebted Poor Countries (HIPC) programme underway, though some question the speed and significance of the benefits granted to date. Some countries (eg Mozambique and Uganda) depend on overseas development assistance for as much as 50 per cent of government expenditure. Clearly this is not a 'sustainable' situation and leaves in question the notion of national sovereignty. There are also questions regarding the conditions attached, and the role of different groups in designing the Poverty Reduction Strategies which governments must prepare in order to receive debt relief, the degree of national 'ownership' of such an externally imposed poverty focus and the PRSP's measurable impact on poverty (Booth, 2001).

More attention is needed on how the benefits of debt reduction or debt forgiveness will be distributed through society, for instance by increasing access to health care or education. Is it reasonable to expect that the same national governments that in many cases incurred the debt through military expenditure, prestige projects or graft will be able to oversee a fair and poverty-focused distribution of benefits? Will these programmes simply encourage them to borrow again, repeating the cycle? How to bridge the need for such poverty-focused programmes to be constructed on in-country priorities and debate, with the desire by Western donors to ensure that benefits do indeed reach poor people rather than being appropriated by the elite? There is continuing tension between micro-management of the process by aid agencies and their protestations of the need for 'country-ownership'.

One symptom of continuing economic decline in many African countries, despite the 'successes' in structural adjustment periodically announced by the World Bank, is provided by the increased numbers of African migrants attempting to enter Europe, Canada and the United States, legally or illegally. Some of these migrant workers experience tragic ends, such as a young legal immigrant to the US from Mali, a street vendor in New York City, named Amadou Diallo, who was shot 41 times in 1999 while trying to enter his front door, unarmed, by an elite group of New York Police. One should also think of the hundreds of Africans who die trying to cross from Morocco to Spain in small boats.

The post-Cold War world has been dominated by Western liberal economic models. Twenty years ago, the beginnings of structural adjustment (eg Mali, 1982–83 and most other African governments since then) aimed at radically revising the responsibilities and powers of government, through a mix of measures including cuts in employment, reduced services and 'cost recovery' for education, health and other services, devaluation, increased tax and reduced expenditure, cuts in government support for agriculture, credit and privatization of state-owned enterprise. Assessing the benefits and costs of these major shifts in policy portrays a mixed experience, with views divided according to place and ideology. Mkandawire (Chapter 6) fails to find the promised benefits (eg internal savings that would be invested or increased external investment) after 20 years of such 'structural adjustment', and he concludes that 'maladjusted' African economies are not able to benefit from globalization.

These debates mirror in the African context the general unease felt by labour, environmental and human rights groups which have been actively lobbying against the uncontrolled growth of free trade at the WTO in Seattle, Prague and Cancún. Such misgivings finally found mainstream articulation in the report of the World Commission on the Social Dimensions of Globalization, chaired jointly by the Presidents of Tanzania and Finland (WCSDG, 2004).

In his speech delivering the report of WCSDG, President Benjamin Mkapa of Tanzania juxtaposed 'decisions' and 'actions':

At Monterrey, donors made commitments to increase Official Development Assistance by US$16,000 million a year by 2006. Even if these commitments were to be met, which as matters stand is highly unlikely, this is still only a third of the actual requirements of at least US$50,000 million a year in additional Official

> *Development Assistance if MDGs are to be met. In reality, in 2002 Official Development ment Assistance from OECD countries increased by a mere US$6000 million over the previous year. Reviewing this trend, the 2004 edition of the OECD's Development Co-operation Report concludes that such levels of increase, while a step in the right direction, are nowhere close to ensuring Monterrey commitments are met, and MDG's achieved.* (Mkapa, 2004)

The other themes President Mkapa emphasized were debt relief, removing rich country barriers to imports from Africa (such as the huge subsidies that the US, EU and Japan still pay their farmers) and, above all, the need for a system of public accountability for the new institutions of economic globalization.

However, rather than place discussion of Africa squarely within international debates about globalization in the manner in which Tanzania's president did, 'the African problem' is still too often seen as unique, and is projected through the lens held by outsiders – aid agencies, journalists and politicians – that bring a set of unspoken assumptions and interests. The aid industry has a particularly ambiguous position, needing Africa's poverty to justify itself and gain additional resources, while also needing the occasional success to demonstrate 'aid effectiveness' and combat 'compassion fatigue' among taxpayers (Hanlon, 1991, 1996; Hancock, 1992; Moeller, 1999; Vaux, 2001). A cynic might see the setting of the Millennium Development Goals to be achieved in 2015 as a means to ensure themselves at least a medium-term future. Competition among Cold War rivals has been replaced by competition between aid agencies, to develop and present rival approaches and policy thrusts. Behind a language of 'partnership' and 'country-driven' strategies, the practice remains firmly to push and shove governments to follow the principles and policies espoused by those in Washington, The Hague, London, Tokyo or Paris.

Aid agencies vie with each other for the best rhetoric and catchy buzzwords, for the new approach which will radically transform the development prospects of a particular country, whether it be the World Bank's Comprehensive Development Framework, the Poverty Reduction Strategies, the Sustainable Livelihoods framework or the sector approaches, donor round tables and National Sustainable Development Strategies of yesterday and today. These have spawned a bewildering cycle of acronyms, methods and approaches pushed by rival aid agencies, each requiring the recipient nations to master a new language, reporting requirements and associated training manuals.

The aid machinery is currently being driven by the International Development Targets agreed in 1997 – reaffirmed by the Millennium Assembly of the UN in 2000 and again at the Johannesburg Earth Summit – which include the pledge to halve the number of those living in poverty by the year 2015. While this constitutes an estimable commitment, all attention is now focused on 'poverty plans and targets' to the neglect of the priorities of last year and the year before. It seems as though the aid community finds it impossible to focus on more than one thing at a time.

African countries are far more vulnerable to such donor whims, because of their far greater reliance on aid and debt relief. Countries like India have donors queuing up to be allowed to give them money, and can politely tell a bossy donor that they have little need of their money. Indeed, the Indian government has recently told its donor nations that it will only be accepting aid from the largest six agencies, because of the transaction costs and general hassle associated with servicing the donors' agendas. By contrast, many African states depend for their economic and political stability on the flows of income and investment provided by the West and must therefore dance to their tune. As tunes change, so governments learn new steps. Countries like Mali and Burkina Faso, which gain 15–20 per cent of their GNP from aid monies, have seen a steady stream of policy changes. These include economic liberalization, agricultural adjustment measures, decentralization, privatization of the key sectors, restructuring of government services – a standard set of measures which differ little from country to country, only the timing and degree of pressure differing between Ouagadougou and Bamako, Maputo and Lusaka.

The land question

Since *Africa in Crisis* was published, the land issue in Africa has risen rapidly up the political agendas of both governments and donors. The drama of rival land claims in southern Africa (especially in Zimbabwe) has received most public attention and press coverage, but contests over land tenure are underway in Kenya, Mali, South Africa and Botswana (Woodhouse et al, 2000) and elsewhere on the continent. In the West African country of Côte d'Ivoire, one-third of the country's population have come from neighbouring states, above all Mali and Burkina Faso. Over the last generation, they have made their homes and established cocoa and coffee farms on land bought or borrowed from local people. But such inflows of migrants have eaten up the land reserves in many southern areas, bringing tension and conflicts between newcomers and local people, who want now to take back 'their' land. But who do these farms belong to – the indigenous forest dwellers or those who have invested their capital and labour in clearing, planting and maintaining their holdings? Government policy has been unclear, sometimes favouring the newcomer, and other times supporting indigenous peoples. New legislation passed in 1998 now clarifies the rival claims by making it impossible for non-Ivorians to hold land as property.

Land issues have been highlighted in a number of recent collections, which take a variety of perspectives. Adams (2000) presents a picture of political vacillation and institutional constraint to help explain the snail's pace process of land reform in South Africa since 1994. Lund (1993, 2001) and Berry (2001) both provide perspectives on land as contested property, based on detailed fieldwork in West Africa. These studies show the complexity of land issues and the need to understand the bargaining strategies of different actors within a broader social, economic and political context (Woodhouse et al, 2000). Questions about land tenure and rural livelihoods have been taken up in two edited collections (Bryceson et al, 2000; Toulmin and Quan, 2000). There are also excellent contributions on these themes from the francophone world by Le Roy et al (1996), Delville (1998) and Traoré (2001). Agricultural production and food security are taken up in Chapters 1 and 5; while Chapter 2, which deals with fishing as a livelihood, brings another perspective to these issues.

Box 0.3 *Women's claims to land at risk*

Processes of differentiation and individualization of land rights within the context of growing land shortages have resulted in the increasing concentration of land in male hands. In several countries, it has been reported that daughters are finding their inheritance rights contested and eroded (Odgaard, 1997). For example, women are losing their rights in land around the homestead, which they had formerly been able to inherit and pass on to their daughters, because such land is deemed suitable for cash crops, which are controlled by men. In some cases, these problems have been accelerated by codification of customary law. But, at the same time, the growing incidence of divorce, single parenthood and male labour migration, and the increase in avenues of formal education, have meant that more women have been forced to take responsibility for family members in the countryside. As a result, in some cases fathers now support their daughters' claims to family land, underlining the argument that inheritance rights accompany those who take responsibility for the welfare of the living.

Source: Tsikata & Whitehead (2004)

Environment and development

Environment was the focus of *Africa in Crisis*, which argued that hunger and famine were the result of long-term political and economic policies and systems, rather than the weather. A product of the mid-1980s, the author, advisers and editor of *Africa in Crisis* were influenced by the shift taking place in thinking about food security. Maxwell sees this as a shift from a production to a consumption focus – a rippling through development studies of the work of Sen (1981),[15] on entitlements and the patent failure of technically driven solutions (Maxwell, 2001a; Maxwell, 2001b). Farmers were not getting enough for their crops, while there had been a systematic bias against long-term sustainable management and investment in the agricultural economy. Agriculture had been seen for too long by government as a sector which should generate surplus for the rest of the economy.

Even today, the idea that farmers require a reasonable return is not always appreciated. For example, Mali's cotton farmers announced in summer 2000 that they would refuse to grow cotton because of the low price offered by the parastatal marketing board, and then found themselves berated by government ministers, who declared it their national duty to grow cotton for the country. Coffee farmers in Tanzania and Kenya have uprooted their coffee trees and planted food because of the low price they have been receiving through marketing channels they distrust.

World commodity prices of particular interest to many Africa countries have followed a long-term decline, and most prices now stand at less than half the level that they were in 1970–80 (see Table 0.1). Low farm-gate prices for cotton are linked in part to farm subsidies paid to US, EU and Chinese cotton producers, while coffee prices are so low mainly because of massive introduction of Robusta coffee onto the market by Brazil and Vietnam.

Table 0.1 *Percentage change in primary commodity world prices, 1970–98*

	Period			
	1970–80	*1980–90*	*1990–98*	*1980–98*
Cotton	13	−36	−24	−51
Cocoa	35	−65	27	−55
Coffee	5	−74	48	−61
Palm oil	−22	−64	123	−20

Source: Kherallah et al (2002)

Primary producers are also receiving a lower and lower share of the price paid by consumers for the final product, because of increasing levels of corporate concentration in global supply chains. Thus, for example, it is reckoned that of a café latte sold for US$1.50, the farmer gains a mere 2 cents (Oxfam Canada, 2002). Such absurd inequities have helped spur the fair-trade movement to establish schemes for purchase of coffee, tea, fruits and nuts from smallholder farmers. Currently only 3–4 per cent of total consumption in rich country markets, such schemes nevertheless demonstrate clearly an alternative way of doing business and put further pressure to reform the inadequacies of the mainstream trading system.

But much of the damage to farming has also been caused by outsiders bringing in half-baked solutions for problems they don't understand. Rene Dumont was one of the first to point this out in his classic study, *False Start in Africa* (Dumont, 1969). Examples can be drawn from the groundnut scheme in the 1940s onwards. Badly thought-out aid projects, elite-oriented government policies plus conflict have rendered a large proportion of people vulnerable to food scarcity, illness and 'environmental bankruptcy'.

Africa in Crisis showed that a large proportion of people didn't get enough to eat even in a normal year, and that Africa as a whole was becoming steadily less able to feed itself. At the same time, commodity prices were low and had been falling, energy prices were high and rising, so that most countries were less and less able to import their needs, and face rising levels of debt while trapped in a downward spiral. Sadly, much of this is still the case. When export prices are high, governments seize the opportunity to capture such rent, rather than giving their farmers a share in this good fortune.

Current assessments of Africa's malaise focus special attention on governance and institutions, both within Africa and at global levels. Back in 1985, there were only just the first suspicions that humankind might be bringing about climate change. Explanations provided for the great droughts of the 1970s and 1980s differed, from being caused by land degradation and loss of tree cover (Africans responsible for their own troubles), to changes in ocean currents (broader global change), while some began to consider possible impacts of global warming on Africa's peoples and livelihoods. In a recent controversial book, *Late Victorian Holocausts*, Davis (2001) reviews the ENSO data and argues that colonial powers took advantages of societies and governments weakened by ENSO-induced drought and famine in the late 1800s to extend Western hegemony. This book suggests that the line of research begun by Rodney's classic work, *How Europe Underdeveloped Africa* (1981; originally published in 1974) has not died.[17]

In 1985, environment was still considered to be largely an issue for Western, industrialized rich countries, who had the incomes to afford the luxury of worrying about green issues. Most African countries were more concerned by the struggle to achieve economic growth. While the 1972 Stockholm conference had raised the issue, it was not until 20 years later at Rio that the environment 'took off' as a policy issue at national and global levels, with funding to match. Almost all ministries of the environment in African capitals date from 1992. The Johannesburg Summit of 2002 assessed how far the lofty ambitions expressed at Rio have found a means to be enacted. Its accounting of the balance sheet of rhetoric vs action on the environment and development front found that most Rio pledges remained unfulfilled. Taking a page from international bankers who 'restructure' debt, diplomats in Johannesburg gave nations more time – another ten years – in what was called the Johannesburg Implementation Plan. This has put particular focus on the WEHAB[18] agenda, to generate support for concerted action on the interlinked issues of water, energy, health, agriculture and biodiversity.

While 'mechanisms' and 'modalities' for 'implementation' of such Johannesburg Summit priorities are being instigated, rural Africans continue to suffer – typically in 2004 – a major infestation of desert locusts (FAO, 2004), the spread of a deadly virus in the sweet potato crop (Wambugu, 1995; NRI, 2003), drought in some parts (UNICEF, 2004c), and flood in others (SADC, 2004).

Global climate change and Africa

There is now a strong consensus on the general lines along which global climate change is likely to affect Africa, although the details are still subject to uncertainty (IPCC, 1998). Climate extremes will increase, as will variability. This will add stress to semi-arid environments; however, the specific impacts will depend on land use. Water stress is likely to grow, especially if one accepts the climate change models that show a decrease in rainfall in the Sahel and southern Africa. Low-lying coastal zones, especially in western Africa, where dense urban populations are to be found, may be flooded by rising sea-levels. Storm surges may more heavily affect some east African coasts where mangroves have already been heavily harvested for export to the Middle East. Wildlife – vital to Africa's tourist economy – will also likely suffer, and African safaris become less attractive.

Food production and agricultural exports could suffer yield decreases from a number of sources – more frequent drought affecting rainfed grain, more frequent frosts affecting fruit in higher altitude, sub-tropical Africa; although freshwater fisheries may increase in productivity (a point taken up in Chapter 2). The question of agricultural yields is complicated by the fact that in many areas maize has become a more popular crop than older, more drought-resistant small grains (sorghum and millet). Food aid has for a long time come in the form of maize. People have grown used to the taste, and maize is easier to market nationally. Thus at a time when international crop-breeding centres such as ICRISAT in India are able to make available improved, drought-resistant sorghum seed, African ministries of agriculture are likely to find that fewer farmers want to use them.

The habitat of disease vectors will also shift. Malaria is already being seen more frequently at higher elevations in East Africa. A warmer environment will increase the propagation of many insects and affect the incidence of yellow fever, dengue fever, river blindness (onchocerciasis), and sleeping sickness (trypanosomiasis).

Water scarcity is growing

The political and economic character of the 'environmental' problems faced by Africa are neatly exemplified by growing water scarcity. At first glance, the problem seems to be one of physical availability. Africa has only about 9 per cent of the planet's freshwater resource, and this water is very unevenly distributed. Mauritania has only 0.01 per cent of the continent's total, while the Democratic Republic of Congo has 25 per cent of mean yearly renewable water resources in the whole of Africa. Giulia Carbone, UNEP's programme officer for sustainable tourism, recently noted that:

> *presently, some 206 million Africans live in water stressed or water scarce countries. By 2025 the number will rise to about 700 million as population continues to grow. Of these, roughly 440 million will live in countries with acute water scarcity – less than 1,000 cubic metres per person per year.* (cited by Smith, 2004)

Average water availability per person at the moment is 5720 cubic metres per capita per year, and the world average is 7600 cubic metres.

However, policy decisions favouring large-scale hydropower development, large-scale commercial irrigation and the privatization of urban water supplies are as important as the physical distribution of surface and ground water in producing a water crisis. Poor rural and urban Africans face a water *access* crisis that is compounded only partly by climate and site. If 1000 cubic metres of water were equitably distributed by efficient, non-wasteful systems, it could meet basic human needs as well as production requirements. But this assumes a polity where power is used for the common good and priority given to hydraulic efficiency rather than financial return on investment.

Controversy over privatization of urban water in South Africa suggests that profit still trumps human needs (Ngwane, 2003). At the international scale the transfer of massive amounts of water from Lesotho's highlands to South Africa's industrial and urban heartland benefits South African and international capital and the government of Lesotho (through payments), but the losers are the local Basotho, who have been displaced from their lands with insufficient and poorly administered compensation (Logan, 2004, pp30–3).

New thinking about African environment

New thinking and much new data now exist concerning what was once simply called 'environmental degradation'. The resilience of the African land and the people who work it have often been underestimated. Evidence from many studies at village and household level clearly demonstrate the buoyant spirit and adaptability of Africa's rural population. Far from passive victims of environmental disaster, contributing further to their own impoverishment, field-level studies show a dramatically different picture. This demonstrates that rural dwellers are pro-active, inventive citizens seeking new opportunities and ways of generating more sustainable livelihoods for themselves and their families (Toulmin and Guèye, 2003).

Wiggins (2000) shows that there has in fact been a continuous growth in food production and yields in many parts of the continent. Equally, studies by Tiffen et al (1994) demonstrate that farm output has responded remarkably well to increased demand in most places, such as around Kano, northern Nigeria, and Maradi, southern Niger (Mortimore and Adams, 2001). This growth can be expected to continue so long as farmers have reasonable access to markets for sale of produce and access to inputs.

Brock and Coulibaly (1999) describe livelihood management and diversification among farmers in Mali in this more optimistic way as do a series of other authors who study smallholder farmers in various parts of the continent (Scoones, 1995; Leach and Mearns, 1996; Raynaut, 1997; MacKenzie, 1999). The historical picture to environmental change is given by McCann's *Green Land, Brown Land, Black Land* (1999), while *Haramata* and the IIED's Dryland Programme's Issue papers are a regular source of new thinking and evidence for sustainable livelihoods and environmental management in Africa's more marginal lands.

Approaches to environment and development have also greatly changed from identifying technical fixes, to institutions and market-related 'solutions'. They have shifted from assuming that Western technology can solve the problem, to seeing how best to build on and strengthen indigenous knowledge and skills. The change in soil conservation approaches provides an exemplar of this, from use of machinery within large donor-funded projects in the 1970s to using improved local techniques, spread by farmers in the late 1980s and 1990s (Reij et al, 1996).

Back in the mid-1980s, the term 'biological diversity' was scarcely known outside a tiny circle, while now it graces an international convention and growing body of programmes and activities. The great weight it now receives is owed to its recognized importance in commercial, technical and cultural fields. Indigenous peoples' rights to benefits from genetic material that are part of their human ecosystem and livelihoods system are now widely recognized – though often denied in practice and debated legally. In the case of wildlife, such biodiversity represents an asset of great value through the revenues generated by tourism.

The challenge is to see how tourism can bring benefits to the broader community to whom such wildlife resources belong, and with whom they coexist. There are examples of community conservation programmes which aim to achieve a fairer distribution of benefits, such as the well-known Campfire initiative in Zimbabwe (Metcalfe, 1994; Duffy, 2000) and Maendeleo Kwa Uhifadhi in Kenya (Coffman, 2004). But there are also contrary examples, such as in the world-famous Ngorongoro Crater area, where the Maasai have been systematically denied their basic rights and continually harassed in the hopes of edging them out of this area in order to make it more attractive to adventure tourists. There is connivance between nature conservation groups in the north and state structures within Tanzania who benefit from the enormous revenues so derived (Brockington, 2002).

There have also been attempts to rewrite the legislation to deny rights and claims of the Maasai (Lane, 1996; Shivji and Kapinga, 1998).

Institutional approaches can, therefore, be just as destructive as 'techno fixes'. Ecotourism is only one of a growing number of systems that involve payment for environmental or ecological services. That is, rural people are supposed to receive payment from end-users or intermediaries for the work rural dwellers do in maintaining or conserving natural beauty, biodiversity, watersheds and water quality, sequestering carbon and mitigating natural hazards (eg preventing landslides by conserving forested hillsides). In Africa it remains to be seen whether and how rural people will actually be the beneficiaries of such schemes (as opposed to local elites or government officials) and what unexpected consequences there may be (Aukland et al, 2002; Landell-Mills and Porras, 2002).

The participatory approach, heralded at Rio, is now seen as an essential part of the rhetoric of government and donor aid policy. While often a pale imitation in practice, nonetheless it offers an opening and opportunity for people to play a greater role in the management of their affairs. However, Toulmin (2001) has warned of a green cul-de-sac, and Adams (2001) has warned against the imposition of 'green' rhetoric without policy back-up. Others have suggested that some attempts at conservation in Africa have further marginalized small farmers and pastoralists (Tandon, 1995; Wisner, 1995b) and presented evidence that 'environmentalism' in Africa cannot be separated from the struggle for sustainable livelihoods and women's rights.

Globalization of culture

Culture, films and music from different parts of Africa have become commonplace and part of world culture. Of global reputation are Nobel-prizewinning novelists, film directors, musicians and singers, footballers, runners, models and designers, graphic artists, painters and sculptors from Africa. African scientists run world-class institutions devoted to the improvement of agriculture, insect science, progress of health. The African Diaspora has produced leaders in many countries outside Africa in all fields from religion and philosophy to economics, marine science and the business world.

Equally strong, however, is the reverse flow of culture – what Ben Barber refers to as McWorld (Barber, 1995): Michael Jackson videos, Schwarzenegger movies, pornographic magazines, drugs, fast food, Gap and Gucci fashion. The arms dealers and mercenaries also flock to Africa. While we do not accept the simplistic contradiction that Barber poses between Jihad and McWorld, there is no denying the powerful influence of Western popular culture in Africa and some of its negative side effects. Richards (1996) relates teenage fighters in the forests of Sierra Leone who amuse themselves between battles by watching Rambo videos.

If Africa is to develop its own way forward through the 21st century, does it not need to interest its children and youth in their own past, their own philosophical and religious ideas, their own artistic and design creations? This question is complex. Richards explains that for the unemployed, futureless youth fighting in the forest, the story of Rambo, a similarly young, miseducated and misunderstood, indeed, *excluded* man, his rebellion and his triumph, strike a deep chord

(Richards, 1996, pp57–8). One youth tells him that the impact of the Rambo video is as great as reading Shakespeare's *Macbeth*, where 'Macbeth strips the mask of public service to reveal naked personal ambition beneath' (p58) – another dramatic vision bound to appeal to young people who have become cynical about their successive governments' devotion to public service. A piece of popular culture has been remade through interpretation by these young men in Sierra Leone, as they express their humanity (and not barbarity) despite the terrible violence of the war.

Whether practitioners know it or not, whenever they engage in 'participatory action research' or one of its multivocal cousins in the course of grassroots development work in Africa, they are asking people to reflect on who they are, who they have been and who they want to be. This is the core of what Freire called the pedagogy of the oppressed (1972), as he practised it in northeast Brazil, Allende's Chile and Guinea-Bissau. Although such ordinary Africans are not professional philosophers, they, too, in their own ways are seeking (with Mudimbe, 1994), the 'idea of Africa'. Africa's women in rural development projects and protests over urban sanitation are *implicitly* pursuing the recovery of an understanding of Africa, while Mudimbe and others such as Serequeberhan (1997) pursue and construct that understanding *explicitly*.

Another, darker, side of the question of culture in Africa is the oppression of minority cultures by the majority. UNDP's *Human Development Report* for 2004 puts the situation very clearly:

> *Accommodating people's growing demands for their inclusion in society, for respect of their ethnicity, religion, and language, takes more than democracy and equitable growth. Also needed are multicultural policies that recognize differences, champion diversity and promote cultural freedoms, so that all people can choose to speak their language, practice their religion, and participate in shaping their culture – so that all people can choose to be who they are.* (UNDP, 2004)

Loss of continental leadership

Who speaks on behalf of Africa and takes up the challenges raised by the great thinkers of the Independence period, such as Senghor and Nyerere? Are there voices that are distinguishably African against the backdrop of globalized culture? Nelson Mandela still has this charisma and authority, but his voice is muted with age. Mandela has been replaced as South Africa's president by a more remote and controversial man, Thabo Mbeki, who is best known for stalling the provision of anti-retroviral drugs to pregnant women with HIV/AIDS because he didn't accept the link between AIDS and HIV. Two generations of African revolutionary intellectuals and leaders have come and gone, many of them dying violent deaths: Nkrumah, Lumumba, Fanon, Neto, Mondlane, Machel, Amilcar Cabral and Chris Hani. Today, the main African politicians speaking for their continent are more modest and cautious in their vision. Presidents Mbeki, Obasanjo and Wade, each of whom contributed to the creation of the New Partnership for Africa's Development (NEPAD, see below, p31), have also pledged to lead the

UN's Millennium African Partnership. The latter aims to make African leaders responsible for achieving better governance and the rule of law, instead of relying on the IMF and others to lay down conditions.

Writers such as Wole Soyinka, Ngugi wa Thiongo and Nadine Gordimer provide irreverent commentary on the temptations of power. Journalists have come to play an increasingly valuable part in challenging how governments do business and investigating the spoils of office, but several have paid the price. A few activists are starting to make their names heard over key issues, such as Wangari Mathaai and the Green Belt Movement in Kenya, where the government's seizure of land is being challenged. But, to date, Professor Mathaai remains a rare female figure in a largely male circle.

A mobile intellectual class

Much of the African intellectual elite spends time out of Africa, in the universities of North America and Europe, in the UN system and increasingly in the global private sector. Such a brain drain is much bemoaned, given the need of their homelands for new thinking and innovative approaches, but there is also return movement. People go back and forth, bringing experience and ideas from elsewhere to contribute to the development of their own countries. Thus, there is a positive side to the increasingly cosmopolitan nature of the African Diaspora, bringing new energy and insights into lobbying, action on social development questions, inflows of capital and business acumen, debt forgiveness, health care and pharmaceuticals.

Arguments Old and New

What we're arguing

What were the main arguments underlying *Africa in Crisis*? How has the analysis and emphasis changed over the last 20 years? What have been the major shifts in arguments and in the broader context? What are the key points underlying our analysis?

Our arguments:

- There is much that is positive happening in many parts of Africa which needs higher profile, and to act as a source of inspiration. Africa's peoples show remarkable resilience and adaptability to difficult conditions. Where there are both reasonable stability and new economic opportunities, people demonstrate great effectiveness in harnessing their skills and assets to improve their living conditions. African governments and aid agencies need to learn how to provide an enabling policy and institutional environment that enhances such energy.
- There are also terrifying challenges from conflict, disease and breakdown of social structure and organization. These demand global attention, the mobilization of resources and commitment for them to be addressed. These are

long-term challenges that will need the re-affirmation of support from the broader global community.

- It takes time to construct a new compact between citizens and the state, recognizing the strengths of African society, while enhancing principles of accountability, transparency, rights and responsibilities. This is also a long-term project, to develop checks and balances within state and civil society structures, and mechanisms for review and assessment within the African community.

A growing Pan-African and international consensus?

Kofi Annan's speech to the UN Millennium Assembly in June 2000 argued for the need for benefits from globalization to be shared more equally across the world, because the global market cannot guarantee the achievement of broader social objectives. These ideas were repeated by the World Commission on the Social Dimension of Globalization in their report, *A Fair Globalization* (WCSDG, 2004). However, in Africa today one continues to see in an extreme form the global disparities of wealth and their consequences for human health, well-being and security, and for the environment. Africa should receive particular attention, requiring a special effort, with African governments and civil society making common cause with outsiders to give greater priority to reducing poverty. This will include the need to open up rich countries' markets to African producers, make more rapid and deeper cuts in debt, and better focused development assistance. Among the greatest challenges will be tackling low agricultural productivity and the major threats from disease such as malaria and HIV/AIDS.

How to accomplish this?

In 2001, President Mbeki of South Africa jointly presented with the presidents of Algeria and Nigeria a Millennium Partnership of the African Recovery Programme (known as MAP),[19] central elements of which are human rights and the rule of law. Mbeki saw that these must be addressed not only for themselves but also because they damage the credibility of African governments and discourage overseas investment in the continent.

> *The MAP programme is a declaration of a firm commitment by African leaders to take ownership and responsibility for the sustainable economic development of the continent. Our starting point is a critical examination of Africa's post independence experience and acceptance that things have to be done differently to achieve meaningful socio-economic progress …* (Mbeki, 2001)

He acknowledged that if African countries are to take charge of such a programme themselves, and impose discipline on their fellow member states, the principle of non-interference in each other's affairs will need to be re-examined. He pledged that African governments would impose conditionality upon themselves, rather than always submitting to pressures from the IMF and World Bank.

At about the same time, President Abdoulaye Wade of Senegal also led a group of African leaders seeking a means to re-define broader development goals outside the orbit of the Washington consensus. His so-called Omega Plan[20] focused mainly on agriculture, education, health and infrastructural development. These two initiatives met together in what has developed into NEPAD, which has become the common approach of a new Pan-African consensus.

The NEPAD Programme of Action (2001) describes three initiatives related to the fundamental conditions for sustainable development in Africa:

- the Peace, Security and Political Governance Initiative;
- the Economic and Corporate Governance Initiative;
- sub-regional and regional approaches to development.

NEPAD then discusses priority sectors, and resource mobilization, focusing on capital flows and global market access issues. While NEPAD is seen as providing a new start to global engagement with Africa, there is nothing startlingly new in NEPAD. Many elements stem from earlier Pan-African debates. However, NEPAD helps provide a more coherent vision while there also seems to be political will behind the vision. In addition, mechanisms have already been put into place to pursue this vision, with projects under the headings of agriculture, private-sector promotion, infrastructure and regional integration underway.

Critics see NEPAD as acceptable to the West because the plan is committed to reshaping Africa to fit an agenda that is still set outside Africa: namely the development of infrastructure and regional integration for the more efficient exploitation of Africa's petroleum, mineral wealth, water, soil, forests and tourist potential by transnational corporations. Trade unions, public-sector workers and small farmers have expressed concern with this strong infrastructure priority when coupled with another major stated priority: private-sector development. It is also unclear whether and how the African governments committed to NEPAD will be able to continue to hold out for major structural changes in the global economy (as they did by joining the Group of 20 at the WTO meeting in Cancún over the need to reduce US and European subsidies to farmers) when NEPAD takes the architecture of the global economy for granted. These critiques, worries and concerns have been tabled by dozens of NGOs and other institutions in Africa and overseas (ICCAF, 2002; Bond, 2002a,b,c,d) and are also summarized by Booker et al (2003).

In 2004, UK's prime minister Tony Blair created a Commission for Africa. Its mandate is to make a comprehensive assessment of the way to tackle Africa's priorities – 'economic issues, education, conflict resolution, health, the environment, HIV/AIDS and governance' – through a 'fresh look at Africa's past, present, and future' (BBC, 2004). The commission is to report by February 2005, but already as the commission met in Addis Ababa, Ethiopia, in October 2004, there were doubts about whether it could deal with the root causes of Africa's problems. On the eve of that commission meeting:

> *church leaders running development programmes in 18 African countries [were] appealing to the Commission for tougher action on a range of issues, from corruption, to the sale of arms in conflict zones, and the need to invest in disaster prevention in vulnerable countries. A declaration to the Africa Commission from church leaders involved in relief and development across Africa, also urges action*

*on the 'immoral double standards' in the world trade system that 'trap the poor',
and for a greater voice for ordinary Africans as they seek to hold their governments to account.* (Ekklesia, 2004)

Fine rhetoric only?

By 2004 it was clear that for most African countries the Millennium Development
Goals (MDGs) will not be fulfilled and that Africa's decline has not been arrested.
Britain's Chancellor and the World Bank President pointed this out at the beginning of 2004 (Brown and Wolfenson, 2004). With Prime Minister Blair's establishment of a Commission for Africa, the dance of former colonized and former
colonizer came full circle. Bob Geldof, who led Band Aid in the 1980s, was
appointed to Blair's commission, along with Michel Camdessus, former head of
the IMF, Meles Zenawi, prime minister of Ethiopia and Tanzania's president, Ben
Mkapa.[21]

One African writer has this to say about Blair's Commission for Africa:

*[T]he commission is not likely to gather new information on how to tackle criti-
cal issues adversely affecting Africa's development, such as: the Draconian international debt burden owed by African nations, estimated at US$300bn by the
American Friends Service Committee; runaway agricultural subsidies give a cow
in Europe more in benefits a day than the typical small-scale African farmer;
continued lack of fiscal transparency and accountability of many African governments; the loss of Africa's best minds due to stifling professional, political, economic and social circumstances; and the need for Africa to integrate its economy
rapidly to enjoy economies of scale in global markets.* (Akukwe, 2004)

The British Overseas Aid Group (BOAG), which combines UK development
agencies, ActionAid, Christian Aid, Cafod, Oxfam and Save the Children, has
welcomed the new commission, but they cautioned that it be judged by actions
and not words alone. Meanwhile, little attention is being paid to another commission's report: that of the World Commission on the Social Dimension of
Globalization, co-chaired by the presidents of Tanzania and Finland, and set up
by the International Labor Organisation. This important analysis asserts what US and
British policy has consistently denied. Economic globalization without an agreed
ethnical and regulatory framework will not bring benefit to poorer countries and
people. The market-place cannot be the sole arbiter of all value among human
beings on a finite planet. Gathering dust on bookshelves in the US Department of
State and the British Foreign Office (and elsewhere) undoubtedly also sit other less-
than-well-thumbed reports: the Brandt Commission's *North–South* (Brand, 1980)[22], various publications of the Julius Nyerere's South Commission (see www.southcentre.org)
and the Independent Commission on International Humanitarian Issues' *Winning
the Human Race*[23] (ICIHI, 1988).

Will this new commission succeed in getting to the root causes of Africa's problems, finding and implementing real solutions? Chukwe-Emeka Chikezie, Executive Director of the Africa Foundation For Development (AFFORD, www.
afford-uk.org) offered this opinion:

Obviously, the commission will need to listen carefully to Africans in their diversity, from the great and the good to the genuinely grassroots (and, of course, the usual suspects). But more importantly, the commission will need to ask the right questions in the right way and involve Africans in setting the agenda. The tendency to wheel in people to speak to an agenda already set behind closed doors will waste valuable time. Most of us, in any case are suffering from acute 'consultitis' we're all researched out... And this is one reason why countless commissions and enquiries never make a difference. Those who should actually own the process of shaping their own destiny are marginalised, excluded, overlooked, patronised. Solutions arrive, but they mean nothing to those who are at that point frustrated and alienated. (Chikezie, 2004)

Signs of Success

Besides the major institutional changes taking place in Africa – establishment of the African Union, NEPAD, regional economic and peacekeeping cooperation – other, less visible signs of vitality and new beginnings can be noted. Since *Africa in Crisis*, there has been a steady outpouring of books and articles illustrating that some things are going right in Africa. The emphasis on crisis should not mask a lot of positive local practice that is bringing improvements in livelihoods and welfare for poor people in many parts of the continent. Paul Harrison's *Greening of Africa* was the first of such; followed by Tiffen, Mortimore and Gachuki's *More People, Less Erosion*; and Leach and Mearns's *The Lie of the Land*: a new look at trends in the African environment that debunks the gloomy myths which have abounded regarding a downward spiral of impoverishment, environmental degradation and disaster.

Small-scale agricultural, horticultural and livestock production is developing in many small projects and larger programmes assisted by local and international non-governmental organizations (Murwira et al, 2000). Micro-credit and 'home town' credit schemes are becoming more common (Honey and Okafor, 1998; Kates and Mabogunje, 2004), as is women's access to credit and productive inputs. Agroforestry, artisanal fishing and small-scale mining (MMSD Project, 2002), as well as new forms of profit sharing from eco-tourism are all adding to the livelihood security of at least some rural Africans. Crop breeding has produced a new rice variety called Nerica ('New Rice for Africa') in West Africa that combines high yield with the hardiness of ancient African rice (Harsh, 2004). Haggblade (2004) has compiled successes in a variety of agricultural areas in a number of African countries including cassava, maize, cotton, small-scale dairy and horticulture.

There is talk of 'Africa's lion economies' to rival the Asian 'tigers' who have grown well over the past two decades. However, the analogy with fierce and energetic wild animals now looks less than appropriate, given the Asian financial crises of the late 1990s. The Asian tigers have all the appearance of moth-eaten stuffed animals at present, barely managing to stay on their feet. In talk of African success stories, there has been repeated reference to Ghana, Uganda, Mali and Mozambique, which are recognized as having swallowed the bitter economic medicine spooned out by the World Bank and IMF, and bringing with it improved levels of economic growth and more healthy public finance. Some, including Mkandawire in this volume, question whether even the moderate achievements of this handful of African countries are sustainable. Another question is how much growth at national level is 'trickling' down in the form of improved incomes and more secure livelihoods for poor people.

There are also signs of success in social development. Africa is home to innovative programmes to heal the psychological traumas of war (Green and Honwana, 1999). There are programmes to reintegrate child soldiers into society, to achieve racial and inter-ethnic reconciliation and to provide veterans with livelihoods. There are also creative forms of local conflict resolution being taught and practised in Kenya, Uganda, Somalia, South Africa and elsewhere, some of which are mentioned by Parlevliet in this book. At the same time, new approaches to schooling are being tried in Mali where primary children can now spend the first few years learning and developing basic skills in their mother tongue language, rather than being forced to sink or swim in the French language. Similarly, in Senegal, there has been increased emphasis by NGOs on civic education programmes in local languages, to encourage literacy and inform local debate about the rights and responsibilities of community and state structures (Guèye and Ly, 1996).

Running Out of Time?

A senior analyst at the All Africa Council of Churches commented on Africa's challenge:

> *Political independence was from the beginning perceived by the pioneering Pan-Africanists as a response to colonial hegemony. However, both the religious and economic projects have been profoundly influenced by the hegemony (stability) of east/west ideology. Hardly any element of modern Africa has been left untouched by the rise and the subsequent ignominious fall of modern east/west ideology. Indeed, it is fair to say that modern Africa was premised on the stability offered by that ideological paradigm. In the ensuing vacuum, Africa faces its own fractured hegemony of ethnicity which, rather than functioning as a unifying factor, promises to keep alive the most vexing of the continent's strengths. Africa is face to face with its most profound strengths and weaknesses. (Miller, 1993)*

More than a decade later, Africa is still trying to balancing those strengths and weaknesses. Recent institutional changes, including deepening of democracy in several nations, increasing regional cooperation and Pan-African linkage through the new AU and NEPAD certainly attempt to build on the continent's strengths. However, production and its basis – the health and education of the people – continues to lag. Twenty years of 'adjustment' have not yielded the economic growth promised nor have the benefits of a globalizing economy reached many in Africa. The 'crisis' in the title *Africa in Crisis* is, we regret to say, the same crisis Timberlake described. Our understanding of the crisis today is more complex, and the spatial scales that link its hotspots and weak points are global and local in a manner a book written in 1985 could not have understood. But there is, still, a crisis. Concerted international, national and local efforts are needed to overcome continuing threats posed by hunger, disease, conflict, economic stagnation, unplanned urbanization and climate change. Is time running out? Certainly for the African children who died preventable deaths today. Credibility and legitimacy of international and national institutions may also be running out if little or no progress is made towards achieving the Millennium Development Goals in Africa by 2015. The mid-term review of the MDGs in September 2005 will provide a key moment for judging how far donors and recipient governments have made progress.

How Can Our Book Contribute?

This remapping of Africa is a project built on a partnership between Western and African writers and researchers, with an advisory group of distinguished Africans to help ground-truth our chapters and interpretation. We would like this to be a metaphor for the kind of solidarity possible within a vision of globalization from below – a vision within which African nations take their rightful place among the community of nations and African people control their own resources and fate. To encourage development of that vision of a new Africa further, we have provided a short, schematic 'Agenda for Action' at the end. We have drawn from the rich material offered by this book's authors in producing this end piece. It should, however, be considered a beginning and not an end or conclusion. We want the Agenda for Action to provoke discussion, debate and action.

The structure of our book might also be taken as metaphorical and indicative of the complexity of the challenges and how they interlink. We move from the human ecological realities of land, water, food and health through institutional questions that span economics and governance at several scales. Each of the contributions in these sections is critical but also highlights some progress and elements that, when combined, constitute an agenda for action. That action will create, not just observe remotely or dispassionately record, a new map of Africa.

Notes

1. An UNCTAD report that analysed Africa's export commodities in the period 1980–2000 found that 12 of the 14 main commodities which African exports are were affected by extreme price volatility, and nine of them had declined in price (UNCTAD, 2004).
2. Compare, for example, the opposite point of view, the follow-up contribution of the UN Research Institute for Social Development to the World Summit on Social Development, entitled (in contrast to the economistic 'unseen hand' beloved of Thatcherites) *Visible Hands* (in the plural!). See UNRISD (2000).
3. 1999 data from World Trade Organization (www.wto.org/english/res_e/statis_e/chp_1_e.pdf), 1985 and 1970 data from Robinson-Rojas Archive (www.rrojasdatabank.org/mmexpe2.htm); UNCTAD (2004) found that Africa's share

of global *nonfuel* exports dropped from 6 per cent to about 4 per cent between 1980 and 2000. The World Bank (2003) is vehement about the deterioration in Africa's world trade position and its developmental consequences: 'Over the last three decades, Africa has been marginalized from world trade. Africa's share of world exports has dropped by nearly 60 per cent from 3.5 per cent in 1970 to 1.5 per cent by the end of the 1990s. This dramatic decline in Africa's export market share represents a staggering income loss of US$70 billion [US$70,000 million] annually, an amount equivalent to 21 per cent of the region's GDP and to more than *five times* the US$13 billion [US$13,000 million] in annual aid flows to Africa.'

4. FAO (2002) lists 21 in sub-Saharan Africa, 14 in Latin America and the Caribbean and 6 in the South Pacific Islands. Thirty-two of these countries are LDCs and/or small island developing states (SIDS). Dependence on a single commodity is more pronounced in tropical countries, notably with respect to sugar, coffee, bananas, cotton lint and cocoa beans.

5. Common Market for Eastern and Southern Africa – commanding, in theory, a total population of 380 million and intra-regional trade among members totalling US$2400 million (see www.ictsd.org/html/weekly/29-05-01/story3.htm).

6. Besides the EAC, SADC, ECOWAS, COMESA, there are the Economic Community of Central African States (CEEAC), the Arab Maghreb Union (AMU), and the Inter Governmental Authority on Development (IGAD) that takes in the countries of the Horn of Africa and East Africa. The last of these, IGAD, has at the moment only a security and developmental function, dealing with Conflict Prevention, Management, and Resolution, and Humanitarian Affairs; Infrastructure Development (Transport and Communications); and Food Security and Environment Protection. It may in the future develop a regional trading function and link up with one of the other blocks.

7. The scale of displacement by violence is hard to visualize. In Mozambique alone in the 1980s some 4.5 million rural people were displaced by war (UNEP, 2002b).

8. A companion study also produced by UN Habitat puts the figure at 61 per cent (UN Habitat, 2003b, p35).

9. The Millennium Development Goals (MDGs) are a set of concrete targets in the range of 2015–2020 in eight areas: poverty, education, gender equality, child mortality, maternal health, HIV/AIDS and other diseases, environment and global partnership (see www.un.org/millenniumgoals/ and www.bond.org.uk/networker/april04/opinion.htm).

10. The World Summit on Sustainable Development (Johannesburg Earth Summit) complemented and expanded the MDGs with a series of 36 'priority actions and commitments', most of them fairly concrete, such as to '[h]alve, by the year 2015, the proportion of people who are unable to reach or to afford safe drinking water and the proportion of people who do not have access to basic sanitation' (see www.un.org/esa/sustdev/csd/csd11/csd11_framework_ministerial.pdf).

11. 'The HIV/AIDS pandemic continued its deadly assault on sub-Saharan Africa in 2003, taking an estimated 2.3 million lives, infecting an additional 3 mil-

lion people ... Africa remains the epicentre of the global crisis, accounting for almost 80 per cent of the 3 million fatalities worldwide and over 60 per cent of the 5 million new infections' (Fleshman, 2004).

12. See www.whitehouse.gov/news/releases/2003/01/20030129-1.html. The excuse given is that US authorities are not convinced that WHO approval of the use of generic ART in combined, single doses is based on adequate data, a point consistent with the danger of widespread viral resistance to these drugs if they are not effectively administered. See de Waal in this volume. Time will tell if this 'scientific' quibble is genuine or a delaying tactic while the US spends its global AIDS funds on more expensive patented drugs by its own pharmaceutical companies.

13. The Bill & Melinda Gates Foundation announced a US$200 million grant to establish the Grand Challenges in Global Health initiative, a major new effort and partnership with the National Institutes of Health (NIH). The initiative will identify critical scientific challenges in global health and increase research on diseases that cause millions of deaths in the developing world (www.grandchallengesgh.org/ArDisplay.aspx?ID=34&SecID=291).

14. 'Angola alone has an estimated 10 million land-mines and an amputee population of 70,000, of whom 8,000 are children' (UNICEF, 2004a).

15. For a critical review of the literature on famine, see Wisner et al (2004, pp127–66).

16. Some African leaders paid close attention to this analysis. Julius Nyerere President of Tanzania, had it translated into Swahili (Dumont, 1976).

17. See also Rau's *From Feast to Famine* (1991) as well as a number of other works that explore the colonial role in undermining self-provisioning food systems in Africa (Palmer and Parsons, 1977; Du Mont, 1983; Rotberg and Rabb, 1985).

18. Five key sustainability areas identified at the World Summit on Sustainable Development in Johannesburg: water (and sanitation), energy, health (and the environment), agriculture, and biodiversity (and sustainable ecosystem management).

19. The MAP is available as a pdf document (www.uneca.org/nepad/).

20. The Omega Plan is available as a pdf document (www.uneca.org/nepad/).

21. Total list of commissioners: Fola Adeola, chairman of FATE foundation, Nigeria; K Y Amoako, United Nations Under-Secretary-General, Ghana; Senator Nancy Landon Kassebaum Baker, US; Rt Hon Hilary Benn, MP, Secretary of State for International Development, UK; Rt Hon Gordon Brown, MP, Chancellor of the Exchequer, UK; Michel Camdessus, Africa Personal Representative, France; Bob Geldof, musician and founder of Live Aid, Ireland; Hon Ralph Goodale, PC, MP, Minister of Finance, Canada; Dr William S Kalema, Chairman of the Board of the Uganda Investment Authority; Trevor Manuel, Minister of Finance, South Africa; Linah K Mohohlo, Governor, Bank of Botswana; His Excellency Mr Benjamin William Mkapa, President of the United Republic of Tanzania; Ji Peiding, NPC, Standing Committee Member and Vice Chairman of the Foreign Affairs Committee, China; Tidjane Thiam, Group Strategy and Development Director, Aviva PLC, Côte D'Ivoire; Dr Anna Kajumulo Tibaijuka, Under-Secretary-General & Executive Director of UN HABITAT, Tanzania; Meles Zenawi, Prime Minister of Ethiopia.

22. See www.brandt21forum.info/BrandtCommission2.htm for more information about the Brandt Commission.
23. Co-chaired by Prince Sadruddin Aga Khan (www.amaana.org/agakhan/sadruddin3.htm) and Prince El Hassan bin Talal (www.princehassan.gov.jo/).

References

Abrahamsen, R (2001) *Disciplining Democracy: Development Discourse and Good Governance in Africa,* Zed Books, London

Abudulai, S (2001) 'Land Rights, Land Use Dynamics and Policy in Peri-urban Tamale', in C Toulmin, P L Deville and S Traoré (eds) *The Dynamics of Resource Tenure in West Africa,* James Currey, Oxford

Adams, M (2000) *Breaking Ground: Development Aid for Land Reform,* Overseas Development Institute, London

Adams, W (2001) *Green Development,* 2nd edn, Routledge, London

Africa Recovery (1998) 'Africa the Fastest Growing World Region, IMF Says', *Africa Recovery,* vol 12, no 2 (November), p12, www.un.org/ecosocdev/geninfo/afrec/subjindx/122econ.htm

Agbenyega, O, Kasanga, K, Longbottom, J and Oppong Nkrumah, K (2001) 'The Role of Institutions in Mediating Access to Land in Peri-urban Kumasi'. Phase 2 report of 'Further Knowledge of Livelihoods Affected by Urban Transition, Kumasi, Ghana', project report, University of Birmingham, Birmingham

Ake, C (1996) *Democracy and Development in Africa,* Brookings Institution, Washington, DC

Akukwe, C (2004) 'Is Blair's New Africa Commission Letting the Cat out of the Bag?', *AxisofLogic.com,* 25 March, www.axisoflogic.com/artman/publish/printer_5875.shtml

Albugre, C (2000) 'Still Sapping the Poor: A Critique of IMF Poverty Reduction Strategies', Global Exchange, San Francisco, www.globalexchange.org/campaigns/wbimf/imf0600.html

Aukland, L, Moura Costa, P, Bass, S, Huq, S, Landell-Mills, N, Tipper, R and Carr, R (2002) *Laying the Foundations for Clean Development: Preparing the Land Use Sector. A quick guide to the Clean Development Mechanism,* IIED, London

Barber, B (1995) *Jihad vs. McWorld,* Times Books, New York

Bayart, J-F (1993) *The State In Africa: The Politics of the Belly,* Longman, Harlow

BBC (2004) 'Blair Launches Africa Commission', 26 February, http://news.bbc.co.uk/1/hi/world/africa/3490382.stm

Berry, S (2001) *Chiefs Know Their Boundaries: Essays on Property, Power and the Past, Asante, 1896–1996,* African Social History Series, Heinemann, Oxford

Bond, P (2001) *Against Global Apartheid: South Africa Meets the World Bank, IMF and International Finance,* University of Cape Town Press, Cape Town

Bond, P (2002a) 'Zimbabwe, South Africa, and the Power Politics of Bourgeois Democracy', *Monthly Review,* vol 54, no 1 (May), pp32–45, available at www.monthlyreview.org/0502bond.htm

Bond, P (2002b) 'NEPAD', *Znet,* www.ifg.org/analysis/un/wssd/bondZnet.htm

Bond, P (2002c) 'Thabo Mbeki's New Partnership for Africa's Development: Breaking or Shining the Chains of Global Apartheid?', *KAIROS-Africa*, www.web.net/~iccaf/debtsap/nepadfpif.htm

Bond, P (2002d) *Fanon's Warning: A Civil Society Reader on the New Partnership for Africa's Development*, Africa World Press, Trenton, NJ

Booker, S, Minter, W and Colgan, A-L (2003) 'Africa Policy Outlook 2003', Silver City, Foreign Policy in Focus, NM and Washington, DC, March, www.presentdanger.org/papers/africa2003_body.html

Booth, D (2001) 'PRSP Processes in 8 African Countries: Initial Impacts and Potential for Institutionalisation', paper for presentation to the WIDER Development Conference on Debt Relief, Helsinki, 17–18 August, www.wider.unu.edu/conference/conference-2001-2/parallel%20papers/1_2_booth.pdf

Boseley, S (2004) 'Scientists Herald Malaria Breakthrough', *Guardian Unlimited*, 15 October, www.guardian.co.uk/medicine/story/0,11381,1328014,00.html

Bourne, D (2003) 'Are PRSPs Making a Difference? The African Experience', *Development Policy Review*, vol 21, no 2

Brandt, W. (1980) *North–South: A Program for Survival*, MIT Press, Cambridge, MA

Brock, K and Coulibaly, N (1999) 'Sustainable Rural Livelihoods in Mali', *IDS Research Report 35*, IDS, Sussex

Brockington, D (2002) *Fortress Conservation: The Preservation of the Mkomazi Game Reserve, Tanzania*, James Currey, London

Brown, G and Wolfenson, J (2004) 'A New Deal for the World's Poor: If We Really Want to Achieve Our Targets, This Is Crunch Time', *Guardian Unlimited*, www.guardian.co.uk/comment/story/0,3604,1149063,00.html

Brundtland Commission (1987) *Our Common Future*, World Commission on Environment and Development, Oxford University Press, Oxford

Bryceson, D, Kay, C and Mooij, J (eds) (2000) *Disappearing Peasantries? Rural Labour in Africa, Asia and Latin America*, Intermediate Technology Publications, London

CDD (2000) 'Corruption and Other Constraints on the Land Market and Land Administration in Ghana: A Preliminary Investigation', *CDD Ghana Research Papers No.4*, Centre for Democracy and Development, Accra

Centre for Development Studies (2003) *The Comparative Research Programme on NGOs*, Bergen University, Bergen, www.svf.uib.no/sfu/ngo/index.htm

Chabal, P and Daloz, J-P (1999) *Africa Works: Disorder as Political Instrument*, IAI/Heinemann/James Currey, London

Cheru, F (1989) *The Silent Revolution: Debt, Development and Democracy*, Zed Books, London

Chikezie, C-E (2004) 'The Commission for Africa: Who's Framing Who?' Bond.org, 4 April, www.bond.org.uk/networker/april04/opinion.htm

Coffman, J (2004) 'Buying (into) and Selling Conservation among Maasai in Southern Kenya', in W Moseley and B I Logan (eds) *African Environment and Development*, pp161–88, Ashgate, Aldershot, Hants

Colclough, C (2004) 'Education for All: "What are You Doing to Provide Us with an Education?"', *UN Chronicle Online*, www.un.org/Pubs/chronicle/2004/issue2/0204p52.asp

Cour, J-M and Snrech, S (eds) (1998) *Pour preparer l'avenir de l'Afrique de l'Ouest: une vision à l'horizon 2020, Etude à long terme en Afrique de l'Ouest*, Club du Sahel/ OECD, Paris

Curtis, M (2004) 'Africa's Plight Can't Be Explained by a Pop Song', *Guardian Weekly*, 10–16 December, p31

Davidson, B (2004) *The African Slave Trade*. James Currey, London; originally published in 1961 as *Black Mother,* Little, Brown & Co, New York

Davis, M (2001) *Late Victorian Holocausts: El Niño and the Making of the Third World in Environment & Ecology*, Verso, London

Davis, M (2004) 'Mega-slums', *New Left Review*, 2nd Series, March/April, pp5–34, www.newleftreview.net/NLR26001.shtml

de Waal, A (1997) *Famine Crimes: Politics and the Disaster Relief Industry in Africa*, Indiana University Press, Bloomington, IN

Delville, P (1998) *Quelles politiques fonocières pour l'Afrique rurale?: Reconcilier pratiques, legitimité et légalité*, Karthala, Paris

Duffield, M (2001) *Global Governance and the New Wars: The Merger of Development and Security*, Zed Books, London

Duffield, M (2002) 'Reprising Durable Disorder: Network War and the Securitization of Aid', in B Hettne and B Oden (eds), *Global Governance in the 21st Century: Alternative Perspectives on World Order*, pp75–105, Expert Group on Development Initiatives (EGDI), Swedish Ministry for Foreign Affairs, Stockholm

Duffy, R (2000) *Killing for Conservation: Wildlife Policy in Zimbabwe*, James Currey, London

Dumont, R (1969) *False Start in Africa*, translated from French (*L'Afrique noire est mal partie*) by Phyllis N. Ott, Frederick A Praeger, New York, NY

Dumont, R (1976) *Afrika Inakwenda Kombo,* Swahili translation of *L'Afrique noire est mal partie,* East African Literature Bureau, Nairobi

Ekklesia (2004) 'Commission for Africa Consults Churches on Action', The Ekklesia Society website, 16 November 2004, available at www.ekklesia.co.uk/content/news_syndication/article_041116africa.shtml

FAO (2002) 'Dependence on Single Agricultural Commodity Exports in Developing Countries: Magnitude and Trends', in *FAO Papers on Selected Issues Relating to the WTO Negotiations on Agriculture*, FAO, Commodities and Trade Division, Rome, www.fao.org/DOCREP/005/Y3733E/y3733e0d.htm

FAO (2004) 'The Latest Situation', Rome: FAO/Desert Locust Information Service, 15 October, www.fao.org/news/global/locusts/locuhome.htm

Ferraz, B and Munslow, B (1999) *Sustainable Development in Mozambique*, James Currey, Oxford

Fleshman, M (2004) 'Toll Mounts in Global AIDS Pandemic', *Africa Recovery*, vol 17, no 4 (January), www.un.org/ecosocdev/geninfo/afrec/vol17no4/174aids.htm

Freire, P (1972) *Pedagogy of the Oppressed*, Penguin, London

Gary, I (2001) 'Oil for Us, Hope for Them: U.S. Trade with Africa Should Stress Value of Human Rights', Catholic Relief Services, www.catholicrelief.org/get_involved/advocacy/policy_and_strategic_issues/philly.cfm

Gillan, A (2004) 'Kenya to Seek Extradition of "Miracle Birth" Pastor', *Guardian Unlimited*, 3 September, www.guardian.co.uk/uk_news/story/0,1296356,00.html

Godlewska, A and Smith, N (eds) (1994) *Geography and Empire*, Blackwell, Oxford

Government of Australia (undated) 'International health – how Australia compares', Australian Institute of Health and Welfare, www.aihw.gov.au/publications/health/ihhac/ihhac-c03e.pdf

Green, E and Honwana, A (1999) 'Indigenous Healing of War-Affected Children in Africa', *IK Notes,* Children and Armed Conflict Unit, Essex University, UK, www.essex.ac.uk/armedcon/story_id/000116.pdf

Guardian (2001) 'Children of the Etireno', 4 October, www.guardian.co.uk/g2/story/0,,562823,00.html

Guèye, B and Ly, M A (1996) *LOHU: MARP Adaptée en Langue Pulaar Dakar*, ARED/IIED, Dakar, Senegal

Guyer, J (ed) (1987) *Feeding African Cities*, Indiana University Press, Bloomington, IN

Haggblade, S (ed) (2004) *Building on Successes in African Agriculture*, 2020 Vision Focus 12, IFPRI Washington, DC, www.ifpri.org/2020/focus/focus12.htm

Hancock, G (1992) *Lords of Poverty: The Power, Prestige, and Corruption of the International Aid Business*, Monthly Review, New York

Hanlon, J (1991) *Mozambique: Who Calls the Shots?*, James Currey, Oxford

Hanlon, J (1996) *Peace without Profit: How the IMF Blocks Peace-Building in Mozambique*, Heinemann, London

Harrison, P (1987) *Greening of Africa,* Penguin, London

Harsh, E (2004) 'Farmers Embrace African "Miracle' Rice", *Africa Recovery,* vol 17, no 4 (January), www.un.org/ecosocdev/geninfo/afrec/vol17no4/174rice.htm

Honey, R. and Okafor (eds) (1998) *Hometown Associations: Indigenous Knowledge and Development in Nigeria*, Intermediable Technology Publications, London

HPTN AIDS Timeline (2001) www.hptn.org/Web%20Documents/CommunityProgram/HPTNAIDSHIVGlobalTimeline.pdf

Huband, M (2001) *The Skull Beneath the Skin: Africa after the Cold War*, Westview, Colorado

Human Rights Watch (2003) *World Report: Africa Overview,* www.hrw.org/wr2k3/africa.html

Human Rights Watch Africa (1999) *Africa: Human Rights Developments*, www.hrw.org/worldreport99/africa/

Hyden, G, Olowu, B and Okoth-Ogendo, H W (1999) *African Perspectives on Governance*, Africa World Press, Trenton

ICCAF (Inter-Church Coalition on Africa) (2002) *Debt, Structural Adjustment and Jubilee: NEPAD*, ICCAP, Toronto, www.web.net/~iccaf/debtsap/nepad.htm

ICIHI (Independent Commission on International Humanitarian Issues) (1988) *Winning the Human Race: The Report of the Independent Commission on International Humanitarian Issues,* Zed Books, London

IIED (International Institute for Environment and Development) (1999) *Land Tenure and Resource Access in West Africa: Issues and Opportunities for the next Twenty Five Years*, IIED, London

ILO (International Labor Organisation (2004) *A Fair Globalization*, Report of the World Commission on the Social Dimensions of Globalization, ILO, Geneva, www.ilo.org/public/english/wcsdg/

InterWorks Europe (1998) 'Is the International Aid System in Recession?', http://homepage.eircom.net/~cosgrave/papers/recess1.html

IPCC (Intergovernmental Panel on Climate Change) (1998) *The Regional Impacts of Climate Change: An Assessment of Vulnerability*, Cambridge University Press, Cambridge

IRIN (United Nations Integrated Regional Information Networks) (2002) 'Central Africa: Five Million Dead from Violent Conflict in Last Decade', ReliefWeb, 19 April, www.reliefweb.int/w/rwb.nsf/0/927db5088ccf965c49256ba3001ad237?OpenDocument

IRIN (United Nations Integrated Regional Information Networks) (2004) 'SUDAN: Thousands of IDPs Dying Every Month – WHO', *IRINNews.org*, 14 September, www.globalsecurity.org/military/library/news/2004/09/mil-040914-irin02.htm

Jones, S and Nelson, N (eds) (1999) *Urban Poverty in Africa: From Understanding to Alleviation*, Intermediate Technology Publications, London

Kalb, M K and Kalb, M G (1982) *Congo Cables: The Cold War in Africa: From Eisenhower to Kennedy*, Macmillan, New York

Kasanga, K (1994) *Land Tenure Systems and Ecological Degradation in Northern Ghana*, Royal Institution of Chartered Surveyors, London

Kasanga K (1998) *Rapid Urbanization, Land Markets and Gender Insecurity in Peri-urban Kumasi*, Institute for Land Management and Development, Kumasi

Kasanga, K, Cocrane, J, King, R and Roth, M (1995) 'Land Markets and Legal Contradictions in the Peri-urban Area of Accra: Informant Interviews and Secondary Data Investigations', *LTC Research Paper*, No 127, Land Tenure Center, Madison, WI

Kasanga, K and Kotey, N (2001) *Land Management in Ghana: Building on Tradition and Modernity*, IIED, London

Kasfir, N (ed) (1998) *Civil Society and Democracy in Africa,* Frank Cass, London

Kates, R and Mabogunje, A (2004) 'Sustainable Development in Ijebu-Ode, Nigeria: The Role of Social Capital, Participation, and Science and Technology', CID Working Paper No 102, Harvard University Cambridge, MA, www.cid.harvard.edu/cidwp/102.htm

Kherallah, M, Delgado, C, Gabre-Madhin, E, Minot, N and Johnson, M (2002) *Reforming Agricultural Markets in Africa*, IFPRI & John Hopkins Press, Baltimore

Kilama, W (2004) *Africa Fighting Malaria*, www.fightingmalaria.org

King, K (1996) *Jua Kali Kenya: Change and Development in an Informal Economy, 1970–95*, East African Educational Publishers, Nairobi

Kjekshus, H (1976) *Ecological Control and Economic Development in East African History,* University of California Press, Berkeley, CA

Kotey, N (2001) 'Compulsory Acquisition of Land in Ghana, the 1992 Constitution: Opening New Vistas?,' in C Toulmin, P L Deville and S Traoré (eds) *The Dynamics of Resource Tenure in West Africa*, James Currey, Oxford

Landell-Mills, N and Porras, I T (2002) *Silver Bullet or Fools' Gold? A Global Review of Markets for Forest Environmental Services and their Impact on the Poor*, IIED, London

Lane, C (1996) *Ngorongoro Voices: Indigenous Maasai Residents of the Ngorongoro Conservation Area in Tanzania Give their Views on the Proposed General Man-*

agement Plan, Forest, Trees and People Programme, Lantbruks University, Sweden

Lane, C (1998) *Custodians of the Commons: Pastoral Land in East and West Africa,* IIED, London

Larbi, W (2000) 'Land Use and the Disposal of Stool/Skin/Family Lands: Problems and Solutions', paper presented at the Institute of Local Government Studies, Accra

Leach, G and Mearns, R (eds) (1996) *The Lie of the Land,* Heinemann, Portsmouth, NH

Le Roy, E, Karsenty, A and Bertrand, A (1996*) La sécurisation foncière en Afrique,* Karthala, Paris

Logan, I (2004) 'Ideology and Power in Resource Management', in W Moseley and I Logan (eds), *African Environment and Development,* pp17–40, Ashgate, Aldershot, Hants

Lund, C (1993) 'Waiting for the Rural Code: Perspectives on a Land Tenure Reform in Niger', *Drylands Issues Paper,* No 44, IIED, London

Lund, C (2001) 'African Land Tenure: Questioning Basic Assumptions', in B Tor and C Lund (eds) *Politics, Property and Production in the West African Sahel: Approaches to Natural Resources Management,* Nordic Africa Institute/Transaction, Uppsala

Mabogunje, A (undated) *Cities as Arenas of Accelerated Social Transformations,* UNESCO, Managing Social Transformations Programme, UNESCO, Paris, www.unesco.org/most/wien/akin.htm

McCann, J (1999) *Green Land, Brown Land, Black Land,* Heinemann, Portsmouth

Machipisa, L (2000) 'EDUCATION-AFRICA: Calls for Global Campaign to Abolish Primary School Fees', InterPress Service, 6 December, www.aegis.com/news/ips/2000/IP001209.html

MacKenzie, F (1999) *Land, Ecology, and Resistance in Kenya,* Heinemann, London

Manby, B (1999) *The Price of Oil: Corporate Responsibility and Human Rights Violations in Nigeria's Oil Producing Communities,* Human Rights Watch, New York, www.hrw.org/reports/1999/nigeria/

Manby, B (ed) (2003) *Sudan, Oil, and Human Rights,* Human Rights Watch, New York, www.hrw.org/reports/2003/sudan1103/

Maxwell, S (2001a) 'The Evolution of Thinking about Food Security', in S Devereaux and S Maxwell (eds) *Food Security in Sub-Saharan Africa,* pp13–31, ITDG Publishing, London

Maxwell, S (2001b) 'Agricultural Issues in Food Security', in S Devereaux and S Maxwell (eds), *Food Security in Sub-Saharan Africa,* pp32–66, ITDG Publishing, London

Mbeki, T (2004) 'Briefing by President Thabo Mbeki at the World Economic Forum Meeting: Millennium Africa Renaissance Program – Implementation Issues', *African Union Summit,* 28 January, www.au2002.gov.za/docs/speeches/mbeki010128.htm

Mekendamp, M, van Tongeren, P and van de Veen, H (eds) (1999) *Searching for Peace in Africa: An Overview of Conflict Prevention and Management Activities,* European Platform for Conflict Prevention and Transformation, Utrecht

Mengisteab, K and Daddieh, C (1999) *State Building and Democratization in Africa,* Praeger, Westport, CT

Mengisteab, K and Logan, B I (eds) (1995) *Beyond Economic Liberalization in Africa: Structural Adjustment and the Alternatives,* Zed Press, London

Metcalfe, S (1994) 'The Zimbabwe Communal Areas Management Programme for Indigenous Resources (CAMPFIRE)', in D Western and R M Wright (eds) *Natural Connections: Perspectives in Community-based Conservation,* pp161–91, Island Press, Washington, DC

Millennium Development Goals (2000) 'Millennium development goals', www.developmentgoals.org/Education.htm

Miller, H (1993) *Peace and Reconciliation in Africa: A Preliminary Survey of Ecumenical Perspectives and Initiatives,* Mennonite Central Committee Occasional Papers, Akron, www.mcc.org/respub/occasional/19.html

Mkandawire, T and Soludo, C (1999*) Our Continent/Our Future: African Perspectives on Structural Adjustment,* IRRC/CODISIRA/Africa World Press, Ottawa

Mkapa, B (2004) 'Speech by the President of the United Republic of Tanzania and Co-chair of the World Commission on the Social Dimension of Globalization, His Excellency Benjamin William Mkapa, at the Presentation of the Report of the Commission to the Governing Body of the International Labour Organization', Geneva, 24 March, www.ilo.org/public/english/wcsdg/docs/mkapa2.pdf

Mlawa, H and Green, R (eds) (1998) *Through Structural Adjustment to Transformation in Sub-Saharan Africa,* Dar es Salaam University Press and African Book Collective, Dar es Salaam, Tanzania and Oxford

MMSD Project (Mining, Minerals, and Sustainable Development) (2002) *Breaking New Ground,* Report of the MMSD Project, Earthscan, London

Moeller, S (1999) *Compassion Fatigue: How the Media Sell Disease, Famine, War and Death,* Routledge, New York

Møller, B (2001) 'Conflict Prevention and Peace-Building in Africa', background paper for the Danida Conference on Conflict Prevention and Peace-Building in Africa, Maputo, 28–9 June, www.copri.dk/publications/WP/WP%202001/28-2001.doc

Mortimore, M and Adams, W M (2001) 'Farmer Adaptation, Change and "Crisis" in the Sahel', *Global Environment Change,* vol 11, no 1, pp49–57

Mudimbe, V (1994) *The Idea of Africa,* James Currey, London

Murwira, K, Wedgwood, H, Watson, C and Win, E with Tawney, C (2000) *Beating Hunger: The Chivi Experience: A Community-Based Approach to Food Security in Zimbabwe,* Intermediate Technology Publications, London

Nairobi Peace Initiative (2003) *Report of Part II of a Peacebuilding Practitioners' Regional Workshop on Conflict Early Warning and Response Methodology and Application,* Nairobi Peace Initiative, Nairobi, www.carleton.ca/cifp/docs/NairobiPeace.pdf

Natural Resource Institute (NRI) (2003) *The Identification, Incidence and Control of Sweet Potato Viruses in East and South Africa and Assessment of Host Plant Resistance for Sustainable Development,* Greenwich University/NRI, London, www.nri.org/spv/

NEPAD (New Partnership for Africa's Development) (2001) *New Partnership for Africa's Development,* www.uneca.org/nepad/

Ngwane, T (2003) 'Sparks in the Township', *New Left Review*, vol 22, July–August, www.newleftreview.net/NLR25603.shtml

OCHA (Office of the UN Co-ordinator for Humanitarian Affairs) (2004) 'South Africa: Country Profile', www.irinnews.org/AIDS/south_africa.asp

Odgaard, R (1997) 'The Gender Dimension of Naykysa Rural–Rural Migration in Mbeya Region', in S Ngware, R Odgaard, R Shayo and F Wilson (eds) *Gender and Agrarian Change in Tanzania*, pp46–70, DUP Ltd, Dar es Salaam

Ouédraogo, J-B (1996) *Violence et communautés en Afrique noire*, L'Harmattan, Paris

Oxfam Canada (2002) 'Coffee companies unoer fire as millions face ruin', www.oxfam.ca/news/MakeTradeFair/Launch02.htm

Oyebade, A and Alao, A (eds) (1998) *Africa after the Cold War: The Changing Perspectives on Security*, Africa World Press, Trenton, NJ

Palmer, R and Parsons, N (eds) (1977) *The Roots of Rural Poverty in Central and Southern Africa*, University of California Press, Berkeley, CA

Quaker United Nations Office (QUNO) (2001) Quaker Consultation on Peaceful Prevention of Violent Conflict, Focus Africa, 2nd Annual Gathering, 30 September–5 October, QUNO, New York and Washington, DC, www.afsc.org/quno/Resources/QPN2001report1.htm

Quaker United Nations Office (QUNO) (2002) Quaker Consultation on Peaceful Prevention of Violent Conflict, Focus Africa, 3rd Annual Gathering, 23–27 September, QUNO, New York, Bujumbura and Gitega, Burundi, www.afsc.org/quno/Resources/QPN2002report.htm

Raychaudhuri, S (1999) 'Is Globalization Bypassing Africa?', *Africa Recovery*, vol 13, nos 2 & 3 (September), www.un.org/ecosocdev/geninfo/afrec/vol13no2/03undp.htm

Raynaut, C (ed) (1997) *Sahels, diversité et dynamiques de relations sociétés-nature*, Karthala, Paris

Reader, J (1997) *Africa: Biography of a Continent*, Vintage, New York

Reij, C, Scoones, I and Toulmin, C (eds) (1996) *Sustaining the Soil: Indigenous Soil and Water Conservation in Africa*, Earthscan, London

Reuters (2004) 'Darfur Death Toll Reaches 70,000 – U.N. Agency', Reuters, 15 October, http://reuters.com/newsArticle.jhtml?type=worldNews&storyID=6515089&section=news

Richards, P (1996) *Fighting for the Rain Forest: War, Youth and Resources in Sierra Leone*, Heinemann, London

Rischard, J (2002) *High Noon: 20 Global Problems/20 Years to Solve Them*, Basic Books, New York

Roberts, M (2003) *Pillage and Plunder: An Anthology of African Dictators*, South Australia, Flinders University, Adelaide, www.ssn.flinders.edu.au/global/africa/marcroberts/

Rodney, W (1981) [1974] *How Europe Underdeveloped Africa*, Howard University Press, Washington, DC

Rotberg, R and Rabb, T (eds) (1985) *Hunger and History*, Cambridge University Press, Cambridge

SADC (Southern African Development Community) (2004) *Southern Africa Flood and Drought Network*, http://edcw2ks40.cr.usgs.gov/sa_floods/index.asp

Salih, M (2001) *African Democracies and African Politics*, Pluto Press, London

Samatar, A (1999) *An African Miracle: State and Class Leadership and Colonial Legacy in Botswana Development*, Heinemann, London

Scoones, I (ed) (1995) *Living with Uncertainty: New Directions in Pastoral Development in Africa*, Intermediate Technology Publications, London

Sen, A (1981) *Poverty and Famines*, Oxford University Press, Oxford

Serequeberhan, T (1997) 'The Critique of Eurocentrism and the Practice of African Philosophy', in E C Eze (ed) *Postcolonial African Philosophy: A Critical Reader*, pp141–61, Blackwell, Oxford

Shivji, I (1998) *Not Yet Democracy: Reforming Land Tenure in Tanzania*, Drylands Programme, IIED, London

Shivji, I and Kapinga, W B (1998) 'Problems of Land Tenure in Tanzania: A Review and Appraisal of the Report of the Presidential Commission of Enquiry into Land Matters', paper prepared for the IIED and presented at the Land Policy Workshop held at Arusha, 15–19 January 1995

Simon, D (1997) 'Urbanization, Globalization and Economic Crisis in Africa', in C Rakodi (ed) *The Urban Challenge in Africa: Growth and Management of Its Large Cities*, United Nations University Press, Tokyo

Simon, D, van Spengen, W, Dixon, C and Närman, A (1995) *Structurally Adjusted Africa: Poverty, Debt and Basic Needs*, Pluto, London

Smith, M (2004) 'Development – Africa: Water Management Crucial to Growth', IPS, 16 March, http://ipsnews.net/interna.asp?idnews=22878

Steyn, P (2004) '"(S)hell in Nigeria": The Environmental Impact of Oil Politics in Ogoniland on Shell International', in W Moseley and B I Logan (eds) *African Environment and Development*, pp213–28, Ashgate, Aldershot

Tandon, Y (1995) 'Grassroots Resistance to Dominant Land-Use Patterns in Southern Africa', in B Taylor (ed) *Ecological Resistance Movements: The Global Emergence of Radical and Popular Environmentalism*, pp161–76, State University of New York Press, Albany, NY

Thebaud, B (2004) *Portrait de Famille: Guide De Recherche Participative*, ARED/IIED, Dakar, Senegal

Tiffen, M, Mortimore, M and Gichuki, F (1994) *More People, Less Erosion: Environmental Recovery in Kenya*, Wiley, New York

Timberlake, L (1985) *Africa in Crisis*, Earthscan, London

Toulmin, C (2001) 'Lessons from the Theatre: Should This Be the Final Curtain Call for the Convention to Combat Desertification?', *WSSD Opinion Papers*, London

Toulmin, C and Guèye, B (2003) 'Transformations in West African Agriculture', *IIED Drylands Issue Paper No. 123*, IIED, London

Toulmin, C and Quan, J (eds) (2000) *Evolving Land Rights, Policy and Tenure in Africa*, Natural Resource Institute, London

Toulmin, C, Delville, P and Traoré, S (eds) (2001) *The Dynamics of Resource Tenure in West Africa*, James Curry, Oxford

Traoré, S (2001) 'Straying Fields – Difficulties in Enforcing the Customary Principle of Shared Pastoral Land Management in the Ferlo, Senegal', in C Toulmin, P L Delville and S Traoré (eds) *The Dynamics of Resource Tenure in West Africa*, James Curry, Oxford

Tripp, A (1997) *Changing the Rules: The Politics of Liberalization and the Urban Informal Economy in Tanzania*, University of California Press, Berkeley, CA

Tsikata, D and Whitehead, A (2004) 'Securing Women's Land Rights: Approaches, Prospects and Challenges', paper presented to the Land in Africa Conference, London, 8–9 November, IIED, NRI, RAS

Turshen, M (1999) *Privatizing Health Services in Africa*, Rutgers University Press, New Brunswick, NJ

UN (2004) *Progress toward Millennium Development Goals 1990–2003*, UN, Department of Economic and Social Affairs, Statistics Division, New York, http://millenniumindicators.un.org/unsd/mi/pdf/Goal_2-final.pdf

UNAIDS/WHO (1998) *Report on the Global HIV/AIDS Epidemic June 1998*, www.who.int/emc-hiv/global_report/rep_html/report6.html

UNCTAD (2004) *Economic Development in Africa: Trade Performance and Commodity Dependence*, United Nations, New York

UNDP (1999) *Human Development Report 1999*, UNDP, New York

UNDP (2003a) 'Human Development Report 2003 Charts Decade-long Income Drop in 54 Countries', 8 July, http://hdr.undp.org/reports/global/2003/pdf/presskit/HDR03_PR2E.pdf

UNDP (2003b) *Human Development Report 2003*, UNDP, New York

UNDP (2004) *Human Development Report 2004*, UNDP, New York, http://hdr.undp.org/reports/global/2004/

UNECA (UN Economic Commission for Africa) (2002a) 'Recent Economic Trends', in *Economic Report on Africa 2002: Tracking Performance and Progress*, Chapter 1, www.uneca.org/era2002/ERA2000/Chapter1.pdf

UNECA (UN Economic Commission for Africa) (2002b) 'Africa's Economic Growth Insufficient to Meet Poverty Reduction Goals, Brussels Meeting Concludes', www.health.fgov.be/WHI3/krant/krantarch2002/kranttekstnov2/021120m07un.htm

UNEP (2002a) 'The Driving Forces for the Scenarios', *African Environmental Outlook*, UNEP, Nairobi: www.unep.org/aeo/266.htm

UNEP (2002b) 'Urban Areas', *African Environmental Outlook*, Part G, UNEP, Nairobi, www.unep.org/aeo/203.htm

UNESCO (2004) *EFA Global Monitoring Report 2004. Regional Overview: Sub-Saharan Africa*, http://portal.unesco.org/education/en/ev.php-URL_ID=23023&URL_DO=DO_TOPIC&URL_SECTION=201.html

UNFPA (undated) '34 million friends: Frequently asked questions', www.unfpa.org/support/friends/faqs.htm#support

UN-Habitat (UN Human Settlements Programme) (2003a) *The Challenge of Slums: Global Report on Human Settlements 2003*, Nairobi, UNCHS, www.unhabitat.org/global_report.asp

UN-Habitat (UN Human Settlements Programme) (2003b) *Slums of the World: The Face of Urban Poverty in the New Millennium?* Nairobi, UNCHS www.unhabitat.org/programmes/guo/documents/SlumReport.pdf

UNICEF (2003) *End Decade Database*. UNICEF/WHO/UNFPA estimates of maternal mortality ratios, maternal deaths and lifetime risk for 1995 (Table 1), www.childinfo.org/eddb/mat_mortal/

UNICEF (2004a) *Impact of Armed Conflict on Children: Land-mines: A Deadly Inheritance*, www.unicef.org/graca/mines.htm

UNICEF (2004b) *Child Trafficking*, UNICEF Innocenti Research Centre Florence, Italy, www.unicef-icdc.org/research/IIS/CP2.html

UNICEF (2004c) 'Drought Increases Risk of Malnutrition in Northern Somalia', *ReliefWeb*, 6 January, www.reliefweb.int/w/rwb.nsf/0/b436c57ec39077c6 85256e14005aa470?OpenDocument

UNOCHA (2004) 'Rwanda: Census finds 937,000 died in genocide', 2 April, www.reliefweb.int/w/rwb.nsf/UNID/F308B7EC24168C9885256E6A00558 A7D?OpenDocument

UNRISD (2000) *Visible Hands,*UNRISD, Geneva

USIP (United States Institute for Peace) (2001) 'AIDS and Violent Conflict in Africa', Special Report 75, USIP, 15 October, Washington, www.usip.org/pubs/ specialreports/sr75.html

Vaux, T (2001) *The Selfish Altruist,* Earthscan, London

Wambugu, F (1995) 'Control of African Sweet Potato Virus Diseases through Biotechnology and Technology Transfer', Biotechnology Seminar Paper, International Service for National Agricultural Research (ISNAR), April, Netherlands, www.isnar.cgiar.org/ibs/papers/wambugu.pdf

WCSDG (World Commission on Social Dimension of Globalization) (2004) *A Fair Globalization: Creating Opportunities for All*, ILO, Geneva, www.ilo.org/ public/english/wcsdg/

Whitehead, A and Tsikata, D (2001) 'Policy Discourses on Women's Land Rights in Sub-Saharan Africa', paper prepared for the UNRISD Project on Agrarian Change, Gender and Land Rights, UNRISD, Geneva

Whitehead, A and Tsikata, D (2003) 'Policy Discourses on Women's Land Rights in Sub-Saharan Africa: The Implications of the Return to the Customary', *Journal of Agrarian Change*, vol 3, nos 1–2, pp67–112

Wiggins, S (2000) 'Interpreting Changes from the 1970s to the 1990s in African Agriculture through Village Studies', *World Development*, vol 28, no 4, pp631–62

Wisner, B (1992) 'Health of the Future/Future of Health', in A Seidman et al (eds), *21st Century Africa*, pp149–82, Africa World Press, Trenton, NJ

Wisner, B (1995a) 'Bridging "Expert" and "Local" Knowledge for Counter-Disaster Planning in Urban South Africa', *GeoJournal*, vol 37, no 3 (November), pp335–48

Wisner, B (1995b) '*Luta*, Livelihood, and Lifeworld in Contemporary Africa', in B Taylor (ed) *Ecological Resistance Movements*, pp177–200, SUNY Press, Albany

Wisner, B, Blaikie, P, Cannon, T and Davis, I (2004) *At Risk: Natural Hazards, People's Vulnerability and Disasters*, 2nd edn, Routledge, London

Woodhouse, P, Bernstein, H, and Hulme, D (2000), *African Enclosures? The Social Dynamics of Wetlands in Drylands*, James Currey and Africa World Press, Oxford and Trenton, NJ

World Bank (2003) *Africa Region Trade Progress Note*, The World Bank, June, Washington, DC, www.worldbank.org/afr/trade/wb_assistance_2003_03.pdf

World Bank (2004) 'Ecowas Leaders, World Bank Head Push Regional Approaches on Trade, Infrastructure and Peace', *allAfrica.com*, 24 March, http://allafrica. com/stories/200403240042.html

WHO (World Health Organization) (2003) *World Health Report 2003,* WHO, Geneva, www.who.int/whr/2003/en/

WHO (2004) 'Recent outbreaks of cholera in Africa', WHO, Geneva, www.who.int/csr/don/2004_02_18a/en/

Part I
HUMAN ECOLOGY

1
Land-based Livelihoods

Mamadou Baro and Simon Batterbury

Introduction

African farmers and pastoralists have been meeting their everyday needs in diverse ways for many centuries. While this process has increasingly been recognized since the late colonial period, a major development since the publication of Lloyd Timberlake's *Africa in Crisis* (Timberlake, 1985) has been the emergence of support to 'livelihood security' and the incorporation of 'sustainable rural livelihoods' in the rationales and thinking of government-led projects and the many international development agencies working in Africa. Researchers too have focused renewed attention on how diverse rural societies enhance their welfare and development options in many corners of the continent.

In this chapter, we explore the fundamental components that shape everyday livelihoods, focusing on dryland West Africa. We look at the constraints that continue to imperil the achievement of livelihood security, as well as the measured (but very diverse) ways in which rural communities piece together income generation, participation in institutions and subsistence activities to ensure their welfare and survival. We provide brief examples from Mali and Niger to illustrate some of these household responses. We conclude that secure rural livelihoods are attained not only by households and individuals using their skills, knowledge and labour to assemble assets and entitlements, but also by finding ways to negotiate the risks created by poor governance, economic uncertainty, conflict and vulnerability to natural hazards. Ultimately, rural programmes and development schemes in rural Africa have to address the broader political and economic contexts in which livelihoods are nested.

What are Rural Livelihoods?

Scoones (1998) suggests that livelihoods are 'the capabilities, assets (including both material and social resources) and activities required for making a living', a definition that echoes the early formulation of rural development stalwarts Chambers and Conway (1992). They are essentially the activities that people do to 'get by' – to survive and to meet their everyday needs – as well as those more entrepreneurial and profit-focused activities that are best summarized as 'getting on' – striving towards better conditions of material well-being (Davies et al, 1998). African farmers, pastoralists and households 'assemble' a portfolio of livelihood strategies based upon a combination of their skills, knowledge and response to opportunity, but livelihood strategies are ever-changing and involve a constellation of components and networks.

'Getting by' aims to ensure a regular supply of food and other important assets, and is achieved through what scholars refer to as 'coping strategies' (Mortimore, 1989), or processes of 'adaptation' to the environmental and social conditions in which they live (Netting, 1993; Batterbury and Forsyth, 1999). While many empirical studies have documented these strategies in near-subsistence societies, this type of analysis can also be applied to conditions where commercial activity and markets are highly important – where rural people are involved in producing and selling commodities, and responding to the unstable employment and life-chances that this can involve. In times of hardship, 'getting by' can easily become the quotidian norm: the search for wild plants and other foodstuffs to supplement the household diet, for example, is now a regular feature of life in the Koro region of Mali, as we explain below.

Since rural poverty is still endemic in Africa, we can surmise that 'getting on' over a life course has only been achieved by a minority of rural people. These include skilled entrepreneurs, those who have been able to exploit and develop their asset base, or those who have inherited and consolidated familial claims to ample labour, livestock or land for farming or herding. An elevated position in stratified society, sometimes coupled with a strong position in political networks, provides labour and assets (either by birth, marriage, new political alliances, conquest or resulting from colonial policy).

Different development philosophies have supported rural livelihoods, which were caught up in colonial projects to develop new territories from the late 19th century. As we show in the next section, many of these efforts were unsuccessful at promoting a structural shift towards more sustainable and lucrative livelihood systems in West Africa. On the one hand, there have been modest efforts to provide much-needed credit or subsidized technologies to poorer households 'in situ'. On the other hand, the colonial and post-colonial demand for commodities (particularly cotton, cocoa, coffee, palm oil and groundnuts in West Africa) has favoured not only a new class of landed commodity producers, but also led to the emergence of new labour regimes based around contract farming or sharecropping, and encouraged labour migration to those regions (Bryceson, 1999; Baker, 2000). Also, West Africa's farming systems must be set within the context of Africa-wide de-agrarianization and the emergence of limited urban and industrial employment in certain regions (Bryceson and Jamal, 1997; Bryceson et al, 2000; Beall, this volume).

Seeking livelihood security is not just a question of mobilizing one's labour and assets to find food or work: it can become a highly political act, for example when it embroils individuals in land tenure battles or wage bargaining, or leads to

the establishment of politically active local organizations and federations. Livelihoods are embedded within broader structures and forces, including political
networks (Bebbington, 1999). The livelihood system is central to the achievement of certain outcomes, but heavily influenced by context and by the disposi-
tion of 'capital' assets of different types. In order to understand a livelihood system
one must consider more than how a household obtains and allocates food and
other essential resources (Ellis, 1998; Ellis, 2000; Francis, 2000). The household
juggles 'capitals' – natural resources as well as labour, capital, time and tools in
response to a number of external signals and constraints, to manage everyday
decision-making. In this chapter, two examples from Niger and Mali illustrate
how this is done, before we return to the broader implications of livelihoods
analysis in the context of West Africa's changing fortunes.

Unfolding Livelihoods in West Africa

The networks in which rural households and livelihoods in Africa are embedded
have their origins at multiple scales, from the family farm (Bélières et al, 2002) up
to price-setting mechanisms for the commodities that some farmers produce.
Although households (of different forms and levels of complexity) are the best
place to begin understanding rural livelihoods, the social arrangements and institutions that make household activities possible are broader and more complex.

The post-colonial era saw expansion of commodity production in agriculture,
alongside resource-extractive industries and some very limited industrialization.
Africa's new policy-makers hoped that all three would be of general benefit to
national development. There was also a renewed hope that rural people and their
labour would fuel modernization and economic take-off of the well-ordered type
that had existed in the region's more affluent entrepots like Lomé, Dakar and
Freetown in the late colonial period. But in the 1970s, economic growth turned
to recession with the drying up of investment and the high oil prices, coupled
with an unfortunate lack of effective governance in several countries (Bryceson
and Bank, 2001). In the 1980s the severe hardship resulting from climatic perturbations (as in the Sahel) and other emergencies resulted in international donor
support for an increasing range of projects including irrigation supply, infrastructure and famine relief. The largest scheme was the Senegal River Valley Project,
which constructed two major dams (Manantali and Diama) encompassing Senegal, Mauritania and Mali. The extensive areas of irrigation opened up by the project
were designed to shift recession agriculture in riparian areas along the Senegal river
into these new irrigated areas (Baro, 1993).

By the late 1980s there was optimism in the region that the threat of famine
had receded, and market-led growth of the rural sector would be sustained, fed in
part by growing urban populations and foreign exchange earned for some successful commodities like cotton, gold and uranium. Yet this optimism was short-lived.
Drought returned, combined with continued population growth, a loss of economic opportunities and the application of perverse subsidies. Complex emergencies persisted, including those in Liberia, Sierra Leone, northern Niger and
Mali, and the Casamance region of Senegal and The Gambia. Conflict reduces

agricultural productivity in affected areas and has serious long-term consequences for household stability. Even areas not directly affected by conflict often suffer from its effects. In addition, malaria and the HIV/AIDS pandemic have taken their toll on the productive members of poor households. As the rates of HIV/AIDS infection increase in West Africa, productivity is reduced, negatively affecting food availability.

Economic policies in West Africa have been dominated by the presence of large government loans taken from the International Financial Institutions (IFIs), known as structural adjustment until their reworking as Poverty Reduction Strategy Paper (PRSPs) in the late 1990s. These have had mixed success, often creating hardship through removing subsidies for agricultural inputs and some state-support networks, but promising increased commodity sales or business activity through removal of market price controls. The latter, however, often require kick-starting through financial credit or skills training, both in short supply in the region. West African livelihoods are also affected by commodity pricing and trade rules. The most famous example in recent years has been the collapse of the Malian and Burkinabé cotton industry which, after a period of growth, has been affected by subsidies given by the USA government to its less efficient producers, who now dominate the world market as a result (Watkins and Sul, 2002).

In the drylands of West Africa in the 1970s and 1980s the combination of incipient famine and policy failure led many rural dwellers to buffer increased risks by refocusing their income generation on more diverse activities, often with increased economic migration to urban environments, or to more affluent rural areas like northern Côte d'Ivoire, Togo and Senegal (Bélières et al, 2002). These migrant routes have been used on and off by Sahelian peoples for hundreds of years. Although the data are partial, one can also chart an increase in other buffers against vulnerability – more business activity with greater spatial reach, the sale and purchase of livestock by farmers, and a diversification of cultivars and petty trade (Mortimore and Adams, 2001).

Weakly developed rural markets characterize the remote and poorly serviced regions of West Africa. Price controls and regulatory systems, monopolies, complex systems of foreign exchange, and a general under-capitalization and lack of assets in the rural sector, are all to blame. In sub-regions with sufficient market opportunities, as well as communication and transportation infrastructures, markets can help buffer against localized droughts or food shortages. However, in many regions of the Sahel, market structures are rudimentary enough that these simple transfers cannot occur, or prices are beyond the reach of poorer individuals. In these regions, it is more likely that localized production shortages translate directly into localized food insecurity.

The new millennium began with sanguine and realistic hopes for the agrarian and pastoral sectors. The political and economic conditions that frustrate local-level livelihood security are persistent. 'Livelihoods thinking', therefore, has emerged as a viable rural development paradigm at a time when the very conditions it was designed to understand and ameliorate make the achievement of livelihood security very difficult. What Bryceson and Bank call 'post-modern liberalism' (2001, p11) now recognizes that ambitious development schemes have been unsuccessful (partly in response to adverse world markets and globalization trends) and attention has turned to more modest, less ambitious goals – equitably distributed 'entitlements' to food, land etc (Sen, 1981) and 'livelihood security'. The feeling among donor agencies is that rural policies should be more careful, targeted and sustainable – few people are now hopeful of large-scale modernization of the rural sector in Africa. Key to this is more effective local governance – exploiting the positive feature of the drive to decentralize fiscal and decision-making powers down to local people, but not in an uncritical fashion that ignores local politics and status (Engberg-Pedersen, 2002). Decentralization (Ribot, Chapter 8, this volume) has a mixed record since it can also empower local elites at the expense of the poor, and has been used to create a power base for central government and political parties in the countryside.

Two Cases

Diversification in response to stress Fandou Béri, Niger

Niger, one of the poorest countries on the continent and with 'no realistic short-term prospects of accelerated development' (Kelley, 2002, p643) experienced a crisis of national political legitimacy, fiscal shortfalls and a withdrawal of international aid in the 1990s. The effects in rural areas, particularly those distant from major towns and cities, were severe. As already meagre state support, NGO activity and commercial opportunities were scaled back, Zarma farmers in the south-west of the country, even those relatively close to the capital city, fell back upon adaptive strategies built around their own rural and urban activities. Livelihood strategies therefore became vital, as vulnerability worsened over several years (Batterbury, 2001).

In the 1970s farmers had emerged from a drought and a previous economic downturn. In 1975 a new political regime under President Kountché came to power, fuelled by uranium revenues that supported agricultural extension agents, a reliable primary education system, medical services and rural cooperatives. But uranium exports collapsed again in the 1980s at a time when the Sahel was once more experiencing drought conditions. This resulted in increased taxation, wage freezes and price reforms, all under a structural adjustment model introduced with IFI loans. The rural support systems begun under Kountché decayed and there was a balance of payments crisis, and frequent changes of government (with two military coups since 1996 alone). By the late 1990s, even rural areas situated quite close to major population centres were without the rural support services they had previously enjoyed. Several international aid donors pulled out of the country or scaled back their activities. Devaluation of the regional currency, the CFA franc, in 1994 raised the cost of imports, but benefited the international livestock trade and Niger's few exports.[1] In sum, Niger was seeing 'development in reverse'.

Fandou Béri is a small Zarma village located about 55km east of Niger's capital city, Niamey.[2] Rainfed agriculture is dominated by millet, the staple crop, grown in the short wet season from June to October. Livestock ownership by the Zarma is widespread, and a few Peulh (Fulani) pastoralist families also live permanently close by the settlement. In this community, typical of so many in dryland West Africa, monetization of the economy first occurred at the beginning of the 20th century, creating a household demand for cash to pay for taxes and, increasingly, consumer items. Cotton was once grown, but such commercial crops are very rare today. The last major development initiative in the village, a commercial seed project, finished acrimoniously in 1989.

The 'vulnerability context' here has always required inventiveness and adaptability. Fandou Béri exemplifies a trend seen elsewhere in this region – increasing local mobility and a changing pattern of labour, resources and skills. In the 1950s, for example, male migration was rare, land for farming and forage was more abundant than today and the community was more reliant on its own food sources. Influenced strongly by two droughts in the mid-1960s and the regional one of 1972–74, diversification was also aided by improvements in 'connectivity' through transport improvements and road building. Access to markets and to Niamey was improved. This helped women to earn and spend their own income, independently from men.

Four traditional household and individual livelihood diversification activities, aside from crop production, developed in this period. These were the increased ownership of livestock by Zarma farmers, labouring for other people, engaging in business activity, and seasonal or long-term migration. Strategies are mixed and matched by individuals to maintain a portfolio of income sources, and some people fare better than others at 'productive bricolage' – the juggling of livelihood activities (Batterbury, 2001), each of which requires different levels of start-up capital and labour. In the larger households, labour of the household members can be deployed more easily to minimize risk, resulting in easier 'switching' between these activities; building up some but de-emphasizing others, depending on profits and labour availability. Older men and women (particularly male lineage elders and the senior wives of polygynous households) have always been able to command more labour and capital. Young Zarma women generally lack these assets and social power, which can set off intra-household conflict over their daily workloads and labour inputs.

Some examples drawn from Table 1.1 illustrate the diversity of livelihood responses in 1997. Household 2 is large and complex, comprising the village chief and his relatives. His ability to command land assets for farming is good, but he experienced a harvest shortfall and financial difficulties that year. So his large livestock herd acted as a tradable asset. Household 6, managed efficiently by a prominent woman entrepreneur, invested in fuel-wood collection and sales to maintain an above-average income. Three Peulh families (hh 14–16) are denied secure land access by their ethnicity and status in the community. But they combine good crop yields obtained with large inputs of manure and careful crop management on small, loaned plots with maintaining large animal herds – rather than through economic migration or trading.

An outcome of livelihood diversification is increased livestock ownership and sales, a trend seen right across the Sahel among farming peoples in the late 20th century (Batterbury and Warren, 2001). Livestock ownership ranges from a single sheep or goat to large herds of cattle or even camels. All are 'bankable' investments, and three-quarters of household heads bought and sold livestock (primarily sheep and goats, but with some cattle). Livestock provide financial security and are easily

Table 1.1 *Comparing farm and non-farm activities for households in Fandou Béri in 1997*

House-hold number	Millet harvest (bottes, a local grain measure)	Household millet requirements (bottes, a local grain measure)	Soil flux on main field (bulked samples) (t ha⁻¹ yr⁻¹)	Annual household income (CFA franc)	Annual household expenditure (CFA franc)	Household financial balance (CFAfranc)	Household animal ownership (Tropical Livestock Units)	Number of migrants in family	Total household size	Local petty trading	Remarks – household status
1	146	300	41.09	179,425	188,650	−9,225	2	0	12	son	Some influence
2	153	400	41.48	542,125	507,450	+34,625	73	1	8	no	Chief. Cash income from taxation
3	191	360	44.23	250,825	820,100	−569,275	12	4	27	no	Religious leader
4	146	300	40.27	208,300	351,800	−143,500	6	2	8	no	Religious leader
5	129	300	38.85	119,225	169,000	−49,775	3	3	12	Hh head	
6	178	250	37.66	375,875	246,700	+129,175	13	1	8	no	Wife is prominent entrepreneur
7	161	200	26.43	137,475	110,900	+26,575	7	0	8	no	
8	235	200	35.28	215,925	227,350	−11,425	5	0	7	Hh head	
9	174	330	42.73	183,225	264,100	−80,875	9	0	9	no	
10	270	250	45.28	262,025	320,575	−58,550	22	3	16	Hh head	
11	191	360	46.46	209,800	224,885	−15,085	5	2	10	Hh head	
12	74	150	40.06	N/A	N/A	N/A	18	2	8	no	Religious leader
13	187	200	33.12	196,050	200,750	−4,700	10	1	3	no	
14	144	300	38.95	224,125	316,600	−92,475	74	2	5	no	Peulh
15	67	300	41.89	206,925	136,600	+70,325	51	0	6	no	Peulh
16	210	450	N/A	414,825	366,000	+48,825	141	1	4	no	Peulh

Source: Batterbury (2001). In 1997, US$1 = CFA 625 (approx).

liquidated when cash is required urgently. The Zarma, like other predominantly agricultural peoples, see the logic in increasing livestock ownership because of its relative stability, but they resist adopting a true agro-pastoral livelihood system since, culturally, it is farming and attachment to land that distinguishes them from the Peulh. Conversely, the Peulh cannot become full-time farmers because they are denied long-term land tenure by the Zarma. They do practise agriculture on small, loaned plots that have such high inputs of animal manure that their yields far outpace the Zarma (Table 1.1). Peulh are also entrusted with the feeding and watering of Zarma animals, and manure 'contracts' are struck with the farmers (exchange of crop stubble grazing for manure). Thus, both ethnic groups systems converge around agro-pastoralism as much as practicalities and entrenched power relationships allow.

A small market for wage labour is available, mostly in the cultivation season and (unlike in Mali, below) confined to men. Agricultural labour was first hired during drought periods in the 1950s, but then at a very modest level since the Zarma were accustomed to deploying family labour (in some cases, former slaves) on their farms. A quarter of adult men worked as paid labourers on the fields of others by 1997, mainly doing essential weeding work and harvesting. They are paid about CFA 750–1000 a day (US$1.20–$1.60); one son earned CFA 22,500 (US$36) this way in a single season, enough to purchase two male sheep or one and a half sacks of millet in July 1997.

The Zarma have always engaged in market trading. Business activity frequently requires travelling to Niamey (two hours by bus) and other market centres, to exploit price differentials. Local market trading and livestock sales are also important, and clearly most activities are seasonal. Some 25 per cent of household heads trade locally, often through marking-up and reselling products like paraffin, matches, kola nuts or foodstuffs (their younger sons engage more infrequently in this activity, preferring the migration option). Women's net profits from business frequently exceed those of their menfolk. Girls begin their income-earning activities at an early age, selling jewellery made from beads bought in the local market, or selling foodstuffs. Foyutto[3] (*Ceratotheca sesamoides*) and crickets, a seasonal snack, are also collected and sold at the regional market. In adulthood, crops such as groundnut, sesame and pois de terre are grown by both men and women separately but in small quantities and are either consumed or sold depending on how much is produced. Incomes vary from CFA 5000–10,000 on average per month per woman engaging in petty commerce and other income-generating activities. Old women specialize in making mats and baskets from local grasses. Fuel-wood sales – the first link of the chain supplying the Niamey market – are dominated by one woman in the village and are lucrative (Batterbury, 2001).

Out-migration is, in the eyes of many, the most problematic strategy for policymakers to comprehend and manage, and yet it is a deep-seated and widespread response to the vagaries of Sahelian life (Rain, 1999; Batterbury and Warren, 2001). Many men are absent from the village in the dry season, and sometimes for years at a time. Seasonal migration relieves reliance on the locality and its sporadic rainfall and undercapitalized markets, and it is one of the main strategies used to earn cash. The Zarma have always migrated widely, notably to Nigeria and Ghana, but by the late 1990s it was most common for them to travel to northern Côte d'Ivoire to work as mobile traders. Some 34 per cent of all men in the village in 1997 had migrated seasonally out of the area, primarily to Côte d'Ivoire but one or two had also gone to northern Nigeria. According to those interviewed, this migration stream has increased since the 1950s. Remittances go to pay for food, rituals and social obligations, especially cloth for wives and for bride wealth payments. Two household heads earned CFA 250,000 (US$400) and CFA 50,000 (US$80) respectively for a single year, but some men cannot even marshal the necessary resources to depart at the beginning of the dry season. In Côte d'Ivoire the migrants stay with other Zarma and live communally, borrowing start-up funds, if necessary, and begin to trade locally in textiles or other head-loaded goods. Although most men do return with cash and goods, some stay away for a long time, or send for their families to join them, and a few do not return at all. Incomes, and the desire to return, are dependent on the economic and political situation in the destination countries. Widespread xenophobic reactions to migrant labourers in Côte d'Ivoire from 2000 have now slowed, perhaps temporarily, the migrant stream to that country (Batterbury, 2001).

These diverse livelihood activities have effects upon agricultural systems, and upon the local landscape (Osbahr and Allan, 2003). In households with high migration rates, soil erosion was found to be higher on their agricultural plots (Warren et al, 2001). This is because in sending household labour to distant locations, weeding and tending of household fields can suffer. Thus there is some correlation between the long-term decline in soil fertility on agricultural land and the emergence of a more diverse economy where the need for cash draws labour to other activities. This is one downside of livelihood diversification, although local people do not perceive it in that way. Diversification and non-farm income sources are closely related to changes in the local landscape – both influence each other.

The Cercle de Koro, Mali

The Cercle do Koro is situated in Mali's 5th region, comprising the area south of the Dogon Plateau and north of the Burkina Faso frontier. With a similar population density to southwestern Niger (median 18.4 people per km²), there is a localized shortage of agricultural land. The livelihood systems of 12 widely dispersed villages in the region were studied in 1996 as part of a project on food security in this sub-region (Baro, 1996).[4]

The study showed similar trends in coping strategies to the Zarma case, and broadly similar climatic conditions and income levels prevail, despite evident differences in political context and ethnicity. Since the 1960s there were two decades of single-party rule in Mali (under Modibo Keita and then Moussa Traoré), during which the widespread Sahelian famines occurred, and the national balance of payments was in deficit. Mali also saw an increase in international assistance and more agricultural support to small farmers over the period. In 1992, a democratically elected government under Alpha Oumar Konaré took power, and a political and administrative process of decentralization began, with elections held to form newly decentralized rural communities in 1999 (Brock and Coulibaly, 1999). There was also a system of government purchases of grain quotas from rural villages until 1982, followed by the gradual liberalization of markets and

Table 1.2 *Livelihood strategies of households in different agro-ecological zones*

Livelihood strategies	% of households				
	Total	High Plateau	Gondo Plain	Sourou Plain	Séno
INCOME					
Livestock sales	24.6	35.3	11.8	14.3	33.3
Loans	10.1	5.9	17.6	7.1	9.5
Paid work	10.1	0	23.5	0	14.3
Gifts from parents	5.8	11.8	0	14.3	0
Selling beer	2.9	5.9	0	7.1	0
Artisanal work	5.8	11.8	0	14.3	0
Other business activity	18.8	5.9	23.5	7.1	33.3
OTHER COPING MECHANISMS					
Purchase of millet	8.7	5.9	11.8	21.4	0
Gathering bush produce	2.9	0	0	7.1	4.8
Reduction in meals	1.4	5.9	0	0	0
Migration	2.9	0	5.9	0	4.8
Use of food reserves	4.3	11.8	0	7.1	0

Source: Baro (1996).
Note: Sample size = 134

trade. Farmers may avail themselves of agricultural credit more easily than in Niger, especially in areas of cotton and rice production (Davies, 1996).

As in Fandou Béri, agrarian systems in Koro region illustrate a strong adaptation to spatial and temporary variability in drought and rainfall. The sample in the survey included farmers of the distinctive Dogon ethnic group (72 per cent), as well as Peulh herders and agro-pastoralists (10 per cent) and Mossi farmers (18 per cent). Each group has culturally distinctive strategies for farming, herding and settlement. In Koro, livelihood strategies differ by geographical location (there are four principal geographical zones) but also according to the 'capability' (Sen, 1981) of individuals and their skills and household networks. At the time of survey, the sale of livestock and engagement in other business activities were the most common practices used by households to gain access to needed cash, but the range of options used was broad.

This co-existence of multiple livelihood options offers a degree of autonomy to individual households. Three different classes of adaptive strategies were noted in the survey. First, there were measures that could be used at any moment and which are local, employed as a reflexive response to changing conditions. A reduction in food intake and the rationalization of low food stocks is practised almost annually as food stocks decline prior to the new autumn harvest, but especially during times of hardship. The consumption of wild foodstuffs is also prevalent (Table 1.3). Some 34 per cent of households depend on these activities for subsistence.

Wild foods were collected by all households in our survey, despite their scarcity during times of drought, during which less palatable species are consumed.

Table 1.3 *Wild foods consumption by agro-ecological zone*

Zones	% households eating wild foods in survey period, 1996
High Plateau	13
Gondo Plain	41.9
Sourou Plain	41.9
Séno	31.4
Total	34.1

Source: Baro (1996).
Note: Sample size = 134

Some 30 per cent of households mentioned the Baobab tree as a food source. There are other trees, shrubs and wild plants of which the leaves and fruits are eaten, some of them much less palatable.

The securing of short-term loans in grain and cash figured in all the case study villages and suggests a certain solidarity among households. In each zone, between 6 and 18 per cent of respondents admitted taking loans in times of hardship. A little less than a third of households borrowed small quantities of cereals from neighbours, parents or local traders during the long dry season, in the hope of returning the same quantity of grain at harvest time. In the case of borrowing from traders, however, 50 per cent more grain was generally demanded on returning the loan. In effect, traders exploited price differentials.

Table 1.4 *Wild foods consumption by agro-ecological zone: Most important food sources*

Plants	% of households eating commonly available or wild foods				
	Total	High Plateau	Gondo Plain	Sourou Plain	Séno
Baobab *Adansonia digitata*	31.8	33.3	50	23.1	10
Tamarind *Tamarindus indica*	9.1	0	0	15.4	20
Karité (Shea nut) fruit *Vitellania paradosea*	6.8	0	11.1	7.7	0
Doum palm	6.8	0	16.7	0	0
Louo *Leptadenia hastata*	9.1	66.7	11.1	0	0
Bere *Boscia senegalensis*	25	0	0	53.8	40
Jujubes *Ziziphus mauritania*	2.3	5.6	0	0	0
Others	9.1	5.6	0	0	30

Source: Baro (1996).
Note: Sample size = 134

More drastic actions result in a reduction in asset stocks – through livestock sales or semi-permanent migration from the region. As in Fandou Béri, the build-up of livestock herds is increasingly part of normal life and over half of households surveyed had either cattle or sheep. The region is also known for its weaving: cloth destined for family use may be sold in times of food stress in exchange for cereals, and local market trading of foods and other goods occurs. Other objects sold off for cash include clothing, guns and bicycles. But sales of some of these items are reserved for situations of extreme hardship, since they are almost impossible to replace in the short term. Peulh herders react to hardship by pursuing a similar combination of livelihood sources as seen among their sedentary neighbours – combining less livestock mobility with exchanges of milk for cereals, as in Fandou Béri.

Livelihood systems involve, as Beall (Chapter 3, this volume) notes, social networks of trust, that in this region allow for occasional loans and borrowing from neighbours. It appears that this practice is most common in villages with established community organizations. Revolving credit systems permit the use of the communal fund for cereals purchase during bad years.

Migration is established and widespread in the culture of several of the ethnic groups present in the region, and unlike in Fandou Béri, it also involves young women who migrate as agricultural workers or who depart to the capital city of Bamako, and other urban areas for brief periods. In harder times, men may migrate to work as labourers elsewhere in the region, exchanging their work for a small quantity of cereals on a daily basis. Migration patterns in the region have been influenced by the devaluation of the CFA franc in 1994, which raised local prices. Also critical has been the situation in Côte d'Ivoire where at least 2 million Malians were resident in the 1990s before rising xenophobia made them increasingly unwelcome. About 15 per cent of households in the survey reported that migration was highly important to livelihoods. Some 44 per cent of migrants headed to Côte d'Ivoire, the majority to work on plantations of cocoa and coffee, and 27 per cent went to Bamako. Less affluent households, particularly on the Sourou Plain, where 60 per cent of households saw at least one of their members leave on migration in 1996, saw it as an exit from difficult food security or disadvantageous tenure conditions.

All of these strategies have limitations. As in Niger, daily living continues to be harsh, there are scant opportunities for income-generating opportunities in local towns like Koro, and the benefits of political reform are slow in coming to the region. The livelihood strategies employed in the survey clearly show the same process of 'productive bricolage', mixing and matching strategies and exploiting near and distant opportunities. It appears that over 50 per cent of income came from agriculture in 1996, but many other activities were pursued. As in Niger, and as other studies have suggested, it is those households of larger than average size that have the flexibility of labour and skills to weather difficult periods (Toulmin, 1992; Davies, 1996; Brock and Coulibaly, 1999). The study also found that the difference in food security between households in the same village was greater than that between villages, due partly to the different constitution and size of households.

Although we have presented the many ways in which people respond to resource constraints, the reality is that the majority are extremely vulnerable to climatic and other stresses and basic needs are far from met. A basic multivariable index placed 40 per cent of those surveyed in the category of 'extremely vulnerable' to food insecurity in 1996 (Baro, 1996, p64). At this time, there was an alarmingly high level of chronic malnutrition, estimated at 43 per cent of the children in the households surveyed. Livelihood insecurity, therefore, is endemic in Koro.

Conclusion

Common threads emerge from our two case studies. First, it is safe to say that for the majority of rural people in West Africa, 'getting by' involves a more complex range of activities and strategies than 20 years ago, although comparative evidence is hard to find. At that time, the Sahel was suffering extreme drought – coping strategies were seen as short-term responses to a natural crisis. But viewed over the longer term, we can see that coping and responding to vulnerability form part of everyday practice and are deeply etched into labour patterns and the evolving relationship between towns and countryside, between rich and poor. Concern that the West African drylands had been pitched into high levels of dependency on aid funds by the droughts of the 1970s proved to be too dramatic. Agricultural systems have proven resilient, livestock herds have been rebuilt, and business and migrant activity have helped to recapitalize areas once devastated by food shortages and hardship (Mortimore and Adams, 2001). In addition to some of the trends described above, rural people are maintaining and extending kin and social networks that extend far beyond their localities. The colonial period initiated some of these movements, which had their roots in tax avoidance and new employment opportunities, but it is rural Africans that have sustained and deepened them.

Second, in many senses the range and diversity of livelihood strategies are increasing, both in response to adversity, and to the widening range of choice offered by the gradual arrival of global linkages throughout the rural Sahel. Local migration offers limited opportunities for agricultural work and trading and forms part of normal kinship and marriage relations. There are other options, but these can be short-lived or (as in the case of artisanal gold mining) risky. Rural to urban migration – particularly to seek work, or to start secondary and higher education – tends to extend out of the Sahel and into neighbouring countries, given the paucity of opportunity, high levels of urban poverty and already saturated labour markets in Sahelian cities like Niamey and Bamako. Violence and conflict in both Niger and Mali have been on a small scale and generally contained, but the established high-volume migration destinations have suffered changing fortunes – in Côte d'Ivoire, the largest economy in the CFA franc zone and a major destination for Sahelians seeking urban and rural jobs, political instability and civil war have seen hundreds of thousands of Sahelians expelled or returning to their countries. At times Nigeria, Togo, Benin and Ghana have also experienced instability or declining labour markets. The response of many Sahelians has become increasingly daring, particularly in regard to immigration controls in Europe and North America. There are many cases of individuals travelling on foot across the Sahara to North Africa where they await opportunities to enter Europe. Sahelians can also be found working in the mines of South Africa, the oilfields of Gabon or in the kitchens of

Tokyo restaurants. There are sufficient numbers of migrants established semi-permanently overseas to provide some villages in Senegal and Mali with a healthy flow of remittances, with complex arrangements (including internet transactions) to make capital transfers back to their natal villages. The remittance economy generates mixed feelings in West Africa. Migrants in Fandou Béri, who had established links in Côte d'Ivoire, regret their absence but have long viewed the migrant trail as a proving ground for young men, with its rewards limited in wealth but abundant in life experience. The Sahel is thus experiencing its own version of globalization.

Third, it is important not to idealize rural livelihoods. Rural life in Africa is hard, given current rates of illness and mortality, low income levels and other hardships, some noted in the chapter. Livelihood diversity is a response to the risks and uncertainty that characterize rural life. It is in part a function of the Sahel's diverse and unpredictable ecology, that makes pure agriculture or pastoralism an unreliable enterprise. Equally, the modern-day uncertainties that surround land access and tenure arrangements in countries now experimenting with land titling, decentralization and Western legal systems demand their own response from households.

Many Sahelians see livelihood diversification as bittersweet. The fact that hundreds of thousands of people are seeking business opportunities, and travelling widely to do so, accords with a neo-liberal model for West Africa – one in which the towns and cities develop stronger labour markets and continue to grow, and where economic modelling suggests freer markets will lead to growing prosperity for all (Cour, 2001). This process, if it were true, would absolve governments from doing too much about rural poverty – particularly those that still dream of the modernization and transformation of rural areas. Such a stance would also help governments resist calls that the state should intervene more directly to ensure that basic needs are being met in the countryside. What need is there to do this if people are getting by on their own, more or less successfully?

However, this position is unrealistic, and absolves the state from its fundamental responsibilities. Livelihood diversification can never be taken to its logical conclusion because of labour and immigration controls enforced by Western nations, because of the import duties placed on African commercial produce and the endurance of 'tied' development aid that does little to increase the volume or quality of solid urban and rural employment opportunities (Bryceson, 1999). Whatever one's view of livelihood diversification, it is clear that in the new millennium, rural Africans are busy and active, trying to negotiate their way out of the African 'crisis'. They take advantage of opportunity, even as they suffer the costs of Africa's global position and history.

Notes

1. US$1 = CFA 760, September 2000. By June 2005 the rate was US$1 = CFA 533.
2. Livelihoods in Fandou Béri were assessed in a project funded by the UK Economic and Social Research Council from 1996 to 1999 and in linked investigations into erosion patterns, agricultural practices and indigenous knowledge systems in this same community. See Batterbury (2001), Warren

et al (2001) and Osbahr and Allan (2003) for greater detail. These and many related papers can be obtained from the first author.
3. A local herb, which is gathered early in the dry season.
4. The study was conducted in 1996 for the agency CARE (see Baro, 1996). The villages studied were Bénébourou and Gakou Timiri on the Sourou Plain; Léré, Pel, Gansagou and Madougou on the Gondo Plain; Douna Bana and Anakila on the Séno; and Tourgo and Déguéré on the Dogon Plateau. Communities ranged in size from 150 to 2800 people; 134 households were surveyed in total, of which 24 were female-headed.

References

Baker, K (2000) *Indigenous Land Management in West Africa: An Environmental Balancing Act*, Oxford University Press, Oxford

Baro, M (1993) 'Mauritania and Irrigated Development Projects: The Case of the Gorgol Perimeter', in T Park (ed) *Risk and Tenure in Arid Lands: The Political Ecology of Development in the Senegal River Basin*, University of Arizona Press, Tucson

Baro, M (1996) *L'étude des systèmes de vie en milieu paysan du cercle de Koro-Mali*, CARE International

Batterbury, S (2001) 'Landscapes of Diversity: A Local Political Ecology of Livelihood Diversification in South-western Niger', *Ecumene*, vol 8, no 4, pp437–64

Batterbury, S and Forsyth, T J (1999) 'Fighting Back: Human Adaptations in Marginal Environments', *Environment*, vol 41, no 6, pp6–11, 25–30

Batterbury, S and Warren, A (2001) 'The African Sahel 25 Years after the Great Drought: Assessing Progress and Moving towards New Agendas and Approaches', *Global Environmental Change*, vol 11, no 1, pp1–8

Bebbington, A (1999) 'Capitals and Capabilities: A Framework for Analyzing Peasant Viability, Rural Livelihoods and Poverty', *World Development*, vol 27, no 12, pp2021–44

Bélières, J-F, and Bosc, P-M, Faure, G, Fournier, S and Losch, B (2002) 'What Future for West Africa's Family Farms in a World Market Economy?', Issue Paper No 113, Drylands Programme, International Institute for Environment and Development, London

Brock, K and Coulibaly, N (1999) 'Sustainable Rural Livelihoods in Mali', *Research Report 35*, Institute of Development Studies, Sussex

Bryceson, D (1999) 'African Rural Labour, Income Diversification and Livelihood Approaches: A Long Term Development Perspective', *Review of African Political Economy*, vol 80, pp171–89

Bryceson, D and Bank, L (2001) 'End of an Era: Africa's Development Policy Parallax', *Journal of Contemporary African Studies*, vol 19, no 1, pp5–23, Carfax Publishing, New York

Bryceson, D and Jamal, V (1997) *Farewell to Farms: De-agrarianisation and Employment in Africa*, Ashgate Press, Aldershot

Bryceson, D, Kay, C and Mooij, J (eds) (2000) *Disappearing Peasantries? Rural Labour in Africa, Asia and Latin America*, IT Publications, London

Carney, D (ed) (1998) *Sustainable Rural Livelihoods: What Contribution Can We Make?*, Department for International Development, London

Chambers, R and Conway, G (1992) 'Sustainable Rural Livelihoods: Practical Concepts for the 21st Century', IDS Discussion Paper No 296, Institute of Development Studies, Sussex

Cour, J (2001) 'The Sahel in West Africa: Countries in Transition to a Full Market Economy', *Global Environmental Change*, vol 11, no 1, pp31–48

Davies, S (1996) *Adaptable Livelihoods: Coping with Food Insecurity in the Malian Sahel*, Wiley, Chichester

Davies, S, Bhargava, P, Jena, B, Mathur, K, Mukerjee, M and Upma, S (1998) 'Making Livelihoods Work: Women, Men and Children in Rajasthan', *Final Report to ESCOR*, Department for International Development/Institute of Development Studies, London/Brighton

Ellis, F (1998) 'Household Strategies and Rural Livelihood Diversification', *Journal of Development Studies*, vol 35, no 1, pp1–38

Ellis, F (2000) *Rural Livelihoods and Diversity in Developing Countries*, Oxford University Press, Oxford

Engberg-Pedersen, L (2002) *Endangering Development: Politics, Projects, and Environment in Burkina Faso*, Praeger, Westport, CT

Francis, E (2000) *Making a Living: Rural Livelihoods in Africa*, Routledge, London

Hussein, K and Nelson, J (1998) 'Sustainable Livelihoods and Livelihood Diversification', IDS Working Paper 69, Institute of Development Studies, Brighton

Kelley, T (2002) 'Squeezing Parakeets into Pigeon Holes: The Effects of Globalization and State Legal Reform in Niger on Indigenous Zarma Law', *New York University Journal of International Law and Politics*, vol 34, no 3, pp635–710, New York University, New York

McDowell, C and de Haan, A (1997) 'Migration and Sustainable Livelihoods: A Critical Review of the Literature', *IDS Working Paper 65*, Institute of Development Studies, Brighton

McMillan, D (1995) *Sahel Visions*, University of Arizona Press, Arizona

Maxwell, S and Smith, M (1992) 'Household Food Security: A Conceptual Review', in S Maxwell and T Frankenberger (eds) *Household Food Security: Concepts, Indicators, and Measurements: A Technical Review*, UNICEF and IFAD, New York and Rome

Mortimore, M (1989) *Adapting to Drought: Farmers, Famines and Desertification in West Africa*, Cambridge University Press, Cambridge

Mortimore, M and Adams, W (1999) *Working the Sahel: Environment and Society in Northern Nigeria*, Routledge, London

Mortimore, M and Adams, W (2001) 'Farmer Adaptation, "Change" and Crisis in the Sahel', *Global Environmental Change*, vol 11, no 1, pp49–58

Netting, R (1993) *Smallholders, Householders,* Stanford University Press, California

Osbahr, H and Allan, C (2003) 'Indigenous Knowledge of Soil Fertility Management in Southwest Niger', *Geoderma*, vol 111, nos 3–4, pp457–79

Rain, D (1999) *Eaters of the Dry Season: Circular Migration in the West African Sahel*, Westview Press, Boulder

Scoones, I (1998) 'Sustainable Rural Livelihoods: A Framework for Analysis', IDS Working Paper 72, Institute of Development Studies, Brighton

Sen, A (1981) *Poverty and Famines: An Essay on Entitlement and Deprivation,* Clarendon Press, Oxford

Timberlake, L (1985) *Africa in Crisis: The Causes, the Cures of Environmental Bankruptcy,* Zed Press/New Society Publishers, London/Philadelphia

Toulmin, C (1992) *Cattle, Women and Wells,* Clarendon, Oxford

Warren, A, Batterbury, S and Osbahr, H (2001) 'Sustainability and Sahelian Soils: Evidence from Niger', *The Geographical Journal,* vol 167, no 4, pp324–41

Watkins, K and Sul, J (2002) 'Cultivating Poverty: The Impact of US Cotton Subsidies on Africa', Oxfam Briefing Paper, Oxfam UK, Oxford

2

Fishing Livelihoods: Successful Diversification, or Sinking into Poverty?

Pierre Morand, Oumar Ibrahima Sy and Christophe Breuil

Introduction

Every year, international agencies publish many reports about the situation in Africa, which focus almost entirely on the urban–rural divide that is analysed and interpreted with reference to the dynamics of farming alone. However, in some African countries, especially in West Africa, the livelihoods of an increasing number of rural and peri-urban communities are based on fishing. This means that such people have specific features and behaviour patterns, which are not understood nor taken into account when designing development policies. Drawing on recent research into fishing and fishing communities in West Africa, this chapter shows why this needs to be remedied and describes some of the initiatives already taken in this regard.

Diverse People and Livelihoods

The description of someone whose livelihood is based on fishing covers a wide range of circumstances. The most obvious is that of a fishermen in the strict sense, that is someone who 'goes on the water' to catch fish. However, someone who owns his boat must be distinguished from someone who goes on board as a crew member or apprentice, whether paid or unpaid. In some cases, the captain of a boat may not be its owner, the latter being an investor, usually with a fishing background.

At one end of the scale, the boat may be relatively light, made by a local craftsman and have no motor or be equipped with an outboard motor that can easily be removed when the boat is beached after a fishing trip. This is referred to as 'canoe (*pirogue*) fishing' (or simply small-scale fishing). At the other end, if the boat is heavy and decked, if it can only berth at ports equipped with quays, if it is fitted with a cabin, an inboard diesel motor and hydraulic winches to lift heavy fishing equipment, this is known as industrial fishing.[1] These two forms of fishing are, however, distinguished not just by their technical characteristics but especially by their entirely different social and financial origins and their very different modes of organization. Canoe fishing, which is always based on local initiatives, is still far more common than industrial fishing in almost all West African countries, both in terms of production (Table 2.2, columns 3 and 4) and, to an even greater extent, the number of workers involved. It is in fact the development over the last few decades of this type of fishing that has employed hundreds of thousands of people and also encouraged the establishment of many related jobs, thereby providing a livelihood for an ever-growing number of families.

The distinction between canoe fishing and industrial fishing applies not only to the way the fish is caught but also to the many other occupational activities connected with fishing. For example, there are many people who buy and sell fish, such as those who collect fish when the boats come in, who sell on to other traders. Some people, especially women, work in fish smoking, drying and salting. There are also all kinds of casual labourers, paid by the day or on a piecework basis, at the landing sites and fish markets: porters, packers etc. Finally, many people do not handle fish but supply inputs or services to the fishermen or traders: suppliers of motors for fishing boats, canoe manufacturers, people who guard and maintain the canoes on land, canoe motor mechanics, suppliers of wood for smoking the fish, suppliers of ice, hauliers and so on. The vast majority of these jobs have developed around canoe fishing, although there are some exceptions, including the small traders who specialize in buying and selling the other accidental fish caught by the industrial tuna fishing fleet and landed at the port of Abidjan (Romagny et al, 2000).

In some coastal countries, a substantial industry has grown up, processing and packing fish mainly for export. The factories get their supplies from both the industrial fishing fleet[2] that lands its catches only in the few ports equipped with infrastructure and from the dealers who collect the fish landed from canoes at the many beach landing sites. These factories make a major contribution towards maintaining and boosting canoe fishing, while providing employment for the female population in many coastal towns.

In addition to the workers in the fisheries sector described above, there are many other people (children, old people, the sick and unemployed) who live with them, depend on their income and are usually more numerous, within each household, than those who are active. They too must of course be counted as people whose livelihoods depend on fishing.

Fisheries as a Growing Livelihood Opportunity

Assessment of the current position

The importance of the fisheries sector for the livelihoods of West African communities cannot be appreciated simply on the basis of statistics relating to the number of boats or the number of fishermen. Many other people are engaged in

Table 2.1 *Employment in the fisheries sector in Senegal, excluding the river basin*

Year	Catch		Processing				Marketing		Total jobs
			Artisanal	Industrial					
	Canoe fishing	Industrial fishing		Freezing	Canning	Fish meal	Artisanal, small-scale	Industrial	
1976	49,001	1829	24,501	3,262	1310	100	98,002	45	178,050
1996	57,067	3351	171,201	11,143	2590	115	342,402	152	588,021

NB: The many jobs in small-scale processing and marketing must be considered as part-time, insofar as most of them are held by women who devote a large proportion of their time to household and family tasks.

Source: Sy (1998)

a range of other trades and services related to fishing, but are not usually accounted for under this heading, as they form part of the huge informal sector found in most African countries. However, studies have shown that for each person working full-time in sea fishing, between 5 and 9 jobs are created in the wider sector, the highest ratio (a ninefold multiplier) being recorded in Senegal, where processing and marketing activities are highly developed as shown in Table 2.1.

However, in the absence of a specific study for each country, a more modest figure of 7 should be assumed for the job creation ratio. This falls to 3.5 for professional fishing in inland waters, where the annual production landed per fisherman is smaller, and down to one-to-one for fishing practised in conjunction with many other activities since, in this case, a large proportion of the small catch is used for family consumption.

Finally, to get a rough calculation of the total number of people whose livelihoods depend on fishing, the total number of estimated jobs in the sector should be multiplied by a factor of 2.3. The application of such ratios to statistical data covering the number of canoes or fishermen thus allows the importance of fishing for the people of several West African countries to be assessed as in column eight of Table 2.2.

It can thus be seen that in four out of five countries, the proportion of people whose livelihoods are heavily or mainly based[3] on fishing is between 5 and 10 per cent, while this proportion is as much as 23 per cent in the case of Senegal.

A growing trend

The current situation, where fishing occupies an extremely important place within the livelihoods of West African communities, is partly the result of recent developments. Data from the national fishery administrations show that the seagoing canoe fleet of six countries on the West African Atlantic shoreline (Mauritania, Senegal, Cape Verde, Gambia, Guinea-Bissau and Guinea Conakry) has increased by a factor of at least six during the last 50 years, in other words an average rate of increase of 3.6 per cent per year. However, as the size and average number of crew members of the canoes have also increased by a third over the same period, rising from 3 or 3.5 people to 5 or more,[4] the numbers of fishermen may be taken

Table 2.2 *Estimated importance of fishing for livelihoods in five West African countries*

Fishing area: sea (m) or inland (c)		Production of canoe fishing (t/year)	Share (%) of canoe fishing in total production	Number of fishing canoes	Number of jobs for fishermen stricto sensu (in canoe fishing)	Estimated number of jobs in other parts of the sector (mainly processing and trade; secondarily in the industrial component, on board and on land)	Estimated number of people heavily dependent on fishing for their livelihoods
Guinea (1, 2)	m	**53,000**	65 to 70	**2400**	**12,000**	*100,000*	*375,000 (or 6 % of the total population)*
	c	*2500*		**1200**	**2500**		
Mali (3)	c	**60,000 to 130,000**	*100*		Full-time: 20,000 part-time: 70,000	*140,000*	*759,000 (or 7.6% of the total population)*
Ghana (4, 5)	m	**300,000**	*77*	**8700**	**96,500**	*400,000 to 450,000*	*> **1,500,000** (or 8.6% of the total population)*
	c	**50,000**			*40,000*		
Mauritania (6, 7)	m	**50,000**	*20 to 25*	**2746**	**10,000 to 14,000**	**> 50,000** (including **5500** in the industrial component)	*165,000 (or 6.7% of the total population)*
	c	*3000*		*1500*	*3000*		
Senegal (8, 9)	m	**250,000 to 325,000**	*80*	**10,600**	**57,100**	**525,000** (including **17,350** in the industrial component)	*194,000 (or 23% of the total population)*
	c	*8000*		**3000**	*6000*		

In bold: figures provided by the authors numbered in the first column and referenced below. The other figures are calculated using the ratios described in the text or are estimated figures (in italics). All the data are from the period 1990–98. Within that period, the most recent data available for each country have been used. The total national production used to calculate column 4 come from the FAO yearbook (average values 1995–98). The total population figures used for the ratio in column 8 are from the United Nations (1996). 1. Domain et al (1999); 2. Greboval (1997); 3. Breuil et al (1996); 4. Koranteng (1990); 5. Chaboud and Charles-Dominique (1991); 6. FAO (1999); 7. Bru and Hatti (2000); 8. CEP (2000); 9. Sy (1998).

to have increased by a factor of at least 8, resulting in an estimated average annual growth rate of 4.2 per cent. Such a figure appears to be substantially higher than the average annual rate of population increase in West African countries, which fluctuated between 2.6 and 3.2 per cent over the second half of the 20th century. It stands in even sharper contrast to the annual rate of increase in the active farming population, which did not exceed 1.7–1.9 per cent over the years 1960–90 in West Africa (Quesnel, 1996).

Another way of assessing the phenomenon is to observe the increasing number of fishing communities settled along the coast or on the banks of rivers and lakes. In many places, new clusters can be seen that did not exist ten or more years ago. These 'fishing camps' have become more numerous around the new lakes formed behind the major hydroelectric dams constructed over the last two decades (eg the reservoirs of Akosombo, Kossou, Sélingué and Manantali). In addition, fishing communities have settled around the hundreds of lakes formed recently by the building of small dams in Côte d'Ivoire and Burkina Faso. New fishing camps are also appearing on the banks of natural bodies of water, such as the upper Niger basin in Guinea and the large island of Bol in the heart of Lake Chad, which is now home to a cosmopolitan community of fishermen who arrived at the end of the 1980s. This also applies to the camps recently set up along the 'Grande Côte' of Senegal, the southern part of the Mauritanian coastline and the Boké region in the northeast of Guinea.

The picture is not uniform, either in time or space: each country has experienced its own period of strong growth in canoe fishing, often associated with a particular economic situation. In Guinea, for example, economic liberalization in the 1980s seems to have played a part in the sharp expansion of the canoe fleet in that country, from 1788 to 2356 units between 1989 and 1996 (Chavance, 2002). This phase of strong growth seems to have come to an end along the Senegalese coast, where the numbers of canoe fishermen rose from 13,600 to 49,000 people between 1960 and 1976 (an increase of 8 per cent per year), reaching 57,100 people in 1996 (an increase of 0.7 per cent per year). The wave of growth flowed on towards Mauritania, which now plays host to fishermen from Senegal and whose canoe fleet has increased fourfold between 1991 and 1997, rising from 677 to 2746 units. Another demonstration of this unevenness comes from the large Sahelian wetland of the inner Niger delta in Mali which was hard hit by drought between 1973 and 1993. It experienced only a slight rise in the numbers of fishermen, tending instead to be the source of migrants heading for new fishing areas, particularly the reservoirs formed behind the major dams (Herry, 1994; Kassibo, 2000). Despite these variations, the overall trend towards rising numbers of people engaged in fishing in West Africa is clear. Moreover, it would appear that this development is even more marked as regards occupations connected with fishing, especially post-catch activities (see below).

The increase in numbers of people working in the fisheries sector is of course partly because of general demographic growth, but it would appear also to be owing to factors specific to fishing. The sector appears to be more than maintaining its share of the active population in West Africa, whereas other primary and rural sectors of activity have, over the same period, lost a relative share of numbers to the towns. What could be the explanation? There are few studies of demography dealing specifically with fishing communities, but such studies as have been done (Herry, 1994) show that natural growth (fertility less mortality) among fishing groups is around 3 per cent per year, which barely differs from that of the West African population as a whole.

The Attraction of the Fisheries Sector

The high growth rate in the canoe fishing sector results from the fact that thousands of people have turned to this activity as a main source of livelihood. They have chosen fishing in preference to previous activities or those practised by their parents. How did this happen and what are the attractions of fishing?

Two livelihood patterns linked to fishing activity

Describing the historical and socio-economic processes that have encouraged the growth in canoe fishing requires some initial scene-setting. It is important to remember the extreme seasonal and inter-annual variations in climatic conditions that prevail in tropical areas, as a result of which very few aquatic environments have permanently high availability of fish. In view of this natural phenomenon, West African communities have developed two livelihood strategies based on fishing:

- a sedentary lifestyle in which fishing is a seasonal pursuit combined with other activities providing supplementary income: the model of the 'multi-active sedentary fisherman' or 'farmer fisherman' (Cormier-Salem, 1991);
- mobility in search of fish and opportunities for marketing fish, using specialist gear and, usually, giving up farming: the model of the 'migrant fisherman' (Haakonsen and Diaw, 1991).

This bipolarity has long been known, since it emerges from work done long ago by ethnographers and the colonial administration (analysed by Chauveau, 1986). The second model was seen as specific to a small number of ethnic groups: the Wolof of Guet-N'Dar and the Lebou of the Cape Verde Peninsula (Senegal), the Fanti and Ga/Adangme of the Gold Coast and the Bozo along the river Niger in Mali. These groups appear to have been the first to include families whose livelihood strategies were entirely based on fishing, with all the constraints (mobility), equipment (large canoes) and know-how (navigation) that this implies. This singular way of life resulted in a particular mindset and this is why these groups continue to be thought of as the 'real fishermen'. However, the first model of livelihood strategy long remained the most widespread and common in West Africa, probably because it is the safest: the farmer fisherman produces his domestic needs in cereals and can thus feed his family without depending on the market. By contrast, the migrant professional fisherman is exposed to a larger number of risks of all kinds. However, he has the advantage, when everything is going well, of deriving substantial monetary income from the sale of fish, which enables him more easily to move within the now dominant market economy.

The expanding canoe fishing sector

Settlement of 'professional fishermen' from elsewhere

Until the end of the 19th century, only a few ethnic groups on the Senegalese coast and what is now Ghana were really specialized in navigation and fishing. It was then that migratory flows from these two locations began to increase, leading successive waves of fishermen to colonize almost the entire West African coastline, within the space of three or four generations (Chauveau, 1986). More specifically, 'Ghanaian' pioneer groups spread from The Gambia to the Congo, broadly overlapping the area of expansion of the 'Senegalese' pioneers that extended from Mauritania to Côte d'Ivoire (Haakonsen and Diaw, 1991).

A very similar phenomenon arose around inland waters: the Bozo from the upstream area of the inner Niger delta, whose lifestyle was that of 'migrant professional fishermen', spread towards the centre and then the downstream areas of this vast wetland zone. Subsequently, in the 1970s, these same groups fanned out into the new lake areas in West Africa, created as a result of dam construction (Kassibo, 2000), as well as upstream of the river Niger in Guinea.

In this way, most of the coastal, river or lakeside areas of West Africa received people from at least one of these groups of migrant professional fishermen during the 20th century. In each of these areas, this influx was a determining factor in the local development of canoe fishing.

Farmer-fishermen convert to professional fishermen

In places where pioneer groups of professional fishermen settled, there were usually indigenous communities who, although relying mainly on farming, were not indifferent to the opportunities provided by aquatic resources. They engaged in gathering activities (such as collecting shellfish) or fishing with light equipment, such as traps, harpoons or individually operated nets, with a preference for shoreline, estuary or lagoon environments (Cormier-Salem, 1991; Bouju, 1999). The temporary and then permanent settlement of groups of migrant professional fishermen alongside them had the effect of encouraging some of these farmer fishermen to undertake more intensive fishing activities at sea, until they themselves became fully professional fishermen. This is what happened with the Nyominka of Sine-Saloum (Senegal) and, more recently, the Soussou in Guinea.

However, some indigenous communities spurned the opportunity to learn sea fishing and remained attached to their ancient practices of coastal and lagoon fishing combined with farming (eg the Baga and Nbalou in Guinea – Bouju, 1999). In the case of freshwater or confined bodies of water (lagoons) and where indigenous communities had long made a relatively substantial investment in fishing, the arrival of migrant professionals using much more efficient and thus potentially destructive techniques was often perceived as negative. Far from being imitated by the local people, in many places these migrants and their methods were rejected.

However farmer-fishermen (or the sons of farmer-fishermen) elsewhere came to specialize to a greater extent in fishing after having contact with migrant fishermen settled in their communities, some of them becoming full-time professionals.

This on-site trend played a part in the process of development of canoe fishing in areas where that activity was still underdeveloped in the mid-20th century.

New groups enter the fishery sector

In some countries, the variety of communities involved in the fisheries sector now extends far beyond the confines of groups formerly considered as 'fishermen' or 'coastal dwellers'. In fact, many canoes are crewed by descendants of families from the Sahelian hinterland who used to specialize in transhumant herding or rainfed agriculture. In Mauritania, the estimated number of Moors who have recently come into fishing in this way is 3000, representing around 30 per cent of total canoe fishermen[5] (FAO, 1999). In Burkina Faso, where most fishing areas involve recently created artificial water bodies, young Mossi farmers have taken up fishing, initially on a seasonal basis and then permanently.

The reason for this new influx into fishing is unclear. It is undoubtedly linked to some extent to the phenomenon of young rural dwellers seeking incomes and employment. One of the entry points seems to be the seasonal jobs available at landing sites. In Senegal, taking this type of casual employment has proved to be a springboard for boys into the better paid occupation of crewing fishing boats. However, this is not true everywhere: in some traditional inland fishing centres (such as the river Niger in Mali) new entrants are kept well away from actually catching fish.

Apart from such inland situations, which represent ancient patterns of economic organization based on complementarity between ethnic groups, it can be said that the origins of those taking jobs in the fisheries sector are gradually becoming of less importance, at least as regards sea fishing. Being a fisherman no longer means having to belong to a particular ethnic group. This lowering of identity barriers to entry into the sector encourages the growth in numbers.

Processes amplifying growth in fishing activity

Apart from the three key processes described above, other factors have encouraged the development of the sector.

The first concerns the expansion in areas becoming accessible or profitable for fishing. This expansion in itself stems from three causes: motorization and the increased size of canoes, which has made the high seas (up to 20 nautical miles), formerly reserved for industrial fishing fleets, available to canoe fishing; the creation of reservoirs by almost all countries in West Africa to expand the production of hydroelectric power; and the building of roads which has enabled the supply chain to reach areas rich in fish but which, owing to isolation, were little exploited until recently. All these 'new' fishing areas have proved particularly welcome for migrants and new fishermen.

The second factor results from the development of the sector in terms of diversification and differentiation. Over the years, new sub-sectors have emerged that seek to gain maximum value from fishing on the basis of the characteristics of the catch on one hand and the needs of the market on the other. This includes the rapid transport of fresh fish for sale in urban markets (quite a recent development since it has gone hand-in-hand with the expansion and greater accessibility of road transport), the production of fish meal (from small pelagic fish) and export of fresh or frozen processed produce by air to Europe and Asia, while not compromising the existence of more traditional industries based on smoking and drying. Such diversification generates not only more added value but also increased demand for labour and operators of all kinds, thereby increasing the number of jobs in the sector for every fisherman onboard.

Explanatory factors

Increased need for cash

One of the main factors that has encouraged the growing professionalization of canoe fishing is that this activity can generate cash income on an almost daily basis, since almost the entire production is sold on return from each fishing trip, with the exception of the usually very small share set aside for family consumption. At the same time, the cash requirements of rural communities are growing since, in many regions, an increasingly large share of commodities, such as rice and oil, is no longer produced in the village but purchased in the shop or from travelling traders. In addition, products such as sugar and tea that are more and more sought-after also have to be purchased in the market. Furthermore, some goods and products that used to be considered as 'luxuries' (such as foam mattresses, plastic shoes, battery-operated cassette players and bicycles) are now seen as essentials. Finally, more and more cash is required for social events.

Few other livelihood opportunities

The second factor encouraging people to take up canoe fishing and associated trades relates to the lack of other livelihood opportunities available in rural areas. Various aspects need to be borne in mind here:

- the growing shortage of farmland, in the context of current fallowing systems;
- the low profitability of rainfed African cereal cultivation, facing heavy competition in urban markets from rice, wheat and imported flour;
- the risky nature of rainfed cultivation in the Sahel, and increased frequency of years with inadequate rainfall;
- the lack of access to paid work in the towns for uneducated rural people;
- the problem of survival for those in the informal sector.

Who gets hooked on fishing and why

However, the main reason for increasing numbers in canoe fishing is related to the consistently favourable market situation, which allows for a long-term increase in price paid to producers and dealers – except at times of seasonal over-production. This is due in part to sustained local and national demand: the urban population is growing fast and increasingly equipped with refrigerators, while fish has no real competition in the market for animal protein at affordable prices, except from poultry.[6] In addition, the harvest from the sea has a growing international market, since there is a structural deficit in supply on a world scale. In West Africa, canoe fishing provides a growing share of the quantities exported.

The fisheries sector is also relatively open access. This is because of the relatively low level of investment capital required to acquire the means of production and to the scope for social mobility, in terms of access to jobs in fishing and to fishing areas, although this last point must be qualified to some extent.

In economic terms, coming into the canoe fishing sector as the owner of a fishing unit requires a relatively modest investment in relation to the expected profits. This investment depends on the environment (it is usually higher in sea as opposed to river or lake fishing) and also varies according to the level of specialization in the type of fishing activity undertaken (Table 2.3). The average outlay on equipment in relation to number of fishermen is around CFA 90,000 to 265,000 per person, which may be taken as the estimated cost of creating one job. This figure is low in comparison with industrial fishing (around CFA 12 million – Henry and Moal, 1998) and other economic sectors. Moreover, this investment barrier may be crossed more easily still by means of a collective strategy, as shown by the example of the 'seine unions' on the Aby Lagoon in Côte d'Ivoire (Verdeaux, 1989) or the multi-owner fishing units of Sine Saloum in Senegal (one fisherman owns the canoe, another the motor etc). However, even though the level of investment required is not a substantial barrier, direct access to the profession of self-employed fisherman remains problematic for new entrants in view of the very high level of know-how required, especially for sea fishing. An investor may, however, have a canoe built and entrust it to a captain who will be responsible for operating it on his behalf.[7]

Table 2.3 *Capital requirements for canoe fishing*

Type of fishing unit	Number of workers	Boat (s)		Outboard motor(s)		Fishing gear and miscellaneous (in capital)	Total equipment outlay
		Number and type	Capital	Number and type	Capital		
Seine net fishing unit (inshore fishing)	20	1 large fishing canoe	1,800,000 to 2,000,000	1 x 30 hp motor	800,000 to 900,000	2,000,000 to 2,400,000	4,600,000 to 5,300,000
Set gillnet fishing unit (inshore fishing)	6	1 fishing canoe	400,000	1 x 15 hp motor	500,000	500,000	1,400,000
'Migrant professional' household (inland waters)	10	1 pinnace for migration	600,000	1 x 15 hp motor	600,000	600,000 to 800,000	2,000,000 to 2,200,000
		2 fishing canoes	200,000	Nil			
'Farmer fisherman' household (inland waters)	5	2 fishing canoes	200,000	Nil		250,000	450,000

Source: based on updated data from Bauman et al (1994) and Kebe (1997) in CFA francs (CFA1 = US$0.0015)

The situation is different as regards jobs in the marketing sector, which require few particular skills and involve only a very modest initial investment (from CFA 50,000). This is where many independent small operators are found, representing the majority of those working in the fisheries sector (Table 2.1), having taken advantage of the fact that fish marketing networks have always remained open, with a low level of intervention on the part of government. Some state fish marketing boards have been set up (such as 'Opération Pêche' in Mopti, Mali and the SMCP[8] in Mauritania), but they have not established restrictive policies, unlike the boards set up to handle farm produce.

Finally, for those with no seed capital and just their labour power to offer, the fisheries sector provides many opportunities for work as casual labourers or apprentices with fishing boat captains and traders. Access to these jobs is easy during the seasonal boom in activity at landing sites and wholesale markets.

As regards the degree of open access to wild fish resources, it is important to distinguish between:

- the open seas and very large lakes, such as Lake Chad, which are technically difficult to exploit and monitor and are, de facto, freely accessible to those able to venture there; however, modern constraints related to the boundaries of territorial waters are beginning to bite, although the ability of governments to patrol these borders is still weak;
- inshore and estuary waters, both of which the indigenous coastal communities are usually still keen to control, although they do not always have the means to prevent the intrusion of better equipped migrant fishermen; and
- lagoon and inland waters, over which indigenous people claim community ownership and where they have real capacity to control access, although this does not necessarily mean that migrant fishermen from elsewhere cannot gain access.

In the last case, although foreign fishermen must request authorization and pay local taxes to the customary authorities in order to operate in these waters, it is unlikely that they will in the end be refused access, as their powerful fishing techniques enable them to afford to pay a high fee, which is clearly of interest to the host authorities.

All this shows that the system of access to fishery resources is multifaceted and quite flexible. It tends to be much more favourable to new arrivals and migrants than the system of access to land, the latter being almost exclusively based on lineage rights.

However, changes in the institutional framework of access to water and fishing resources are beginning to emerge with the decentralization initiatives launched in several West African countries in the 1990s. These reforms make some moves towards more institutionalized forms of community-based management (see below: case studies), which strengthen the position of indigenous communities. This may increasingly hinder free access by migrant fishermen to foreign waters in the future, particularly inland.

How easy is it to leave fishing?

Finally, there is another explanation for the growth in numbers in the fisheries sector: while there is a flow of incomers, there are very few people leaving the sector, because of the difficulties people face in taking up other activities.

The first of these difficulties relates to the pattern of life for migrant fishermen: because of their frequent moves, their status as foreigners which penalizes them in social and political relations and the fact that they live close to the water in remote areas that are not accessible in all seasons, fishermen are a people 'apart'. This has many negative consequences, one of which is the low school enrolment rate of children in fishing communities. This is often below 20 per cent and, in all cases, systematically lower than the average rates in the wider population. Under the circumstances, the children of fishermen have little chance of getting into better forms of employment.

Furthermore, owing to social factors, a shift in strategy from being a farmer-fisherman to becoming a migrant fisherman tends to be irreversible. Abandoning cultivation for several years or, worse still, leaving ancestral lands over which the family had customary use rights means that those who become migrant fishermen cannot usually return to farming especially as arable land becomes increasingly scarce. Moving from farmer-fisherman to migrant fisherman therefore seems, to a very large extent, to be a one-way journey.[9]

Consequently, there are only two pathways for a self-employed fisherman: upward mobility which involves becoming a dealer or ship owner with several canoes, or downward mobility, which means becoming an assistant or labourer working for other fishermen. This latter path is often the result of a process by which the fisherman, having had no luck, eventually finds himself unable to renew his equipment.

Effects on Livelihood Security and Sustainability

Having described the variety of people who depend on the fisheries sector in West Africa and the causes for the constant rise in their numbers, we now turn to examine the sustainability and security of their livelihoods.

How renewable are fish stocks?

Fishing experts have long thought that, as a result of the open access system characteristic of most aquatic resources, fishing tends to develop beyond the limits of sustainability, exhausting resources through excess offtake. However, the recent history of fisheries (see for example Pavé and Charles-Dominique, 1999, on West Africa), as well as new scientific knowledge, has altered the picture. In fact, for this type of fishery, there have been virtually no cases of collapse of the total catch from an aquatic ecosystem, despite the extraordinary rise in fishing effort over the last few decades. Since the 'Gordon-Schaefer' reference model for fishery management (Gordon, 1954) did not provide a satisfactory explanatory framework in the face of this evidence, it is now tending to be replaced by a 'plateau response' model which better incorporates the multispecies nature of the resource and gives a better account of historical, local and regional dynamics.

According to this model (based notably on observations and studies of Regier, 1973; Marten and Polovina, 1982; Morand and Bousquet, 1994; Laë, 1997; Welcomme, 1999), increased effort over the first phases of development of a fishery allows larger catches to be made up to a maximum Y_{max}. After this, catches stabilize and the 'full exploitation' or plateau phase is reached, which extends over a wide scale of additional increase in effort. It is only beyond an extremely high level of effort that there is a theoretical (but rarely observed) possibility of a fall in overall catch occurring.

The catch volume (Y_{max}) achieved during the full exploitation phase corresponds to the old notion of 'potential fish yield', which depends on the size and biotic features of the ecosystem as well as environmental conditions. As regards the length or duration of the plateau phase, this reflects the resilience of the resource as a whole and its foundation (ie the aquatic ecosystem) in the face of intensified exploitation. This resilience brings into play many bio-ecological mechanisms whose overall result is the increasing proportion of short-lived species (Pauly et al, 1998) and, therefore, an accelerated turnover in resource biomass. This acceleration enables the ecosystem to sustain the same level of annual offtake despite the fact that the biomass present in the water at any given time is shrinking.

In parallel with these developments in ecological parameters, fishermen alter their practices because catches per unit of effort fall, as witnessed by the usual observation: 'there are fewer fish now than before'. In an attempt to maintain their individual yields and incomes, fishermen will therefore turn to areas they did not previously fish (eg the open sea), cast more nets per trip or seek to catch smaller fish, particularly by using finer mesh or more efficient nets, such as monofilament[10] nets. These responses from the fishermen contribute towards even greater intensification.

Although fishery experts all agree that most inland and coastal West African waters are currently at an advanced stage of full exploitation, there is no sign that we are coming dangerously close to the cut-off point that would lead to a collapse in the total catch. It is therefore possible that a substantial increase in the number of fishermen or in fishing effort in the years to come will lead merely to stagnation in fishing output, as has already been observed over the last decade. Such a scenario is not desirable, since it would have serious consequences for fishermen's livelihoods.

Effects on household income and wealth

While total catch can indeed be sustained over a wide scale of increased effort, the same is not true for the efficiency of fishing, as measured by the volume of catch per unit of effort (for instance per hour's fishing) and the total annual catch per boat. These ratios are the ones that have the most direct influence on fishermen's incomes and they are falling.

Commonly, the fishing boat captains try to maintain production, despite the decreased availability of the resource, by increasing the length of fishing trips, and thereby expenditure on fuel and supplies as well as wear on equipment. Their operating income should fall, in view of the increase in operating costs. However, by good fortune, a concomitant increase in the price of fish – caused by rising demand – has more or less offset this rise in costs. This has made it possible to maintain economic viability. However, if new canoes enter the fishery, the overall situation will be more critical.

Changes to the fishery, such as the smaller proportion of large fish and the increase in species with a short life cycle, also have an impact on levels of income through:

- a possible drop in the average species value (per kilo) of the catch; and
- an increase in the sensitivity of fishing to environmental fluctuations. Short cycle species have much larger inter-annual biomass variations (Caverivière et al, 2002) than long-lived species whose populations are made up of several age groups.

Moving into the full exploitation phase consequently has a negative impact on the average level and stability of incomes for fishermen, so that some of them will have difficulty in renewing their equipment and will become impoverished.

Safety and health concerns

To maintain their catches and income, fishermen are obliged to increase the length and range of their fishing trips. Fishermen travel further and further out to sea into areas operated by industrial vessels which, at night, may collide with the canoes and whose trawling gear may destroy the nets set by canoe fishermen. On the Senegalese coast, where large canoes stay at sea for up to eight days and travel as much as 20 miles or more from the coast, accidents are common, especially when there is a deterioration in weather conditions.

Furthermore, the livelihood strategy adopted by professional fishermen, based on seeking out where the best possible income may be obtained from fishing, implies changing their place of residence, on a seasonal or longer basis. Permanent settlement in a new area is, however, rare: moving is usually repeated several times during the life of a fisherman and his household. During the settlement phase following a move, fishermen will live in a 'camp', for anything from a few months to more than a decade. In such camps, daily living conditions are harsh, with no latrines or large trees, few drinking water sources and frequent flooding contaminating such wells as do exist. Moreover, the tracks leading to these camps are often almost impassable, making it difficult to evacuate the sick when necessary. In the circumstances, it is not surprising that children's survival and adults' working capacity are seriously affected by waterborne diseases (diarrhoea, bilharzia and malaria) and lack of access to medical care.

Effects on social cohesion and peace

The involvement of an increasing number of people in the fisheries sector and their increased mobility are likely to give rise to more tension and conflicts. However, it is important to be clear about the nature and location of such conflicts, as they are not necessarily found where one would expect.

Despite the increasing scarcity of the resource and increased struggle to catch fish at sea, clashes on the water between canoes are rare because of the rules of conduct to which fishermen are much attached: for example, a shoal of fish always 'belongs' to the first canoe that finds it. Disputes relating to technical incompatibility of fishing gear are more common but there again, the fishermen are usually able to get together to discuss and establish rules to put an end to such conflicts.

The most serious conflicts take place on land and relate to issues such as settlement rights (activities sharing and trading terms), reflecting the social relations within groups of migrant professional fishermen and between them and indigenous communities (Fay, 1994). Many factors determine how harmonious or conflict-ridden such relationships may be. For example, in economic terms, limited initial involvement of indigenous communities in fishing may be a favourable factor in establishing good relations with migrants, because of complementarity between the activities of the two groups. In the same way, participation of women and young members of the indigenous community in trade and casual work associated with fishing can be advantageous. On the other hand, requests for access to farm land, often put forward by migrant fishermen seeking to grow cereals for subsistence, tend to be badly received by the indigenous population who are sometimes themselves suffering from shortage of land and consider such requests as a breach of the rule that the two groups' activities should be clearly separate and non-competitive.

In addition, migrant fishermen who are not nationals of the host country are often the victims of discrimination by government policies designed to allow nationals to maintain control of the fisheries sector. Other scenarios, such as accusations of political plotting or the resurgence of xenophobia, are even more critical and can lead to expulsion of migrant fishermen. Unfortunately, such crises have become common in West Africa.

Migrant fishermen are vulnerable not only in their places of settlement, but also when out fishing, especially when their trips are extended and become veritable expeditions in search of new, under-exploited fishing areas, ranging over several hundred kilometres and lasting several weeks. In this case the fishermen will leave the territorial waters of their country of origin or settlement to try their luck along the coast of neighbouring countries. For example, Senegalese fishermen may find themselves fined or even imprisoned by the maritime authorities of Guinea-Bissau or Mauritania, the latter having recently invested in armed coastguard vessels.

Coping Strategies at Micro- and Macro-levels

Household and group strategies in Kayar, Senegal

Origin of the Kayar fishing community

Kayar is a village in the region of Thiès, 50km from Dakar, with an estimated population of 20,000. At the end of the 19th century, the inhabitants of this Lebou and Wolof village were engaged in agriculture during the rainy season and in local fishing for the rest of the year. It was only from around 1940 that some inhabitants began to turn professional, continuing their fishing activities throughout the year, as a result of the relatively continuous availability of fish throughout the year, because of specific maritime conditions and the geographical proximity of Dakar, a rapidly expanding consumer market.

Fishing activities gradually became dominant and the village acquired a degree of renown for its produce that was marketed in the large colonial town nearby. This encouraged the government to begin construction of a tarmac road from Kayar to Dakar in 1951, giving a further boost to fish marketing and the specialization of Kayar's people in fishing. During the 1970s, as a result of drought, the last few inhabitants still farming fell back completely and for good on fishing.

Another process contributed towards the development of Kayar as a major centre for canoe fishing: the arrival of migrant fishermen from St Louis, in northern Senegal, from the 1940s. These migrants were particularly attracted by the opportunities to market fish from Kayar in nearby urban markets, especially Dakar. Having initially settled on a seasonal basis, they have remained more or less permanently, and they now account for 30 per cent of the total canoe fleet. This figure rises to 40 per cent during the intensive phase of the fishing season, when numbers are swelled by seasonal migrants, from December to May.

Under the impact of these two phenomena and overall demographic growth, the number of fishermen in Kayar rose from 814 to 5000 between 1948 and 1999, that is an average annual growth rate of 3.6 per cent.

At the same time as the number of fishermen increased, the canoe fleet has also developed, with the introduction of motors as of 1952 and the appearance of new types of canoes. These are larger than the old ones and allow for new types of fishing, such as seine net fishing for small pelagic fish using powerful canoes working in tandem, fishing at sea for several days using canoes equipped with ice boxes to keep the catch fresh etc. Fishing areas were therefore expanded and fished more intensively, which led to an increase in volume landed from 4500 tonnes in 1948 to 40,000 tonnes in 1999, an average annual rise of 4 per cent. This production, although it has now reached its ceiling, had an estimated commercial value of CFA 5 billion in 1999.

Local mechanisms for managing resource conflicts

Cohabitation between the two groups, natives of Kayar on the one hand and migrant fishermen originating from St Louis on the other, has often been difficult. The main cause of tension between the groups has long been the issue of using two competing and incompatible types of fishing gear: lines and gillnets. Although the former were used by both groups, use of the latter was a speciality of the fishermen originating from St Louis. Apart from the fact that gillnets allow for a large catch, they directly hinder use of lines. Local people from Kayar were therefore keen to get rid of gillnets, but those from St Louis, who used gillnets, argued that the sea does not belong to anyone. As a result, this matter has caused recurrent conflict since the 1960s. Finally, a body known as the 'Kayar/St Louis Solidarity Committee' (CSKSL) was set up in the early 1990s and succeeded in marking out separate fishing areas for the two types of gear. Both groups of fishermen as well as the local government are represented on this committee, with a small group appointed to monitor enforcement of the agreed measures.

Such measures, accompanied by penalties in the event of breach of the rules, help not only to reduce tension between the two groups but also to conserve fish breeding areas where only lines, which cause little disturbance, are now entitled to operate.

Diverse local incomes despite constraints

To maintain income from fishing despite the natural ceiling reached in total catch, several community-based strategies have been developed.

The first of these strategies relates to diversification in modes of operation and exploitation of fish resources, leading to the production of a wide range of products whose quality and price are adapted to various segments of the national and international market. Figure 2.1 portrays the diverse types of operator involved from catching the fish through to distribution and shows the 'client–supplier' relationship between them. Various sub-sectors can be seen, one of which (now accounting for 5 per cent of the catch) is geared towards industrial processing for export.

Another strategy is designed to support the sale price of fish by limiting daily landings. At the initiative of the 'Kayar/St Louis Solidarity Committee' (CSKSL), the first attempt of this type was made in 1992. It consisted of limiting the number of fishing trips using seine nets to one per day, in order to avoid oversupply of small pelagic fish that cause a sharp drop in prices. As of 1994, the same committee

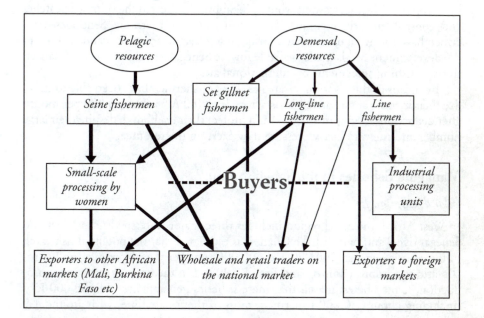

Figure 2.1 *Diagram of main stakeholders in the fish production and processing sector (Kayar, Senegal)*

initiated a comparable measure in respect of line fishing which targets species intended for the European market: when the canoes come in, the number of 15kg boxes of fish may not exceed three. In addition, the committee has established a floor price for the sale of different categories of fish, in consultation with the dealers. These various measures have had two effects:

• prices have held up better and brought increased income derived from selling fish;
• variable costs have gone down to some extent,[11] since trips are often cut short or are less frequent.

Another positive result is some reduction in competition between line fishing crews, meaning that fewer risks are taken at sea.

Protecting the interests of canoe fishing against outside threats

The CSKSL is a member of the CNPS (Senegalese national fishermen's association) which engages in active lobbying at an international level, with the support of northern NGOs. When fishing agreements with the European Commission (see Kaczynski and Fluarty, 2002) were last renegotiated in 2002, representatives of the CNPS were part of the Senegalese delegation that travelled to Brussels on several occasions. Their presence helped to ensure rejection of one of the main European demands, which related to access for European industrial vessels to the Kayar trench, considered by scientists as one of the most important areas for biological renewal of fish stocks on the main coast of Senegal. Fishing in the trench by European industrial trawlers would probably have affected the volume of catches and, consequently, the income of Kayar fishermen. Furthermore, Senegalese fishermen have formed a union that is struggling to secure access for canoe fishing to the development funds made available for the Senegalese fisheries sector financed through fishing agreements or international aid.

By means of these various strategies, Kayar fishermen have been able to stabilize their income at a relatively satisfactory level (CFA 55,000–80,000 per month after deduction of equipment costs) and protect their livelihood, despite their large number and the very heavy pressure they exert on the resource.

Managing fisheries in the Sahelian zone[12]

Inland Sahelian fisheries

In West Africa, the Sahel region includes three major watersheds: the Niger and Senegal rivers and part of Lake Chad. It is estimated that the potential fish catch in this area is between 200,000 and 400,000 tons per year depending on hydro-climatic conditions (Bonzon and Breuil, 1992). On the basis of this annual production, it may be estimated that these fisheries generate around 600,000 jobs (including about 230,000 fishermen, most of them part time) with around 1.9 million people depending heavily on this sector for their livelihoods. Consequently, inland fishing in the Sahel is critical to development of the countries concerned, especially in terms of combating poverty.

In seeking to understand the management problems facing Sahelian fisheries, two of their main characteristics should first be considered:

- First, these fisheries are very heavily dependent on environmental conditions. The amount of water received by the region is subject to extreme variation, within and between years. Consequently, the size of aquatic environments varies considerably over time, and some bodies of water are not permanent.
- Second, associated with the above, the communities involved in fishing frequently resort to multiple activities as part of their livelihood strategies (Sarch and Allison, 2000). Households do not depend for their survival on income from catching fish alone. Wives usually have their own occupations in processing and marketing fish, other trading activities or market gardening. Men may be involved to varying degrees, as occasional fishermen, farmer fishermen (the most numerous) and full-time fishermen, the latter most often being migrants, sometimes more or less settled.

Key issues in Sahelian inland fisheries management

The plateau response model, discussed earlier, also applies to Sahelian fisheries, since these are multispecies fisheries whose productivity and sustainability depend primarily on the quality of aquatic environments and hydrological conditions. The risk of a collapse in fish stocks due to excess fishing is very low in this type of fishery, at least in the absence of destructive fishing techniques (chemical poison, explosives etc) and provided that a minimum quantity of breeding fish, however small, survives at the end of the dry season (Welcomme, 1999). However, environmental degradation is the key problem, and one that fishery managers should tackle as a priority, rather than the risk of over-fishing. Changes in the aquatic environment (eutrophication, pollution, damming, silting up, destruction of banks) are usually caused by activities such as intensive agriculture (irrigated sugarcane and rice cropping), mining, sand extraction etc. Unfortunately, fishermen have very few means at their disposal to combat this degradation.

The third issue relates to government policy and the conflicting interests and claims of different groups. As regards policy options, mention can be made of two scenarios frequently observed in the newly established fisheries in the reservoirs formed behind dams:

- Who should have preferential access to the resource: migrant fishermen or indigenous fishermen? A choice must be made between these two options knowing that the strength of claim asserted by each of the two groups is not the same, that the results in terms of sector performance (level and regularity of production) will not be the same either and that management of the system will differ as a result.
- Which processing and marketing networks should be encouraged, bearing in mind the fact that stakeholders involved in marketing fresh fish and processed products are usually not the same and that the distribution of value added will be very different depending on which sector is involved?

Sound management of inland Sahelian fisheries must focus primarily on efforts to combat environmental degradation and trade-offs between socio-economic priorities and their distributional consequences. To facilitate resolution of such problems, specialists in Sahelian fishery management are now calling for a differentiated approach depending on the type of fishery. In this regard, they distinguish between river fisheries (usually associated with flood plains), major natural lakes (such as Lake Chad), reservoir lakes and, finally, small stretches of water.

Institutional aspects of inland Sahelian fisheries

In most countries, the prevailing situation since independence and until the early 1990s was that the state, considering itself as the owner of water resources, attempted to apply a centralized management model, at least on paper. This was based on levying fishing duty, services supporting technology transfer and applying national regulations intended to prevent the supposed risks of 'overexploitation' (eg minimum mesh size for nets). This management model was based on a poor understanding of management requirements and profoundly out of step with existing practices, leading to many problems. Another weakness of the approach was its uniform deployment throughout the country, leaving no possibility of adapting management to the specific features of the different types of fishery. Moreover, this management mode, primarily based on coercion, generated substantial institutional costs for no appreciable benefit. All of this militated in favour of redefining relations between the state and resource-users.

From the end of the 1980s, most Sahelian states began the process of changing the governance of fishing, especially attempting to involve stakeholders to a greater extent in management. This process was consolidated in the early 1990s as a result of new approaches to fishery management at international level, particularly the adoption by the FAO of the Code of Conduct for Responsible Fisheries in 1995. Some of the principles in the code are particularly relevant to the management of Sahelian fisheries: the need for attention to the conservation of aquatic environments; the promotion of more adaptable management models (such as the plateau response model) that take account of social and economic parameters in management decisions; the participation of stakeholders in management on the basis of joint management systems; and acknowledgement of the role played by fishing as a social safety net. Finally, at the end of the 1990s, the emergence of decentralization policies in most states of the Sahelian region encouraged the establishment of legal frameworks for community participation in fishery planning, at least in the form of consultation procedures.

How effective have these new management methods been? As regards the environmental issue, little progress has been made despite the establishment of institutions at sub-regional level for coordinated watershed management (eg OMVS and ABN[13]) and despite local efforts at environmental education and rehabilitation. Environmental policies come up against budget problems and resistance to change from other watershed users. In addition, the fishery administrations do not have the capacity to defend vigorously the sector's interests within national and regional bodies.

On the other hand, as regards the second key issue (trading-off socio-economic priorities), genuine progress has been recorded over the last decade following the implementation of co-management policies. This is illustrated by two examples below.

Joint management mechanisms in Mali and Burkina Faso

For historical reasons, these two countries have not followed the same approach to promoting joint management. As Mali is a country with a strong fishing tradition, the national authorities have built on existing institutional structures. Burkina Faso, on the other hand, had plenty of scope to work out completely new arrangements. In both cases, policies were implemented by government to lay the foundations for participation by fishing communities, as in Mali, or to set up genuine co-management mechanisms, as in Burkina Faso. These various policies include:

- *Clarifying ownership rights and restricting open access* Legislation in Burkina Faso (the 1997 forestry code) has gone furthest in this respect in that it has replaced national permits with sub-national permits at regional level to limit the mobility of migrant fishermen. It has also established legal systems appropriate to the different types of fishery, such as the introduction of a specific permit scheme governing access to fish resources in the major artificial lakes. Malian legislation passed in 1995 introduced the concept of 'fishing property', whereby local government is now better able to control access to resources in accordance with the new powers given to them by the laws on decentralization.
- *Developing regulations specific to the local context* In both countries, legislation provides for the drafting of rules for individual fisheries, provided that these are at least in line with the minimum conservation measures laid down in national law. In Mali, these regulations take the form of 'local fishing agreements'. The laws passed in Burkina Faso in 1997 provide for the drafting of 'schedules of conditions' for fishing in the major reservoirs.
- *Community participation in management measures* In Mali, fishing councils provide the forum where the public authorities and communities come together to determine new contractual relations and have an important role to play in preparing draft local agreements. Recent initiatives around Lake Sélingué show that these draft conventions are beginning to incorporate unwritten rules based on customary law. In Burkina Faso, co-management is undertaken by joint management committees, which have equal representation from the communities and the public authorities. These committees are responsible for preparing a management plan that they will monitor and evaluate.

It is now acknowledged that joint management is one of the pillars of sustainable development in the field of natural resource management, which also holds true for Sahelian fisheries. Experience to date has shown that participatory management systems provide more powerful groups with plenty of scope to exercise their influence, and there is no certainty that these leaders' perceptions of management will always be compatible with the aim of combating poverty more generally. Because of this, parallel government action must be taken to build the capacity of the most vulnerable groups and monitor the impact of participatory management on different people.

Conclusions

The rapid growth in canoe fishing in West Africa over the 20th century, especially the second half, raises many questions. As a result of this growth, canoe fishing is now one of the main sources of income and wealth for populations in the region. In view of the fact that this sector is entirely based on African skills and capital, should this be seen as an exemplary success story for economic development of the continent? Or should one be alarmed to note that a growing number of people are basing their livelihoods on the exploitation of resources whose availability is limited by nature?

As a consequence of the growing influence of international experts in the field of environment and fish biology, it is the second perception that now dominates within international agencies. Increasingly conservationist policies are being promoted, with many projects to establish protected areas designed to give fish shelter from fishermen. One may wonder whether these policies are realistic and ethically acceptable in the social and economic context of West African countries. They stand in strong contrast to the policy previously supported by international aid, that is 'support to development of the sector', which was and is based on grants of equipment or incentives to investment and training. Finally and most importantly, conservationist policies overlook the importance of the social safety net provided by fishing in West African countries over the last few decades.

This does not mean that we should ignore the danger that continued rapid expansion in numbers and fishing capacity would pose for fishing communities. It is therefore urgent to design and establish new policies so that these communities may avoid a crisis. To this end, policies should support work along the following lines: capacity development to ensure greater value added of landed output; greater coherence between regulations governing access to resources; promotion of local regulatory practices that have shown their worth; protection of traditional livelihood strategies based on multiple activity; integration of migrant fishing into local development in the host areas; and empowerment of communities through educating young people. Such activities would seem essential to prevent the exposure of fishing families to increasing social and economic risks and to enable them to improve their incomes.

Notes

1. In the case of industrial fishing, the shipowner is always separate from the crew; in fact, this is usually a company whose capital is often of foreign origin.
2. For example, when tuna or large prawns are required that only industrial fishing techniques can catch.
3. But not 'exclusively', as it is uncommon in Africa for all the active members of a household to devote their entire working time to a single sector of activity.
4. The 1960 census of Senegalese fishing (excluding the river) counted 13,600 men and 3900 canoes, while the 1996 census showed 57,100 men and 10,600 canoes. This development results from the appearance of new types of larger canoe allowing the use of pelagic seine nets (in the 1970s) and fishing trips

extending over several days (in the 1980s). These innovations were encouraged by motorization which has become widespread along the coast in the last 50 years.

5. This case is somewhat exceptional, since communities in this country (apart from the Imraguen) had virtually no seagoing tradition and so there was a void to be filled.

6. Since farmed poultry is partly fed on products based on fish meal, increased consumption of eggs and chicken indirectly contributes towards increasing outlets for the fishing industry.

7. It is, however, rare for an investor from outside the sector to risk launching a fishing unit, as the likelihood of cheating (especially as regards the quantities produced) is extremely high.

8. Société Mauritanienne de Commercialisation du Poisson = Mauritanian fish marketing board.

9. Bearing in mind the risky nature of such a move, some households try to do more fishing while continuing to pursue other activities, which involves some of the household members going away to fish while the others remain on the family land to cultivate. This livelihood strategy seems to be the best and most desirable (Fay, 1994; Béné et al, 2000). However, it is not always possible: only households with considerable labour power and material resources can implement it.

10. This type of net, which allows for a large catch but is costly to use because it is very difficult to repair, is a growing success with fishermen. It is prohibited in some countries (such as Senegal) as it is thought to be dangerous for the environment because it does not degrade.

11. These costs represent the largest share of operating costs (about 75 per cent), fuel being the most important item of expenditure. The longer and more numerous the trips are, the higher this item of expenditure will be.

12. The information in this section is drawn from various technical reports produced in connection with the FAO/DFID Sustainable Fisheries Livelihood Programme in West Africa (PMEDP-SFLP) (www.sflp.org).

13. OMVS: Senegal river valley development office; ABN: Niger river basin agency.

References

Bauman, E, Fay, C and Kassibo, B (1994) 'Systèmes de pêche et stratégies globales', in J Quensière (ed) *La Pêche dans le Delta Central du Niger*, IER-ORSTOM-Karthala, pp401–6

Béné, C, Mindjimba, K, Belal, E and Jolley, T (2000) 'Evaluating Livelihood Strategies and the Role of Inland Fisheries in Rural Development and Poverty Alleviation: The Case of the Yaéré Floodplain in North Cameroon', paper presented at the 10th Conference of the International Institute of Fisheries Economics and Trade, Oregon State University, 10–14 July

Bonzon, A and Breuil, C (1992) 'Priorités pour l'aménagement et la planification du développement des pêches continentales dans la région du Sahel', FAO Fisheries Report No 481, FIPP/R481, FAO, Rome

Bouju, J (1999) 'Autochtones, migrants et technotopes ou l'appropriation des espaces sociaux de production', in F Domain, P Chavance and A Diallo (eds) *La pêche côtière en Guinée: ressources et exploitation*, IRD/CNSHB, pp211–31

Breuil, C, Cacaud, P and Quensière, J (1996) *Proposition d'un document de politique des pêches et de la pisciculture au Mali*, PNUD/MLI/91/005, FAO, Rome

Bru, H and Hatti, M (2000) *Pêche artisanale et lutte contre la pauvreté. République islamique de Mauritanie*, PNUD/FAO

Caverivière, A, Thiam, M and Jouffre, D (eds) (2002) *Le poulpe Octopus vulgaris. Sénégal et côtes nord-ouest africaines*, IRD éditions, Coll. Colloques et Séminaires, Paris, p385

CEP (2000) 'Note de conjoncture no 9 et note de conjoncture no 10, situation du premier semestre 2000 et situation du deuxième semestre 2000', Cellule d'Etudes et de Planification, Ministère des Pêches (Sénégal)

Chaboud, C and Charles-Dominique, E (1991) 'Les pêches artisanales en Afrique de l'Ouest: état des connaissances et évolution de la recherche', in J R Durand, J Lemoalle and J Weber (eds) *La recherche face à la pêche artisanale* (Research and small-scale fisheries), Vol 1, ORSTOM éditions, Coll. Colloques et Séminaires

Chauveau, J (1986) 'Une histoire maritime africaine est-elle possible? Historiographie et histoire de la navigation et de la pêche africaines à la côte occidentale depuis le XVème siècle', *Cahiers d'Etudes Africaines*, vol 26, nos 1–2, pp173–235

Chavance, P (2002) 'Un essai de reconstruction d'un demi-siècle d'évolution des pêcheries en Afrique de l'Ouest, Premiers résultats et difficultés rencontrées, in M Ba, P Chavance, D Gascuel, D Pauly and M Vakily (eds) *Actes du Symposium de Dakar, Sénégal*, 24–28 June, ACP-EU Fisheries Research Report

Cormier-Salem, M (1991) 'Pêcheurs migrants et paysans-pêcheurs: deux modèles de gestion de l'espace irréductibles', in J R Durand, J Lemoalle and J Weber (eds) *La recherche face à la pêche artisanale* (Research and small-scale fisheries), Vol 2, ORSTOM éditions, Coll. Colloques et Séminaires, pp621–30

Domain, F, Chavance, P and Diallo, A (eds) (1999) *La pêche côtière en Guinée: ressources et exploitation*, IRD/CNSHB

FAO (1999) *Evaluation des stocks et aménagement des pêcheries de la ZEE mauritanienne*, CPACE/PACE Series 99/64

Fay, C (1994) 'Organisation sociale et culturelle de la production de pêche: morphologie et grandes mutations', in J Quensière (ed) *La pêche dans le Delta Central du Niger*, IER-ORSTOM-Karthala

Gordon, H (1954) 'The Economic Theory of Common Property Resources: The Fishery', *Journal of Political Economy*, vol 62, no 2, pp124–42

Greboval, D (1997) 'Schéma directeur pêche et pisciculture', Rapport Technique FAO no 5, TCP/GUI/4556

Haakonsen, J and Diaw, C (eds) (1991) *Migration des pêcheurs en Afrique de l'Ouest*, DIPA/WP/36

Henry, F and Moal, R (1998) *Compétitivité de la pêche maritime en Afrique: Mission d'études, d'évaluation et de prospective*, Secrétariat d'Etat à la Coopération et à la Francophonie, Coll. Rapport d'Etude

Herry, C (1994) 'Démographie des pêcheurs', in J Quensière (ed) *La Pêche dans le Delta Central du Niger*, IER-ORSTOM-Karthala, pp123–41

Hugon, P (1998) 'Ajustement structurel, emploi et rôle des partenaires sociaux en Afrique francophone', *Cahiers de l'emploi et de la formation*, no 28, p53, OIT

Kaczynski, V and Fluarty, D (2002) 'European Policies in West Africa: Who Benefits from Fisheries Agreements?', *Marine Policy*, vol 26, pp75–93

Kassibo, B (2000) 'Pêche continentale et migration: contrôle politique et contrôle social des migrations de pêche dans le Delta central du Niger (Mali)', pp231–46, in J Chauveau, E Jul-Larsen and C Chaboud (eds), *Les pêches piroguières en Afrique de l'Ouest*, Karthala-IRD-CMI

Kebe, M (1997) *Coûts et revenus en pêche artisanale: résultats du suivi d'unités de pêche à Hann* (Sénégal), Rapport multigraphié, FAO-DIPA

Koranteng, K A (1990) 'Ghana Canoë Frame Survey 1989', Information Report, 25, Tema, Fisheries Department Research and Utilization Branch

Laë, R (1997) 'Does Overfishing Lead to a Decrease in Catches and Yields? An Example of Two West African Coastal Lagoons', *Fisheries Management and Ecology*, vol 4, pp149–64

Marten, G and Polovina, J (1982) 'A Comparative of Fish Yields from Various Tropical Ecosystems', in D Pauly and G Murphy (eds) *Theory and Management of Tropical Fisheries: International Centre for Living Aquatic Resources Management Conference Proceedings*, vol 9, ICLARM, Manila

Morand, P and Bousquet, F (1994) 'Relations entre l'effort de pêche, la dynamique du peuplement ichtyologique et le niveau des captures dans un système fleuve-plaine', in J Quensière (ed) *La Pêche dans le Delta Central du Niger*, IER-ORSTOM-Karthala, pp267–81

Moss, B (1992) 'Uses, Abuses and Management of Lakes and Rivers', *Hydrobiologia*, vol 243/244, pp31–45

Pauly, D, Christensen, V, Dalsgaard, J, Froese, R and Torres, F Jr (1998) 'Fishing Down Marine Food Webs', *Science*, vol 279, pp860–3

Pavé, M and Charles-Dominique, E (1999) 'Science et politique des pêches en Afrique occidentale française (1900–1950): quelles limites de quelles ressources?', *Natures Sciences Sociétés*, vol 7, no 2, pp5–18

Quesnel, A (1996) 'Population et devenir des agricultures africaines', in F Gendreau, P Gubry and J Véron (eds) *Populations et environnement dans les pays du Sud*, Karthala-CEPED, Paris

Regier, H (1973) 'Sequence of Exploitation of Stocks in Multispecies Fisheries in the Laurentian Great Lakes', *Journal of the Fisheries Research Board of Canada*, vol 30, pp1992–9

Romagny, B, Ménard, F, Dewals, P, Gaertner, D and N'Goran, N (2000) 'Le "faux-poisson" d'Abidjan et la pêche sous épaves dans l'Atlantique tropical Est: circuit de commercialisation et rôle socio-économique', in J-Y Le Gall, P Cayré and M Taquet (eds) *Pêche thonière et dispositifs de concentration de poisons*, Éditions IFREMER, Actes de colloques, 28

Sarch, M and Allison, E (2000) 'Fluctuating Fisheries in Africa's Inland Waters: Well Adapted Livelihoods, Maladapted Management', paper presented at the 10th Conference of the International Institute of Fisheries Economics and Trade, Oregon State University, 10–14 July

Sy, O (1998) *Etude sur l'exploitation des petits pélagiques au Sénégal*, Rapport FAO

Verdeaux, F (1989) 'Généalogie d'un phénomène de surexploitation: lagune Aby (Côte d'Ivoire), 1935–1982', *Cahiers Sciences Humaines*, vol 25, nos 1–2, pp191–211

Welcomme, R (1999) 'A Review of a Model for Qualitative Evaluation of Exploitation Levels in Multi-Species Fisheries', *Fisheries Management and Ecology*, vol 6, pp1–19

3
Urban Livelihoods

Jo Beall

Introduction

One of the most significant demographic and social changes of the 20th century was the inexorable growth of urbanization. This trend seems set to continue well into the 21st century, with Africa being the least urbanized but the most rapidly urbanizing region globally. As with other late developing countries, the cities of Africa are host to a large and growing proportion of the world's poorest people. In a winner-takes-all global economic environment and a context where it has been said that Africa has no 'world cities' (Rakodi, 1998), the prospects for African cities as engines of economic growth and as centres of employment generation are slim. Indeed, for a long time it has been incumbent on Africa's urban poor to carve out a living for themselves, with, without or in spite of global and national economic development, a situation that remains the case across much of the continent today.

For people to secure a sustained urban existence, wages and income need to match the high monetary costs of living in cities. These include rates, taxes, licence fees, transport costs, rents, payment for services and sometimes bribes. Building the assets or incurring debt is a prerequisite for acquiring shelter or security of tenure, and the right to work or access to income-earning opportunities can involve poor people in transaction costs with gatekeepers. So urban poverty is expensive. Second, urban livelihoods depend on safe and secure communities and social networks, which in towns and cities extend beyond those of kin and clan to include neighbours and other forms of associational life. Lastly, livelihoods have to be struggled for and this can involve not only individual and household level efforts but also collective action. As such, acknowledging the politics of urban livelihoods is as important as understanding their economic, physical and social base.

These three dimensions of urban livelihoods – making a living, maintaining social networks and mounting collective action – are explored for the African context, against a consideration of the interpretative frameworks for understanding the livelihoods of the urban poor. The ways in which urban people in Africa construct work opportunities and compose their social and political worlds are reviewed by drawing on research conducted in Johannesburg (Beall et al, 1999) and Kumasi (Korboe et al, 1999) as part of a broader study on urban poverty and governance.[1]

Framing Urban Livelihoods

Framing urban livelihoods means recognizing that they are not simply a matter of making a living or transacting money. Livelihoods also imply the management of relationships, meanings and identity and, as such, a livelihoods perspective forms part of a long social science tradition of seeing economic activities as embedded in social relationships (Polanyi, 1944; Granovetter, 1985; Appadurai, 1986; Granovetter, 1993). At the centre of most analytical frameworks concerned with understanding livelihoods is an empirical focus on rural contexts (Murray, 1999; Francis, 2000; Whitehead, 2000). Making a living in African cities has been explored less often from a livelihoods perspective, with a few exceptions (Beall et al, 1999; Rakodi, 1999; Beall, 2002).

The rapid take-up of a livelihoods perspective as an analytical and operational framework in development studies is testimony to the resonance that the approach has for those concerned to move beyond a money-metric approach to socio-economic analysis. A livelihoods perspective is appealing too because it introduces an element of agency into any understanding of the diverse ways in which people make a living under conditions where structural constraints seem overwhelming. This is especially the case for sub-Saharan Africa, where a legacy of colonialism, adverse incorporation into the global economy, recent histories of armed conflict and 'weak states', as well as inappropriate or harmful interventions by international agencies and development institutions, have provided the backdrop against which people pursue survival and security.

More problematic has been the tendency for livelihoods perspectives fast to become 'livelihoods frameworks' that rigidly codify series of 'capitals' or 'assets' that people have or aspire towards.[2] Frameworks can be useful mechanisms for organizing perplexing and often detailed social analysis for policy-makers and development practitioners. However, they can also become straitjackets that awkwardly accommodate the complexities and micro-politics of everyday life. As Whitehead (2000) has argued in relation to her work on Ghana, there is a problem with the current enthusiasm for conceptualizing social relations and institutions in terms of 'assets' or 'capitals', alongside say physical or financial capitals, when using ideas from anthropology, sociology or political economy. This does not necessarily mean eschewing terms such as social capital, which has become intrinsic to a livelihoods perspective. Rather it is about preserving their more complex meaning. As Whitehead elaborates:

> From the perspective of the latter [political economy], assets are of course relational: systems for access and distribution and systems of exclusionary access are intrinsic to the idea. They become torn out of their relational context in the shift to the language of neo-classical economics to explore livelihoods. (Whitehead, 2000, p7)

This sits well with Fine's (1999) recent argument in relation to social capital, that there is a colonization of the social sciences by economics that tends to drive out approaches that are 'inhospitable' to a functionalist and reducible view of social interactions. To this end, therefore, rather than seeing Africa's urban poor as social capitalists or 'managers of complex asset portfolios' (Moser, 1998, p5), the approach adopted here is closer to that of Bebbington who argues for 'a wide conception of the resources that people need to access in the process of composing a livelihood' (Bebbington, 1999, p2022). Understood in this way a livelihoods perspective offers an integrated framework for thinking about access to resources, whereby 'the distinction between *access* and *resources* breaks down, because *access* becomes perhaps the most critical resource of all' (Bebbington, 1999, p2022). This analytical departure is particularly useful for understanding livelihoods in the African urban context, where social differentiation can be considerable and where for the urban poor, proximity to resources does not translate automatically into access.

Strategies for economic survival and security in urban Africa have been subject to different interpretative treatments, most often associated with the informal sector debate. In the context of weak states, poor economic performance and limited opportunities for waged employment, it was in Africa that the informal sector debate originated (ILO, 1972; Hart, 1973). Initially discussions on the urban 'informal sector' centred on its relationship to the 'formal sector' and whether the relationship was benign or exploitative (Tokman, 1978; Sethurman, 1981). The most common criticisms arising out of the debate centred on the gross oversimplification implied by this artificial dualism and the fact that it ignored the inter-connections between different types of activities. Moreover, the debate concealed stark differentiation and wide variety in the forms of accumulation within the urban economy, both formal and informal.

More recently a range of alternative concepts have emerged to describe the phenomenon of informalization in Africa, with the interdependence of the so-called 'formal' and 'informal' economies being seen as significant within most national economies across the continent and as serving multiple interests globally, such that Meagher (1995, p266) has argued that it is 'part of a global restructuring strategy to defend formal sector profits'. In the literature on the informal or second economy in Africa as well, there is increasing discomfort with the artificial distinction between formal and informal economies, particularly in the context of current 'flexible labour' strategies and the accompanying mechanisms of home-working and out-sourcing. Here the norm is reliance on unprotected and casual-ized labour, often treated as self-employed workers'. Beyond these relationships there are hidden livelihoods that are intermeshed, autonomous entities that may or may not be linked into global, national or even local economies.

These linkages and interdependencies have lead MacGaffey to talk about an all encompassing 'real economy' in Africa, understood as including:

> *all components of economic activity, all transactions monetized and non-mone-tized, official and unofficial, taking place between rural and urban areas of a country, to arrive at a picture of the total economy, which is the 'real economy'.* (MacGaffey, 1991, p10)

For MacGaffey the 'real economy' includes what she prefers to call the 'second economy', being those economic activities that are not officially reported and directly taxable. If Hadjor's (1993, p162) assertion is true that 'the invention of the term "informal sector" was a cynical exercise in making a virtue out of necessity', then the notion of the 'real economy' is a not so cynical effort to value all forms of economic activity and to bring from margin to centre that pole of the economy formerly seen as informal, small-scale, hidden, unrecorded or extra-legal and, concomitantly, as peripheral and insignificant. It is within the context of the 'real economy' that urban livelihoods within the 'second' or 'informal' economy are explored here.

An added dimension provided by a livelihoods perspective is the recognition that, in order to make a living in any economy at all, people draw upon a range of tangible and intangible assets that are crucial for managing and balancing complex sets of activities and decisions. Beyond earnings, savings and other financial assets, African urban dwellers, like their rural counterparts, have assets tied up in themselves.[3] These include their labour, skills, knowledge and health or their connections, such as relationships with family, neighbours and friends. A common assumption is that modern city life undermines family and kinship ties and the mobility and heterogeneity of city populations mean that social networks are generally thought to be less robust in urban areas. Clientalist relations and gatekeeper practices prevent access to the political process in towns and cities as much as in the countryside.

In these and other ways, the urban environment in Africa can be particularly hostile to the construction and maintenance of a secure asset base, not least of all because it is highly monetized and the options for diversifying income are often exaggerated. Important reasons for vulnerability include repeated shocks brought about by economic crisis at the macro-level and, at the micro-level, personal and physical insecurity as a result of high levels of ill health, violence and crime. In Africa these problems are frequently compounded by the prevalence of HIV/ AIDS, armed conflict, internal displacement and the movement of refugees to cities, often requiring hard-pressed urban dwellers to share or compete for limited resources and services in poorly managed cities run by weak and under-resourced local governments. It is against this background that we need to recognize the resilience and adaptability of the urban poor in Africa (Guyer, 1987; Tripp, 1997; Jones and Nelson, 1999; Friedberg, 2001) and the important contribution of Africa's second economy not only to the national accounts but to the reduction and prevention of urban poverty (MacGaffey, 1991; Meagher, 1995; King, 1996).

However, as pointed out elsewhere in relation to urban livelihoods in Africa:

This focus is not meant to obscure the vulnerabilities of people in poverty, or to over-emphasise the options available to them in their efforts to earn incomes, create liveable environments and develop positive social relationships. They frequently pursue these ends in the context of severe structural constraints. Rather, the aim is to point up the significance of the activities of households and communities for policy and planning and to analyse the linkages between the workings of these smaller units and the larger-scale economic, social and political processes operating in, on and beyond African cities. (Beall et al, 1999, p160)

Moreover, a focus on the rugged self-reliance of the urban poor of Africa's second economies should not lead to policy conclusions that rely entirely on the resources of poverty, depleting rather than conserving and restoring the assets of the African urban poor and penalizing them for their very resourcefulness. This issue is taken up again in the conclusion in relation to the policy implications of the argument advanced below.

Making a Living

A powerful obstacle to sustainable urban development and urban poverty reduction in Africa is the inability to provide employment for growing urban populations. This constitutes one of the most intractable problems facing national and local governments. Most urban jobs are concentrated in the public, manufacturing and service sectors with the latter increasing in relative importance as public-sector employment is in decline and manufacturing employment becomes more insecure. Colonial and post-colonial economic policy in Africa was historically interventionist, with heavy protectionism and significant amounts of state production. This generated a rapid and sustained process of industrial transformation in some countries but also resulted in significant levels of unevenness in development across regions and produced a highly segmented labour market with relatively good conditions of work for some and high levels of insecurity and poverty for others.

The economic recession of the 1980s, and the accompanying reform measures imposed on African economies by the international financial architecture, led to policies that favoured export-led growth over import substitution, the promotion of tradables over non-tradables, private solutions over public involvement and a general demand for downsizing, lower wage bills and changes in labour practices. In the worst cases this led to mounting unemployment, while in less severe cases it resulted in the weakening of trade unions and a threat to formal employment contracts. Either way the brunt of the impact of economic restructuring was borne by the African urban poor. Despite the negative effects of these changes on the livelihoods of the urban poor, proponents claim that global economic development has made it almost impossible for governments to sustain protectionist policies, that the losses associated with restructuring will be temporary and that, properly implemented, they will produce significant improvements in both productivity and income distribution.

In the case of Africa it is perhaps too early to tell but in the meantime, responsibility for household well-being is most often borne by those working in the service sector and the informal economy of cities. Compounded by global trade expansion, increased international competition and technological advances, recent decades in Africa have seen, for many urban households, falling real incomes and increased household expenditure, leading to more women engaging in income earning (Kanji, 1995), more children on the streets (Cullen et al, 1997) and more people scavenging the waste dumps of the continent's cities to survive (Beall and Seegmuller, 2001). This said, it is important to recognize differentiation within the informal economy, which can be lucrative for the better off within it, as well as being the last resort of the working poor. MacGaffey (1991) in her work on the Democratic Republic of Congo (DRC) argues that the second economy has eclipsed the salaried sector, which in turn is most valued not for its wages but the access it provides to an even wider and more lucrative range of informal economic activities. What this suggests is that activities within the second economy can represent a preferred set of alternatives to waged or salaried employment. As such the second economy does not mean second best. Rather the first and second economies are bound together by vertical and horizontal linkages that comprise asymmetrical social relationships that benefit some more than others.

People bring personal histories and prior social endowments to their pursuit of livelihoods wherever they are. These, together with structural conditions and their accompanying social relations, influence the ways in which the urban poor form and deploy assets and control the processes involved. Illustrative is the role of women in urban economies. In Africa, women have been involved in production and trade for centuries. As such they are not necessarily new actors in the urban economy and have long played a critical role. A classic portrayal of women's involvement in the African urban economy, and one largely supported by evidence from Johannesburg and Kumasi, is as locally based, small-scale traders or street vendors, operating in micro-enterprises characterized by a lack of capital formation, concentrated in areas such as services or retail and around particular commodities with low profitability. For example, recent work undertaken in Durban, South Africa (Lund et al, 2000) shows that for most women, trade is in low volumes for small returns and the struggle is for survival rather than security, with asset accumulation remaining elusive. While true for many cases, there were also examples from our own research of significant accumulation strategies on the part of women, for example the 'shebeen queens'[4] of Soweto and the significant involvement of women in market trade in Kumasi. Research elsewhere has highlighted the role of women in market trade (Mittullah, 1991), women entrepreneurs in the Nairobi garment industry (McCormick et al, 2001; McCormick and Schmitz, 2001) and elite women entrepreneurs in urban Kinshasa (MacGaffey, 1992). However, as our own research revealed, despite being numerically dominant, women market traders in Kumasi were excluded from decision-making processes about the city's market, and local governance in Johannesburg remains dominated by more powerful forces than the illicit beer brewers and alcohol vendors of the city's townships.

The struggles of women to engage in paid work and micro-enterprises in African cities confirm as myth the notion that access to the second economy is easy simply because it requires limited capitalization and is loosely organized. In reality, powerful clientelist control operates at different levels, hampering entry and barring access. Such institutions are fluid and urban livelihoods in Africa are constantly created and reconstructed in changing political, economic and institutional contexts. In fact, any studies of the economic activities that comprise the urban livelihoods of Africa's urban poor can only be seen as indicative and this is surely the case with our studies of Johannesburg and Kumasi. They will necessarily be incomplete or temporary because circumstances are fluid and workers, producers and traders become more mobile and diversified according to their various endowments and histories. Moreover, people engaged in what are largely hidden livelihoods are reluctant to give details of clandestine or illegal activities. This applies to much of the second economy by virtue of the lack of regulatory definition throughout much of urban Africa and the fact that people avoid taxes, fees and licences, the imposition of which is not always possible when implemented by ineffective local governments.

Maintaining Social Networks and Urban Communities

Making a living in the city involves the forming and nurturing of commercial relationships as production and trading depends on the establishment of personal ties and the development of reputations and bonds of trust. This applies not only in relation to customers but also in relation to the mobilization of finance for business pursuits. How people relate to one another in debt relations is a fundamental component of the urban livelihood experience in Africa. The literature on African entrepreneurs provides a mixed picture in terms of the role of kin in providing loans for business and our evidence suggests that credit is as likely to result from friendships or more formalized relationships. However, the risks involved and the precariousness of material livelihoods in urban Africa mean that investment in social relations, including those based on kin, is taken all the more seriously.

Moreover, declining real per capita incomes in African cities have put increasing pressure on urban households not only to generate income but to engage in multiple strategies for survival and betterment. Many of these involve reciprocal relationships and practices of mutuality. It is in this context that households and kinship networks are particularly important, as people best pursue urban livelihood opportunities from a secure domestic unit.[5] The process of household consolidation itself is often a lengthy and dynamic process in urban areas, particularly for migrants and younger families. Urban household consolidation involves above all the accumulation of resources, achieving security of tenure and becoming engaged in area-based or interest-based networks in the city. This means that urban households often remain fluid in size, composition and location for a long time, as members seek security in the city. Thus it can be argued that the formation and maintenance of urban households are often in themselves a livelihood strategy.

In Africa there are often important rural–urban linkages in the livelihood strategies of urban households. On the one hand people migrate to cities in search of employment and urban workers send remittances to family members in rural areas. On the other, they rely on relatives in the countryside during stringent times, for example for agricultural produce, medicines, family labour or extended periods of childcare (Tacoli, 1998; Beall et al, 1999). What this points to is the fact that the pursuit of livelihoods can include a swathe of responses ranging from labour market involvement to changing patterns of consumption, social networking and the rearrangement of household responsibilities. These responses are put under severe strain during periods of economic stress and as welfare services, however inadequate, are replaced by reliance on the caring capacity of families and communities (Kanji, 1995; Rakodi, 1995; Moser, 1996).

A widespread assumption is that kinship relations and social networks are not as deeply entrenched in urban contexts as in rural situations. However, there was sufficient evidence from the two city studies drawn on here to suggest that individual survival is difficult in cities and that poverty makes cooperative behaviour all the more necessary. In Johannesburg and Kumasi findings suggested that kinship ties, social networks and reciprocal practices of various kinds existed within urban environments and beyond. Indeed, extended family networks spanned the rural–urban divide and were important sources of security. Results from the Kumasi study paralleled those of others (Ferguson, 1999; Francis, 2000) that migration and remittance flows are not necessarily uni-directional but flow from rural to urban areas and vice versa, depending on where they are needed at any one time.

While kinship networks form an important basis of support and mutual self-help, they can be a mixed blessing. Close-knit kinship networks were shown to work well for Kumasi's better-off families, for example those with relatives overseas who contributed towards gains in overall living conditions for the family at home through migration and inward remittances. However, for more marginal households limited resources could be drained by the demands of relatives. Borrowing and begging on the part of destitute kin, with no intention or possibility of repayment, becomes highly problematic for relatives who themselves are already on the edge. As I have argued elsewhere (Beall, 1995) and as the evidence from Johannesburg also confirmed, without basic resources and security in place it is difficult if not impossible for poor families to sustain self-help and mutual assistance.

Another key example from Kumasi related to the increasing commoditization of rites of passage, which could lead to family events such as christenings, weddings and funerals resembling barely disguised extortion rackets. For example, deprivation has lead to funerals becoming occasions where family members haggle over the belongings of deceased relatives rather than the important social events they generally constitute in Ghanaian society. Under conditions of economic and social stress, urban funerals in Ghana have become seemingly fractious, contested affairs, often associated with high levels of acrimony and increased interpersonal violence, rather than opportunities to strengthen social relations and consolidate family ties. In sum, while reciprocal obligations are an important component of urban livelihoods in Africa, they can also erode the social resources and material assets of the poor.

Beyond kinship, connections with friends and neighbours were reported to be of vital importance in both Kumasi and Johannesburg, softening and lubricating the experience of urban life. Broader social networks and associations were found to be an important way for people to access accommodation, glean information about employment opportunities and to build assets through pooling mechanisms or through investing in informal savings clubs such as *susus* in Kumasi and *stokvels* in Johannesburg. Other evidence of cooperation was found in bulk-buying schemes, communal eating arrangements and burial associations, as well as church-based and religious organizations and hometown associations. In the African context, urban social groupings can coagulate around rural linkages and identities, which in turn feed into job-securing networks. In Kumasi rural–urban linkages were assiduously nurtured and in Johannesburg, too, many migrants to the city maintained close links with people from their places of origin. As with hometown associations, burial societies and savings groups, social networks often became semi-formalized and constitutive of a complex web of urban associational life.

Important though such cooperative relationships were, it is important not to romanticize social networks and support. The experience of many cities in Africa mirrors that of Johannesburg, which was particularly redolent with examples of no-go areas, autocratic urban mafias and pervasive fear generated by the activities of anti-social and violent criminal gangs. In many parts of the city warring gangs, taxi-drivers, shacklords, druglords and pimps intimidate entire neighbourhoods and zones. The high levels of crime and interpersonal violence such as rape and murder mean that people across all areas and social classes in Johannesburg are gripped by fear. Such conditions, which are common to many African cities, erode any sense of public safety and challenge community cohesion and collective action. Thus in Johannesburg and in Kumasi, in ways that echo Ferguson's findings for the Zambian Copperbelt (1999), unaffordable land prices and housing costs, together with poor quality and crumbling services, have given rise to levels of insecurity, apathy and disillusionment with urban life and livelihoods, such that organized public action seems a remote possibility.

Mounting Collective Action

MacGaffey's (1998) work on Zaire, now the DRC, takes up the idea that livelihood strategies may be forms of resistance against weak or kleptocratic states. Her position parallels in part de Soto's (1989) more unreservedly optimistic characterization of the informal economy in Latin America, as a peaceful, non-violent and 'hidden' revolution. It also anticipates Tripp's (1997) work on Tanzania, which uses Scott's (1985) notion of the 'Weapons of the Weak' to suggest that the informal economy and the organizations and associations tied to it are mechanisms to assert autonomy, self-reliance and to challenge top-down government. A common thread in this line of argument is that the very existence of the informal or second economy undermines state legitimacy because it provides evidence of the inadequacy of local government to regulate it and makes visible the paucity of official distribution channels, employment and pricing.

Compelling though this argument is, livelihoods pursued by Africa's powerless and often disenfranchised urban poor are invariably little more than a valiant coping mechanism, defensive resistance that does not mount to offensive resistance or a hidden revolution. Nevertheless, they can sometimes add up to a surreptitious struggle by stealth, which Bayat (1997) has described in the case of urban Iran, as the 'quiet encroachment of the ordinary'. As such, the resilience and adaptability of the urban poor in Africa is not in doubt and in this respect research conducted in Johannesburg and Kumasi confirms findings elsewhere in Africa on the inevitability and intractability of the urban informal economy (King, 1996; Tripp, 1997; Jones and Nelson, 1999; Freidberg, 2001).

What the case of South Africa shows is that under certain circumstances that are not always clear, predictable or replicable, the quiet encroachment of ordinary self-help forms of collective action can be scaled up towards more generalized livelihoods goals. Here local branches of organizations such as the Congress of South African Trade Unions (COSATU) and the South African National Civic Organisation (SANCO) have been formed into wider federations operative at the national and city levels and they can and have had considerable positive impact. As the Johannesburg city study illustrates, the scaling-up and scaling-out of urban collective action usually occurs in the context of opposition or protest politics. In less turbulent and more polarized times, various forms of capture can come into play that reduce the effectiveness and autonomy of federated organizations. Moreover, despite the transition to democracy in South Africa, contemporary economic and political conditions as elsewhere in Africa militate against strong trade unions and popular organizations.

In Johannesburg one immediate problem observable was that of local or branch level concerns becoming subverted to national level organizational ambitions. The local branches of COSATU and SANCO had to balance their accountability downwards with accountability upwards, in terms of the aims and objectives of the national organizations. For both organizations this has been made more difficult by having positioned themselves in terms of post-apartheid politics as national movements sympathetic to the ANC but potentially and actually in opposition to many aspects of government policy, particularly as rolled out at city level. In the case of COSATU, for example, an official alliance partner with the dominant African National Congress (ANC), it finds itself in Johannesburg in a head-to-head clash with the ANC-led Metropolitan Council that seeks to downsize the municipal labour force and contract out urban services to parastatals and private operators.

The Kumasi study provided weary illustrations of new problems emerging in Johannesburg. In the Ghanaian city not only were community-based organizations diverted from their own concerns but were actually being created by the state or other developmental institutions for project-based and sometimes political purposes. For example, the Association for the Defence of the Revolution in Kumasi is party politically driven from above and therefore has little impact on advancing urban livelihoods, while Kumasi's local level Unit Committees proved to be far more effective at mobilizing the community towards the goals of local government than at channelling community level priorities or grievances to government. Similarly in Johannesburg there was some anxiety that the Community Development Forums – set up in good faith during the transition from apartheid to democracy, as part of the consultative process accompanying the establishment of Local Development Objectives by the Greater Johannesburg Metropolitan Council – were becoming increasingly partisan and would undermine existing or more inclusive community-based organization. In Kumasi traditional authority structures and ethnic politics served to gate-keep opportunity so that the social resources and livelihood opportunities of the urban poor were deeply embedded in asymmetrical social relationships, with some evidence of similar patterns in post-apartheid Johannesburg.

As with kinship and social networks, collective action was found not to be confined to the urban poor. Private-sector coalitions were shown to be involved in the civic and economic life of Kumasi and Johannesburg and to influence government, such as the associations of market traders in Kumasi and the taxi owners' associations in Johannesburg. As the example of women traders in Kumasi illustrates, such organizations are unlikely to include the weaker operatives in their sectors, but rather seek ways of reinforcing their own interests in the context of the city. Involvement with local government is as likely to be driven by pork-barrel politics as by civic duty or concern for the urban poor, with whom they clash as much as collaborate. To the extent that there is a relationship between local governments and coalitions of less well off entrepreneurs in urban Africa, this appears to depend on the strength and organization of the latter. From our city case studies, examples would be the Aboabo Talia Producers' Association in Kumasi or the Street Vendors Association and the Self-Employed Women's Association in Johannesburg and Durban, which have usefully engaged on behalf of their constituencies with local authorities and more lucrative or formal businesses.

In terms of collective action to advance the situation of Africa's urban poor, the evidence provided by our two city case studies is patchy, showing the potential of formal and large-scale organization, particularly around livelihoods issues, and the pitfalls faced when they come up against either the pork-barrel politics of more powerful associations or their relative powerlessness in the face of structural and macro-level forces operating in and on the city. While the case of Johannesburg offers beacons of hope, the South African case should not be presented either as problem-free or as a blueprint for the continent. The lack of public safety and feelings of fear and insecurity severely threaten associational life in Johannesburg and have proved to have a negative impact on public action in the city. In Johannesburg, law and order has until very recently fallen outside the competencies of local government, making it difficult for the city to do much more than provide tacit support for the establishment of neighbourhood watch schemes and community policing initiatives.

In Kumasi, responsibility for public safety and order has become increasingly informal, with the mayor running personal 'macho' forces and public safety often falling by stint of state neglect into the hands of community 'watchdog committees'. As in Johannesburg, these are often loose associations of young people who patrol neighbourhoods at night without pay but in full expectation of being rewarded for their efforts. There is a thin line in such cases between these efforts being positive local level interventions and a more perverse form of vigilantism. There is a body of evidence to suggest that low levels of social engagement constitute a strong predictor of high levels of crime and violence in urban centres (Kawachi et al, 1997; Moser and Holland, 1997).

Conclusions

The resilience and adaptability of the urban poor in Africa is not in doubt. Nor is the fact that the urban informal economy, of which they form an important and growing part, is an intrinsic and vital part of the continent's real economy. As such, urban growth is a necessary but not sufficient condition for addressing the problem of urban livelihoods. However, where cities are engaging effectively in local economic development, as in Johannesburg, there is no immediate evidence that this necessarily improves the position of the urban poor (Beall et al, 2002). Against a growing realization that cities must respond to a changing global market-place, some, such as Johannesburg, have responded by marketing themselves globally to encourage inward investment but the promise of 'trickle-down' benefits remains just that, a promise.

Urban dwellers, as individuals, within households and as part of more extended networks and groups, construct their livelihoods within broader socio-economic, political, institutional and physical contexts than those contained by urban boundaries. Livelihood networks and income-earning activities, alongside economic and poverty trends in urban centres, are closely linked to national economic performance as well as social and economic development policies decided and executed at different levels, including internationally. The wide range of organizations and processes acting in and upon urban centres in turn comprise the institutional context that is central to urban livelihoods analysis. Informal institutions, social networks and relationships are a vital component of such a context and crucial to the ways in which urban dwellers in Africa make a living, deal with risk and withstand shocks.

Nevertheless, collective action is a strategy that remains important and livelihoods are as much in danger of weak civil societies as weak states. Enabling policies are vital as well and despite macro-economic policy that is eroding formal employment opportunities and conditions of service, South Africa also provides positive examples of how livelihoods can be advanced by government, with local authorities having a constitutional obligation to consult with workers' organizations and street traders' associations on matters affecting them. Responsive government is only one half of the equation, however, with supportive policy frameworks being the other. For social and economic development to be so reliant on the social resources of the urban poor, as is the case in so many African cities today, is to offer the most perverse of incentives and to deplete Africa's most valuable resource, the energy and optimism of its people.

Notes

1. Reference to Johannesburg and Kumasi draws on these two studies unless otherwise stated, being the African city studies conducted under the auspices of DFID-funded Research on Urban Governance, Partnership and Poverty, undertaken between 1998 and 2001.
2. The sustainable livelihoods perspective (Chambers and Conway, 1992) gave rise to a framework adopted by the Department for International Development (DFID) in the United Kingdom (Carney, 1998) and by other agencies, notably UNDP, Oxfam and CARE (Carney et al, 1999), with CARE and DFID having developed the strongest urban focus (Rakodi and Lloyd-Jones, 2002).
3. Natural assets such as access to the commons are more important for rural than for urban livelihoods, although land and security of tenure remain crucial urban issues. Physical assets like shelter and basic infrastructure – such as water, energy and transport – are perhaps more important for urban than for rural dwellers in terms of health and well-being. Similarly, housing can be

multifunctional, potentially providing shelter, a source of income from rent, as well as a location for home-based enterprise.

4. During the apartheid era, some township women illegally sold home-brewed alcohol in their homes. Their homes became known as *shebeens*, the equivalent of pubs or taverns, and they were known as *shebeen* queens.

5. How these units are defined and analysed presents difficulties for both rural and urban contexts, although the concept of 'household' is most commonly used and is employed here as a matter of convenience. It is recognized, nevertheless, that it is an analytical category and covers a wide range of residential forms, groupings of people and functions. The concept 'family' is used to imply a more complex set of relationships and normative assumptions.

References

Appadurai, A (ed) (1986) *The Social Life of Things: Commodities in Cultural Perspective*, Cambridge University Press, Cambridge

Bayat, A (1997) *Street Politics, Poor People's Movements in Iran*, Columbia University Press, New York

Beall, J (1995) 'Social Security and Social Networks among the Urban Poor in Pakistan', *Habitat International,* vol 19, no 4, pp427–45

Beall, J (2002) 'Valuing Social Resources or Capitalising on Them? Limits to Pro-poor Urban Governance in Nine Cities of the South', *International Planning Studies*, vol 6, no 4, pp357–75

Beall, J, Crankshaw, O and Parnell, S (1999) *Urban Governance, Partnership and Poverty in Johannesburg*, Working Paper 12, International Development Department, University of Birmingham

Beall, J, Crankshaw, O and Parnell, S (2002) *Uniting a Divided City: Governance and Social Exclusion in Johannesburg*, Earthscan, London

Beall, J, Kanji, N and Tacoli, C (1999) 'African Urban Livelihoods: Straddling the Rural–Urban Divide', in S Jones and N Nelson (eds) *Urban Poverty in Africa*, Intermediate Technology Publications, London, pp160–8

Beall, J and Seegmuller, R (2001) 'Livelihoods from Solid Waste', unpublished paper, commissioned by CARE International, London

Bebbington, A (1999) 'Capitals and Capabilities: A Framework for Analyzing Peasant Viability, Rural Livelihoods and Poverty', *World Development*, vol 27, no 12, pp2021–44

Carney, D (ed) (1998) *Sustainable Rural Livelihoods: What Contribution Can We Make?*, Department for International Development, London

Carney, D, Drinkwater, T, Rusinow, K, Neefjes, S, Wanmali, S and Singh, N (1999) *Livelihoods Approaches Compared*, Department for International Development, London

Chambers, R and Conway, G (1992) *Sustainable Rural Livelihoods: Practical Concepts for the 21st Century*, IDS Discussion Paper No 296, Institute of Development Studies, Sussex

Cohen, A (1969) *Custom and Politics in Urban Africa: A Study of Hausa Migrants in Yoruba Towns*, Routledge & Kegan Paul, London

Cullen, M, Hossain, T and Verghese-Choudhury, A (1997) 'Children Living, Learning and Working in the City', in J Beall (ed) *A City for All: Valuing Difference and Working with Diversity*, Zed Books, London, pp66–78

De Soto, H (1989) *The Other Path: The Invisible Revolution in the Third World*, Harper & Row, New York

Ferguson, J (1999) *Expectations of Modernity: Myths and Meanings of Urban Life on the Zambian Copperbelt*, University of California Press, Berkeley

Fine, B (1999) 'The Developmental State is Dead – Long Live Social Capital?', *Development and Change*, no 30, pp1–19

Francis, E (2000) *Making a Living, Rural Livelihoods in Africa*, Routledge, London

Freidberg, S (2001) 'Gardening on the Edge: The Social Conditions of Unsustainability on an African Periphery', *Annals of the Association of American Geographers*, vol 91, no 2, pp349–69

Granovetter, M (1985) 'Economic Action and Social Structure: The Problem of Embeddedness', *American Journal of Sociology*, vol 91, pp481–510

Granovetter, M (1993) 'The Nature of Economic Relationships', in R Swedberg (ed) *Explorations in Economic Sociology*, Russell Sage Foundation, New York

Guyer, J (ed) (1987) *Feeding African Cities: Studies in Regional Social History*, Manchester University Press, Manchester

Hadjor, K (1993) *Dictionary of Third World Terms*, Penguin, London

Hart, K (1973) 'Informal Income Opportunities and Urban Employment in Ghana', *Journal of Modern African Studies*, no 11, pp61–89

ILO (1972) *Employment, Incomes and Equity: A Strategy for Increasing Projective Employment in Kenya*, International Labour Organization, Geneva

Jones, S and Nelson, N (eds) (1999) *Urban Poverty in Africa: From Understanding to Alleviation*, Intermediate Technology Publications, London

Kanji, N (1995) 'Gender, Poverty and Economic Adjustment in Harare, Zimbabwe', *Environment and Urbanization*, vol 7, no 1 (April), pp37–55

Kawachi, I, Kennedy, B and Lochner, K (1997) 'Long Live Community: Social Capital as Public Health', *The American Prospect*, November/December, pp56–9

King, K (1996) *Jua Kali*, James Currey, Oxford

Korboe, D, Diaw, K and Devas, N (1999) *Urban Governance, Partnership and Poverty in Kumasi, Working Paper 10*, International Development Department, University of Birmingham

Lund, F, Nicholson, J and Skinner, C (2000) *Street Trading*, University of Natal, Durban

MacGaffey, J (1991) 'Historical, Cultural and Structural Dimensions of Zaire's Unrecorded Trade', in J MacGaffey (ed), *The Real Economy of Zaire: An Anthropological Study*, James Currey, London

MacGaffey, J (1992) 'Initiatives from Below: Zaire's Other Path to Social and Economic Restructuring', in G Hyden and M Bratton (eds) *Governance and Politics in Africa*, Lynne Rienner, Boulder, CO

MacGaffey, J (1998) 'Creatively Coping with Crisis: Entrepreneurs in Zaïre's Second Economy', in B McDade and A Spring (eds) *African Entrepreneurship: Themes and Realities*, University Press of Florida, Gainesville

McCormick, D, Kimuyu, P, and Kinyanjui, M (2001) 'Kenya's Garment Industry: An Institutional View of Medium and Large Firms', IDS Working Paper no 531, Institute for Development Studies, University of Nairobi, Kenya

McCormick, D and Schmitz, H (2001) *Manual for Value Chain Research on Homeworkers in the Garment Industry*, Institutes for Development Studies, University of Nairobi and University of Sussex, Nairobi and Brighton. Available at www.ids.ac.uk/ids/global/valchn.html

Meagher, K (1995) 'Crisis, Informalization and the Urban Informal Sector in sub-Saharan Africa', *Development and Change,* no 26, pp259–84

Mittullah, W (1991) 'Hawking as a Survival Strategy for the Urban Poor in Nairobi: The Case of Women', *Environment and Urbanization,* vol 3, no 2 (October), pp13–22

Moser, C (1996) *Confronting Crisis: A Comparative Study of Household Responses in Four Poor Urban Communities,* Environmentally Sustainable Development Studies and Monograph Series No 8, World Bank, Washington, DC

Moser, C (1998) 'The Assets Vulnerability Framework: Reassessing Urban Poverty Reduction Strategies', *World Development,* vol 26, no 1, pp1–19

Moser, C and Holland, J (1997) *Urban Poverty and Violence in Jamaica,* World Bank, Washington, DC

Murray, C (1999) 'Changing Livelihoods: The Free State, South Africa, 1990s', Working Paper 4, Multiple Livelihoods and Social Change Working Papers, Institute for Development and Policy Management, University of Manchester

Polanyi, K (1944) *The Great Transformation: The Political and Economic Origins of Our Time*, Beacon Press, Boston

Rakodi, C (1995) 'The Household Strategies of the Urban Poor: Coping with Poverty and Recession in Gweru, Zimbabwe', *Habitat International,* vol 19, no 4, pp447–71

Rakodi, C (1998) 'Globalization Trends and sub-Saharan African Cities', in Fu-Chen Lo and Yue-Man Yeung (eds) *Globalization and the World of Large Cities, Tokyo, New York and Paris*, United Nations University Press, pp314–51

Rakodi, C (1999) 'A Capital Assets Framework for Analysing Household Livelihoods Strategies: Implications for Policy', *Development Policy Review*, vol 17, no 3, pp315–42

Rakodi, C and Lloyd-Jones, A (eds) (2002) *Supporting Urban Livelihoods,* Earthscan, London

Scott, J (1985) *The Weapons of the Weak: Everyday Forms of Peasant Resistance,* Yale University Press, New Haven and London

Sethurman, S (ed) (1981) *The Urban Informal Sector in Developing Countries: Employment, Poverty and Environment,* International Labour Organization, Geneva

Tacoli, C (1998) 'Beyond the Rural-urban Divide', *Environment and Urbanization,* vol 10, no 1, pp3–5

Tokman, V E (1978) 'An Exploration into the Nature of Informal-formal Sector Relationships', *World Development,* vol 6, nos 9–10, pp1065–75

Tripp, A (1997) *Changing the Rules: The Politics of Liberalization and the Urban Informal Economy in Tanzania,* University of California Press, Berkeley and Los Angeles

Whitehead, A (2000) 'Continuities and Discontinuities in Rural Livelihoods in North-east Ghana between 1975 and 1989', Workshop Paper for Multiple Livelihoods and Social Change Project, Institute for Development Policy and Management, University of Manchester

4

The Challenge of HIV/AIDS

Alex de Waal[1]

Introduction

The HIV/AIDS epidemic is already causing regression in Africa. It further threatens to set in motion processes that will profoundly and negatively transform society, development and governance in Africa, amounting to social involution.

A generalized HIV/AIDS epidemic, such as is occurring in southern Africa and is emerging elsewhere on the continent, is not just another shackle on progress, like malaria or poor rural roads. It is a structural or systemic change. Alan Whiteside of the University of Natal, who has led the way in framing the wider impacts of the epidemic (Barnett and Whiteside, 2002), has described HIV/AIDS as a 'Darwinian event' (Whiteside, 2004). As of late 2003, AIDS and related causes have killed about 20 million Africans, with more than 30 million currently living with HIV, making it the largest killer on the continent.

But it is not just the numbers of people killed that makes HIV/AIDS an event of evolutionary significance: it is the way in which the human immunodeficiency virus, at generalized epidemic levels, is changing the very ecology of *Homo sapiens* as a social being. The virus is able to evade the normal evolutionary pressures towards reduced virulence at the levels of cell and individual host (Hutchinson, 2003). Unusually for a lethal virus, HIV can do so at the level of the host population as well: achieving individual lifetime risk among hosts approaching 100 per cent ('saturation') without jeopardizing its own continued transmission. With adult prevalence of 20 per cent ('semi-saturation' level), the influence of the virus is ubiquitous and systemic, although often invisible to the casual observer or to the macro-economist equipped with conventional methodological tools. At these levels, HIV is capable of achieving an impressive symbiosis with *Homo sapiens*, not just as a biological organism but also as a social collectivity. It will do so in part by creating new patterns of social and economic activity, marked by extreme poverty, low levels of education and disintegration of most existing social structures. It is an alarming regularity of demographic history that one calamity is commonly the cause of a secondary disaster of comparable scale. In southern Africa,

HIV/AIDS has already contributed to food crises of unusual scale and profile, and with a disturbing likelihood that the full recovery of rural livelihoods will be impossible (de Waal and Whiteside, 2003). The epidemic is eroding education systems (Husain and Badcock Walters, 2002). Unlike most historic disasters, the HIV/AIDS epidemic is a long-wave event, and in turn its secondary impacts are likely to be long-term and systemic rather than transient disruptions. One of the likely outcomes of such secondary impacts is that they increase a population's susceptibility to high rates of HIV transmission.

Such a symbiosis between HIV and humankind would be marked by a social developmental trap in which progress becomes impossible. In this chapter, the concept of 'involution' is applied to this phenomenon, borrowing from Clifford Geertz, who defined it as 'the overdriving of an established form in such a way that it becomes rigid through an inward over elaboration of detail' (1963, p82). It displays 'late Gothic' features, including 'increasing tenacity of a basic pattern; internal elaboration and ornateness; technical hair-splitting, and unending virtuosity', and results in an incapacity to achieve either stability or development. In the context of HIV/AIDS, social involution manifests itself in a tenacious determination to continue business as usual, or at least to fit responses to the epidemic into existing categories. This is an effort that requires ever more short-term and expedient stratagems, which in turn exacerbate the socio-economic damage inflicted by the epidemic. The survival of *Homo sapiens* as a species is not endangered: rather the mutual evolution of HIV and its host takes the two on a different trajectory of joint ecological accommodation. The first part of this chapter outlines the risk of this trap. The second part focuses on the paradox – 'grotesquely obscene' in the words of Stephen Lewis, the UN Secretary General's Special Envoy for AIDS in Africa[2] – that such a catastrophic regression might occur at a time when the medical technology for treating (if not curing) AIDS is available and (in global terms) affordable. How, in this context, is the involutionary trap to be avoided?

HIV/AIDS and its Potentially Devastating Impacts

Overcoming HIV/AIDS in Africa is an intellectual task as much as a practical, policy-making and political one. But while a high level of biological-scientific intelligence has been directed against the virus, the efforts of the social sciences have lagged.

The epidemic's full capacity to inflict structural regression has only become apparent very recently. Although the HIV/AIDS epidemic in Africa is two decades old, several characteristics have disguised its implications. The first is its novelty: no epidemic has had comparable implications for human progress for at least four centuries.[3] Hence we collectively lack the cultural archive for responding to such a threat. Second, there is a 7–10-year lag between an individual being infected with HIV and she or he developing AIDS. This means that the HIV/AIDS epidemic follows two curves: first, HIV prevalence rises, but without a commensurate increase in AIDS morbidity and mortality. Only after the best part of a decade do numbers of AIDS deaths climb. This provides both a window of opportunity for responding and an excuse for complacency and inaction. It also means that, with prevalence rates still rising, we are still experiencing the first phase of the epidemic. Everything experienced so far is small in comparison with what the future holds.

A third reason is that the measurement tools we have for monitoring the wider impact of the epidemic are blunt, misleading and take time to produce. The most powerful indices for national and international policy-making are aggregate economic indicators such as GDP. Most macro-economists have thus far posited a modest impact of HIV/AIDS on GDP, namely a reduction in annual growth of between 0.4 and 1.5 per cent. This is well within the range of outcomes that could occur because of external economic shocks such as drought or commodity price changes, fiscal mismanagement or global economic slowdown. Until very recently, influential economic analyses such as those of the World Bank posited that HIV/AIDS might actually increase GDP per capita, because the reduction in economic activity would be less than the loss of population (Over, 1992; World Bank, 1999, p32). This latter conclusion came about because of technical peculiarities in the calculation of the production function. Economic indicators are artifices, a rough cut of reality. When their findings are not only so profoundly counter-intuitive, but also challenged by careful analyses of the role of human capital, they need to be questioned.

The construction of new aggregate indicators for economic activity in societies impacted by HIV/AIDS is an important task that is beyond the scope of this chapter. I have addressed some of these challenges elsewhere (de Waal, 2003b), focusing on the need more accurately to measure women's labour, dependency ratios and household livelihoods. International agencies working on HIV/AIDS speak of the need to see the world through an 'AIDS lens': developing such methodologies is part of grinding the lens (Whiteside et al, 2003).

The final reason why the systemic implications of the HIV/AIDS epidemic have been so well disguised is the level of denial surrounding the disease. Most deaths due to AIDS are not publicly attributed to this cause. For example, politicians in Kenya routinely succumb to 'a long illness bravely borne'. The Kenyan government, newly committed to tackling AIDS, missed a chance for breaking the silence that continues to surround the disease, when a senior government official died in mid-2003. This silence feeds the stigma and discrimination that afflict so many people living with HIV and AIDS, many of whom say that this stigma is worse than the disease itself. A similar state of denial surrounds a full acknowledgement of its implications. A kind of obligatory optimism pervades much of the debate, with advocates and policy-makers insisting that over 90 per cent of African adults are still HIV negative, that Africa will eradicate AIDS etc. It is indeed peculiarly tragic that the epidemic unfolded just as South Africa was throwing off centuries of racial oppression, the Cold War was ending, and the prospects for democracy and development in the continent suddenly seemed brighter than for decades.

The short-term impacts of the HIV/AIDS epidemic are primarily sickness and death of mature adults. Sickness contributes to distortions in both household and public spending, away from productive investment into health care. It lowers the productivity of labour. This lowers savings and investment rates and thereby reduces economic growth. Labour supply contracts and household dependency rates rise.

In the longer-term, structural impacts will emerge. The most significant of these is shortened adult life expectancy and its manifold implications. Although recognized in micro-studies of the impact of HIV/AIDS on rural communities (Barnett and Whiteside, 2002; Baylies, 2002; Rugalema, 2002) thus far this factor has not been fully included in even the most sophisticated modelling exercises. The most well-known of the latter, the projection of possible outcomes for the South African economy by Bell et al (2003), focuses on the inter-generational accumulation or loss of assets and skills, including educational achievement. Bell and his colleagues' exercise is a useful advance on most of the earlier World Bank models, in that for the first time the implications for the next generation of loss of human capital through early death of adults are modelled.

The decision by Bell et al to use South Africa as their case study limits its usefulness. First, the model overlooks the concentration of human and physical capital among a minority with lower HIV prevalence than the national average. Second, by dealing with the one African national economy with sufficient resources to respond to the epidemic without foreign aid, the model overlooks the scenario in which there is no economic path that avoids stagnation or collapse.

The next step is to build models that analyse the spillover effects of losses in human capital into fixed capital and possible non-linear interactions with institutional functioning. Malcolm McPherson, who pioneered the development of non-linear models focusing on human capital loss, has described the process as akin to 'running Adam Smith in reverse' (McPherson and Goldsmith, 1998; McPherson et al, 2000; McPherson, 2003). I have drawn attention to the likely structural impact on institutional functioning and governance, calling it 'running Max Weber in reverse' (de Waal, 2003a).

The fundamental point to recognize is that a drop in adult life expectancy (LEA) from about 40 years to about 20 or 25 represents a structural change in social functioning unlike anything witnessed in modern history. Normally, life expectancy at birth (LEB) is used as the indicator for longevity. But LEB is (like all such aggregates) a statistical construct that requires careful scrutiny if it is to be used in the changed context of a population impacted by AIDS. For example, the LEB of South Africa in 2000 of 50.4[4] years was slightly longer than Chad's at 49.3, and perhaps ten years less than it would have been without HIV/AIDS. But the life expectancy of a 20-year-old in South Africa was 36.6, comparable to that of a Sierra Leonean (35.6) and lower than a Chadian (42.0). The reason for this discrepancy is that the majority of mortality in Chad is accounted for by deaths of children under five (51 per cent), whereas in South Africa only a small minority of deaths are of young children (15 per cent). Bear in mind that these figures refer to a South African population only beginning to feel the impacts of AIDS. By 2010, demographers predict that a further ten years will have been cut from LEA, and three-quarters of teenagers will not expect to live to see their sixtieth birthdays (Dorrington et al, 2002).

This dramatic foreshortening of LEA entails structural changes that are simply not captured in any of today's macro-economic models, predictions and policies. Savings rates will plummet, implying that NEPAD's goal of raising domestic savings from 19 per cent to 33 per cent of GDP will be unrealizable. Returns to education will fall, implying a structural reduction in the level of educational capital in the population. Complex institutions will not function, because the long career trajectories on which they are founded will disappear. The majority of people will not live to see their grandchildren, with unknown implications for the functioning of family structures. Of the above, only the truncation of inter-generational transfers of assets and skills has thus far been incorporated into any quantitative modelling exercises.

The potentially catastrophic implications of lower LEA underline the social and economic rationale for prolonging the lives of people living with HIV and AIDS through anti-retroviral therapy (ART). But, as discussed below, it is improbable that ART can be provided on a rapid enough scale to reverse the fall in LEA.

A drop in LEA of this kind is a wholly different prospect to the normal constraints on economic development that economists are used to dealing with. It is unlike problems such as illiteracy, malaria or physical infrastructure damaged by neglect or warfare. The challenge in these familiar cases is increasing the rate of human and physical capital accumulation. Even without a state and development policies and programmes, societies function and growth occurs. A case in point is stateless Somalia which (without a generalized AIDS epidemic) has continued to function as an economy and even prosper (Little, 2003). In an AIDS-impacted country, for any sector that requires domestic mobilization of human and physical resources, or that depends upon a domestic market, the prospects for growth may be zero.

When the prevalence of HIV reaches 35–40 per cent of adults, a teenager's lifetime chance of contracting HIV approaches 80–90 per cent.[5] For the virus, this is approaching the optimal situation in which saturation coverage of the host population is achieved, without killing off the host before onward transmission occurs. At 25 per cent prevalence, lifetime risk is above half. At such levels, behavioural change on the scale needed to reduce prevalence is exceptionally difficult because incidence of new infections is only a fraction of incidence of all transmission, with the majority of the latter being super-infection of an individual who is already HIV positive. Lifetime HIV risk is therefore substantially over-determined, and near-universal adherence to the 'ABC' of HIV prevention – abstinence, being faithful to one lifetime partner, and using condoms – is necessary to reduce incidence. There are some indications of lower prevalence among young women in southern African cities, but so far not on the scale to represent anything but a slowing in the upward climb of national prevalence levels.

Moreover, one of the insidious effects of HIV is the way in which it contributes to the socio-economic conditions favourable to its own proliferation. At household and community level, HIV/AIDS increases poverty and inequality, and contributes to lower educational levels in the population. These are all risk factors in susceptibility of communities to high levels of HIV. By reducing institutional capacity and functioning, the epidemic reproduces the problems of poor schooling and health care, again reinforcing the conditions that make for susceptibility. In short, as HIV saturates a society, it may create a low-level form of 'equilibrium' in human society – in short, the end-point of protracted social involution.

The case for systemic economic and social non-performance rests in part on the objective implications of high levels of AIDS sickness and death. Thus far, that is what we have mostly seen: diversion of expenditure, loss of human capital and the halting and reversal of development trends. Increasing inequality is also emerging as an important effect, both within countries (as AIDS-affected households become poor and stay that way) and internationally (as the epidemic accentuates the flight of the skilled and ambitious). The second and arguably more significant element is the subjective one. When young adults anticipate a short life, they will behave differently. Thus far, the subjective anticipation of longevity and other life chances has not been systematically studied, so we are not in a position to move beyond informed conjecture.[6] Psychologists, social workers and AIDS activists have all focused upon the reaction and world-view of the individual who learns that she or he is HIV positive. This is important. But only a small proportion of those who are living with HIV in Africa are aware of their sero status. This number will increase as voluntary counselling and testing (VCT) services expand in tandem with increased provision of ART and related treatments.

However, the key factor driving the subjective expectation of longevity and life chances is not individual knowledge of HIV status. Rather, it is a sense of inevitability about contracting HIV and the experience of seeing one's immediate elders falling sick and dying in large numbers. In a generalized epidemic, no adult who is sexually active can afford not to think about the possibility of being HIV positive. When an AIDS epidemic has been sustained for more than a decade, these deaths become so common that no young person can avoid considering the likelihood of dying in her or his twenties or thirties. And the prospect of surviving to old age, but being bereft of almost all one's peers, is scarcely more attractive. In such a situation, statistical LEA comes to correspond to the subjective expectation of longevity.[7] And in turn, subjective expectation of longevity must be a powerful influence on a range of behaviours and decisions, all of them critical for economic development and social sustainability.

For our purposes, involution can be identified as the systemic behavioural counterpart of denial and the consequent paralysis and regression of systemic socio-economics. It is the brave but futile attempt, by individuals, societies, institutions and governments, to preserve a basic normality when the world has changed. Involution thus implies the multifaceted regress brought about simultaneously by the epidemic and by governments' failure to adopt suitable policies.

While denial has been a consistent theme of writing on AIDS, its ramifications have less often been addressed. In her investigation of children orphaned by AIDS in Botswana, Marguerite Daniel (2003) applies the concept of social involution, drawn specifically from the work of Thayer Scudder and Elizabeth Colson, who used it to explain social responses exhibited by central African communities displaced by big dams (Scudder and Colson, 1982). In turn they drew on an extensive literature concerned with social and psychological responses to extreme stress (Laughlin and Brady, 1978; Dirks, 1980). This framework implies a three-stage socio-cultural process. First is involution, a set of expedient attempts, including denial and cultural conservatism, aiming to salvage the status quo. This is followed by the institutionalization of those expedient strategies that have proved effective in the short term. Finally, these strategies operate inter-generationally, becoming a set of norms and institutional principles for young people emerging into adulthood. Social involution thus represents the coalescing of these maladaptive responses. Daniel's work from Botswana demonstrates these processes at work in the adoption, neglect and exploitation of children orphaned by AIDS. He concludes disturbingly that rather than creatively responding to the problem, the Batswana are desperately trying to recreate a vanishing and unsustainable set of social norms.

Similar processes are evident in the realm of economic behaviour, both by individuals and states. Heads of households, tending to regard AIDS as individual misfortune rather than collective disaster (cf Baylies, 2002), follow standard 'coping' strategies that fail to work – but see no alternative. Economic policy-makers persist in the fiction that they can achieve all the varied targets they have set themselves. Denying the profound impacts of the HIV/AIDS epidemic, they thereby avoid the tough task of prioritizing their goals and abandoning those that cannot be achieved. A state's energy is focused on maintaining a dysfunctional status quo. Comparable maladaptations can be witnessed in the economic regress of post-Soviet Russia, where the collapse of production witnessed an outflow of resources to trade and exchange (Burawoy, 1997).

Governments have a well-documented propensity to pursue policies contrary to their own interests, such as unwinnable wars. In her classic study of this phenomenon, Barbara Tuchman asks whether 'in modern states there is something about political and bureaucratic life that subdues the functioning of intellect in favour of "working the levers" without regard to rational expectations' (Tuchman, 1985, p473). We can define 'policy involution' as this proclivity taken to the extreme, continuing to elaborate on a failing policy system when state and society are imperilled by the HIV/AIDS epidemic.

Positive Anomalies

Any pessimistic argument, such as this one, must deal with the positive anomalies provided by the cases of Botswana and Uganda. Now almost matched by Swaziland in 2003, Botswana has held for a decade the dubious distinction of having the world's highest-measured national HIV prevalence. However, it failed to stick to the pessimistic script in two respects. First, AIDS deaths did not climb as high and as fast as predicted (Grassly et al, 2003). Most probably, this was because in the 1990s, HIV prevalence estimates were biased upwards because of the erroneous assumption that pregnant women attending antenatal clinics in small towns were representative of the general rural populace. In fact, it appears that rural prevalence was lower than in the small towns from which surveillance data were taken, so that more systematic rural surveillance has flattened the curve.[8] However, more recent (2003) estimates for prevalence at 38 per cent are likely to be very accurate. Second, the economy of Botswana has continued to grow at a record pace, with the national budget moving into deficit only in 2003. However, the most substantial contribution to Botswana's economic miracle has been diamonds, which are still hugely profitable despite the additional costs incurred by the national mining company Debswana in providing for ARTs and other treatment for those in its workforce who are HIV positive.

Uganda is a more intriguing case. Although the precise interpretation of the statistics is open to question, there is no doubt that Uganda witnessed a fall in national HIV prevalence from about 12 per cent in 1993 to about 6 per cent ten years later. The Ugandan AIDS 'success story' has been politically important for the Ugandan government and for the international AIDS industry, which is desperately in need of a positive example from Africa. Many different reasons for the success have been mooted, including: the promotion of abstinence and faithfulness, the promotion of condoms, the visible leadership role of President Museveni and his insistence that all his government makes speeches on the subject, the national multisectoral plan for AIDS, the involvement of the NGO sector, and the empowerment and education of women and girls. These explanations need careful scrutiny. Those who have tried to cast a critical eye over the statistics have been pilloried by the Ugandan government (Parkhurst, 2002). The figures do, in fact, tell a more complex story, with some impressive reductions in prevalence and some less impressive falls and some locations with no fall at all. But, the big picture remains that Uganda has seen HIV levels fall and has also registered impressive economic growth and poverty reduction. How?

For some the reason for Uganda's success has little to do with the government's AIDS policies. This explanation runs something like this. There are distinct patterns to the HIV/AIDS epidemic. In urbanizing or socially disrupted societies, the epidemic grows rapidly in a steep 'S' curve. In rural societies, marked by less population mobility and greater social cohesion, the epidemic grows in a slow incline (cf Barnett and Whiteside, 1999, 2002). Southern African countries are examples of the former, Tanzania and Ethiopia the latter. Uganda during the period 1979–86 was an example of the former, owing due to the civil war that engulfed most parts of the country including the formerly prosperous rural areas in the south and centre. The near-genocidal counter-insurgency of the second Obote regime contributed to massive population disruption, the collapse of health and education provision and local government, and migration to cities such as Kampala. The victory of Museveni's National Resistance Army (NRA) in 1986 brought peace to most of the country. People returned home. Uganda being extraordinarily fertile and Ugandans of all kinds being famously ready to sustain a livelihood through farming, the country went through a rather unusual process after 1986: a return to rural life. This process was abetted by the NRA's policy of reforming, democratizing and strengthening local government by the inflow of capital following Museveni's encouragement to the Ugandan Asians (expelled in 1971) to return and resume their businesses, and by the re-opening of rural schools and the government's policy of encouraging girls' education. This return to rural life would imply a switch from a 'disrupted' pattern of epidemic to a 'rural' pattern. And indeed, HIV incidence began to fall in 1988, a fact that can be retrospectively inferred from the prevalence data.

In 1988, the famed national policies on HIV/AIDS were not yet functioning fully. The national AIDS budget was small (just US\$21,675,000 for 1987–92). The strongest argument in favour of the efficacy of the behavioural change programme is that it was most effective at its earliest stages, when it was domestically designed and implemented (Low-Beer and Stoneburner, 2003), while focusing on the essential 'ABC' message of behavioural change.[9] The 'social cohesion' hypothesis supplies a potential answer to the question of why similar programmes have not worked elsewhere, despite more plentiful resources: it takes both social cohesion and a well-designed and implemented communication strategy for success.

Meanwhile, Uganda's impressive economic performance was facilitated by several unusual factors. First, the economy was in such bad shape in 1986 that growth of 7 per cent per annum or so was to be expected. Second, the country benefited from major assistance flows and inward capital investment. Third, very large numbers of educated Ugandans were outside the country during the war years, and returned when peace came. Coming from the UK, Kenya and Sudan – countries with fewer HIV cases – the returning exiles had lower HIV levels. Lastly, the agrarian economy of Uganda is unusually resilient to the loss of adult labour associated with HIV/AIDS (Barnett and Blaikie, 1992). With well-distributed rainfall, fertile soils and perennial crops such as bananas, which can be cultivated with modest labour inputs, Uganda's farmers are less likely to succumb to destitution than those in less well-endowed areas.

Uganda's success, therefore, provides less solace for other hard-hit countries than is widely imagined. In particular, no other African country is undergoing a comparable process of rural renaissance. To the contrary, rural Africa is in crisis and African countries are urbanizing. In most regimes, even Uganda itself is set on a course of rapid growth based on neo-liberal precepts, alongside a decay in governance, that may ultimately undermine the social basis for its erstwhile success.

Avoiding the Trap

Medical intervention in the form of an active, effective vaccine would hold out the prospect for halting the HIV/AIDS epidemic and stemming these processes of involution and regression. But for at least a decade and probably longer this is extremely unlikely. It is more likely that there will be partially effective treatments, such as ART, affordable and accessible microbicides and possibly a partly effective vaccine (ie one that reduces the susceptibility to transmission but does not eliminate it).

ART holds out the promise of transforming the landscape of the HIV/AIDS epidemic. Since 2001, ART has become hugely cheaper and simpler. Rather than costing tens of thousands of dollars and requiring a regimen of dozens of pills per day, the drugs themselves have come down in cost to a dollar a day, administered in just two pills. But the major obstacle to providing ART at scale is not the drugs themselves but the health infrastructure, including the trained personnel necessary for administering the treatment. The full treatment package involves more than ART: it includes VCT, prevention of mother-to-child transmission, treatment of opportunistic infections, nutritional support and healthy living assistance, and quite possibly micro-credit and other support to people living with HIV and AIDS in order for them to sustain a livelihood for themselves and their families.

A second challenge is ensuring adequate patient compliance. There are fears that poorly administered ART, for example self-administration by patients who purchase the drugs in the market, might contribute to the development of drug-resistant strains of HIV. Some leading virologists have warned of the disastrous implications of widespread drug resistance, implying that treatment should not be rolled out at scale. Fortunately, the dangers of treatment interruptions are not as severe as were earlier feared. Pilot studies have demonstrated high rates of compliance in Africa,[10] but it must be borne in mind that one of the requirements for entering an ART pilot is a demonstrated good record of treatment compliance, so these levels will not be replicated when ART is taken to scale.

In the scenario of universal ART, which prolongs healthy life by a decade, many of the worst societal implications of truncated LEA will be avoided. But what will be the implications? Will African states be transformed into conveyer belts for rolling out foreign-funded ART?

Developments in 2001–03 have meant that, whatever the virological implications, enormous international resources will be spent on ART. At their special summit in Abuja in April 2001, African leaders called for the mobilization of both national and international resources to combat HIV/AIDS. Their domestic target was 15 per cent of national budgets to be allocated to health, a target not met by a single African government within two years. Internationally, UN Secretary General Kofi Annan called for the establishment of a Global Fund to fight AIDS, TB and Malaria.[11] This was endorsed by the UN General Assembly Special Session on HIV/AIDS in June 2001, and the Global Fund began disbursing its first funds in January 2003. By September 2003, the Global Fund had commitments of over US$1500 million and had disbursed US$131 million. In January 2003, President George Bush promised US$15,000 million over five years to fight HIV/AIDS in Africa and the Caribbean, two-thirds of it new money. Meanwhile the World Bank and bilateral donors have also increased their spending on HIV/AIDS.

Apart from the Bush promise, very little of this money is additional to global aid budgets (which stand at about US$55,000 million annually): most is diverted from elsewhere. And, despite the dramatic reductions in ART cost, treating AIDS is still expensive.

There is a powerful moral case for providing treatment, of a kind readily available in rich countries, to people living with HIV and AIDS who happen to be citizens of Africa. The moral case has been made effectively and emphatically by treatment activists, many of them living with HIV themselves and allies in international civil society such as Oxfam and Médecins Sans Frontières. But has the moral argument been won at the price of abandoning decades of lessons about socio-economic development (Levine, 2003)?

There is a pragmatic economic case for treatment. The 2001 report of the Commission on Macroeconomics and Health argued that spending on health in general is a good investment. Globally, expenditure of an additional US$60,000 million on essential health care in developing countries (a figure that excludes ART provision, which was prohibitively expensive at that time) was estimated to yield a total of US$366,000 million in additional global income. Although the CMH did not directly address the cost-effectiveness of ART, a number of studies in the business sector in Africa (almost all in South Africa) have done precisely this, and concluded that for most private companies, providing ART to employees has a better return than not doing so (Rosen et al, 2003). The returns are better for more skilled and senior staff, but as the costs of ART fall, it is increasingly viable for unskilled workers as well. A similar case has yet to be argued for people working in the informal sector, smallholder farmers and mothers, but will doubtless be made before long. The wider the social benefits from sustaining life (keeping schools functioning, sustaining family structures), including the positive impacts on the next generation (children stopped from becoming orphans, skills and knowledge handed on), the stronger the economic case for treatment will be.

Making the case involves putting a new value on human capital and finding ways of measuring social capital – including the unremunerated contributions of women hitherto invisible in macro-economic statistics. This in turn requires the adoption of more inclusive methodologies for compiling national accounts, and revising the economic models which have thus far predicted such modest impacts on GDP.

To the extent that the financial resources available for HIV/AIDS are diverted from other aid budgets, they risk starving other sectors. The quality of AIDS aid may also be lower than other forms of assistance. The emergent 'best practice' for development assistance is direct budgetary support to governments committed to poverty reduction, and subject to mutual accountability based upon joint evaluation of development outcomes. Such an assistance modality is premised on the high transaction costs and relative inefficiency of project and programme aid. However, most AIDS funding is programmed in such traditional ways, and risks burdening recipient countries with complex reporting procedures and conditionalities. Would it not be more sensible for donor countries to request that HIV/AIDS programmes and policies be incorporated fully into national budgets and development strategies, and then support the entire package? Does not separate AIDS funding risk re-imposing precisely the same kind of external development dictat that has had so little success?

If the international resources mobilized for HIV/AIDS are indeed additional, then another important set of issues arises. How to absorb these funds within existing macro-economic frameworks? These frameworks are designed to achieve the best conditions for containing inflation, stimulating investment, ensuring growth and reducing poverty, and the associated conditionalities are integral to countries' eligibility for debt relief under the HIPC initiative. This approach is unlikely to change, both because it has demonstrated benefits and because it is pivotal to maintaining the current global economic policy framework. Even when macro-economic doctrines are shown to be inappropriate – as for example the 1980s insistence on structural adjustment contributed to a damaging run-down in health and education services – economic policy-makers have been notoriously slow to change. Therefore, finance ministries and the Bretton Woods Institutions are likely to resist calls for HIV/AIDS funding to be regarded as 'exceptional' and exempt from tight budgetary frameworks. And, if they do back down on this issue, it will not be far.

This dilemma was illustrated by a proposed US$52 million Global Fund three-year grant to Uganda for HIV/AIDS, offered in 2002. Initially, the Ministry of Health estimated that it would need US$150 million for AIDS alone every year (Wendo, 2002a). But this relatively modest grant would have taken the Ministry of Health expenditure through the ceiling of US$107 million agreed with the Ministry of Finance. Thus, Finance instructed Health either to refuse the grant or to accept it but stick to the spending ceiling, returning the balance of the health budget to the treasury (and thus making the grant spurious). Charles Wendo, the medical journalist following the story, noted that 'the Ministry of Finance has fixed a ceiling below the floor' (Wendo, 2002b). After protracted negotiations, a compromise was reached whereby the grant was scaled down somewhat, stricter controls were placed on its usage, but AIDS spending was placed outside the government's overall fiscal framework. 'The ceiling has burst!' one AIDS activist exclaimed (Wendo, 2003). Subsequently, the Ministry of Finance has moved to ensure that Global Fund grants are retained within the overall health budget, though the implications of this are uncertain (Wendo, 2004).

Both sides have valid points to make. Health argues that the HIV/AIDS epidemic is exceptional and that, as with national emergencies such as wars, spending limits must be waived. It continues that unless ART is provided to citizens, including the staff who run the crucial institutions of state (including the Finance Ministry itself), then the capacity to administer anything will be in peril. Finance replies that HIV/AIDS is a long-term spending proposition and therefore cannot be regarded as an emergency measure, and that exceeding spending limits threatens the prospects for growth and poverty reduction, without which there is no chance of tackling HIV/AIDS or indeed any other social problems. Underpinning the arguments on both sides is an acceptance of the reality that countries such as Uganda are simply too poor to be able to spend the money needed to keep their citizens alive.

A related challenge is that of limited human resources and absorptive capacity for health programmes. Countries are caught in a vice of increasing requirement for health services and declining capacity, due to both AIDS mortality and the international brain drain. In recent years, the issue of limited absorptive capacity has sometimes been used by donors as an excuse for parsimony. The alleged incapacity of recipient countries to spend money disbursed was used as an alibi for inaction. But, whatever the donor motivation, the issue is real. The implementation rates for the World Bank's Multi-country Assistance Program have been very disappointing. For example, US$59.7 million was committed to Ethiopia in January 2001, and by May 2003 only 30 per cent had been spent. Those accustomed to the inefficiencies of Ethiopia's Ministry of Health and its disinclination to make HIV/AIDS a priority assumed that the country lagged behind performance elsewhere in Africa. However, in the 2003 review of the Progrm, Ethiopia was actually one of the star performers. The average rate of disbursement for Program funds was a meagre 12 per cent.

Countries such as Uganda, Malawi and Mozambique already have half or more of their national budgets supported from aid resources, a level widely regarded as the maximum for effective aid provision. Can such countries really absorb more external resources? The Global Fund grants to Malawi, which will certainly test if not exceed that country's capacity to dispense the funds effectively, will be a critical experiment in absorptive capacity. Given the problems of dealing with inefficient and slow bureaucracies with fixed rules and limited human resources, is a parallel NGO route an option? This has many attractions: grass-roots organizations, churches and local and international NGOs are often more rapid, creative, 'close to client' (in the language of health systems specialists) and trusted than governments. Emergent organizations such as associations of people living with HIV and AIDS are another possible delivery route, in this case with the obvious advantage that their members have a clear personal interest in the effectiveness of the programme. One challenge of the NGO route is regulation and quality control. A second is sustainability: ART provision is a lifetime commitment, not a three-year project. A further challenge is the implications of refocusing NGO priorities away from other goals such as human rights and democratization.

A recurrent lesson of development and social protection programmes is that domestic design and ownership is a crucial ingredient of success. This was one conclusion drawn from the review of structural adjustment programmes of the 1980s (Cornia et al, 1987; Stewart, 1995, pp126–7). This would also seem to be the case of HIV/AIDS programmes. The successful programmes in Senegal and Uganda were begun at an early stage of the epidemic and with modest external funding. The Ethiopian army's HIV/AIDS programme, regarded as a model of its kind, was set up in 1996 and ran for its first few years without any external funds (Tsadkan, 2002).

The availability of undreamed of funds for HIV/AIDS programming also brings dangers. Another recurrent lesson from development and humanitarian action is that plentiful resources can create as many problems as they solve. 'Development' can generate its own institutional discourses that ultimately become self-justifying, irrespective of whether they have a real positive impact on the lives of the people they are supposed to be assisting. Humanitarian programmes that don political blinkers in order to act expeditiously can end up supporting the very political pathologies that feed the crises themselves. The international assistance industry as a whole can build a 'citadel of expertise' that is impenetrable by civic action and democratic scrutiny.

Currently, too often the first focus for HIV/AIDS programmes is securing funding rather than trying to understand the problem at hand. Frank evaluations are rare. Even the best AIDS programmes usually fail to achieve their objectives (cf Campbell, 2003). Given the extraordinary challenges in the way of success, such failures should not be a cause for embarrassment, let alone cutting off funds. But one of the unfortunate downsides of the obligatory optimism that pervades the AIDS industry is that unrealistic expectations are set. Failures, however legitimate, are not adequately analysed.

A third important lesson from the recent history of assistance is that the political implications of external funding may be as significant as the economic impacts. As African governments have received larger proportions of their resources from foreign donors, and less and less from domestic taxation, their domestic accountability has withered at the expense of sensitivity and responsiveness to donor requirements.

As mentioned, the flood of money to support AIDS work has been organized separately from (and to some extent, in contradiction to) the practices of budgetary support, donor policy harmonization and mutual accountability to development outcomes – the 'enhanced partnership' vision that helped motivate NEPAD (ECA, 2001). If pursued consistently and sensitively, the 'enhanced partnership' should enable African countries to retain considerable discretion in policymaking, within the broad framework of poverty reduction strategy papers (PRSPs) agreed with both citizens and donors. However, PRSPs have paid far too little attention to HIV/AIDS and its impacts. For the most part, despite the rhetoric of 'mainstreaming' HIV/AIDS, programming is confined to the health sector. This shortcoming reflects, first, an ongoing denial about the extent of the problem, along with the fact that PRSPs were set in motion before specialists realized the gravity of the impacts of HIV/AIDS.

Second, it reflects an inadequate conceptualization of 'mainstreaming', which confines largely to including HIV/AIDS information and prevention activities in the programmes of every sector. In fact, effective mainstreaming has been extremely rare. One of the few good examples is the Ethiopian military, where the AIDS programme was distinguished by a participatory discussion of the importance of the disease for the army's core functions. This led to the realization by commanders of different ranks that the functioning of their respective units depended on them pursuing effective AIDS prevention and impact mitigation policies (Tsadkan, 2002). This in turn was possible because the programme was initiated jointly by the Chief of the General Staff and the army medical corps. Unusually for an army, HIV rates remained low during the period in which the programme was implemented. Where such an analysis is missing, 'mainstreaming' remains little more than bringing health and awareness activities into non-health institutions.

Leaving aside questions over the quality of AIDS funding, the sheer amount of money alone is certain to have major repercussions for the functioning of political systems.

The HIV/AIDS epidemic poses dangers for democracy. The impoverishment and declining state capacity it entails is likely to jeopardize the standing and legitimacy of states (Mattes, 2003). Civil society and democratic participation are already suffering (Manning, 2002). Democracy in Africa is defined not only by constitutional procedure and popular representation, but autonomy of national decision-making from foreign control. The deepening aid dependence of AIDS-impacted countries jeopardizes this external axis of democracy (Rana, 2003). As more external resources pour in to a poor country, there will inevitably be competition among potential recipients (among different ministries, between government and the NGO sector, among NGOs etc). One of the most important public-policy choices for Africa of the decade – whether to prioritize ART over other possible uses for scarce resource – is being taken with public discussion. Once resources are available for ART, decisions will need to be made as to whom to treat first. Such decisions will not be taken solely on medical criteria. Either rationing will be instituted transparently and democratically, or it will be done through the market and political favouritism. Given that the rationing of treatment is a version of triage, even the faintest suspicion of bias could contribute to political tension (Cheek, 2001). The current inequity in access to treatment reinforces both national and global inequality: elites can escape the trap by buying themselves an exclusionary lifestyle (including access to ART) or by leaving the continent altogether.

In the context of the dismal record of development and humanitarian programming in Africa, the challenges of effectively combating HIV/AIDS may appear insuperable. Not only are the funds and capacities inadequate, but the problems attendant on receiving resources are themselves depressingly formidable. Yet, when we change our focus to look at the resources required on a global scale, the problem seems to shrink. Bush's promised US$15,000 million is tiny in comparison with the US$87,000 million request for US activities in Iraq and the nearly US$400,000 million annual budget of the Pentagon (itself larger than sub-Saharan Africa's total GDP). On a global scale, these sums are certainly not inflationary.

Meanwhile, while Africa may lack the skilled personnel in its public health sector, if we take into account the African health professionals working outside the continent, let alone the potential for non-African expertise, the capacity problem begins to disappear.

For most African countries, the national scale is simply not big enough to allow for coherent and sustainable action against the HIV/AIDS epidemic. For a small, poor country with high rates of AIDS, there may be no route to avoid the involution trap. We may find that regional integration or unification and new forms of development partnership are necessary for Africa to overcome AIDS.

However, resource mobilization is only one part of the story: the other part is to create the social conditions that limit HIV transmission. Currently, social and economic planning for growth is conducted without reference to the possible implications for social susceptibility to the HIV/AIDS epidemic, and indeed accelerated growth seems in most cases to presuppose urbanization. While analysis and policy-making concerning HIV/AIDS remain at the level of public health, there is little chance of concerted action to sustain the kinds of social structures that may protect against susceptibility to high levels of HIV transmission.

Conclusion

The accumulation of evidence and analysis shows that the HIV/AIDS epidemic in Africa will have implications far in excess of any other epidemic diseases that have occurred in modern history. As the epidemic enters its third decade, HIV prevalence continues to rise, AIDS deaths increase rapidly, and the third 'impact' wave is upon us. These secondary impacts of the epidemic are far-reaching and systemic. An unprecedented drop in adult longevity threatens to undo the basic fabric of affected societies over a very long period of time. Thus the HIV/AIDS epidemic represents a fundamental transformation, with implications that are extremely hard to predict.

Among the known impacts of HIV/AIDS are major demographic shifts, shortened adult life expectancy, and adverse trajectories for savings, investment, education, health and the intergenerational transmission of assets and skills. However, the methodologies for measuring these effects, assessing them across sectors and integrating them into coherent frameworks and models are weak. For the most part, African governments and their international partners are still using old-style linear thinking and policies, which are increasingly inappropriate. African societies are struggling to cope, and increasingly households and communities are failing to cope. They are clinging to a fading illusion of normality, denying the reality of the catastrophe because they simply do not have the tools with which to overcome it. Rather than adopting the radical measures required, they hold on to existing frameworks for public policy and international assistance, forever tinkering and elaborating them to sustain an illusion of action and effectiveness. We face involution and a real prospect of continental regression.

Can an African and international response to HIV/AIDS prevent societies from falling into the AIDS involution trap? Will the provision of treatment halt the decline? Or will it only exacerbate existing problems, overwhelming governmental capacity and deepening inequalities, allowing a fortunate elite to escape from the immiseration and collapsing life chances of the majority? Is there sufficient recognition of the deep structural causes of vulnerability to HIV to form the basis for a new approach to socio-economic development? Or are the vested interests in the current policy frameworks sufficiently great to block the kinds of creativity necessary for such radical change? Will today's irresponsible caution prevail?

Between 2004 and the end of the decade, the number of people dying from AIDS in Africa is likely to double. At best, the wider scale use of ART will blunt this catastrophic rise in mortality. We appear to be in the early stages of a massive natural experiment in exploring how much punishment Africa's already poor and vulnerable societies can take. New ways of thinking and acting must emerge from Africa and the world community to ensure that AIDS-impacted societies can continue to function amid this turn of events. We need, in short, a new social contract for the era of AIDS.

Notes

1. Director, Justice Africa. This chapter has benefited from comments by Lincoln Chen, Malcolm McPherson and Alan Whiteside.
2. Opening address, International Conference on AIDS and Sexually-Transmitted Diseases in Africa (ICASA), 22 September 2003.
3. The historical comparisons that spring to mind are the Black Death in 14th-century Europe, the ravages of smallpox and measles on post-contact American populations in the 16th century and syphilis in Europe in the same century. The demographic catastrophes of late-19th-century China, India, Brazil and east Africa are the most recent comparable calamity, but those had more complex causes.
4. All figures from WHO life tables accessed April 2003.
5. The precise lifetime probability depends upon the age pattern of transmission and other factors.
6. Given that we are witnessing changes of a systematic nature and scale, that have only just begun, it is not only justifiable but necessary to move beyond the empirical evidence base into informed projection of this nature, ie based on models that have proved their efficacy. To insist on inductive rigour is to condemn oneself to be always behind the curve.
7. Note that in Africa, LEB, as a statistical construct from a bimodal mortality pattern, does not reflect any such subjective anticipation of longevity. In countries with high child mortality, LEA may be longer than LEB.
8. Zimbabwe's drop in reported HIV prevalence from 2000–03 is most likely caused by the same set of factors.
9. 'ABC' refers to the sexual behaviours that limit the risk of HIV transmission, namely abstinence, being faithful to one lifetime partner and using condoms.
10. 'Ugandans Outdo Americans in Aids Drugs Compliance', *The Monitor* (Kampala), 5 September 2003.
11. The addition of TB and malaria was made primarily out of deference to Thabo Mbeki who was uncomfortable with the focus on AIDS.

References

Badcock-Walters, P (2003) 'Educator Mortality in KwaZulu-Natal: A Consolidated Study of Impact and Trends', paper presented at Scientific Meeting on The Empirical Evidence for the Demographic and Socio-Economic Impact of Aids, Durban, 26–28 March

Barnett, T and Blaikie, P (1992) *AIDS in Africa: Its Present and Future Impact*, John Wiley, London

Barnett, T and Whiteside, A (1999) 'HIV/AIDS and Development: Case Studies and a Conceptual Framework', *European Journal of Development Research*, vol 11, no 2, pp200–34

Barnett, T and Whiteside, A (2002) *AIDS in the Twenty-First Century: Disease and Globalization*, Palgrave Macmillan, London

Baylies, C (2002) 'The Impact of AIDS on Rural Households in Africa: A Shock Like Any Other?', *Development and Change*, vol 33, no 4, pp611–32

Bell, C, Devarajan, S and Gersbach, H (2003) *The Long-run Economic Costs of AIDS: Theory and Application to South Africa*, World Bank, Washington, DC

Burawoy, M (1997) 'The State and Economic Involution: Russia through a China Lens', in P Evans (ed) *State-Society Synergy: Government and Social Capital in Development*, University of California Press, Carlifornia

Campbell, C (2003) '*Letting Them Die': Why HIV/AIDS Prevention Programmes Fail*, International African Institute in association with James Currey, London

Cheek, R (2001) 'Playing God with HIV', *African Security Review*, vol 10, no 4

Commission on Macroeconomics and Health (2001) *Macroeconomics and Health: Investing in Health for Economic Development*, WHO, Geneva

Cornia, G, Jolly, R and Stewart, F (1987) *Adjustment with a Human Face*, Oxford University Press, Oxford

Daniel, M (2003) 'Children without Parents in Botswana: The Safety Net and Beyond', paper presented at Scientific Meeting on Empirical Evidence for the Demographic and Socio-Economic Impact of AIDS, Durban, 26–28 March

de Waal, A (2003a) 'How Will HIV/AIDS Transform African Governance?', *African Affairs*, vol 102 (January), pp1–24

de Waal, A (2003b) 'HIV/AIDS and Emergencies: Challenges of Measurement and Modelling', paper for the RIACSO Consultation, 'Vulnerability in the Light of the HIV/AIDS Pandemic', Johannesburg, September

de Waal, A and Whiteside, A (2003) '"New Variant Famine": AIDS and Food Crisis in Southern Africa', *The Lancet*, vol 362, pp1234–7

Dirks, R (1980) 'Social Responses during Severe Food Shortages and Famine', *Current Anthropology*, vol 21, pp21–44

Dorrington, R, Bradshaw, D and Budlender, D (2002) *HIV/AIDS Profile in the Provinces of South Africa: Data for 2002*, University of Cape Town, Centre for Actuarial Research, Cape Town

ECA (2001) *The Compact for Africa's Recovery*, ECA, Addis Ababa

Geertz, C (1963*) Agricultural Involution: The Process of Ecological Change in Indonesia*, University of California Press, California

Grassly, N, Walker, N, Mahy, M and Timaeus, I (2003) 'Comparison of Survey and Model-Based Estimates of Mortality and Orphan Numbers in Sub-Saharan

Africa', paper presented at Scientific Meeting on The Empirical Evidence for the Demographic and Socio-Economic Impact of AIDS, Durban, 26–28 March

Husain, I and Badcock-Walters, P (2002) 'Economics of HIV/AIDS Mitigation: Responding to Problems of Systemic Dysfunction and Sectoral Capacity', in S Forsythe, *The State of the Art: AIDS and Economics,* Policy Project, Washington, DC

Hutchinson, J (2003) 'HIV and the Evolution of Infectious Diseases', in G Ellison, M Parker and C Campbell (eds) *Learning from HIV and AIDS*, Cambridge University Press, Cambridge

Laughlin, C and Brady, I (eds) (1978) *Extinction and Survival in Human Populations*, Columbia University Press, New York

Levine, R (2003) 'Is AIDS Rewriting the Rules?', Guest Editorial, *International AIDS Economics Network,* vol 17 (April)

Little, P (2003) *Somalia: Economy without State*, International African Institute in Association with James Currey, London

Low-Beer, D and Stoneburner, R (2003) 'Behavior and Communication Change in Reducing HIV: Is Uganda Unique?', *African Journal of AIDS Research*, vol 2, no 1, pp9–21

McPherson, M (2003) *Non-Linear Macro Effects of HIV/AIDS: An Overview*, USAID EGAT/ED/HEW and Centre for Business and Government, JFK School of Government, Harvard, mimeo

McPherson, M and Goldsmith, A (1998) 'Africa: On the Move?', *SAIS Review*, vol 28, 153–67

McPherson, M, Hoover, D and Snodgrass, D (2000) *The Impact on Economic Growth in Africa of Rising Costs and Labour Productivity Losses Associated with HIV/AIDS*, JFK School of Government, Harvard

Maingi, J (2004) 'A Long Illness Bravely Borne', *Index on Censorship*, January, www.indexoncensorship.org

Manning, R (2002) 'AIDS and Democracy: What Do We Know?', paper prepared for *AIDS and Democracy: Setting the Research Agenda*, IDASA, Cape Town

Mattes, R (2003) *Healthy Democracies?*, Institute of Security Studies, Pretoria

Over, M (1992) *Macroeconomic Impact of AIDS in Sub-Saharan Africa*, World Bank, Africa Technical Department, Population, Health and Nutrition Division, Technical Working Paper No 3, Washington, DC

Parkhurst, J (2002) 'The Ugandan Success Story? Evidence and Claims of HIV-1 Prevention', *The Lancet,* vol 360, 78–80

Rana, A (2003) *HIV/AIDS and the Limits of Liberal Politics*, Justice Africa, London

Rosen, S, Simon, J, Vincent, J R, MacLeod, W, Fox, M and Thea, D M (2003) 'AIDS Is Your Business', *Harvard Business Review*, Boston

Rugalema, G (2002) 'Coping or Struggling? A Journey into the Impact of HIV/AIDS in Southern Africa', *Review of African Political Economy*, vol 26, no 86, pp537–45

Scudder, T and Colson, E (1982) 'From Welfare to Development: A Conceptual Framework for the Analysis of Dislocated People', in A Hansen and A Oliver-Smith (eds) *Involuntary Migration and Resettlement: The Problems and Responses of Dislocated People*, Westview Press, Colorado

Stewart, F (1995) *Adjustment and Poverty: Options and Choices*, Routledge, London

Tsadkan Gebre-Tensae, T (2002) *HIV/AIDS in the Ethiopian Military: Perceptions, Strategies and Impacts*, Centre for Strategic and International Studies, Washington, DC

Tuchman, B (1985) *The March of Folly: From Troy to Vietnam*, Abacus, London

Wendo, C (2002a) 'Uganda Hopes Fund Will Bring Long-Term Progress', *The Lancet*, vol 360, 6 July, p66

Wendo, C (2002b) 'Uganda Stands Firm on Health Spending Freeze', *The Lancet*, vol 360, 7 December, p1847

Wendo, C (2003) 'Uganda and the Global Fund Sign Grant Agreement', *The Lancet*, vol 361, 15 March, p942

Wendo, C (2004) 'Ugandan Officials Negotiated Global Fund Grants', *The Lancet*, vol 363, 17 January, p222

Whiteside, A (2004) 'The HIV/AIDS Epidemic in an Historical Perspective', paper for International Conference, Louvain-la-Neuve, Belgium, 11–13 March

Whiteside, A, Barnett, T, George, G and van Niekerk, A (2003) 'Through a Glass Darkly: Data and Uncertainty in the AIDS Debate', *Developing World Bioethics*, vol 3, no 1, pp49–76

World Bank (1999) *Confronting AIDS: Public Priorities in a Global Epidemic*, World Bank, Washington, DC

5
Food Security

William G Moseley and B Ikubolajeh Logan

Introduction

The broad goal of this chapter is to explore the political economy of food security discourse and monitoring in Africa:

- in terms of the conceptualization of hunger in mainstream discourse; and
- by linking hunger discourse to the technical approaches to hunger monitoring that have been adopted 'on the ground'.

We argue that the conceptualization of hunger is a discursive process in which the meanings assigned to key concepts (for example, hunger, famine, vulnerability, food security, food insecurity) often reflect the ideological position and interests of major donors.

The discussion follows two main thematic thrusts. First, we present a generalized overview of the conceptual nuances in food security discourse, especially as they pertain to the definition of food security/insecurity and vulnerability. Second, we propose that the conceptual untidiness of this discourse often reflects itself as logical shortcomings in the design and implementation of hunger mitigating strategies. We make the specific case that there is a discursive link between mainstream interpretations of food security and vulnerability, which requires the conceptualizations of hunger as a supply-side problem. This discursive process, in turn, makes it possible for famine early warning systems to approach hunger mitigation without addressing fundamental problems of political economy. Finally, we make some recommendations for best practice.

The chapter is organized into five sections following this introduction. The first section is used to examine some of the definitional problems encountered in the food security literature, and sets the stage for the second section where we attempt to illuminate the discursive process between food insecurity, vulnerability and what we consider to be the supply-side dilemma. The third section is used to describe the main famine early warning systems, as backdrop for a critical assessment of these systems in the fourth section. The final section is used to provide some recommendations for best practice. The chapter also includes three text boxes exploring various dimensions of food security in three specific African country contexts (Zimbabwe, Sudan and Malawi).

Food Security: The Definitional Quandary

Food Security and Nutrition: The Global Challenge (Kracht and Schulz, 1999) is considered by many to be one of the most definitive, contemporary works on global food security. The 32 contributors to the volume, including some of the best-known names in the field, deal with many aspects of food security. Yet one comes away from the volume without obtaining a clear, cohesive and well-articulated definition of this complex and rather elusive subject. That a tome of this stature should avoid providing a standard definition of food security is testimony to the ideological contentiousness surrounding the subject (although the book does adopt an explicit neo-liberal tone).

The definitional difficulty surrounding food security takes many forms. One of the most palpable of these is curious usage in which antonym is used as synonym, seemingly without much loss of communication. It is, therefore, not unusual to find food security and food insecurity being used interchangeably in the same context. Besides this interesting lexical attribute, food security is employed, sometimes ambiguously, at multiple scales, ranging from the household (even intra-household) through the local, national and regional levels. The World Bank (1986, p2), for example, defines food security as 'access by all people at all times to enough food for an active, healthy life'. This definition seems implicitly to cover the totality of population at every scale in the spectrum. Another usage of food security focuses on the status of communities and households. For example, Frankenberger and Goldstein (1990, p21) define the term to be a condition in which '[t]he viability of the household as a productive and reproductive unit is (not) threatened by food shortage'. In these terms, food insecurity may be thought of as inadequate access to sufficient amounts of food during all or part of the year for a healthy and active life (either through insufficient subsistence production or limited ability to acquire food through other means, for example purchase, barter or informal reciprocity arrangements). To avoid the definitional quagmire, some commentators, for example, Leroy et al (2001) have found it easier to state what constitutes food security than to define the term. To paraphrase them, food security includes the following checklist:

- economic and physical access to food;
- food self-sufficiency (described as sufficient food for a healthy and active life);
- security of access, which implies political and economic stability;
- sustained access over a long period (Leroy et al, 2001).

Ostensibly, food insecurity exists when one or more of these conditions are absent. Interestingly, Leroy et al conflate food security with food self-sufficiency, concepts which others (eg Maxwell and Frankenberger, 1992; Moseley and Logan, 2001) find to be quite different. The juxtaposition of food security and food self-sufficiency, like that of food security and food insecurity, sometimes introduces interpretational difficulties where none should exist.

Increasingly, since the seminal work of Sen (1981), the various elements of food security are being encapsulated in the idea of household food entitlements (defined as legitimate claims on food resources). A fundamental idea underlying Sen's characterization of the problem is that national food audits, using the food balance sheet approach, do not always or necessarily provide insights into household food security. The typical audit is couched in terms of an aggregate supply–demand problem in which national supply (production + stocks + imports) is compared to national demand (total population × caloric need per capita). Although not a useless exercise, national audits (where sufficient supply is often defined as national demand plus 10 per cent) (Geier, 1995) might satisfy national goals without accounting for the differing abilities of households to access food, even when it is available on the market. To phrase the problem more baldly, strategies designed to achieve national food goals do not necessarily and concomitantly achieve household food security. By contrast, it is reasonable to suppose that when household food entitlements are obtained, national food security goals would, of necessity, also be achieved.

Although the idea of household food entitlements is now centrally located within food security discourse, the macro-level approach, which underlies national audits, is still alive. Indeed, while the professional development community sometimes aspires to micro-scale analyses, food monitoring systems are guided by the view that food security is essentially a macro-scale issue that can be addressed through provincial, national and regional audits. These monitoring systems are designed primarily to predict and monitor national food production and the potential for widespread hunger (famine) in a region or country. The predictions then serve as guides for the development of strategies for delivering emergency relief to avert famine. Although the early warning business has become increasingly professional and technical, critics (eg Watts and Bohle, 1993; Swift, 1996; Moseley and Logan, 2001) question the value of initiatives that are based on problematic macro-level assumptions and also fail to question the underlying political economy causes of famine and poverty. In the next section, we elaborate on how discourse informs these systems to avoid the political economy of hunger.

Vulnerability Discourse, Monitoring Practice and Food Aid

Food insecurity and vulnerability

Food monitoring practices are built on the assumption that it is possible to identify vulnerable populations, monitor changing conditions and deliver targeted food aid in the event of insurmountable production shortfalls. In this context, the food insecure are those populations that exhibit high levels of vulnerability to changing conditions and might, therefore, require aid.

In the food monitoring literature, the food insecure, often differentiated in terms of those who suffer from temporary versus chronic shortages, are defined to include the rural and urban poor, refugees from civil conflicts and those suffering from the effects of environmental crises (cf Siddle and Swindell, 1990; O'Connor, 1991). Sometimes, the temporarily food insecure are distinguished from those who are chronically food insecure by the fact that the former are experiencing short-term adverse conditions with which they cope in a variety of ways, including, for example, use of savings and sale of livestock. Food monitoring systems are designed implicitly to tackle the vulnerability of this latter group, more so than the former.

Vulnerability and its various components have been defined by a number of scholars. Swift (1989) notes that vulnerability is a function of inadequacy, both in terms of immediate entitlements (eg food production and income) and household assets, which serve as buffers in times of crisis. Vulnerability is, therefore, a result of immediate entitlement failure and the extent to which buffers have been exhausted. Robert Chambers (1989, p1) defines vulnerability as:

> *the exposure to contingencies and stress, and difficulty coping with them. Vulnerability, thus, has two sides: an external side of risks, shocks and stress to which an individual or household is subject; and an internal side which is defenseless, meaning a lack of means to cope[1] without damaging loss.* (Chambers 1989, p1)

Watts and Bohle (1993, p45) essentially build on Chambers' definition and identify vulnerable groups as 'those most exposed to perturbations, who possess the most limited coping capability, who suffer the most from crisis impact and who are endowed with the most circumscribed capacity for recovery'. There are at least three aspects of vulnerability contained in these different definitions:

1. risk[2] of exposure to entitlement failure;
2. limited ability to cope in the short term with entitlement failure; and
3. limited ability to recover (ie resiliency) from entitlement failure.

One of the conceptual difficulties facing food monitoring is that vulnerability, like food security, does not possess a consistent definition. In particular, the food discourse uses the term in ways that make it unclear whether it is a cause or outcome of food insecurity or indeed the same thing as food insecurity.

As cause (of hunger), vulnerability is used to refer to the totality of social and economic factors in the production system that leaves communities susceptible to the vagaries of nature. On the other hand, when vulnerability is used to indicate outcome, the focus is on populations facing crises (Sutherland et al, 1999; Kracht and Schulz, 1999). Thus, vulnerability as cause of hunger is process-determined and would seek to examine the underlying structural causes that expose populations to famine and hunger. Vulnerability as outcome, however, describes the economic, social and nutritional state or condition of a population. This view of vulnerability as outcome is closely associated with USAID Famine Early Warning System (FEWS) which defined vulnerability as 'a consequence, rather than a cause' (Downing, 1991, p5). Downing actually argues that it is misleading to define vulnerability as cause because such a definition would establish a causal link between the term and negative outcomes (for example between vulnerability, drought and famine).

Whether vulnerability is defined as cause or outcome has significant conceptual and methodological implications for famine warning systems. In particular, the emphasis of agencies like USAID on vulnerability as outcome precludes the kinds of political economy analyses that would be critical to a definition that examines cause. Dilley and Boudreau (2001, p237) suggest that the conceptual difficulty facing mainstream discourse (and monitoring practitioners) can be avoided by couching food insecurity in a framework built on three related pillars: event(s), susceptibility to it (them) by a community or household, and resulting outcome(s). In this sense, vulnerability becomes three inextricably interlinked prongs that make it possible to explore processes (environmental, political, social, cultural), map out the susceptibility of different groups to them, and assess possible outcomes. In this framework, the same event, for example a drought, will have different ranges of susceptibility for different households and communities, and have different outcomes, which may or may not be linked to food insecurity. It also becomes possible for one event (drought) to precipitate another (resource disputes, policy failures) and so on. Tracing processes in this way would make the outcomes much easier to understand and possibly even to predict.

Vulnerability as a supply-side problem, monitoring practice and food aid

Food aid has long represented a significant portion of international assistance to Africa, particularly for some donors such as the United States. Along with this type of assistance has developed a science and practice of famine early warning. Donor interest in early warning systems is multifaceted. First, developed countries do not want to be caught unaware of a crisis, as they were with the Sahelian famine in the early 1970s. This concern is not only humanitarian, but geopolitical as famines often lead to large-scale migration, cross-border tensions and potential conflict. Second, donor nations have been inherently suspicious of African governments, often claiming that they exaggerate the magnitude and depth of food shortages in order to garner handouts. Or that African governments do not distribute food aid based on an objective assessment of needs but based on other, often political, considerations. Donor-supported monitoring systems are thought to provide a more objective assessment of potential food shortages. Finally, economists in particular have been concerned that poorly targeted food aid dilutes price incentives that might normally encourage local producers to step up production efforts in years of shortage. These market concerns have spurred donor demand for systems that accurately identify those households that truly need food assistance.

Historically, early warning systems have served as a trigger for food aid. Increasingly, however, practitioners have sought to bridge the relief–development gap with interventions designed to reduce vulnerability (Ross et al, 1994). The definition of vulnerability as outcome becomes significant at this crossroads between conceptual discourse and the planning practices that it informs. Many hunger-mitigating initiatives have a supply-side focus (that is, initiatives designed to increase food supply). The supply-side focus is present in policies adopted by the World Food Council in the 1980s to increase food supply as a prerequisite for overall economic development and also in the various international conferences held on the subject during the 1980s and 1990s (Isis International, 1996). More recently, the supply-side ideology has become dominant in US Title II food-aid policies, which, with its several thousand million dollars budget, aims at improving the physical and economic access of people to 'sufficient, safe and nutritious foods to meet their daily dietary needs and food preferences for an active and healthy life' (Fanta Project, 2002; see also Paarlberg, 2000; Shane et al, 2000; Timmer, 2000).

The dominance of the supply-side orthodoxy in planning is paradoxical given that it is built on the definition of vulnerability as outcome. If vulnerability is, indeed, merely an outcome, then its solution must not be sought on the supply side, but on the demand side (in the sense that poor populations need income). We argue that the mainstream planning praxis oriented at supply-side solutions is part of a conceptual sleight of hand to avoid analyses of political economy. By promoting the idea of vulnerability as outcome, agencies like USAID can either choose to ignore process completely, or to address it only in a limited, superficial and apolitical way, that does not threaten the agendas and interests of the forces that create and perpetuate hunger (van Rooyen and Sigwele, 1998; Teklu, 1999). For a discussion of the recognition, and non-recognition, of the underlying causes of food insecurity in Zimbabwe and Malawi see Boxes 5.1 and 5.3.

Box 5.1 *Food security as the third* chimurenga[3] *in Zimbabwe*

Food security in Zimbabwe is being tackled on three major fronts:

1. as part of a national strategy to combat drought and famine;
2. as part of regional (southern Africa) strategy; and
3. as part of a continent-wide strategy.

Underlying all of these efforts is land reform, and in each case, the drive for food security has taken on aspects of a political liberation struggle. Locally the battle is being waged between the ruling ZANU-PF on the one hand, and commercial farmers and the opposition Movement for Democratic Change on the other. Both the Commercial Farmers Union (CFU) and the Movement for Democratic Change are viewed by the state as agents of neo-colonialism. Internationally (both regionally and globally), Zimbabwe's land reform programme has pitted the ZANU-PF against a host of foreign interests, most notably, the British government and the EU.

Zimbabwe's drive for national food security is tied at the continental level to the New Partnership for Africa's Development (NEPAD), a programme initiated and promoted by South Africa's Thabo Mbeki. NEPAD is an economic revitalization plan that invokes portions of a Senegalese initiative, Omega, and the Millennium Partnership for African Recovery Programme (MAP), which has the blessings of the World Bank and the West. NEPAD is viewed by many to be the economic dimension of the African Union (AU), launched in Durban, South Africa, in July 2002. In general, NEPAD seeks to replace a decade or more of World Bank/IMF vision for economic recovery in Africa with some home-grown alternatives. Zimbabwe has located its food-security struggle in the same light as NEPAD – a struggle to rid Africa of neo-colonialist interests, which impoverish the continent's peoples rather than help them to develop. In this sense, the Zimbabwe state views its food-security struggle, especially as they relate to land reform, to be a template for the struggle for real African economic freedom envisioned in NEPAD.

At the regional level, Zimbabwe's food-security struggle has become tied to a political and economic struggle against genetically modified grain. In the midst of a severe drought that has caused widespread famine in the region, several countries, including Malawi and Zambia, have refused US food aid because of fears that the genetically modified maize would cause health problems to humans, infect chicken and cattle, and replace local strains, thereby making the region completely dependent on US seed imports. Zimbabwe, which has not received part of the aid, has used a July 2002 SADC ministerial meeting on the matter to express its strong support for the refusal of genetically modified grain into the region (*Zimbabwe Herald,*[4] 25 July 2002, p7).

As part of a national strategy to combat drought and famine, food security is managed through a number of programmes, perhaps the most notable being the 'Africa 2000 Sustainable Agricultural Programme', which focuses on the production of small grains in marginal agricultural areas. The programme was initiated in 1998 with funding from Belgium and focuses on the drought-prone regions of the country. Among other things, the programme aims to promote indigenous grain species that are adaptable to drought, empower smallholders, especially women, reduce the use of expensive inorganic inputs and promote storage and marketing options for rural communities (*Zimbabwe Herald*, 2 August 2002, pB6). Another important element of the national food-security drive is food aid through NGOs. Both the sustainable agricultural programme and food aid have become politicized as part of the 'second liberation struggle'. The state has accused NGOs of fermenting political instability in rural areas, and has banned a number of them, including the World Food Programme, Oxfam and Save the Children, from distributing food in certain regions of the country. The Movement for Democratic Change and the CFU claim that the government has banned the distribution of food aid only in areas that have voted against the ruling party in recent elections. Food security has, therefore, been placed at the centre of national politics. Nowhere is this more palpable than in the area of land reform.

Zimbabwe's land reform programme has the attention of the whole southern African region, the British government, the EU, the Commonwealth and the newly formed AU. Proponents of land reform (and these include non-ZANU-PF supporters) claim that it is long overdue. The state claims that the programme has been a resounding success.

> *Despite scepticism that the land reform programme would kill the agriculture economy, crops such as tobacco that were not affected by the drought have increased both in quantity and earnings due to the land reform programme's newly settled farmers ... Were it not for the drought, the country's maize production was set to increase dramatically because the area that had been put under maize was considerably bigger than in previous years.* (*Zimbabwe Herald*, 25 July 2002, p8)

According to the government, as a result of land reform, total acreage under cultivation in the country in 2002, is reported to have increased by 8 per cent over 2001 levels. Despite the drought, commercial, resettlement and small-scale farmers in Mashonaland are reported to have produced excess maize, cotton, paprika, tobacco and rapoko (*Zimbabwe Herald*, 10 July 2002). The CFU and the Movement for Democratic Change lambast these positive government assessments as politics as usual (www.samara.co.zw/cfu/news/news.htm, *Guardian*[5]). They decry the subdivision of parcels under the resettlement scheme and predict that production shortfalls will occur even with good rains. In particular, they point to the lack of international support for the programme which, they predict, will only lead to more difficult economic and political times in the country.

True, Zimbabwe's land reform progress is being observed closely by, among others, South Africa and Namibia, the Commonwealth, the World Bank and a host of other international interests; and it has not generated a lot of support. The state believes, however, that both the attention given to the programme and its lack of international support stem from the fact that it is a new 'liberation struggle' against the political, economic and cultural agents of globalization. In particular, the state views the programme as an example of the struggles that await the AU for legitimate economic and political freedom in Africa.

Food security has taken on strong political overtones on all fronts. Unfortunately, the political focus threatens to divert attention from other important elements of food security, including short-term hunger mitigation, and long-term, sustainable agricultural production.

Source: Moseley and Logan (2004)

The above discussion is focused largely on the narrowly defined use of food-security monitoring and food aid for humanitarian purposes. It must be acknowledged, however, that food aid sometimes is used to achieve political ends, both by national elites and donor countries (eg de Waal, 1997). Government officials often have a say in the distribution of food assistance and they may use this power to reward supporters and punish opponents. While famine early warning systems have, in part, been put in place to thwart this possibility, government functionaries may steadfastly and openly resist the food distribution patterns suggested by these systems or covertly influence monitoring results through manipulation of the data collection process. In the case of the former, donors may compromise distribution schedules and patterns in order to secure the cooperation of the government (see Box 5.2 on Sudan). In the latter situation, chronically under-funded, ground-level data collection efforts are often easy to manipulate when they are carried out largely by government civil servants.

Donors themselves are not above using food aid to achieve political goals. The United States has long used food aid as a means of dumping surplus agricultural production in Africa (Diven, 2001). More recently, the United States has used food aid as a tool in its ongoing fight to encourage the use of GMO food crops around the world (see Box 5.1 regarding Zimbabwe). Food aid has also been used as an instrument of war in Sudan (Box 5.2).

Box 5.2 *Food aid and complex emergencies in Sudan*

Food insecurity in Sudan has been exacerbated by a 19-year-old civil war between the Muslim central government based in Khartoum and the Sudanese People's Liberation Army (SPLA), the main rebel group in the Christian South. The situation has resulted in the loss of more than 2 million lives. It has been described as a complex emergency wherein food insecurity is related to a mix of political, economic, social and natural causes (FEWS, 1997b).

The United States government is one of the biggest suppliers of food aid to southern Sudan. This assistance, along with that of other countries, is delivered through a consortium of NGOs known as Operation Lifeline Sudan. In order to monitor food needs, Operation Lifeline Sudan employs the household food economy approach (FEWS, 1997b).

Both relief food and starvation have become weapons in this protracted civil war. Operation Lifeline must rely on the goodwill of the government or rebel groups to deliver food. As such, the SPLA or the government control the food spigot. As Maren (1998, p12) notes, 'Both the government and the rebels have choked off villages, stolen cattle and burned and looted crops. As a result, people have been living on relief food supplied by a consortium of UN agencies and relief groups known as Operation Lifeline Sudan.' Maren (1997) asserts that food is a resource for fighting wars as soldiers are fed first or food is sold to purchase weapons and ammunition.

In a similar vain, Autesserre (2002) has argued that food aid has become the main channel for US Sudan policy. The US has sought to aid South Sudan because of pressure from groups on the religious right (who wish to support the Sudanese Christians) and more recently because of concerns about Khartoum's role in supporting international terrorism. The US, however, has been unwilling to support the South Sudanese openly owing to American corporate interests that exploit gum Arabic and oil in North Sudan. By providing food aid, the US is able to contradict directly Khartoum's strategy of starving the South into submission and help the rebel movement and army. An important advantage of using food aid for these purposes is that, because of Western prejudices about Africa as a starving continent, few people question the underlying motivations of US assistance.

Source: Moseley and Logan (2004)

Description of Famine Early Warning Systems in Africa

In this section we outline four monitoring systems, to be followed by critical assessment in the next section. The big players in African early warning today are the FAO's Global Information and Early Warning Systems (GIEWS), the World Food Programme's Vulnerability Assessment Mapping (VAM) and the USAID's Famine Early Warning System (FEWS). To a lesser degree, the Save the Children Fund (SCF-UK), with their Household Food Economy Approach, is a significant monitoring player in a few countries. These international efforts interact with a number of national early warning units that receive varying levels of technical support from one or several of the aforementioned players. These systems approach early warning with different conceptual machinery.

The earliest approach, and one the FAO and several national early warning units continue to use, is the food balance sheet approach. The food balance sheet approach is used to establish whether there is adequate food supply to meet demand by calculating national foods needs (population × per capita grain needs) and comparing these needs to the sum of agricultural production, stocks and net imports (imports – exports) (SADC, 1998). The unit of analysis is the country as a whole (although smaller geographical units are sometimes analysed).

USAID and others (Swift, 1985; Eele, 1994) began to develop indicator-based approaches to famine early warning in the 1980s. This approach uses a finite number of indicators, not all of them measured in the same units, that are assumed to capture various aspects of the vulnerability of populations in a given area (FEWS and FSTAU, 1997). The FEWS' indicator-based approach of USAID relies on vegetation indices derived from satellite imagery (eg Normalized Difference Vegetation Index) to bolster production estimates and it assembles a wide range of government-collected data related to food supply, food access and health. Data describing food access includes food prices, labour prices and local terms of trade (between grain and animals for example). Data describing health conditions is collected as downstream indicators of a hunger problem. Examples of such measures include morbidity, mortality and malnutrition figures (Eele, 1994; Kennedy and Sullivan, 1994; FEWS, 1997a). The trajectories of these indicators are analysed over time to determine whether food-security conditions might be deteriorating or improving. These indicators are also often combined into a general index of vulnerability (FEWS, 1997a; FEWS and FSTAU, 1997). The indicator approach is still used by USAID FEWS and others in many African countries, especially where data availability is limited.

The USAID FEWS indicator approach is founded on a number of basic assumptions, including:

- famine is the culmination of a process rather than a catastrophic event;
- famine has observable indicators;
- there is a progression of indicators that reflects the degree of vulnerability to famine;
- indicators will vary between places and through time; and
- some indicators appear early enough to permit mitigating action to be taken (FEWS, 1997a, p12).

USAID FEWS began to use a modified income estimation or maize equivalency approach in Zimbabwe in 1996–97 as a result of concerns over the indicator-based approach (Eilerts and Vhurumuku, 1997; FEWS and NEWU, 1998; Moseley and Logan, 2001). This approach has also been used on an experimental basis in other southern African countries. FEWS Zimbabwe assembles data from secondary sources (mainly the government) on food production, cash income and transfers/entitlements for sub-national territorial units known as communal land areas. These sources of food and income are then converted to a common metric of per capita maize equivalents by communal area (maize is used as a common metric as it is the staple food in Zimbabwe and accounts for a large proportion of most rural diets). The sum of maize equivalents (from different sources of food and income) is then compared to a threshold value of 250kg of maize per capita per annum to determine if there is a shortfall or surplus.

The SCF-UK household food economy approach has been automated and comes as a standalone computer package known as RiskMap (SCF-UK, 1997; Seaman, 2000; Moseley, 2001a). This approach attempts to determine aggregate need through the development of an understanding of processes operating at the household level. The approach begins by dividing a country up into food econ-omy zones or areas where the majority of households have similar access to mar-kets and strategies for obtaining food and income. Research is then undertaken to develop profiles for poor, modal and rich households in these different zones for a normal year. These profiles detail a household's sources of food and income, as well as asset levels, surplus production, coping strategies and markets used. By monitoring year to year, zone level production, income sources and food markets, it becomes possible to determine household level impacts based upon the under-lying understanding of normal year prices and sources of food and income. While the household food economy approach uses indicator-type data for monitoring purposes, it also attempts to understand the structure of sources of food and income for different types of households in order to interpret better the effect of aggregate data trends on food security. Among others, Save the Children uses this approach as a key monitoring agency in countries such as Ethiopia and Sudan. Key elements of this approach have more recently been incorporated into the Africa-wide monitoring efforts of WFP VAM and USAID FEWS (FEWS NET, 2002; WFP, 2002).

Critical Assessment of Early Warning Systems in Africa

In this section, we first examine the impact on monitoring of the view that vulner-ability is an outcome; and then the impact on monitoring recommendations of the view that the solution to hunger is only a supply-side problem. We try to show that the two issues are related to the unwillingness of the mainstream to address political economy problems.

Of the monitoring methods examined, the food balance sheet approach is most emblematic of supply-focused conceptualizations of food security. The major problem with this method is that it equates food supply with food access (an issue brought to the attention of monitoring experts by Sen (1981)). While food supply or availability might be sufficient at the national level, it may be inac-cessible to certain segments of society owing to high prices or insufficient income. For example, Franke and Chasin (1980) discuss how food commodity crops were being exported from the Sahel region in the early 1970s (indicating adequate sup-ply at the regional level) while villagers were dying of starvation. Furthermore, Malawi and Zimbabwe, once thought of as major maize producers in southern Africa, are now recognized as having long-standing hunger problems among cer-tain segments of the population (see Box 5.3 regarding Malawi). The persistence

Box 5.3 *Bungled policy and Malthusian obfuscation: Vulnerability in Malawi*

The root causes of food insecurity in Malawi are often described in terms of a vicious cycle of overpopulation, land scarcity and environmental degradation (eg UNICEF, 1993; Minde et al, 2001; Place and Otsuka, 2001). As one of Africa's most densely populated (250 persons/km^2 in parts of the south) and chronically food insecure countries, this assessment holds a certain amount of appeal.

However, this explanation breaks down when confronted with evidence that a lack of land is not the key constraint facing many Malawian smallhold farmers, but insufficient labour at key junctures in the agricultural season (eg Pearce et al, 1996; Alwang and Siegel, 1999; Moseley, 2000). Malawi's history of labour out-migration in the colonial and post-colonial periods and policies emphasizing maize monocultures better explain current problems facing Malawian smallhold farmers.

Malawi's history of labour out-migration in the colonial and post-colonial periods may have inhibited the normal process of agricultural intensification that Boserup (1965) and like-minded scholars (eg Turner et al, 1993; Mortimore and Adams, 2001) have described in other parts of Africa. Malawi was viewed by the British as a backwater colony and a labour reserve for other colonies in the region that had more developed mining activities. In 1950, about half the male workforce was working outside the indigenous agricultural economy, either in neighbouring countries or on plantations in Malawi (Barber, 1961). Although this out-migration has subsided, many Malawians continue to look outside the rural economy for employment opportunities. Boserup (1965) herself acknowledged that removal of labour from the subsistence economy could lead to a situation of continued low yields.

Colonial and post-colonial government policies have also placed a heavy emphasis on the cultivation of maize monocultures. The 'success' of these policies is reflected in the fact that nearly 70 per cent of the land under cultivation in the 1990s was in maize (Majid and Adams, 1998). Malawian farmers traditionally planted the majority of their food crops as polycultures, that is as a mixture of complementary crops in the same field.

The British colonial administration encouraged maize cultivation in a number of its southern African protectorates, including Nyasaland (now Malawi). This allowed for regional maize trade and a stable food supply for mineworkers in South Africa and Northern Rhodesia. Malawi's first post-colonial government under Hastings Banda (1966–94) also strongly encouraged maize production. Maize production was encouraged in order to meet national food self-sufficiency objectives and to garner foreign exchange on the regional maize market (Pryor, 1990). Former President Banda also benefited personally from expanding maize production in Malawi. Under Banda, the maize economy of Malawi was tightly controlled, from seed sales to the retailing of maize meal, through the President's personal ownership of key companies (Majid and Adams, 1988).

The transition from polycultures to maize monoculture has had serious implications for farm labour. Rather than inter-planted crops harvested over multiple time-frames, farmers are now faced with one concentrated harvest period. This 'telescoping' of labour demands into very distinct periods has contributed to serious labour bottlenecks at critical junctures in the agricultural season (Moseley, 2000). Weed control, nitrogen fixing, decreased soil erosion and reduced insect-related crop loss are also benefits of inter-cropping that have been lost.

Although the dominance of maize monocultures has declined somewhat in recent years with changes in government policy, 50 years of government directives emphasizing maize monocultures are difficult to reverse. The latest food crisis in Malawi (Vidal, 2002) has also been exacerbated by neo-liberal policy prescriptions that eliminated government subsidies for agricultural inputs over the past ten years and, only last year, forced the government to sell off its emergency reserves of maize grain. A lack of strategic reserves has meant that the government has had to go back on the open market to purchase maize, often at inflated prices, in an attempt to address the current shortfall.

Source: Moseley and Logan (2004)

of the food balance sheet approach can be explained in terms of its technical simplicity and focus on inadequate supply as the cause of food insecurity.

The other three early warning methodologies reflect a more nuanced understanding of vulnerability (giving attention to food availability and access), yet all tend to describe vulnerability as a condition rather than a historical process. This, as well as their narrow use for food-aid decisions, means that they are unlikely to inform the longer term resolution of food insecurity. Each of these systems also face technical impediments, a few of which we will describe below.

While the indicator-based approach is an improvement over food balance sheets in that it tries to account for access, there are a number of concerns related to its conceptual validity, interpretation and usefulness to policy-makers. First, there is the question of how to weight each of the indicators when constructing a composite index of vulnerability. Often, this involves a degree of arbitrariness (eg counting all of the indicators equally). Second, it is difficult to interpret the meaning of a composite vulnerability index in relation to the situation in other countries that might have an index composed of different indicators with different weights. Finally, while the approach allows statements about relative vulnerability in different areas of a country, it is generally incapable of quantifying actual food deficits and policy-makers sometimes find it difficult to understand or interpret the meaning of an abstract vulnerability index.

The maize equivalency and household food economy approaches account to varying degrees for levels of access and are able to quantify a food shortfall in deficit years. The major problem with the maize equivalency approach is that it is data-intensive and its deficit predictions are highly reliant on the quality of data employed. For example, Moseley and Logan (2001) found that the grain harvest numbers used by this approach in some areas of Zimbabwe were unrealistically low. The method also assesses the situation in terms of the average individual, disguising potentially large disparities in food production and income between different segments of the population in the same area.

The major shortcomings of the Risk Map approach are also its strong points, that is, data collected by wealth group in terms of homogeneous production zones (interesting but difficult to obtain data). In describing household food economies, and identifying those that are more vulnerable (ie more exposed to, and less capable of, coping with fluctuations), the Risk Map approach suggests that underlying conditions, in combination with environmental or economic perturbations, are what create food insecurity. While this approach perhaps comes closest to depicting vulnerability as a cause of food insecurity, the end-users of the system still employ its output for the targeted delivery of food aid. These structural descriptions of vulnerable households could be used as a starting point to ask why some households produce little in the way of crops, have minimal incomes and have few reserves to deal with shortfalls. The answers to these 'why' questions could lead to some interesting development initiatives that actually address the root causes of food security. Unfortunately donors have chosen not to use information on the structure of household food economies for anything more than the targeting of food aid (eg Hammond and Maxwell, 2002).

It is worth mentioning that the monitoring systems we have discussed are largely focused on the continent's rural areas. This focus has been justified by a longer history of famine in rural areas, a relatively small proportion of the population living in urban areas, and past policies that favoured the urban consumer. Despite the lack of attention paid to urban food security in the past, 20 years of structural adjustment policies in Africa have undercut the situation of the urban poor, making this group much more vulnerable (Becker et al, 1994; Potts, 1997; Riddell, 1997; Moseley, 2001b). While there are technical impediments to monitoring hunger among heterogeneous, urban populations pursuing a wide array of livelihood strategies, early warning systems may also see little point in monitoring urban areas if their major concern is to track the evolution of food production. This said, a few attempts are being undertaken to monitor hunger in Africa's urban areas (eg FEWS, 2002).

Recommendations for Best Practice

Climate variability is a long-standing phenomenon in many parts of Africa and history suggests that episodic harvest failures need not lead to famine (and in fact only do so when significant structural vulnerability exists among segments of the population). As argued in the initial sections of this chapter, vulnerability is neither a static condition nor the explicit outcome of climatic vagaries and traditional agricultural systems. Rather, vulnerability has more to do with the distribution of resources and power (ie political economy).

While creating a society of equals is utopian, understanding vulnerability as a cause of food insecurity implies that policy-makers need to consider addressing the worst structural inequities (ranging, for example, from land redistribution in some contexts to fair commodity prices in others) if the vulnerability (a product of social relations) of certain segments of society is ever to be addressed. Unfortunately the international donor community has shown little to no interest in addressing underlying structural problems that perpetuate vulnerability and, as such, ensure some level of hunger every time harvests and incomes fall below normal. Perhaps, this should not be surprising as the Global North has a vested interest in maintaining the current global trading regime, and its associated system of private property, ensuring a continued supply of cheap raw materials. While NGOs continue to launch small-scale projects that often do some good, they are unwilling and incapable of addressing deeper, structural problems. The big financial actors in African development, the World Bank and IMF, continue to make loans that bolster neo-liberal policies that exacerbate inequities, ensuring the persistence of food insecurity in Africa.

While the development community has been reluctant to confront vulnerability as cause, they have been quite willing to monitor populations for hunger and supply emergency relief when the situation appears to be degenerating. This willingness to provide relief is in part humanitarian, and partly geopolitical as famine can lead to unrest and migration. As we have suggested, however, food-security monitoring is an inexact science. While monitoring experts have moved beyond a one dimensional concern with production, vulnerability mapping (allowing one to predict who will be affected by economic or climatic variation) is contingent upon regularly collected, comprehensive and sound socio-economic data – an expensive and rare commodity in Africa. The inexactness of food-security monitoring means that the national or international safety net will always be riddled with holes.

The donor community's unwillingness to address structural inequities, coupled with their desire – yet imperfect capability – to tackle hunger, suggests that we should propose a mid-range remedial solution pending more revolutionary change. Precolonial African history hints that there may be another way to approach food-security monitoring and relief. While precolonial rural African societies were far from egalitarian, they often had a moral economy (Scott, 1976) that acted as a safety net in times of harvest shortfall. The moral economy dictated that wealthy villagers and the extended family provide needy households with interest-free grain loans in times of shortage (to be repaid at the next harvest). Furthermore, the moral economy operated at the local scale, leaving it to villagers (not monitoring systems) to decide when they should go to a neighbour and ask for assistance. While the moral economy has all but been destroyed by market penetration and monetization (Watts, 1983), and a return to the past is impractical, a modern-day substitute for the moral economy deserves further exploration.

One such system is that of local-level grain banks. Local-level grain banks could operate like the wealthy, but supportive, neighbour of yesteryear by providing grain loans in times of shortfall. This loan (in grain) would be repaid in grain with a small amount of interest at harvest time (allowing the grain bank to persist and grow). Grain bank clients are also entirely self-selected, assuming that individuals know better than monitoring systems when they are hungry. While successful grain banks require well-trained and disciplined management (Moseley, 1995: World Neighbors, 2002), the millions of dollars spent on technical equipment and high-salaried staff to run monitoring systems could create thousands of locally self-sufficient grain banks.[6] While grain banks are not without their critics (eg Berg, 1998; Kent, 1998), this proposal is well worth serious consideration and deliberation.

Notes

1. Davies (1996, p238) has defined coping strategies as 'the tertiary activities pursued by people to survive when habitual primary and secondary activities cannot guarantee a livelihood'. In other words, coping strategies are short-term measures undertaken to obtain food when standard sources of income or food fall short of normal levels.
2. The concept of risk in the food-security literature refers to the probability that an entitlement will fail. Risks to food entitlements include variability in crop production and food supply, market and price variability, risks in employment and wages, and risks in health and morbidity for livestock and humans (Maxwell and Frankenberger, 1992).
3. The term *chimurenga* is a local term (in the Shona and Ndebele languages) for liberation wars. The First Chimurenga, or First Liberation War, occurred in 1896–97 against the British. The Second Chimurenga refers to the liberation struggle leading up to Zimbabwean independence in 1980. The land question was central to both of these struggles (Mukunya, 1995).
4. The *Zimbabwe Herald* is the official organ of the ruling party, ZANU-PF and thus expresses a particular perspective.
5. The *Zimbabwe Guardian* expresses the viewpoint of the Commercial Farmers' Union.
6. This also assumes that government policy will not actively discourage grain banks (eg village grain banks were bombed by the Khartoum government in Sudan (deWaal, 1997)).

References

Alwang, J and Siegel, P (1999) 'Labor Shortages on Small Landholdings in Malawi: Implications for Policy Reforms', *World Development*, vol 27, no 8, pp1461–75

Autesserre, S (2002) 'United States "Humanitarian Diplomacy" in South Sudan', *Journal of Humanitarian Assistance*, 18 March, www.jha.ac/articles/a085.htm

Babu, S and Quinn, V (1994) 'Food Security and Nutrition Monitoring in Africa: Introduction and Historical Background', *Food Policy*, vol 19, no 3, pp211–17

Barber, W (1961) *The Economy of British Central Africa*, Stanford University Press, Stanford, CA

Becker, C M, Hamer, A M and Morrison, A R (1994) *Beyond Urban Bias in Africa: Urbanization in an Era of Structural Adjustment*, Heinemann, Portsmouth, NH

Berg, E (1998) 'The Question of "L'Organisation du Monde Rural" or "What's Our Vision for a Developed Rural Economy"', presentation made at workshop, *Community-Level Grain Storage Projects (Cereal Banks): Why Do They Rarely Work and What Are the Alternatives?*, sponsored by Catholic Relief Services, Dakar, Senegal, 19–22 January.

Boserup, E (1965) *The Conditions of Agricultural Growth: The Economics of Agrarian Change Under Population Pressure*, Aldine, Chicago

Chambers, R (1989) 'Vulnerability, Coping and Policy', *IDS Bulletin*, vol 20, pp1–7

Cooper, D and van Zyl, J (1994) 'The Influence of Land Reform on Food Security and Food Self Sufficiency in South Africa', *Food Security South Africa*, pp17–31

Davies, S (1996) *Adaptable Livelihoods: Coping With Food Insecurity in the Malian Sahel*, St Martin's Press, New York

de Waal, A (1997) *Famine Crimes*, Indiana University Press, Oxford

Dilley, M and Boudreau, T (2001) 'Coming to Terms with Vulnerability: A Critique of the Food Security Definition', *Food Policy*, vol 26, no 3 (June), pp229–47

Diven, P (2001) 'The Domestic Determinants of US Food Aid Policy', *Food Policy*, vol 26, no 5, pp455–74

Downing, T (1991) 'Assessing Socieconomic Vulnerability to Famine: Frameworks, Concepts and Applications', FEWS Working Paper 2.1, USAID

Dreze, J and Sen, A (1989) *Hunger and Public Action*, Oxford University Press, New York

Eele, G (1994) 'Indicators for Food Security and Nutrition Monitoring: A Review of Experience from Southern Africa', *Food Policy*, vol 19, no 3, pp314–28

Eilerts, G and Vhurumuku, E (1997) 'Zimbabwe Food Security and Vulnerability Assessment, 1996/97', mimeo, USAID FEWS, Harare

Fanta Project (2002) 'Food Aid and Food Security Assessment', *Food Forum*, vol 60, 2nd quarter, pp11–12

FEWS (1997a) 'Vulnerability Analysis and FEWS', unpublished mimeo, Famine Early Warning System (FEWS), United States Agency for International Development (USAID), Washington, DC

FEWS (1997b) 'Southern Sudan: Monitoring a Complex Emergency', Famine Early Warning System (FEWS), United States Agency for International Development (USAID), Washington, DC

FEWS (2002) 'Harare Urban Vulnerability Update', www.fews.net/current/special/gcontent.cfm

FEWS NET (2002) 'Food Economy Baseline Analysis', www.fews.net/livelihoods/baseline

FEWS and FSTAU (1997) 'Vulnerability Analysis for SADC Countries: A Suggested Approach for Early Warning Units (draft)', unpublished mimeo, USAID Famine Early Warning System (FEWS) and SADC Food Security Technical and Administrative Unit (FSTAU), Harare

FEWS and NEWU (1998) 'Zimbabwe: Current Vulnerability Assessment for 1998/99', mimeo, USAID Famine Early Warning System (FEWS) and National Early Warning Unit (NEWU), (AGRITEX), Harare

Franke, R and Chasin, B (1980) *Seeds of Famine: Ecological Destruction and the Development Dilemma in the West African Sahel*, Allanheld, Osmun, Montclair, NJ

Frankenberger, T and Goldstein, D (1990) 'Food Security, Coping Strategies, and Environmental Degradation', *Arid Lands Newsletter*, vol 30, pp21–7, Office of Arid Lands Studies, University of Arizona

Geier, G (1995) 'Food Security Policy', in *Africa between Disaster Relief and Structural Adjustment*, Frank Cass, London

Hammond, L and Maxwell, D (2002) 'The Ethiopian Crisis of 1999–2000: Lessons Learned, Questions Unanswered', *Disasters,* vol 26, no 3, pp262–79

Isis International (1996) 'Food Security in Women's Hands', *No Short Cut to Food Security*, monograph series, no 2, Isis International, Manila

Kennedy, L H and Sullivan, J (1994) 'Choice of Indicators for Food Security and Nutrition Monitoring', *Food Policy*, vol 19, no 3, pp329–43

Kent, L (1998) 'Why Cereal Bank Projects Rarely Work: A Summary of Findings', Catholic Relief Services, Baltimore

Kracht, U and Schulz, M (eds) (1999) *Food Security and Nutrition: The Global Challenge*, St Martin's Press, New York

Leroy, J, van Rooyen, J, D'Haese, L and de Winter, A (2001) 'A Quantitative Determinant of the Food Security Status of Rural Farming Households in the Northern Province of South Africa', *Development Southern Africa*, vol 18, no 1, March, pp5–17

Logan, B I and Tevera, D (2001) 'Neoliberalism, Regime Survival and the Environment: Economic Reform and Agricultural Transformation in Zimbabwe in the 1990s', *Canadian Journal of African Studies*, vol 35, no 1, pp99–138

Majid, N and Adams, L (1998) 'Combining RiskMap Analysis and Climate Prediction: The Possible Effects of El Nino on the Food Security of Rural Households in Malawi', mimeo, Save the Children Fund (UK), London

Maren, M (1997) *The Road to Hell: The Ravaging Effects of Foreign Aid and International Charity*, Free Press, New York

Maren, M (1998) 'The Faces of Famine', *Newsweek*, 27 July, vol 132, no 4, p12

Maxwell, S and Frankenberger, T (1992) *Household Food Security: Concepts, Indicators, Measurements: A Technical Review*, UNICEF and IFAD, New York

Mekuria, M and Moletsane, N (1966) 'Initial Findings of Rural Household Food Security in Selected Districts of the Northern Province', *Agrekon*, vol 35, pp309–13

Minde, I, Kowero, G, Ngugi, D and Luhanga, J (2001) 'Agricultural Land Expansion and Deforestation in Malawi', *Forest Trees and Livelihoods*, vol 11, no 2, pp167–82

Mortimore, M and Adams, W (2001) 'Farmer Adaptation, Change and "Crisis"', *Global Environmental Change*, vol 11, no 1, pp49–57

Moseley, W (1995) 'Securing Livelihoods in Marginal Environments: Can NGOs Make a Long Term Difference?', in *Policy In The Making, Poverty and Food Economy: Assessing Livelihoods,* Policy Development Unit Discussion Paper No 4, Save the Children Fund, London, pp12–22

Moseley, W (2000) 'Paradoxical Constraints to Agricultural Intensification in Malawi: The Interplay Between Labor, Land and Policy', *Department of Geography, Discussion Paper Series*, no 00-1, University of Georgia, Athens

Moseley, W (2001a) 'Computer Assisted Comprehension of Distant Worlds: Understanding Hunger Dynamics in Africa', *Journal of Geography*, vol 100, no 1, pp32–45

Moseley, W (2001b) 'Monitoring Urban Food Security in Sub-Saharan Africa', *African Geographical Review*, vol 21, pp81–90

Moseley, W and Logan, I (2001) 'Conceptualizing Hunger Dynamics: A Critical Examination of Two Famine Early Warning Methodologies in Zimbabwe', *Applied Geography*, vol 21, no 3, pp223–48

Moseley, W and Logan, I (2004) *African Environment and Development*, Ashgate, Aldershot, UK

Mukunya, S (1995) *Dynamics of History. Book 3,* College Press Publishers, Harare

O'Connor, A (1991) *Poverty in Africa: A Geographical Approach*, Belhaven Press, London

Paarlberg, R (2000), 'The Weak Link between World Food Markets and World Food Security', *Food Policy*, vol 25, no 3, 317–35

Pearce, J, Ngwira, A and Chimseu, G (1996) 'Living on the Edge: A Study of the Rural Food Economy in Mchinji and Salima Districts of Malawi', Save the Children Fund (UK), Lilongwe

Place, F and Otsuka, K (2001) 'Population, Tenure, and Natural Resource Management: The Case of Customary Land Area in Malawi', *Journal of Environmental Economics and Management*, vol 41, no 1, pp13–32

Potts, D (1997) 'Urban Lives: Adopting New Strategies and Adapting Rural Links' in C Rakodi (ed) *The Urban Challenge in Africa: Growth and Management of Its Large Cities*, United Nations University Press, New York

Pryor, F (1990) *The Political Economy of Poverty, Equity and Growth: Malawi and Madagascar*, World Bank and Oxford University Press, New York

Quinn, V and Kennedy, E (1994) 'Food Security and Nutrition Monitoring Systems in Africa: A Review of Country Experiences and Lessons Learned', *Food Policy*, vol 19, no 3, pp234–54

Riddell, B (1997) 'Structural Adjustment Programs and the City in Tropical Africa', *Urban Studies*, vol 34, no 8, pp1297–1307

Ross, J, Maxwell, S and Buchanan-Smith, M (1994) 'Linking Relief and Development', *IDS Discussion Paper #344*, Institute of Development Studies, Sussex

SADC (1998) 'SADC Food Security Quarterly Bulletin – Zimbabwe', www.zimbabwe.net/sadc-fanr/rewu/qfsb/qfsbzw.htm

Save the Children Fund (SCF-UK) (1997) *RiskMap 1.2* (computer database and analytical model for 15 African countries including Mali), Save the Children (UK), London

Scott, J (1976) *The Moral Economy of the Peasant. Rebellion and Subsistence in South East Asia*, Yale University Press, New Haven

Seaman, J (2000) 'Making Exchange Entitlements Operational: The Food Economy Approach to Famine Prediction and the RiskMap Computer Program', *Disasters*, vol 24, no 2, pp133–52

Sen, A (1981) *Poverty and Famines*, Clarendon, Oxford

Shane, M, Teigen, L, Gehlhar, M and Roe, T (2000) 'Economic Growth and World Food Insecurity: A Parametric Approach', *Food Policy*, vol 25, no 3, pp297–315

Siddle, D J and Swindell, K (1990) *Rural Change in Tropical Africa: From Colonies to Nation States*, Blackwell, Oxford

Sutherland, A, Irungu, J, Kang'ara, J, Muthamia, J and Ouma, J (1999) 'Household Food Security in Semi-Arid Africa: The Contributions of Participatory Research and Development to Rural Livelihoods in Eastern Kenya', *Food Policy*, vol 24, no 4, August, 369–90

Swift, J (1985) 'Planning against Drought and Famine in Turkana, Northern Kenya', mimeo, Institute of Development Studies, University of Sussex

Swift, J (1989) 'Why Are Rural People Vulnerable to Famine?', *IDS Bulletin,* vol 20, no 2, pp8–15

Swift, J (1996) 'Desertification: Narratives, Winners and Losers', in M Leach and R Mearns (eds) *The Lie of the Land*, James Curry, Oxford

Teklu, T (1999) 'Food Demand Studies in Sub-Saharan Africa: A Survey of Empirical Evidence', *Food Policy*, vol 21, no 6 (December), pp479–96

Timmer, C (2000) 'The Macro Dimensions of Food Security: Economic Growth, Equitable Distribution, and Food Price Stability', *Food Policy*, vol 25, no 3, pp283–95

Turner, B, Hyden, G and Kates, R (eds) (1993) *Population Growth and Agricultural Change in Africa*, University Press of Florida, Gainesville

UNICEF (1993) *Situation Analysis of Poverty in Malawi*, United Nations in Malawi and Government of Malawi, Lilongwe

van Rooyen, C and Sigwele, G (1988) 'Toward Food Security in Southern Africa: New Roles for Agriculture', *Food Policy*, vol 23, no 6, pp491–504

Vidal, J (2002) 'A Disaster Waiting to Happen', *Guardian*, 3 May, www.guardian.co.uk/Archive/Article/0,4273,4406336,00.html

Watts, M (1983) *Silent Violence: Food, Famine and Peasantry in Northern Nigeria*, University of California Press, Berkeley

Watts, M and Bohle, H (1993) 'The Space of Vulnerability: The Causal Structure of Hunger and Famine', *Progress in Human Geography*, vol 17, no 1, pp43–67

World Bank (1986) *Poverty and Hunger: Issues and Options for Food Security in Developing Countries*, World Bank Policy Study, Washington, DC

World Food Programme (WFP) (2002) 'VAM. Putting Hunger on the Map', www.wfp.org/index.asp?section=5

World Neighbors (2002) 'Mali: Banking On Grain', www.wn.org/WorldFood-Day.asp

Part II
INSTITUTIONAL CHANGE

6

The Global Economic Context[1]

Thandika Mkandawire[2]

Introduction

Globalization is a multifaceted process that defies unique definition. Different authors emphasize different things about causes and effects of globalization, partly because of differences in the definition of the process, partly because of differences in focus and partly because of different ideological predispositions about the process itself. In this chapter I will treat globalization as a process whereby national and international policy-makers proactively or reactively promote domestic and external liberalization. Africa illustrates, perhaps better than elsewhere, that globalization is very much a policy-driven process. While in other parts of the world it may be credible to view globalization as driven by technology and the 'invisible hand' of the market, in Africa most of the features of globalization and the forces associated with it have been shaped by Bretton Woods Institutions (BWIs) and Africa's adhesion to a number of conventions such as the World Trade Organization (WTO) which have insisted on opening up markets. African governments have voluntarily, or under duress, reshaped domestic policies to make their economies more open. The issue therefore is not whether Africa is being globalized but under what conditions the process is taking place and why, despite such relatively high levels of integration into the world economy, growth has faltered.

The word that often comes to mind whenever globalization and Africa are mentioned together is 'marginalization'. The threat of marginalization has hung over Africa's head like the sword of Damocles and has been used in minatory fashion to prod Africans to adopt appropriate policies.[3] In most writing globalization is portrayed as a train which African nations must choose to board or be left behind. As Stanley Fischer, the Deputy Director of the IMF, and associates put it, 'globalization is proceeding apace and sub-Saharan Africa (SSA) must decide whether to open up and compete, or lag behind' (Fischer et al, 1998, p5). *The Economist*, commenting on the fact that per capita income gap between the USA and Africa has widened, states that 'it would be odd to blame globalization for holding Africa back. Africa has been left out of the global economy, partly because its governments used to prefer it that way' *The Economist*, 2001, p12).

Globalization, from the developmental perspective, will be judged by its effects on economic development and the eradication of poverty. Indeed, in developing countries the litmus test for any international order remains whether it facilitates economic development which entails both economic growth and structural transformation. I shall argue that in the case of Africa this promise has yet to be realized. The policies designed to 'integrate' Africa into the global economy have thus far failed because they have completely sidestepped the developmental needs of the continent and the strategic questions on the form of integration appropriate to addressing these needs. They consequently have not led to higher rates of growth and, their labelling notwithstanding, have not induced structural transformation. Indeed the combined effect of internal political disarray, the weakening of domestic capacities, deflationary policies and slow world economic growth have placed African economies on a 'low equilibrium growth path' against which the anaemic Gross Domestic Product (GDP) growth rates of 3–4 per cent appear as 'successful' performance. I will illustrate this point by looking at two channels through which the benefits of globalization are supposed to be transmitted to developing countries: trade and investment.

The chapter is divided into three sections. The first section deals with what globalization and the accompanying adjustment policies promised, what has been delivered and what has happened to African economies during the era of globalization. The second deals critically with some of the explanations for Africa's failure. And the last part advances an alternative explanation of the failure with respect to both trade and access to foreign finance.

The Promise of Globalization and Achievements

The promise of trade

Expanded opportunities for trade and the gains deriving from trade are probably the most enticing arguments for embracing globalization. The Structural Adjustment Programme's (SAP's) promise was that through liberalization African economies would become more competitive. As one World Bank economist, Alexander Yeats, asserts, 'If Africa is to reverse its unfavourable export trends, it must quickly adopt trade and structural adjustment policies that enhance its international competitiveness and allow African exporters to capitalize on opportunities in foreign markets' (Yeats, 1997, p24). Trade liberalization would not only increase the 'traditional exports' of individual countries but would also enable them to diversify their exports to include manufactured goods assigned to them by the law of comparative advantage as spelled out and enforced by 'market forces'. Not only would trade offer outlets for goods from economies with limited markets but, perhaps more critically, it would also permit the importation of goods that make up an important part of investment goods (especially plant and equipment) in which technology is usually embodied.

By the end of the 1990s, and after far-reaching reforms in trade policy, little had changed. The few gains registered tended to be of a one-off character, often reflecting switches from domestic to foreign markets without much increase in overall output (Ndulu et al, 1998; Helleiner, 2002a; 2002b; Mwega, 2002). Indeed some increases in exports of manufactured goods even occurred as the manufacturing sector contracted. According to Francis Ng and Alexander Yeats of the World Bank:

> *no major expansion occurred in the diversity of products exported by most of the Sub-Saharan African countries, although there are one or two exceptions like Madagascar and Kenya. Indeed, the product composition of some of the African countries' exports may have become more concentrated. Africa's recent trade performance was strongly influenced by exports of traditional products which appear to have experienced remarkably buoyant global demand in the mid-1990s.*
> (Ng and Yeats, 2000, p21)

Furthermore recent changes in Africa's exports indicate that no general increase had occurred in the number of industries in which most of the African countries have a 'revealed' comparative advantage. Indeed, after decades of reforms, the most striking trend, one that has given credence to the notion of 'marginalization of Africa', is the decline in the African share of global non-oil exports which is now less than one-half what it was in the early 1980s (Ng and Yeats, 2000) representing 'a staggering annual income loss of US$68,000 million – or 21 per cent of regional GDP' (World Bank, 2000).

The promise of additional resources

A persuasive promise made by BWIs was that adhesion to its policies would not only raise domestic investment through increased domestic savings but would relax the savings and foreign exchange constraints by allowing countries to attain higher levels of investment than would be supported by domestic savings and their own foreign exchange earnings. One central feature of adjustment policies has been financial liberalization. The focus is on the effect of interest rates on 'loanable funds' and as the price variable that adjusts to equilibrate the supply of savings to investment. The major thesis has been that 'financial repression' (which includes control of interest rates and credit rationing by the state) has discouraged savings and led to inefficient allocation of the 'loanable funds' (Shaw, 1973; Fry, 1982). The suggested solution then is that liberalization of markets would lead to positive real interest rates which would encourage savings. The 'loanable funds' thus generated would then be efficiently distributed among projects with the highest returns through the mediation of competitive financial institutions. Significantly, in this view saving precedes investment and growth. After years of adjustment there is little discernible change in the levels of savings and investment (see Table 6.1).

Perhaps even more attractive was the promise that financial liberalization would lead to increased capital inflows and stem capital flight. Indeed, most African governments' acceptance of IMF policies has been based on precisely the claimed 'catalytic effect' of agreements with IMF on the inflow of foreign capital. Governments were willing to enter the Faustian bargain of reduced national sovereignty in return for increased financial flows. Even when governments were sceptical of

Table 6.1 *Savings and investment in Africa 1975–2001:*
Periodical average (as percentage of GDP)

Indicator	1975–84	1985–89	1990–97	1998	1999	2000	2001
Gross Domestic Savings (GDS)							
SSA	19.9	15.7	16.0	14.5	15.6	18.7	17.4
SSA excl. SA & N	14.8	13.4	12.6	11.6	13.5	15.6	15
Gross National Savings (GNS)							
SSA	18.5	11.6	12.4	12.4	12.7	15.3	14.2
SSA excl. SA & N	15.3	9.2	8.6	10.7	11.3	12.7	12.6
Resource Transfers (GDS–GNS) abroad							
SSA	1.5	4.2	3.6	2.1	2.9	3.4	3.2
SSA excl. SA & N	–0.5	4.2	4.0	0.9	2.2	2.8	2.3
Gross Domestic Investment							
SSA	20.5	12.6	16.4	18.6	18.4	17.5	18.4
SSA excl. SA & N	18.3	12.9	17. 6	20.1	20.5	18.3	18.3
Resource Balance							
SSA	–1.8	0.4	–0.5	–4.1	–2.8	1.2	–1.3
SSA excl. SA & N	–5.29	–3.1	–5.2	–8.4	–7.0	–2.6	–3.8

Source: World Bank (2003a)

the developmental validity of BWIs policies, the belief that the stamp of approval of these institutions would attract foreign capital tended to dilute the scepticism.

To the surprise of the advocates of these policies and to the chagrin of African policy-makers, the response of private capital to Africa's diligent adoption of SAPs has, in the words of the World Bank, 'been disappointing'. The market 'sentiments' do not appear to have been sufficiently persuaded that the policies imposed by the BWIs have improved the attractiveness to investors. The much-touted catalytic effect of IMF conditionality has yet to assert itself. The scepticism of private investors about the BWIs stamp of approval is understandable in light of the history of non-graduation by any African country. Indeed, there is the distinct danger that, since economies under BWIs' intensive care never seem to recover, IMF presence may merely signal trouble. The BWIs seem to be unaware of the extent to which their comings and goings are a source of uncertainty among businessmen and evidence of a malaise. This said, there is, nevertheless, a trickle of foreign investment into Africa but this has not been enough to increase Africa's share in global FDI flows (see Table 6.2). The rise in foreign direct investment in the latter part of the 1990s is cited as evidence that globalization and SAPs are working (Pigato, 2000).[4] This celebration is premature. There are a number of significant features of the financial flows to Africa that should be cause for concern over their developmental impact and sustainability.

First, there is the high country concentration of investment with much of the investment going to South Africa. Secondly, there is the sectoral concentration on mining. Little of this has gone into the manufacturing industry. As for investment in mining, it is not drawn to African countries by macro-economic policy changes, as is often suggested, but by the prospects of better world prices, changes in attitudes towards national ownership and sector-specific incentives. Third, there is the problem of the type of investment. The unintended consequence of the policies has been the attraction of the least desirable form of foreign capital. Most of the new investment has taken the form of the highly speculative portfolio investment attracted by 'pull factors' that have been of a transitory nature – extremely high real domestic interest rates on Treasury Bills caused by the need to finance the budget deficit – and temporary booms in export prices which attract large export pre-financing loans (Kasekende et al, 1997). It has also been driven by acquisitions facilitated by the increased pace of privatization to buy up existing plants that are being sold usually under 'fire sales' conditions. Such investments now account for approximately 14 per cent of Foreign Direct Investment (FDI) flows into Africa.[5] Little has been driven by plans to set up new productive enterprises. Some of the new investment is for expansion of existing capacities, especially in industries enjoying natural monopolies (eg beverages, cement, furniture). Such expansion may have been stimulated by the spurt of growth that caused much euphoria and that is now fading away. It is widely recognized that direct investment is preferable to portfolio investment, and foreign investment in green field projects is preferable to acquisitions. The predominance of these types of capital inflows should be cause for concern. However, in their desperate efforts to attract foreign investment, African governments have simply ceased dealing with these risks or suggesting that they may have a preference for one type of foreign investment over others.

Finally, such investment is likely to taper off within a short span of time, as already seems to the case in a number of African countries. Thus, for Ghana, hailed as a 'success story' by the BWIs, FDI which peaked in the mid-1980s at over US$200 million annually due mainly to privatization was rapidly reversed to produce a negative outflow.[6] It should be noted, in passing, that rates of return of direct investments have generally been much higher in Africa than anywhere in other developing regions (UNCTAD, 1995; Bhattacharya et al, 1997). This, however, has not made Africa a favourite among investors, largely because of considerations of the intangible 'risk factor', nurtured by the large dose of ignorance about individual African countries. There is considerable evidence to show that Africa is systematically rated as more risky than is warranted by the underlying economic characteristics.[7]

Capital flight

Not only is Africa still severely rationed in financial markets, but during much of the globalization there is evidence that Africa is probably a net exporter of capital. Paul Collier and associates (Collier and Gunning, 1997; Collier et al, 1999) have suggested that in 1990, 40 per cent of privately held wealth was invested outside Africa and that in relation to the workforce, capital flight from Africa has been

Table 6.2 *Foreign direct investment inflows by host region and economy,*
1982–2002 (millions of dollars, except rows 5–7 which are percentages)

	1982–87	1988–94	1995	1996	1997
1. Developing Countries & SA	19,694	54,540	116,132	150,577	197,041
2. Sub-Saharan Africa	1,059	2,150	3,964	3,815	7,951
3. SSA w/o South Africa	1,034	2,075	2,723	2,997	4,134
4. SSA w/o SA & Nigeria	655	966	1,644	1,403	2,594
2/1	5.4	3.9	3.4	2.5	4.0
3/1	5.3	3.8	2.3	2.0	2.1
4/1	3.3	1.8	1.4	0.9	1.3
	1998	1999	2000	2001	2002
1. Developing Countries & SA	191,845	230,798	246,944	216,220	162,899
2. Sub-Saharan Africa	6,046	8,663	5,364	13,295	7,452
3. SSA w/o South Africa	5,485	7,161	4,476	6,506	6,698
4. SSA w/o SA & Nigeria	4,433	6,156	3,546	5,402	5,416
2/1	3.2	3.8	2.2	6.1	4.6
3/1	2.9	3.1	1.8	3.0	4.1
4/1	2.3	2.7	1.4	2.5	3.3

Source: UNCTAD (2003)

much higher than in other developing country groups. In a recent more systematic attempt to measure the extent of capital flight, James Boyce and Léonce Ndikumana show that for the period 1970–96 capital flight from sub-Saharan Africa was US$193 billion, and with imputed interests the amount goes up to US$285 billion. These figures should be compared with the combined debt of these countries which stood at US$178 billion in 1996 (see Table 6.2). Their conclusion is worth citing at length:

> *The evidence presented in this essay leads to a startling conclusion: far from being heavily indebted, many sub-Saharan African countries are net creditors vis-à-vis the rest of the world. This is because their private external assets, as measured by cumulative capital flight, are greater than their public external debts. For the 25-country sample as a whole, external assets exceed external debts by US$14.5 billion to US$106.5 billion, depending on whether we count imputed interest earnings on the asset side. Region's assets are 1.1 to 1.6 times the stock of debts. For some individual countries, the results are even more dramatic. Nigeria's external assets are 2.8 times its external debt by the conservative measure, and 4.1 times higher when we include imputed interest earnings on capital flight.* (Boyce and Ndikumana, 2000, p32)

So far financial liberalization has not done much to turn the tide. In a World Bank study of the effects of financial liberalization in nine African countries, Devajaran et al (1999) conclude that the effects of liberalization on capital flight are 'very small'. In response to this failure to reverse capital flight, the World Bank economists now argue that the capital flight may indeed be good for Africa:

> *The much-denigrated capital flight out of Africa may well have been a rational response to low returns at home… Indeed Africans are probably better off having made external investments than they would have been if they invested solely at home!* (Devajaran et al, 1999, pp15–16)

The conclusion ignores the obvious fact that the social benefits of citizens investing in their own country may exceed the private benefits accruing to individuals.

All this indicates that financial liberalization in itself may not be the panacea for reducing capital flight. Effective policy measures to reduce capital flight in the African context may need much deeper and more fundamental changes in the economic and political systems. One policy implication of both the reluctance of foreign capital to come to Africa and the huge amounts of wealth held outside Africa has been the calls for policies intended not so much to attract foreign capital but Africa's own private capital. While this is a valid option, the political economy of such attraction and the specific direct policy measures called for are rarely spelled out.[8]

The Failed Promise of Growth

A comparison between Africa's economic performance during the period over which globalization is often said to have taken hold – the last two decades of the 20th century – and earlier periods shows clearly that thus far globalization has not produced rates of growth higher than those of the 1960s and 1970s (see Figure 6.1). Per income growth was negative over the two decades, a serious indictment to those who have steered policies over the decades. This slower rate of growth is not peculiar to Africa as is suggested by some of the 'Afro-pessimist' literature. During the period of globalization economic growth rates have fallen across the board for all groups of countries. The poorest group went from a per capita GDP growth rate of 1.9 per cent annually in 1960–80, to a decline of 0.5 per cent per year (1980–2000). For the middle group (which includes mostly poor countries), there was a sharp decline from an annual per capita growth rate of 3.6 per cent to just less than 1 per cent. Over a 20-year period, this represents the difference between doubling income per person, versus increasing it by just 21 per cent. The other groups also showed substantial declines in growth rates (Weisbrot et al, 2000a; 2000b; 2001). The global decline in growth is largely due to deflationary bias in orthodox stabilization programmes imposed by International Financial Institutions (IFIs).[9]

Explaining the Poor Performance: Has Africa Adjusted?

The poor performance of Africa with respect to the channels through which the positive effects of globalization would be gained (ie increased access to markets

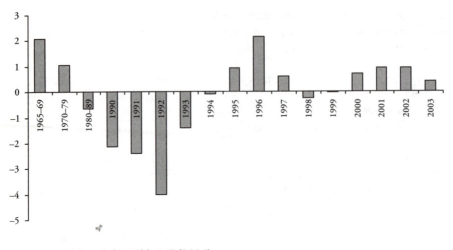

Sources: World Bank (2003b); IMF (2004)

Figure 6.1 *African countries' annual growth rates in GDP per capita, 1965–2002*

and finance) is now widely accepted. There are, however, disagreements over the cause of the failure. The BWIs have adhered to two explanations.

The first one is simply that African countries have rather incomprehensibly persisted with their doomed 'dirigiste' ways and refused to swallow the bitter but necessary pills of adjustment. Inadequate implementation of reforms and recidivism are some of the most common themes running through the literature on African economic policy. In the 1994 report (World Bank, 1994) the World Bank's view was that adjustment was 'incomplete' not because of any faults in the design of the programmes but because of lack of implementation.

The second explanation was that insufficient time had elapsed to reap the gains of adjustment and, therefore, of globalization. Coming from the BWIs, this is a strange position. It was these very institutions that, in dismissing the structuralist argument on the inelasticity of the response of developing countries to economic stimuli, claimed that liberalization would elicit immediate and substantial responses and bring about 'accelerated development' (the promise of the Berg Report (World Bank, 1981)). Indeed, in the early years, the World Bank was so certain about the response to its policies that it measured economic success by simply looking at the policy stance and assuming that this axiomatically led to growth (Mosley et al, 1995).

Today, there is recognition that the axiomatic mapping of policies into performance was naïve and misleading. There are admissions, albeit grudging, to having underestimated the external constraints on policy and the vulnerability of African economies to them. Equally the responsiveness of the economies and the private sector has been overestimated, while the wrong sequence of policies eroded state capacities and responsibilities ('policy ownership'). However it is still insisted that the passage of time will do its job and the posture recommended to African countries has been to sit tight and wait for the outpouring of gains. There is no recognition that the accumulated effects of past policy errors may have made the implementation of 'market friendly' policies in their pristine form more difficult.

By the second half of the 1990s neither of these arguments carried any weight. African countries have made far more adjustments than any other global region. Indeed the BWIs themselves began to point proudly to the success of their pro-grammes, suggesting that enough time had transpired and a large number of Afri-can countries had persevered in their adjustment to begin to reap the fruits of the adjustment process. IMF officials talked about a 'turning point'(Fischer et al, 1998) and that the positive per capita growth rates of 1995–97 (4.1 per cent) 'reflected better policies in many African countries rather than favourable exogenous devel-opments' (Hernández-Catá, 2000). According to Fischer et al:

> *Important structural reforms have been implemented in many African economies in this decade: domestic price controls have been abolished or at least liberalised in several countries; some inefficient price controls have been abolished or at least liberalised in several countries; some inefficient public monopolies have been dis-mantled; and a large number of state enterprises have been privatised. In the external sector, non-tariff barriers have been eliminated in most SSA countries and import duties have been lowered in some, exchange rates have been freed and unified in most countries (with Nigeria a major exception); and restrictions on payments and transfers for current international transactions have been eliminated in 31 out of 54 of SSA countries. Most countries also have eliminated direct con-trols on bank credit and have established market-determined interest rates.* (Fischer et al, 1998)

President of the World Bank James Wolfensohn, for example, reported in his 1997 address to the Board of Governors that there was progress in sub-Saharan Africa, 'with new leadership and better economic policies' (Wolfensohn, 1997). Michel Camdessus, the then Managing Director of the International Monetary Fund, at the 1996 annual meeting of the World Bank and the IMF, said, 'Africa, for which so many seem to have lost hope, appears to be stirring and on the move.' The two vice presidents for Africa at the World Bank, Callisto Madavo and Jean-Louis Sar-bib, wrote an article, appropriately titled 'Africa on the Move: Attracting Private Capital to a Changing Continent' (Madavo and Sarbib, 1997), which gave rea-sons for this new 'cautious optimism'. The then Deputy Managing Director of the International Monetary Fund, Alassane Quattara, would say the following about the good performance: 'A key underlying contribution has come from progress made in macroeconomic stabilization and the introduction of sweeping structural reforms' (Quattara, 1997). The major World Bank report on Africa of 2000 stated 'many countries have made major gains in macroeconomic stabilisation, particu-larly since 1994' and there had been a turn around because of 'ongoing structural adjustment throughout the region which has opened markets and has a major impact on productivity, exports, and investment' (World Bank, 2000, p21). Even the Economic Commission for Africa (ECA), a strident critic of SAP in the past, joined the chorus.[10]

And so by the end of the millennium, African countries had been largely adjusted. There can be no doubt that there has been a sea-change in the African policy landscape. Africa is very heavily involved in 'globalization' and is very much part of the global order and much of the policy-making during the last two decades has been designed deliberately to increase Africa's participation in the global economy. In any case, more devaluations, lowering of tariffs and privatization of marketing were imposed in Africa then anywhere else. By the mid-980s, with the exception of the franc zone countries, most SSA countries had adopted flexible exchange rates policies and there had been major real exchange rate depressions. Major reforms in marketing, including the abolition of marketing boards, had been introduced. Arguments that African countries had refused or been slow to adjust or that enough time had not transpired became less credible, especially in light of the celebratory and self-congratulatory remarks by the BWIs themselves.

However, by 1997 the growth rates had begun to falter. By 1999, in its report on global prospects and the developing countries, the World Bank made a downward revision of the 1999 growth rate 'despite continued improvements in political and economic fundamentals'. The report blamed the poor performance on terms of trade and the Asian crisis. In a sense we had been there before. 'Success stories' have been told many times before and countries have fretted and strutted on this 'success' stage only to be heard of no more. Twenty-six sub-Saharan countries have been, at one time or another, on the lists compiled by the IFIs (see Table 6.3). The terms used have included 'strong adjusters', 'early intensive adjusters', 'globalizers' etc. Of the 15 countries listed as 'core adjusters' by the World Bank in 1993, only three (Lesotho, Nigeria and Uganda) appear in the list of strong performers in 1998 (UNCTAD, 1998). As in the past, the new 'success' or 'recovery' or 'turnaround' was of a one-off nature and attributable to a whole range of things that have little to do with policies – improvements in terms of trade, new sourcing strategies of mining conglomerates, end of conflicts and favourable climate.

Rather than abandon the deflationary policies, supporters of adjustment have simply reframed the question to read: 'Why is it that when the recommended policies are put into place (often under the guidance of – and pressure from – the International Monetary Fund and the World Bank) the hoped for results do not materialise quickly' (Clague, 1997, p1). The answer was: lack of 'good Governance' and of 'good Institutions'. These assertions conceal a clear loss of certainty and a growing sense of intellectual disarray. This is apparent in the World Bank study, *Can Africa Claim the 21st Century?* (World Bank, 2000). Unlike earlier approaches, the report speaks in a much more subdued and less optimistic tone, based more on faith than analysis. There is an admission, albeit grudging, that policies of the past have not worked. The new agenda is much more eclectic and more a reflection of confusion and loss of faith than the discovery of a coherent, comprehensive policy framework. The additional set of reforms is nebulous, eclectic and largely of a more political and institutional character – good governance, participation of and consultation with civil society, democracy etc. Increasingly the World Bank's new solutions suggest that there is little to be done by way of reform on the economic front. The World Bank's projection of African economic performance in the coming decade is depressing reading:

Despite the growth slow-down of the late 1990s, recent performance continues to support the view that fundamental structural change and institutions strengthening will have significant impact on sub-Saharan prospects. The forecast is for a halt to the region's lengthy decline and marginalisation and even for moderate reversal: The longer term (2003–10) outlook is for sustained GDP growth – 3.7 per cent – with per capita income rising 1.3 per cent per year. The primary driving force behind the outlook remains better governance and ongoing reforms to the policy environment. (World Bank, 2001, p152)

Table 6.3 *'Good adjusters', 1981–98*

Country	Number of times listed
Malawi	7
Uganda	5
Kenya	5
Madagascar	4
Ghana	4
Zambia	3
Tanzania	3
Mauritania	3
Mali	3
Côte d'Ivoire	3
Zimbabwe	2
Togo	2
Senegal	2
Nigeria	2
Niger	2
Mozambique	2
Cameroon	2
Burundi	2
Burkina Faso	2
Zaire	1
Namibia	1
Mauritius	1
Lesotho	1
Gambia	1
Chad	1
Benin	1

Sources: Several World Bank reports

Africa Maladjusted: The Low-growth Path

As we noted earlier, adjustment has not led to the promised 'resource mobilization'. The response of the BWIs to the poor performance in resource mobilization has been ambiguous, to say the least. At times they have expressed concern over the decline of investment but blamed it on inflation, the low after-tax, risk-adjusted rate of return on capital which, in turn, has been attributed to macro-economic instability, loss of assets owing to unenforceability of contracts, debt overhang and physical destruction caused by armed conflicts (Hernández-Catá, 2000); at other times this fall in investment has been seen as a temporary phase during which efficient use of existing capacity matters more than accumulation of new capital. Once the economy is placed on an efficient path, it will begin to accumulate, so the argument goes. The BWIs have now reached the conclusion that African economic growth does not respond to investment and that maybe there is 'over-investment' in Africa. In a World Bank paper entitled 'Is investment in Africa Too Low or Too High? Macro and Micro Evidence', Devajaran et al (1999) argue that they find no evidence that private and public capital are productive investments in Africa either in cross-country data or in country case studies. They conclude:

> *First, we should be more careful about calling for an investment boom to resume growth in Africa. Unless some or all of the underlying factors that made investment unproductive in the past are addressed, the results may be disappointing. We should also be more circumspect about Africa's low savings rate. Perhaps the low savings rate was due to the fact that the returns to investment were so low. Also the relatively high levels of capital flight from Africa may have been a rational response to the lack of investment opportunities at home.* (Devajaran et al, 1999, p23)

The patently absurd result comes from the failure to consider the possibility that, given the errors of the past and the maladjustment of the African economies, a much larger 'Big Push' may be required to get African economies on a path in which economies respond to investment. It also fails to take into account that patterns of investment induced by SAPs may not be the kinds associated with high economic growth. Although some of the recent literature modifies the 'capital fundamentalist' argument on the primacy of investment, it continues to place capital accumulation at the centre of the growth process. And in any case investment, growth and productivity tend to move in tandem. Second, in the pre-adjustment era, investment was associated with relatively high growth and significant total factor productivity gains in a significant number of countries.[11] One would therefore have to explain what it is in the adjustment process that produced what is patently an atypical response to investment.

To understand Africa's poor performance in terms of the two channels of globalization – trade and finance – we have to understand the interactions between these and economic growth. The usual procedure is to regress growth on initial conditions, GDP, state variables and policy instruments. In these models export performance and investment rates would be determinants of growth in a unidirectional way. There is a rich theoretical and empirical literature that points to the potential explanatory power of reverse direction by suggesting a more simultaneous process in which the usual 'determinants' of growth are themselves determined by growth.

Slow growth and resource mobilization

Let us start with the investment–savings nexus. Earlier literature by such Keynesians as Michael Kalecki and Nicholas Kaldor suggested that the causal chain may be from growth to both investment and savings and not the other way around. The Kaleckian 'flexible accelerator' view that capital needs are essentially determined by expected output (ie investment demand is driven by expected growth) is a case in point. 'Endogenous growth theories' have revised interest in this matter by suggesting that some of the 'determinants of growth' may themselves be dependent on growth.

Writing on private saving rates Loayza et al (2000) conclude that private saving rates rise with the level and growth rate of real per capita income. Furthermore, the influence of income is larger in developing than in developed countries where a doubling of income per capita is estimated, other things being equal, to raise the long-term private saving rate by some 10 per cent of disposable income. Likewise, a 1 per cent rise in the growth rate raises the private saving rate by a similar amount. In a study of savings transitions, Dani Rodrik argues that there is strong evidence that economic growth tends to have a clear positive effect on the saving rate (Rodrik, 1997). In the specifically African case, Elbadawi and Mwega (2000) and Mlambo and Oshikoya (2001) reach generally similar conclusions, namely that 'causality runs from growth to investment and saving'. The important policy conclusion to this is that that policies that spur development are an indirect but effective way to raise private saving rates and the 'negative focus on saving performance does not seem to be a profitable strategy for understanding successful economic performance' (Rodrik, 2000b, p505).[12]

In this neo-Keynesian view, the poor response of private investors – both domestic and foreign – should not have come as a surprise, what with contractions of domestic markets through deflationary policies and increased competition from imported goods, the collapse of public services and infrastructure and the political uncertainty engendered by policies that have undermined the 'social pacts' that hitherto provided some modicum of social cohesion. And so, despite the fact that a number of countries had been 'adjusted', new credits were not forthcoming. That was mainly because investors did not have the confidence that the countries' growth performances would improve and that the potential returns on their investments would fully materialize, because improvements in trade surplus were caused primarily by demand-repression and deflationary policies. For the BWIs the major explanation for poor response of foreign investment is 'risk' – a not particularly useful piece of information. It seems to me that the greatest 'risk' for investors is investing their money in economies under the grip of policies designed to achieve stabilization (Bird, 2001).[13] It is perhaps this sluggish growth that accounts for the fact that the Institutional Investor rating of Africa deteriorated from 31.8 per cent in 1979 to 21.7 in 1995 (the range is 1–

100) (Collier and Gunning, 1997). It is significant that the two countries that performed well with respect to this index were high-growth economies which were not under the grip of the deflationary policies: Botswana and Mauritius. It is on the basis of these theoretical arguments and empirical observations that there have been calls for an 'investment-led' adjustment process (Mkandawire and Soludo, 1999; Griffin, 2001).

Trade, low growth and absence of structural change

The slow growth discussed above has also had an impact on the growth of exports and diversification by weakening the investment–export nexus crucial to the process. Here again, the orthodox view has been that increased trade or openness measured in various ways is a determinant of growth. Consequently, the major policies with respect to trade have involved trade liberalization and adjustments in exchange rates largely through devaluation.

The failure on the trade front is linked to the failure in the structural transformation of African economies so that they could produce new sets of commodities in a competitive and flexible way. Globalization in Africa has been associated with industrial stagnation and even de-industrialization (Mkandawire, 1988; Stein, 1992; Stewart, 1994). African economies were the quintessential 'late latecomers' in the process of industrialization. I have argued elsewhere (Mkandawire, 1988) that although the writing on African economies is based on the assumption that Africa had pursued import substitution for too long, the phase of import substitution was in fact extremely short – in most countries it was less than a decade.[14] SAPs have called for policies that have prematurely exposed African industries to global competition and thus induced widespread processes of de-industrialization. African economies have somehow been out of sync with developments in other parts of the world. When most economies embarked on import substitution industrialization, financed by either borrowing or debt default, much of Africa was under colonial rule, which permitted neither protection of domestic markets nor running of deficits. And even later when much of industrialization was financed through Eurodollar loans, Africans were generally reluctant borrowers so that eventually much of their borrowing in the 1980s was not for industrialization but to finance balance-of-payments problems.

Every case of successful penetration of international markets has been preceded by a phase when import substitution industrialization was pursued. Such a phase is necessary not simply for the 'infant industry' arguments that have been stated ad infinitum, but also because they provide an institutional capacity for handling entirely new set of economic activities. The phase is also necessary for sorting out some of the coordination failures that need to be addressed before venturing into global markets. A 'revisionist' view argues three main points. First, that substantial growth was achieved during the phase of import substitution industrialization; second, that even successful 'export oriented economies' had to pass through this phase and maintain many features of the import substitution (IS) phase; and finally that important social gains were made.

The IS phase did lead to the initial phases of industrialization. Significantly, UNIDO notes that African countries were increasingly gaining comparative advantage in labour intensive branches, as indicated by revealed comparative advantage (RCA) but then notes:

> *It is particularly alarming to note that the rank correlation of industrial branches by productivity growth over 1980–95 and RCA value in 1995 is very low. Productivity has fallen in furniture, leather, footwear, clothing, textiles, and food manufacturing. An export oriented development strategy cannot directly stimulate Total Factor Productivity (TFP). Policy must focus on increasing technological progress within the export industries – many of which have seen very rapid progress in the application of the most modern technologies (informatics, biotechnological, etc) to their production and distribution system.* (UNIDO, 1999, p245)

Given the conviction that import substitution in Africa was bad and had gone on for too long, there was no attempt to see how existing industries could be the basis for new initiatives for export. The policy was simply to discard existing capacity on the wrong assumption that it was the specific micro-economic policies used to encourage the establishment of these industries that accounted for failure at the macro-level. The task should have been to extend and not reverse such gains by dismantling existing industrial capacity. The rates of growth of manufacturing value added (MVA) have fallen continuously from the levels in the 1970s. UNIDO estimated that MVA in sub-Saharan Africa was actually contracting at an annual average rate of 1.0 per cent during 1990–97. UNIDO shows that for Africa as a whole in ten industrial branches in 38 countries labour productivity declined to an index value of 93 in 1995 (1990 = 100). Increases in productivity were registered only in tobacco, beverages and structural clay products. In many cases, an increase in productivity has been caused by a fall in employment growth (UNIDO).

The decline in total factor productivity of the economy as a whole is attributed to de-industrialization which it defines as 'synonymous with productivity growth deceleration'. Output per head in sub-Saharan manufacturing fell from US$7924 in 1990 to US$6762 in 1996. The structural consequence is that the share of manufacturing in GDP has fallen in two-thirds of the countries (Figure 6.2). The number of countries falling below the median has increased from 19 during 1985–90 to 31 during the 1991–98 period. While admitting such poor performance in manufacturing industry during the era of structural adjustment, supporters of SAP argue that such decline in industrialization is a temporary and welcome process of weeding out inefficient industrialization (Jalilian and Weiss, 2000) and also that insufficient time for adjustment has passed to ensure benefits from globalization through the establishment of new industries. Considering that this argument has been repeatedly deployed since 1985, Africa may have to wait for a long time before the gains from globalization materialize.

Students of historical structural changes of economies inform us that structural change is both cause and effect of economic growth. As Moshe Syrquin (Syrquin, 1994; see also Syrquin, 1995) observes, a significant share of the measured rate of aggregate total factor productivity is owing to resource shifts from sectors with low productivity to sectors with high productivity. We have learnt from the 'new trade theories' and studies on technological development how countries run the risk of being 'locked' in a permanently slow-growth trajectory if they follow the dictates of static comparative advantage.

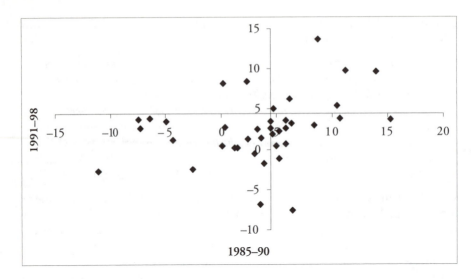

Source: World Bank (2000)
Note: Each point on the graph represents one African country's growth rate for value added in manufactured goods during 1991–98 as a percentage of what it was during 1985–90. The axes are drawn to pass through the median of the 1985–90 period.

Figure 6.2 *Comparative rates of growth of manufactured value added*

To move away from such a path, governments have introduced policies that generate externalities for a wide range of other industries and thus place the economy on more growth-inducing engagement with the rest of the world. For years, UNCTAD economists have pointed to the importance of growth for trade expansion. They have argued that it is the absence of growth, or more specifically an investment–export nexus that accounts for the failure of many countries to expand and diversify their export base. Rapid resource reallocation may not be feasible without high rates of growth and investment.[15] The principle means for effecting export diversification is investment. Many empirical tests of 'causation' have been conducted and suggest that there are good theoretical and empirical grounds for taking the reverse causation seriously as the dynamics of high growth lead to even greater human and physical investment and greater knowledge formation; which, by Verdoon's Law, leads to more productivity and therefore greater competitiveness.

Experience of successful export drives clearly shows a strong relationship between rates of structural change and rates of growth in value added in manufacturing and the rates of growth of exports. Lessons from countries that have embraced trade liberalization and achieved some degree of success suggest clearly that liberalization should be in conjunction with policies that ensure that relative prices will be favourable to export industries (and not just to non-tradables) and that interest rates will support investment and economic restructuring. Successful export promotion strategies have required a deliberate design of an investment–export nexus. Diversification of exports that is developmental needs to go beyond the multiplication of primary commodities and include industrial products. This requires not merely the redirection of existing industrial output to the external but the expansion of such output and investment in new activities. There is a need to design a system of incentives that favours investments that open up new possibilities or introduce new technologies to the country. In this respect infrastructure and human resource development are important preconditions for the success of pro-export policies.

The instruments used to promote investment have included not only public investment but also the provision of subsidized inputs by public enterprises, direct subsidies through tax incentives including exemptions from duties, industrial policy which, in turn, has meant selective allocation of credit and encouragement of investment by cheapening imported investment goods (often by manipulation of exchange rates in favour of the import of plant and equipment and export sector) (Bradford Jr, 1990; Akyüz, 1996). While 'diversification' has always featured in virtually all adjustment programmes, there has been no clear spelling out how this was to be achieved. In most cases, the need for diversification was overshadowed by the short-term pressures to exploit static 'revealed' comparative advantage and reduce public spending. The failure to stimulate new economic activities (especially industrial ones) has meant not only sluggish growth in exports but also failure to diversify.

Under SAP all these instruments have been off limits. Evidence that more successful cases have had some kind of 'industrial policy' has been dismissed on the grounds that African countries had neither the type of government nor the political acumen to prevent 'capture' of these policies by rent-seekers and patron–client networks. Governments have been left with no instrument for stimulating investment and industrial development directly or for creating an environment for robust demand and profitability in which investment, or complementary public inputs such as infrastructure, research and development, education and training, could thrive. It is this passivity that has led to failure for structural transformation and the establishment of an investment–export nexus that would have led to increase and diversification of exports.

Thus, the name given to the policies packages of the BWIs notwithstanding, the 'structural adjustment process has not led to structural changes in Africa'. At first glance, one can see signs of structural change, especially in the decreased shares of industrial and agricultural sectors in overall GDP and the significant increase in services. Such change would seem to be following the norms established by Simon Kuznets and other observers of the structural change in the process of economic development. However, in the case of Africa such an interpretation is misleading because the transformation taking place is perverse, reflecting, as it does, stagnation of the economy, de-industrialization and poor agriculture performance rather than structural change induced by differential productivity gains and changing demand structures induced by increasing incomes (by way of Engel's Law). The expansion of the service sector is evidence of growing informalization, pauperization of the middle classes and 'compradorization' of African economies. Structural adjustment in Africa has thus far meant reversing some of the structural changes that African governments sought to induce as countries are driven back to the production patterns of the colonial era through 'back to the future' adjustment of African economies and through the process of 'de-industrialization'(Singh,

1987; Mkandawire, 1988; Stein, 1992). Ghana is back as the 'Gold Coast' and Zambia is desperately trying to cling to its copper belt.

One should add here that the negative effects of this deflationary process also work through the trade mechanism. For African economies, terms of trade have enormous effects on the performance of economies, a fact that the World Bank now increasingly recognizes as unfavourable trade conditions scuttle its own programme. World Bank economist William Easterly, in an article tellingly entitled 'The Lost Decades: Developing Countries Stagnation in Spite of Policy Reform, 1980–1998' (Easterly, 2001), reaches conclusions that would warm the heart of any member of the 'Dependence School'. In his paper he considers as possible explanations of the poor performance of developing countries the following factors:

- good policies that did not achieve desired results;
- bad economic policies; or
- some third factor like shocks?

Based on his evidence – cross-country regressions and comparison of turning points that relate events in the rich countries to those in the developing countries – his conclusion is that the most likely explanation was point 3. The principal shock he finds was the 'growth slowdown in the industrial world'.

In conclusion, in a situation of generalized low growth rates, Africa is unlikely to experience much diversification. General policies such as 'marked liberalization' or exchange rate devaluations, while perhaps supportive of diversification, are unlikely to induce the shifts in resources essential to tangible diversification.[16] This is because there are structural factors that attenuate responsiveness to new opportunities. The decline of Africa's share in world trade is thus closely related to low levels of growth which in turn is related to de-industrialization. Or as Gerald Helleiner succinctly states, 'Africa's failures have been developmental, not *export* failure per se' (Helleiner, 2002a, p4). Hence failure in trade cannot be explained by simply looking at trade policies. One has to look at the overall growth of the economies and ensuing structural change. As Dani Rodrik (1997) notes, Africa's 'marginalization' is not caused by trade ratios (relative to GDP) that are low by cross-national standards: Africa trades as much as is to be expected given its geography and its level of per capita income. Indeed there is the evidence that suggests that 'Africa overtrades compared with other developing regions in the sense that its trade is higher than would be expected from the various determinants of bilateral trade' (Foroutan and Pritchet, 1993; Coe and Hoffmaister, 1999).[17]

The marginalization of Africa in world trade is the consequence of two factors: first, Africa's GDP per capita has grown slower than other regions; and second, the output elasticity of trade exceeds unity, so that as other countries have grown, their trade volumes have expanded more than proportionately. The dismissal of deliberate, strategic industrial and trade policies to shape Africa's position in the global trading system has left Africa on the low-productivity, low-growth path. The policy implications of this perspective are to stimulate growth, invest in infrastructure and human capital.

WTO context

Africa is the only continent for which it was explicitly predicted that the advent of the WTO trade regime would entail losses. Most of these losses related to trade issues – most specifically the loss of preferential treatment from its erstwhile colonial masters and the European Union under the Lomé Conventions. There is one feature of globalization that Africa's industrialization aspirations will have to confront – the restrictive policy context of the global financial and trade regimes. Much of the industrialization that has taken place elsewhere has been supported by explicit or implicit industrial policy. Both the import substitution and export promotion of the post-World War II period has been the product of industrial policy. New trade arrangements, of which the WTO is emblematic, have changed the environment for industrial policy.

There is considerable debate as to what globalization entails in terms of individual states' capacity to pursue their own development strategies. From one end it is argued that while during much of the post-World War II era, the global order allowed states considerable room for manoeuvre to pursue such national goals as full employment or growth and development, the current wave of globalization has significantly reduced the leverage of governments over the economy. The institutional arrangement said to signal this changed environment for industrial policy is the WTO. Thus it is argued that WTO has changed the environment for development and restricted policy options to promote industry and trade in a manner comparable to pulling up the ladder. A whole range of policies that have been central to virtually every strategy of industrialization are now off limits (Panchamukhi, 1996; Adelman and Yeldan, 2000; Rodrik, 2000a). In other words, while clearly the new world order demands highly intensive involvement by the state in industrialization, the regulatory regimes deny the state the means for such intervention. For the 'late industrializers' such as African countries it is clear that the international trade regime to which they are now tethered makes it extremely difficult for these economies to capture the potential gains from global markets.

This view has been challenged by some authors who argue that the WTO regime still leaves room for catching up, and that developing countries can still embark on deliberate industrialization by exploiting some of the special provisions reserved in the WTO arrangements. Amsden (1999), who has written extensively on the role of industrial policy in the East Asian context, argues that the WTO regime still leaves room for industrial policy initiatives. For Peter Evans, WTO is something still in the making and there is, therefore, the possibility that it can be shaped to serve the interests of developing countries. Adelman and Yeldan (2000), who list the major constraints imposed by WTO on development policy, argue that paradoxically the new regime allows direct government investment in new activities and non-market pressures on individual private firms to develop new types of comparative advantage. This may lead to greater intervention and more targeted discretionary activities by governments wishing to develop their economies (Adelman and Yeldan, 2000).

This debate may ultimately be a fruitless one, given the multiplicity of fora in which 'negotiations' on global issues takes place. Often concessions made in one forum are eroded or nullified by the conditionalities imposed in another forum.

Thus even the interventionist measures which Adelman points to as policy options not disallowed by WTO may simply be off limits under IMF and World Bank adjustment programmes and conditionalities. A country cannot refuse to open all its markets as demanded by the BWIs by appealing to WTO exemptions. Pressures for trade liberalization and the anti-industrial stance of the BWIs institutions have whittled away the positive effects of the provisions that would allow the poor countries to protect their infant industries. This has been particularly so for sub-Saharan Africa which has undoubtedly been subjected to more conditionalities per capita than any other region[18] and where structural adjustment has tended to make it impossible to exploit the special concessions made to African countries in the international agreements such as WTO or Lomé Conventions.

Concluding Remarks

The African policy landscape has changed radically during the last two decades. Liberalization of trade, privatization and reliance on markets have replaced the widespread state controls associated with import substitution. One would expect by now to see some signs of the 'accelerated development' promised by the Berg report in 1981. That adjustment has failed as a prerequisite for development, let alone as a 'strategy for accelerated development', is now widely accepted.[19] These failures can, in turn, be traced to the displacement of developmental strategic thinking by 'an obsession' with stabilization – a point underscored by low levels of investment and institutional sclerosis. The key 'fundamentals' that policy has sought to establish relate to these financial concerns rather than to development. The singular concentration on 'opening' up the economy has undermined post-independence efforts to create, albeit lamely, internally coherent and articulated economies and an industrial structure that would be the basis for eventual diversification of Africa's export base. The excessive emphasis on servicing the external sector has diverted scarce resources and political capacities away from managing the more fundamental basis for economic development. Even the issue of 'poverty' has received little attention, except perhaps when it has seemed politically expedient to be seen to be doing something to mitigate the negative effects of adjustment. SAP, owing to its deflationary bias, has placed African economies on such a low-growth trajectory, which has then conditioned the levels and types of Africa's participation in the global economy.

Over the last two decades, Africans have been faced with not merely a set of pragramatic measures but a full-blown ideological position about the role of the state, about nationalism and about equity, against which many neo-liberals, including Elliot Berg, had ranted for years.[20] It is this ideological character of the proposals that has made them impervious to empirical evidence including that generated by the World Bank itself and it is this that has made policy dialogue virtually impossible. The insistence of 'true believers' on the basic and commonsense message they carry has made dialogue impossible. The assumption that those on the other side are merely driven by self-interest and ignorance that might be remediable by 'capacity building' has merely complicated matters further. Things have not been made easier by the supplicant position of African governments and their obvious failures to manage their national affairs well. These policies were presented as finite processes which would permit countries to restore growth. With this time perspective in mind, countries were persuaded to put aside long-term strategic considerations while they sorted out some short-term problems. The finite process has lasted two decades.

There are obvious gains to participation in increased exchange with the rest of the world. The bone of contention is: what specific measures should individual countries adopt in order to reap the benefits of increased exchange with other nations? With perhaps a few cases, developing countries have always sought to gain from international trade. Attempts to diversify the export base have been a key aspect of policy since independence. Import substitution was not a strategy for autarky as is often alleged but a phase in eventual export diversification. However, for years the integration of developing countries into a highly unequal economic order was considered problematic, characterized as it is by unfavourable terms of trade for primary commodities, control of major markets by gigantic conglomerates, protectionism in the markets in the developed countries together with 'dumping' of highly subsidized agricultural products, volatile commodity and financial markets, asymmetries in access to technology etc. From this perspective gains from trade could only be captured by strategizing and dynamizing a country's linking up with the rest of the world.

It is ironic that while analysis in the 'pre-globalization' period took the impact of external factors on economic growth seriously, the era of globalization has tended to concentrate almost exclusively on internal determinants of economic performance. Today, Africa's dependence on external factors and the interference in the internal affairs of African countries by external actors are most transparent and most humiliating and yet such dependence remains untheorized. Theories that sought to relate Africa's economies to external factors have been discredited, abandoned or, at best, placed on the defensive. The focus now is almost entirely on internal determinants of economic performance – economic policies, governance, rent-seeking and ethnic diversity.

While the attention on internal affairs may have served as a useful corrective to the excessive focus on the external, it also provides a partial view of African economies and can be partly blamed for the pursuit of policies that were blind to Africa's extreme dependence and vulnerability to external conjuncture – a fact that the BWIs have learnt as exogenous factors scuttled their adjustment programmes. Indeed, unwilling to discard its essentially deflationary policies and faced with poor performance among many countries which have been 'strong adjusters', the World Bank's explanations have become increasingly more structuralist-deterministic and eclectic. Even the IMF in the latest World Economic Outlook explains Africa's poor performance in surprisingly structuralist language as it notes that the 'resilience' of growth in recent years 'partly reflected more favourable developments in non fuel commodity prices, which did not contract as much as in earlier global slowdowns, as well as debt relief under the HIPC initiative'. The IMF also notes that, despite the trend towards improved macroeconomic policies in many African countries, 'external current account deficits in many countries in sub-Saharan Africa remain relatively high, reflecting in part continued high debt levels but also low savings rates related to low per capita incomes and structural impediments to economic diversification' (IMF, 2004).

It is now admitted that many mistakes have been made during the past two decades. When errors are admitted, the consequences of such errors are never spelled out. Economists increasingly use the concept of *hysteresis*[21] to account for any 'path dependence' of the state of economic variables on the past history of the economic system or policies. In explaining the failure of their policies, the BWIs argue that past (before-adjustment) policy errors have a lasting effect through hysteresis. Strangely, no such hysteresis is entertained for policies pursued by the BWIs in the recent past. Policy failures, especially those as comprehensive as those of SAPs, can continue to have effects on the performance of the economy long after policy failures are abandoned. It may well be that the accretions of errors that are often perfunctorily admitted have created *maladjusted* economies not capable of gaining much from globalization. Both the measures of 'success' used for African economies and the projections for the future suggest that essentially the BWIs have put Africa's development on hold. This clearly suggests the extreme urgency of Africans themselves assuming the task of 'bringing development back in' in their respective countries and collectively. To benefit from interacting with the rest of the world, African policy-makers will have to recognize the enormous task of correcting the maladjustment of their economies. They will have to introduce more explicit, more subtle and more daring policies to stimulate growth, trade and export diversification than hitherto.

Notes

1. This chapter is also published, slightly revised, as 'Maladjusted Economies and Globalisation', in *Africa Development*, vol 30, nos 1–2, 2005, CODESRIA, Dakar.
2. The author would like to thank Virginia Rodriquez and Nina Torm for research assistance.
3. There is something illogical about juxtaposing globalization and marginalization. Either the process is 'global' and encompasses all spaces on the globe or is only partial, marginalizing certain sections of the planet. Globalization does not necessarily mean that everyone gains; it entails gains and losers, core and periphery, top and bottom, etc. African economies are encompassed by and subordinate to the global economy. Indeed it leaves open the possibility of adverse globalization; as Stanley Fischer, discussing capital flight, states: 'in spite of capital controls, African capital has *de facto* been globalized – albeit in the wrong direction' (that is, the poor performance at the level of macro-economic outcomes, and high levels of connectivity at the levels of policy and institutional reform). In other words, if one focuses on policy and institutional reforms, Africa is highly integrated into, and not marginal within, the world system (Bangura, 2001).
4. Pigato's paper seeks to refute the 'old wives' tale' which claims that, except for the natural resources sector, African countries fail to attract significant FDI. The author claims that reforming countries do not seem to suffer from the unfavourable image and pessimistic perceptions about the continent. And yet Pigato's paper clearly shows the resource bias of the investments, the prepon-

derance of South Africa and its being privatization driven. Even for South Africa, only 16 per cent of investment was in 'Greenfield' activities. The paper is apparently part of the 'awareness initiative' sponsored by the World Bank and the United Nations to 'help boost SSA's image as an investment location' (Pigato, 2000, p2). This may explain the positive image that is painstakingly extracted from a set of data that points in the opposite direction.

5. UNCTAD reports that in 1998 alone foreign direct investment through privatization triggered a total of US$684 million in foreign exchange reserves in sub-Saharan Africa. This is a one-off affair and may explain the jump in FDI in more recent years. Already by 1999 we witness a slowdown in privatization-related FDI.

6. The 'rise and fall' of Ghana as a pupil of the BWIs is recounted in a number of publications (see especially Aryeetey et al, 2000; Hutchful, 2002).

7. A study by the World Bank's International Financial Corporation in which managers were asked questions about specific obstacles to doing business and their interactions with government concludes: 'The first striking finding is that ten out of the fifteen questions elicit the same responses in Africa as is the case worldwide, suggesting that the business environment is no different in these respects: respondents see few problems with regulations for starting new business, price controls, labour regulations, safety or environmental regulations and perceive little threat of terrorist acts. They do find financing problematic, think, unsurprisingly, that taxes are high and/or tax regulations cumbersome; they also find that policy instability and general uncertainty about the cost of regulations pose serious problems to doing business. In all these respects, conditions in Africa are about the same as the world average. This is a very encouraging finding.'

8. In most cases, such a reversal of flows may call for 'amnesty', given the illicit nature of the accumulation of much of the expatriated capital. This raises a host of questions including those of the morality of seeming to reward kleptocracy and the credibility of the 'amnesty'. The credibility of the amnesty will ultimately depend on the legitimacy of the government pronouncing the amnesty and on the adhesion by the domestic class to what is a clearly national and popular development project. 'Amnesty' imposed by outsiders and by officials who belong to the kleptocracy is unlikely to be convincing to either private capital or the general public.

9. In a review of the long, inconclusive literature on the IMF Przeworski and Vreeland (2000) find that IMF programmes lower annual economic growth by 1.5 per cent for each year that a country participates in its programmes.

10. According to ECA:

After two decades of stagnation, from the mid-1990s, African economies started showing evidence of a turnaround. There is now convincing evidence of improved economic performance in a wide range of African countries, with recorded gross domestic product (GDP) growth rates in excess of 6 per cent in several of them. The progress has been largely due to improved policy performance, particularly the adoption of less-distorted macro-economic frameworks, and the improvement in governance in many countries. (UNECA, 1999)

11. Countries such as Côte d'Ivoire, Kenya, Tanzania and even Zaire experienced higher total factor productivity growth than most East Asian countries (Rodrik, 2001).

12. One consequence of the orthodoxy is fixation with austerity not as a programmatic concern over careful use of limited resources but as an ideologically driven clampdown on state-driven activities, since in most cases these measures are often accompanied by removal of constraints on private borrowing leading to profligacy and reduced private savings. In more concrete terms, this has resulted in strengthening the finance ministry and other 'austerity' and debt management institutions at the expense of the 'spending' ministries so crucial to a growth-focused process.

13. And as McPherson and Rakovski (2001) observe, 'Without growth to provide some dynamism, particularly the expectation among investors that growth will continue (and probably accelerate) there has been no incentive for anyone to invest. Thus the slow growth has fed on itself to produce the "tragedy"' (p11). African regional organizations and research institutions have argued for decades that SAPs were anti-developmental because of their deflationary thrust. The 'fundamentals' that SAP have pushed may have been adequate to address stabilization but they were definitely not the 'fundamentals' for development involving growth and structural change (Mkandawire and Soludo, 1999).

14. I have argued this case in Mkandawire (1988).

15. One reason why the contribution of investment to growth in Africa is underestimated may be precisely because its contribution to increasing the flexibility of the economy is ignored.

16. This is the recurring message of the collection of papers edited by Helleiner (Helleiner, 2002b), especially Mwega, 2002 and Ndulu et al, 2002.

17. For a contrary view see the IMF paper by Subramanian and Tamarisa (2001). There is an intriguing suggestion in the paper that, at least among Anglo-Saxon countries, intra-African trade has been much more dynamic than trade with the rest of the world. Subramanian suggests that this is no good for Africa as it means weakening the links with the technologically more dynamic North. He provides no evidence that Africa's import of plant and equipment from the North, the goods that are most important in terms of technological acquisition, has suffered as the result of increased intra-Africa trade.

18. As Tony Killick noted, the spread of SAP has 'given the BWIs an historically unprecedented leverage over the economic policies of sovereign developing country governments, to an extent that would be unimaginable among OECD states' (Killick, 1996, p221).

19. No lesser person than the Chief Economist of the World Bank, Joseph Stiglitz (1998), has called for the transcendence of the Washington consensus in order to place development back on to the agenda. The World Bank has proposed that each country prepare a 'comprehensive development framework' which considers 'structural, social and human aspects' of development (Wolfensohn, 1999).

20. On the state see Bauer (1981, 1984). On nationalism see Johnson (1967). Green characterizes Elliot Berg's economic world-view as 'of a more robust and free competitive market-oriented, comparative advantage-led, neo-liberal political economic world than that portrayed in the AD' (Green and Allison, 1986, p63).

21. A phenomenon observed in some physical systems, by which changes in a property lag behind changes in an agent on which they depend, so that the value of the former at any moment depends on the manner of the previous variation of the latter.

References

Adelman, I and Yeldan, E (2000) 'Is this the End of Economic Development?', *Structural Change and Economic Dynamics*, vol 11, pp95–109

Akyüz, Y (1996) 'The Investment–Profit Nexus in East Asian Industrialisation', *World Development*, vol 24, no 3, pp461–470

Amsden, A (1999) 'Industrialisation under New WTO Law', paper presented at *UNCTAD X: High Level Round Table on Development: Directions for the Twenty-First Century*, Bangkok, 12 February

Aryeetey, E, Harrigan, J and Nissanke, M (2000) *Economic Reforms in Ghana: The Miracle and the Mirage*, James Currey, London

Bangura, Y (2001) 'Globalization and African Development', in R Suttner (ed) *Africa in the New Millennium*, Nordiska Afrikainstitutet, Oslo

Bauer, P (1981) *Dissent on Development*, Weidenfeld & Nicolson, London

Bauer, P (1984) *Reality and Rhetoric: Studies in the Economics of Development*, Weidenfeld & Nicolson, London

Bhattacharya, O, Montiel, P and Sharma, S (1997) 'Can Sub-Saharan Africa Attract Private Capital Flows?', *Finance and Development*, June, pp3–6

Bird, G (2001) 'IMF Programmes: Do They Work? Can They Be Made to Work Better?', *World Development*, vol 29, pp1849–65

Boyce, J and Ndikumana, L (2000) 'Is Africa a Net Creditor? New Estimates of Capital Flight from Severely Indebted Sub-Saharan African Countries, 1970–1996', Political Economy Research Institute, University of Massachusetts, Amherst, MA, pp1–47

Bradford Jr, C I (1997) 'Introduction', in C Clague (ed) *Institutions and Economic Development: Growth and Governance in Less-Developed and Post-Socialist Countries*, Johns Hopkins University Press, Baltimore, MD, pp1–9

Clague, C (1997) 'Introduction', in C Clague (ed) *Institutions and Economic Development: Growth and Governance in Less-Developed and Post-Socialist Countries*, John Hopkins University Press, Baltimore, MD, pp1–9

Coe, D and Hoffmaister, A (1999) 'North–South Trade: Is Africa Unusual?', *Journal of African Economies*, vol 8, pp228–56

Collier, P and Gunning, J (1997) *Explaining African Economic Performance*, Centre for the Study of African Economies, Oxford

Collier, P, Hoeffler, A and Patillo, C (1999) 'Flight Capital as Portfolio Choice', International Monetary Fund, Washington, DC

Devajaran, S, Easterly, W and Pack, H (1999) 'Is Investment in Africa Too Low or Too High? Macro and Micro Evidence', Papers 2519, Country Economics Department, World Bank, Washington, DC

Easterly, W (2001) 'The Lost Decades: Developing Countries Stagnation in Spite of Policy Reform, 1980–1998', *Journal of Economic Growth*, vol 6, no 2, June

Economist (2001) 'Globalization and Its Critics: A Survey of Globalization', *The Economist* (Special Supplement)

Elbadawi, I and Mwega, F (2000) 'Can Africa's Saving Collapse Be Reversed?', *The World Bank Economic Review*, vol 14, pp415–43, World Bank, Washington, DC

Fischer, S, Hernàndez-Catà, E and Khan, M (1998) *Africa: Is this the Turning Point*, World Bank, Washington, DC

Foroutan, F and Pritchet, L (1993) 'Intra-Sub-Saharan African Trade', *Journal of African Economies*, 2 May, pp74–105

Fry, M (1982) 'Models of Financially Repressed Developing Countries', *World Development*, vol 10, no 9, pp731–750

Green, R and Allison, C (1986) 'The World Bank's Agenda for Accelerated Development: Dialects, Doubts and Dialogues', in J Ravenhill (ed) *Africa in Economic Crisis*, Macmillan, London, pp60–84

Griffin, K (2001) 'Macroeconomic Reform and Employment: An Investment-Led Strategy of Structural Adjustment in Sub-Saharan Africa', in T McKinley (ed) *Macroeconomic Policy, Growth and Poverty Reduction*, Palgrave, London

Helleiner, G (2002a) 'Introduction', in G K Helleiner (ed) *Non-Traditional Export Promotion in Africa: Experience and Issues,* Palgrave, New York, pp1–20

Helleiner, G (2002b) *Non-Traditional Export Promotion in Africa: Experience and Issues*, Palgrave, New York

Hernández-Catá, E (2000) 'Raising Growth and Investment in Sub-Saharan Africa: What Can be Done?', *Finance and Development: A Quarterly Magazine of the IMF*, December, vol 37, no 4

Hutchful, E (2002) *Ghana's Adjustment Experience: The Paradox of Reform*, UNRISD/ James Currey, Geneva and London

IMF (2004) *World Economic Outlook*, IMF, Washington, DC

Jalilian, H and Weiss, J (2000) 'De-industrialisation in Sub-Saharan Africa: Myth or Crisis?', in H Jalilian, M Tribe and J Weiss (eds) *Industrial Development and Policy in Africa*, Edward Elgar, Cheltenham

Johnson, H (1967) 'A Theoretical Model of Economic Nationalism in New and Developing Countries', in H G Johnston (ed) *Economic Nationalism in Old and New States*, pp1–16, University of Chicago Press, Chicago

Kasekende, L, Kitabire, D and Martin, M (1997) 'Capital Inflows and Macroeconomic Policy in Sub-Saharan Africa', in G K Helleiner (ed) *Capital Account Regimes*, Macmillan, London, pp141–83

Killick, T (1996) 'Principals, Agents and the Limitations of BWI Conditionality', *World Economy*, vol 19, pp211–19

Loayza, N, Schmidt-Hebbel, K, and Servén, L (2000) 'Saving in Developing Countries: An Overview', *The World Economy Review*, vol 14, pp393–414

McPherson, M and Rakovski, T (2001) *Understanding the Growth Process in Sub-Saharan Africa: Some Empirical Estimates of African Economic Policy*, John F Kennedy School of Government, Harvard University; Belfer Center for Science & International Affairs, Boston, Mass

Madavo, C and Sarbib, J-L (1997) 'Africa on the Move: Attracting Private Capital to a Changing Continent', *SAIS Review*, vol 7, pp111–26

Mkandawire, T (1988) 'The Road to Crisis, Adjustment and de-Industrialisation: The African Case', *Africa Development*, vol 13, no 1, pp5–31

Mkandawire, T and Soludo, C (1999) *Our Continent, Our Future: African Perspectives on Structural Adjustment*, African World Publications, Trenton, NJ, co-published with CODESRIA, Dakar

Mlambo, K and Oshikoya, T (2001) 'Macroeconomic Factors and Investment in Africa', *Journal of African Economies*, vol 10, pp12–47

Mosley, P, Subasat, T and Weeks, J (1995) 'Assessing Adjustment in Africa', *World Development*, vol 23, pp1459–73

Mwega, F (2002) 'Promotion of Non-Traditional Exports in Kenya', in G K Helleiner (ed) *Non-Traditional Export Promotion in Africa: Experience and Issues*, Palgrave, New York, pp159–91

Ndulu, B, Semboja, J and Mbelle, A (1998) 'Promoting Non-Traditional Exports to Tanzania', revised draft for the UNU/WIDER project *Growth, External Sector and Role of Non-Traditional Exports in Sub-Saharan Africa*

Ng, F and Yeats, A (2000), *On the Recent Trade Performance of Sub-Saharan African Countries: Cause for Hope or More of the Same?* World Bank, Washington, DC

Panchamukhi, V R (1996) *WTO and Industrial Policies*, UNCTAD, Geneva

Pigato, M (2000) *Foreign Direct Investment in Africa: Old Tales and New Evidence*, World Bank, Washington, DC

Przeworski, A and Vreeland, J (2000) 'The Effects of IMF Programs on Economic Growth', *Journal of Development Economics*, vol 62, pp385–421

Quattara, A (1997) 'The Challenges of Globalization for Africa', *Southern African Economic Summit Sponsored by the World Economic Forum*, Harare

Rodrik, D (1997) *Trade Policy and Economic Performance in Sub-Saharan Africa*, Swedish Foreign Ministry, Stockholm

Rodrik, D (2000a) 'Can Integration into the World Economy Substitute for a Developing Strategy?', *World Bank's ABCDE-Europe Conference*, Paris

Rodrik, D (2000b), 'Saving Transitions', *The World Bank Economic Review*, 14, pp481–507

Rodrik, D (2001) *The Global Governance of Trade as If Development Really Mattered*, Cambridge, MA

Shaw, E (1973) *Financial Deepening in Economic Development*, Oxford University Press, Oxford

Stein, H (1992) 'Deindustrialisation, Adjustment and World Bank and IMF in Africa', *World Development*, vol 20, no 1, pp83–95

Stewart, F (1994) 'Are Short-term Policies Consistent with Long-Term Development Needs in Africa?', in G A Cornia and G Helleiner (eds) *From Adjustment to Development in Africa: Conflict, Controversy, Convergence, Consensus?*, pp98–128, Macmillan, London

Stiglitz, J (1998) *More Instruments and Broader Goals: Moving toward the Post-Washington Consensus*, The United Nations University/WIDER (World Institute for Development Economics Research), Helsinki

Subramanian, A and Tamarisa, N (2001) *Africa's Trade Revisited*, International Monetary Fund, Washington, DC

Syrquin, M (1994) 'Structural Transformation and the New Growth Theory', in L Pasinetti and R M Solow (eds) *Economic Growth and the Structure of Long-Term Development*, pp3–21, St Martin's Press, New York

Syrquin, M (1995) 'Flexibility and Long-Term Economic Development', in T Killick (ed) *The Flexible Economy: Causes and Consequences of the Adaptability of National Economies*, pp34–63, Routledge, London

UNCTAD (1995) *Foreign Direct Investment in Africa – 1995*, United Nations, Geneva

UNCTAD (1998) *Trade and Development Report, 1998*, United Nations, Geneva

UNCTAD (2003) *World Investment Report*, United Nations, Geneva

UNECA (1999) *The ECA and Africa: Accelerating a Continent's Development*, UNECA, Addis Ababa

UNIDO (1999) 'Domestic Capacity-Building for Enhancing Productivity and Competitiveness in Africa', in A Sall (ed) *The Future Competitiveness of African Economies*, Karthala, Paris

Weisbrot, M, Baker, D, Naiman, R and Neta, G (2000a) *Growth May Be Good for the Poor – But Are IMF and World Bank Policies Good for Growth?* Center for Economic and Policy Research (CEPR), Washington, DC

Weisbrot, M, Naiman, R and Kim, J (2000b) *The Emperor Has No Growth: Declining Economic Growth rates in the Era of Globalization*, www.cepr.net/images/IMF/The_Emperor_Has_No_Growth.htm, Center for Economic and Policy Research (CEPR)

Weisbrot, M, Baker, D, Kraev, E and Chen, J (2001) *The Scoreboard on Globalization 1980–2000: Twenty Years of Diminished Progress*, Center for Economic and Policy Research (CEPR), Washington, DC

Wolfensohn, J (1997) The Challenge of Inclusion, Address to the Board of Governors, Hong Kong, China, *Address to the Board of Governors*, Hong Kong, China, p5

Wolfensohn, J (1999) *A Proposal for a Comprehensive Development Framework*, World Bank, Washington, DC

World Bank (1981) *Accelerated Development in Sub-Saharan Africa: An Agenda for Action*, World Bank Washington, DC

World Bank (1994) *Adjustment in Africa: Reforms, Results and the Road Ahead*, World Bank, Washington, DC

World Bank (2000) *Can Africa Claim the 21st Century?* World Bank, Washington, DC

World Bank (2001) *Global Economic Prospects*, World Bank, Washington, DC

World Bank (2003a) *World Bank Africa Database*, World Bank, Washington, DC

World Bank (2003b) *World Development Indicators*, World Bank, Washington, DC

Yeats, A J (1997) *Did Domestic Policies Marginalize Africa in World Trade?* World Bank, Washington, DC

7

Legal Frameworks

Ann Seidman and Robert B Seidman

Introduction

In the early years of the post-World War II anti-colonial struggle, Ghana's first President, Kwame Nkrumah, declared, 'Seek ye first the political kingdom, and all else shall follow.' By seizing and then using state power, he implied, Africa's former colonies could transform themselves into modern and prosperous states. More than that: he called on the new governments to join together into a continental union, utilizing their continent's rich resources to build a powerful industrialized federation.

A half century later, as the new millennium dawned, colonial rule in Africa lay shattered. Throughout the continent, newly elected post-colonial governments had initially tried to introduce populist programmes. Instead of achieving continental unity and prosperity, however, almost all had become enmeshed in a 'fatal race'. Too often, instead of using state power to improve their people's lot, the new governors adapted to the historically imposed, distorted institutions that perpetuated the continent's poverty and vulnerability.

In many countries, newly written constitutions granted elected parliaments 'the legislative power', sometimes alone, more often in conjunction with an elected president. At first, tyranny's overthrow seemed to promise substantial improvements in the people's quality of life. In Ghana and most of the continent, from the Mediterranean to southern Africa, newly independent governments helped people build new schools and hospitals, and new roads that reached into remote hinterlands. By the century's end, blacks in the former bastion of apartheid, South Africa, could attend schools that, for decades, had barred them. A tiny handful of Africans had joined the captains of industry.

Yet too often, newly elected legislators failed to enact laws to change the institutions, shaped by decades of colonial rule, that blocked most Africans from fulfilling their basic needs. Africans still comprise a significant part of the 80 per cent of the world's population, living in the developing or transitional countries, who receive less than a fifth of the world's output of goods and services. Most of that large majority of the world's peoples struggle for bare survival. Only a wealthy few wax rich and powerful. (In Africa, typically 5–10 per cent of a country's population receives half to three-quarters of their nation's total cash income.)

This chapter briefly describes the institutional problem that underpins the fatal race in Africa. In recent years, some lawmakers throughout the developing and transitional worlds, including some in Africa, have turned to institutionalist legislative theory, here summarized briefly, to guide their efforts to draft and enact more effective laws for democratic social change. As a basis for assessing their efforts, the chapter offers an explanation for past African governors' failures to use law to change the institutions that perpetuate their peoples' poverty and vulnerability. Those failures resulted only in part because of powerful elites' self-seeking greed. They also reflected populist governors' apparent inability to facilitate institutional transformation through law. Finally, the chapter briefly reviews the experiences of some Africans who have initiated attempts to use institutionalist legislative theory as a guide for drafting, assessing, enacting and implementing new laws to improve the majority of Africans' quality of life. At most these comprise first steps, but they do make a start in the process of drafting legislation likely to transform the inherited institutions that have thwarted good governance and development in the vast continent of Africa.

The Roots of African Poverty and Vulnerability

To comprehend the way Africa's inherited institutions perpetuate Africa's poverty requires understanding of not only the *nature*, but also the *causes* of the distorted allocation of resources that denies her peoples the benefit of that vast continent's riches.

The distorted allocation of African resources

As in the colonial era, after independence in most African nations, a wealthy minority, often closely associated with transnational corporate enterprise, continued to employ low-cost labour to export Africa's rich minerals and agricultural resources to the world's industrialized nations. African workers, mainly rural migrants fleeing neglected hinterlands, still earned wages a fourth or less of those in the so-called 'first' world. By the 20th century's end, a tiny handful of factories employed unskilled workers to assemble and process imported parts and materials to produce cheap consumer items – shoes, bicycles, textiles. Importing machinery, equipment and some semi-processed parts and materials, these factories also exported most of their output. African elites bought imported luxury consumer items: cars, television sets, even clothing. Some African countries' exports' value exceeded that of their imports. Nevertheless, every year, most of them paid out more than they earned, not only for high-priced imports but also in the form of profits, interest, dividends and capital flight. The net outflow reflected the way Africa's inherited economic institutions shaped its distorted allocation of resources.[1]

The institutions that distort Africans' human and physical resources

This distorted pattern of African resource allocation did not happen by chance. Historically shaped institutions, defined as repetitive patterns of behaviours,[2] shape the resource allocations that perpetuate the export of Africa's physical, financial and human resources – its external dependence, growing underemployment and deepening poverty. A century and more of colonial rule laid the economic, political and social foundations that underpin the African crisis. In east and southern Africa, colonial governments used laws to impose head and poll taxes, not to raise revenue but to drive Africans to work for the white settlers and companies who seized the vast farms and rich mines that produce crude agricultural and mineral produce for overseas buyers. In western and central Africa, colonial rule spawned the great trading firms that reaped profits by buying African peasants' produce at bare subsistence prices, and selling it abroad for as much as five to ten times more to wealthy elites in industrializing countries. Colonial government ministries drafted and implemented the laws and subordinate legislation that typically maintained the legal framework, the rules of the game, within which those globe-encircling trading, financial and industrial institutions functioned.

Despite political independence, many of those colonial-imposed institutions, and the rules of the game that undergird their basic structures – only marginally altered – persist to this day. Lack of employment opportunities in the African countryside still force rural African youth to seek work in their countries' export-dependent mines, farms and factories. Big wholesale trading firms still purchase small cash farmers' crops at bare subsistence prices. Labour-intensive factories, typically linked to foreign firms, employ unskilled workers for long hours at or below poverty-level wages. Property and contract laws still grease the skids for transnational corporations and a handful of wealthy nationals to reap the profits generated by African workers, producing and marketing African materials – not to meet most Africans' basic needs. Unwilling to risk loans to small 'informal sector' entrepreneurs, both domestically- and foreign-owned banking institutions make loans mainly to big farms, factories and trading companies. Their major enterprises owned or controlled by transnational corporations or a local elite that perceives itself as part of a global economy, African countries still mainly export not only agricultural and mineral wealth, mostly in crude form, but also the economic surpluses produced by African workers. Little altered since the not-so-distant colonial past, these institutions still reproduce Africa's poverty and vulnerability. To change them, governments have to learn to use law and the legal order consciously and cannily. To date, few have done either.

For half a century, a strange paradox persisted: in country after country, populist governors and deputies grasped the reins of formal state power, but they ruled through old, authoritarian, frequently racist institutions that continued to drain the economic surplus out of the country.[3]

In their efforts to resolve that paradox Africa's new governments became enmeshed in a fatal race. Independence opened a window of opportunity to use state power through law to transform those inherited institutions to reallocate resources and build balanced, integrated, self-sustaining national development directed to satisfying their peoples' basic needs. If they did not seize the moment to enact essentially transformative laws, gradually but inevitably the existing institutions seduced them into perpetuating the status quo to benefit themselves and their cronies.

Two handicaps hindered African lawmakers' efforts to win that fatal race: First, everywhere, officials in existing institutions, national and global, sang seductive songs: make haste slowly. No need to change government institutions; like a scalpel, those institutions work for whoever wields them, and *you* wield them now. Incremental change is safe, transformation risky. Things work now, sort of; if you disrupt them, schools may close, transport stop, supply of goods dry up, police disintegrate, army revolt. Be careful: drastic measures will scare away the foreign investors who can bring you funds, market access, managerial skills and technologies.

Second, only a few African governments even tried to enact laws to foster institutional transformation. They did little to restructure their inherited public service and land tenure systems, or the large firms, banks and financial institutions that chained their nations' productive sectors to foreign inputs and markets. Instead, at most, they spent government's scarce revenues and borrowed abroad to expand social services: schools, hospitals and roads. Because they did not restructure lawmaking and implementing institutions to ensure the transparency, accountability and participation required for good governance, many of their officials continued to make arbitrary, too often corrupt, decisions. In Africa, as in much of the Third World, a nearly universal lament moaned, 'We have good laws, but they remain badly implemented.'

In the late 1970s and 1980s, as their countries' terms of trade collapsed, African governments found their nations' economies overwhelmed by foreign debt. Promising rescue, IMF, the World Bank and USAID dictated neo-liberal policies that relied on 'the market' as the universal cure-all. Currencies' values fell, inflation soared. Almost everywhere, the old institutions seemed to win. Instead of populist governments transforming retrograde institutions, too often the institutions seemed to transform governments. Many governments abandoned even the populist rhetoric; cynicism and corruption corroded the very heart of government. By the end of the 1980s, the international aid agencies (the World Bank, to its credit, leading the charge) discovered that even markets need rules and that kleptocrat governments make poor investment climates. 'Good governance' emerged as a leading theme in the development symphony: Government decisions should emerge from accountable, transparent, participatory processes that ensure that decisions reflect, not whim, but the rule of law.

Law and the legal order assumed priority on the development agenda. Aid agencies sent armies of lawyers to help Third World and transitional governments strengthen the courts and draft new legislation. To ensure 'market efficiency' in hopes of attracting foreign investments, not infrequently imposing acceptance of their 'model laws' as a condition for more aid, some urged new 'business legislation': contract and companies law, secured transactions law, intellectual property law, cheque law and banking law. As new business tides lifted everyone's boats, the neo-liberals promised, equity would come later.

Yet still development lagged. The 'have'–'have-not' gap, not only between them and the industrialized 'first' world, but also within African countries, yawned ever more widely. Whether newly emerging populist governments would win the fatal race remained in doubt. Closing the gap between words and deeds, between the laws' words and actual behaviours, between the *law-in-the-books* and the *law-in-action*: in Africa, as throughout the Third World, that emerged as the new millennium's central challenge.

Can African Governments Use Law to Restructure Dysfunctional Institutions?

To lay a sound theoretical basis for a strategy to strengthen Africans' capacity to draft and implement more effective transformative laws, this section will explain why, in the end, governments must resort to law to facilitate democratic social change; and why so many well-meaning post-independence governments so often proved inept in exercising their state power through law to implement institutional transformation.

Can governments induce institutional change through law?

To effect a fundamental transformation of the institutions that have for so long perpetuated African poverty and vulnerability, African governments have little option but to employ law. Law engages the development process at many points: it serves to settle disputes, maintain social stability, state basic societal values and protect valued interests (like human rights and the environment). Here, however, we discuss only law's potential role in restructuring the institutions, the repetitive patterns of social behaviours that for so long have condemned Africans to arbitrary (and sometimes corrupt) governance and deepening poverty.

Some say that government cannot use law to change behaviour. Behaviour, they say, follows folkways, not the law. Inevitably, law lags behind social institutions. Lawmaking always plays catch-up with society, which changes by its own dynamic.

In reality, however, for at least two reasons, governments must govern primarily through *rules*, that is, broadly defined, law.[4] First, governments must convey the detailed prescriptions as to the appropriate behaviours necessary to implement a policy, backed by government's full authority, to many tens of thousands of government officials (sometimes even more), and many millions of a country's inhabitants. Second, to the extent that an elected legislature enacts a law (or a government agency under power granted by an elected legislature promulgates subordinate legislation), a nation's inhabitants will more likely view governmental commands as *legitimate,* and hence obey them.

Some laws plainly constitute a 'but for' cause for behaviour. To provide two examples: *but for* an income tax law, nobody would pay income tax; *but for* an election law, nobody could cast a vote. On the other hand, some laws – like laws prohibiting the sale or use of alcoholic liquor or prohibiting sexual intercourse between persons not married to each other – have generally proven ineffective. Few laws induce *no* changes in behaviour, but the changes may or may not conform to those the laws prescribe. Most laws fall between the two extremes. Most post-independence governments, however, failed to use law to implement promised institutional transformation – and lost the fatal race. The task for interested scholars and others becomes to learn from experience: what laws induce what sorts of behaviour, and why. Then they must use that knowledge to inform lawmaking practice.

How Africans Designed Laws

To develop a bill's substance requires two sets of decisions: first, to draft a bill to help resolve a particular social problem (determining its *priority*); and second, to formulate the bill's details (the *'legislative design'*). Here, we examine the 'legislative design'.

Legislative design

To induce appropriate new behaviours for development in the context of a particular country's unique circumstances, drafters must design *detailed legislative prescriptions*. Instead, inherited drafting institutions have encouraged African lawmakers to enact laws that grant officials broad discretion in making decisions as to how to implement the laws' details.

The importance of legislative details

In conditions of development, the design of a bill's details has crucial significance. To foster development, a law's detailed provisions must effectively alter the existing patterns of behaviour – the institutions – that obstruct, or, in the case of government agencies, fail to effectively implement, development programmes. Long-continued patterns of social behaviours come with stories, myths and legends, valuations attached. Sociologists denote them as 'values and attitudes'. Under whatever title, they comprise the mental frameworks that people use to make sense out of their world.

The English colonies' legal tradition held that law primarily aimed to assert general principles, and left law enforcers to sanction deviants. That tradition hindered drafters from conceptualizing how best to design a bill's detailed prescriptions to ensure appropriately changed behaviours. Instead, they drafted laws in general terms, which granted its implementing officials the discretion to interpret those terms' detailed implications. Being human, the officials' values and attitudes – shaped to fit not the prescribed new behaviours but outmoded existing ones – too often determined their implementing decisions. Inevitably, that put at risk the effectiveness of a new law aimed at inducing institutional transformation.

For transformational bills, lawmakers have no choice but to insist that, at the end of the day, whether in a statute or in subordinate legislation (an implementing decree, agency rule or administrative regulation), the law must prescribe new behaviours required of its addressees – whether members of civil society or implementing officials – *in detail*. The devil lies in those details; they determine the policy's actual shape and whether it will achieve the desired social impact.

How Africans designed their laws

Instead of designing detailed legislative provisions, drafters in Africa, as elsewhere, typically either merely restated general principles, without detailed instructions about who must (or must not) do what, or fell back on one of three methods: slavishly copying foreign laws or 'international best practice' models, criminalizing unwanted behaviours or compromising between competing interests. Sometimes, central office drafters redrafted ministry bills in an archaic language – 'legalese' – that hindered ordinary citizens from understanding them and hence made them less likely to behave as the laws prescribed. Except by chance, laws drafted by any of these methods usually fail to induce the new behaviours required to implement the lawmakers' desired policies.

Why did African lawmakers design laws as they did?

As illustrated by the former British colonies' experience,[5] this dismal result seemed to reflect two interrelated causal factors: the nature of inherited drafting institutions and the way colonial drafting traditions shaped the drafters' own views of their tasks.

ANGLOPHONE DRAFTING INSTITUTIONS

As throughout the developing world, in Anglophonic Africa government officials design most, if not all, bills. In many countries the newly independent countries' constitution typically nominally allocated 'the legislative power' to parliament's elected members. Nevertheless, in practice, in virtually all countries, government ministers and cabinet overwhelmingly dominates the legislative process. Government introduces most bills. Under most electoral systems, party chiefs' endorsement proves essential for MPs' renomination and political advancement so that what cabinet wants parliament to enact, cabinet usually gets.

Typically, ministries prioritize bills, and government drafters assume primary responsibility for drafting them. The term, 'drafters' here refers to more than those who work in a central drafting office (variously named; for example, in South Africa, the Senior State Counsel's chambers; in Zimbabwe, the Solicitor's Office); it also includes the line ministries' senior civil servants assigned to prepare legislation.

When some senior official (usually the relevant minister) authorizes officials to put an idea into the form of a bill, it becomes a *legislative policy*. The officials responsible for drafting translate that policy into the bill's detailed design. In post-independence Africa's formative years, higher political authority and legislators reviewed that design, but rarely changed it; the debate mainly turned on the policy declared in the draft bill. Many, probably most, bills travelled from the drafters' pen to legislators' final vote unchanged. Most post-independence drafters' view of their task remains moulded by colonial drafting traditions.

COLONIAL DRAFTING TRADITIONS

Two sets of English drafting traditions seem to discourage drafters from even attempting to design bills' detailed measures to transform inherited institutions. One goes back to 1869 when Britain's first Chief Parliamentary Counsel, Sir

Henry Thring, insisted on reviewing government bills before their submission to Parliament. Before that, ministries had sent their bills directly to Cabinet, and thence to the Parliament. To counter ministers' objections, Thring claimed his Chambers aimed merely to ensure bills' consistency with existing law and formal legal standards. In reality, Thring promised the impossible. Words and policy, form and substance, inevitably comprise two sides of the same coin: no one can change a bill's wording for either 'legal' or purely 'formal' reasons without changing its substance.

Today's anglophone African drafters still trace their craft lineage back to Thring. Colonial drafters trained in the Chief Parliamentary Counsel's Chambers in London; African drafters either trained in the Chambers in London, Canada or Australia or served as apprentices to London-trained drafters in their own country's central drafting offices. They all learned their trade directly from Thring or someone trained by Thring – unquestioningly adopting the myth that drafter should not even consider a bill's substance.

In addition, most African drafters still accept the British tradition that drafters should draft mainly to instruct judges about how to settle disputes. That implies they need neither investigate the social circumstances that cause problematic behaviours, nor design detailed legislative measures to change or eliminate those causes. Instead, drafters should merely specify the disputants' 'rights and duties'. In short, nobody has any responsibility for designing the legislative details necessary to transform dysfunctional institutions.

These views led African drafters to focus, not on substance, but form. Furthermore, without a legislative theory to guide their enquiries into the causes of relevant social actors' problematic behaviours, they had no basis in either logic or fact to design detailed legislative prescriptions that might facilitate needed institutional transformation. They fell back on drafting broad principles, copying foreign law or formulating compromises between competing interest groups. When they did turn their attention to behaviours, they mainly drafted provisions that criminalized deviance; after all, one of a judge's primary tasks involves setting fines and penalties.

In short, inherited lawmaking institutions and legislative drafting traditions encouraged post-independence drafters in Africa simply to ignore their bills' substantive details' social impact. In the end, far from fostering institutional transformation, the legislation they drafted contributed to Africa's new governors' loss of the fatal race.

Legislative Theory and the Use of Law for Institutional Transformation

In part, poor governance persisted in Africa, as well as elsewhere in the developing world, because drafters (both line ministry officials and central drafting office lawyers) ineptly translated policy's vague generalities into the detailed prescriptions for the behaviours required to implement legislation. At bottom, this reflected the drafters' inability to ground their bills on reason informed by experience, and the absence of lawmaking institutions that required them to do so. Inevitably, part of the new governors' difficulties reflected the power of the institutionalized forces arrayed against them that comprised the challenge they confronted. Unless they managed to use state power through law to tame and ultimately restructure those institutions, they could not effectively alter the distorted resource patterns that condemned their citizens to poverty and oppression. The remainder of this chapter focuses on the potential of institutionalist legislative theory as a guide to lawmakers, including drafters, in designing, enacting and implementing laws likely to facilitate democratic institutional transformation.

As the new millennium dawned, a few Africans, in governments and in civil society, began to use institutional legislative theory to guide the process of drafting proposed legislation's details, a process shaped not by power but the use of facts and logic. That theory offered a logical way of analyzing available country-specific facts about the institutions – the repetitive behaviours – that perpetuated Africa's crisis. It underscored the reality that a bill can effectively resolve a social problem only if it first prescribes *detailed* measures that, in the country's unique circumstances, will likely overcome the causes of the primary role occupant's problematic behaviours; second, if it prescribes *detailed* behaviours for the implementing agency likely to facilitate alteration or elimination of those causes and induce behaviours likely to resolve the problem addressed; and finally, if it prescribes *detailed* procedures and criteria for the implementing agency to employ in decision-making that – characterized by transparency, accountability and the participation of those affected – conform to the requirements of good governance.

Legislative theory's focus on behaviours

Institutionalist legislative theory rests on the premise that, to facilitate effective social change, law must change the behaviour patterns – the institutions – that block the development process. That requires answering the question, *why do people behave as they do in the face of a rule of law?* Built on foundations laid by legal realists, a simple model captures the relationship between the laws and the behaviours of the social actors.

That model starts with a simple concept of how people in a society behave. Individuals and collectivities make *choices* within the constraints and resources thrown up by their physical and subjective environments. Which of those constraints and resources does experience suggest have relevance for explaining how social actors behave in the face of a rule of law?

These social actors may decide to disobey if they anticipate that no agency will effectively implement the law. They also may not conform to a law because of the influence of non-legal factors specific to their country's environment. These include not only subjective factors (like their interests or traditional values) but also objective causes (for example, their circumstances may deny them the opportunity or capacity to obey the law).

The model of how law influences behaviour has a rather non-intuitive consequence. A drafter cannot assume that the circumstances within which a proposed law's addressees *choose* to behave in *this* time and place will present the same range of constraints and resources as affected a superficially similar choice in *another* time and place. It follows that without careful research into specific facts and circumstances, a drafter cannot copy a law from another jurisdiction or time on the assumption that it will induce in *this* jurisdiction today the same behaviours a similar law induced in its place and time of origin. (Call that the Law of Non-Transferability of Law.)

Legislative theory combines this understanding of law's impact on social actors' behaviours with John Dewey's problem-solving methodology (Dewey, 1916; 1925; 1939). That methodology purports to guide drafters in organizing the available facts about the time- and place-specific circumstances as a basis for conceptualizing how to translate policy into effectively implemented law.

A problem-solving methodology

The key to answering the question: why do people behave as they do in the face of a rule of law? is to analyse

- the rule itself;
- the likely behaviour of the relevant implementing agenc(ies); and
- the non-legal constraints and resources likely to influence those actors' behaviours.

These are broad questions, however, and they do not provide either lawmakers in general, or drafters in particular, with ready-made answers. They only guide attention to areas of possible hypotheses – 'educated guesses' – to help explain problematic behaviours. In turn, each hypothesis guides the gathering of the relevant facts required to demonstrate that that hypothesis appears consistent with the available evidence. In that sense, legislative theory offers a map to guide discovery of relevant available facts, and how to structure them in a way that justifies the bill's substantive details. By following that map, lawmakers can assess the likelihood that, at the least possible social cost, a proposed law will prove susceptible of effective implementation and help resolve the social problem addressed.

Legislative methodology pulls the labouring oar in structuring the evidence that the drafters gather. Evidence alone – the infinite detailed 'facts' inherent in the world's social and physical realities – has no particular meaning. Evidence can acquire meaning for conceptualizing the translation of a policy into an effectively implemented law only when drafters structure and present the relevant facts in a logical way. The problem-solving methodology outlines an agenda of steps for structuring available evidence logically to justify a transformative bill's *detailed* provisions.

In contrast to other lawmaking methodologies, the problem-solving methodology guides lawmakers in grounding proposed bills on reason informed by experience; that is, on logically organized relevant facts.

Steps in legislative theory's problem-solving methodology

Legislative theory's problem-solving methodology specifies four steps for grounding proposed bills on reason informed by experience; that is, on logically organized relevant facts.

Step I: *Identifying the difficulty.* This step involves two moves. The *first*, the perception of a social problem sparks off the drafting process; here, the drafters must provide evidence to substantiate their descriptive hypotheses as to the nature and scope of the difficulty's *surface appearance.* The *second* move requires drafters to specify *whose and what behaviours* – the relevant social actors, whose behaviours contribute to the social problems targeted; and provide evidence to substantiate their descriptions of those behaviours.

Step II: *Proposing and warranting explanations.* Effective laws must alter or eliminate the causes of social actors' existing problematic behaviours. Drafters must therefore systematically explore all possible hypotheses as to the *causes of a person's (including the relevant implementing agency officials') problematic behaviours.* Again, to warrant those hypotheses requires marshalling the available evidence, or conducting new research to find the country-specific circumstances that may cause those behaviours.

Step III: *Proposing a solution.* To the degree validated by evidence, drafters' explanations as to the causes of existing behaviours justify an equal degree of confidence in their predictions as to future behaviours. As long as the same causes operate, the behaviours will likely persist. Drafters should formulate their bills' detailed provisions – including adequate detailed implementation devices – in ways logically likely to alter or eliminate the causes of existing problematic behaviours, both of the primary role occupants, and also the implementing agency.

Step IV: *Monitoring and evaluating implementation.* Finally, drafters should build into their bills adequate monitoring and evaluation mechanisms. No law ever works exactly as anticipated. Pressures to pass legislation quickly frequently preclude adequate research. Moreover, laws always function in a world of unceasing change. After a law's passage and implementation, lawmakers require adequate feedback to determine whether the relevant social actors – including the designated implementing agencies – do in fact behave as prescribed, with the desired social consequences.

Legislative theory's explanatory categories

Rarely does a single factor cause behaviour. To prove effective, a law must change or eliminate all the interrelated causes of the actors' behaviours that comprise dysfunctional institutions. To help lawmakers formulate hypotheses as to all the possible causes of problematic behaviours (problem-solving's Step II), institutionalist legislative theory offers a detailed set of categories. An understanding of these categories is the basis for logically designing detailed legislative measures.

Earlier we saw that rules address not only individual's behaviour, but also the implementing agency's expected behaviours as well as all the non-legal constraints and resources of these actors' location-specific environment. The last category, however, remains too broad to help drafters formulate the kinds of detailed hypotheses on which to build effective detailed legislative measures. Legislative theory unpacks that category into:

- *Rule* (the law itself),
- *Opportunity,*

- *C*apacity,
- *C*ommunication,
- *I*nterest,
- *P*rocess, and
- *I*deology

The initial letters of these categories provide an easily-remembered mnemonic, ROCCIPI. The order of the categories has no significance.

Each of these narrower categories may stimulate ideas as to interrelated test-able propositions – hypotheses – regarding possible subjective and objective causes of each set of a person's problematic behaviours. (If a category proves irrelevant for explaining a role occupant's behaviours, a drafter may simply ignore it.)

The *subjective factors* mainly comprise ideas in role occupants' heads. *Interests* (or incentives) include the person's perception of likely costs and benefits – both material and non-material incentives, like power and reference-group esteem. Adoption of interest-related explanations typically leads lawmakers to impose direct conform-ity-inducing legislative measures – punishments or rewards – in an effort to alter those interests. The role occupant's response depends in part on their anticipation of the implementing agency's behaviours (will they get 'caught'?); they seldom merely take into account a law's paper penalty. *Ideology* (values and attitudes) constitutes the second subjective category of behaviours' possible causes. Broadly construed, this category covers all those subjective motivations for behaviours not subsumed under 'Interest'. These range from values, attitudes and tastes, to religious beliefs, traditions, and more or less well-defined political, social and economic ideologies.

Subjective factors – 'Interest' and 'Ideology' – do offer partial explanations of individuals' problematic behaviours – not necessarily those shaped by existing institutional structures. As a result, legislative solutions directed at subjective fac-tors rarely lead to institutional transformation; inherently, instead, they aim only to change individuals' personal interests and ideologies. Those changes may facili-tate implementation of institutional changes, but, of themselves, they cannot change the objective causes of dysfunctional behaviours.

In contrast to subjective factors, ROCCIPI's *objective categories* – Rule, Oppor-tunity, Capacity, Communication and Process – centre the drafters' attention on more powerful interrelated explanations for institutionalized behaviours that may block good governance and development. Hypotheses as to these kinds of causes should stimulate the search for evidence to answers to different kinds of questions.

In reality, people behave as they do, not in the face of a single law, but of a whole cage of laws. Those *rules'* mere existence may help to explain problematic behaviours for four possible reasons, best understood by considering an example. Suppose existing laws forbid putting pollutants into the Niger river or Dar es Salaam's harbour, but people still persist in dumping wastes into those waters. The con-tinued polluting behaviour may continue, first, because the laws do not prescribe implementing officials' behaviours which would effectively prevent those pollut-ing behaviours' causes. Second, the laws' implementing provisions may permit or even authorize agency officials to make decisions through non-transparent, unac-countable processes that enable them simply to ignore the pollution problem (elsewhere, managers of polluting industries have taken advantage of non-transparent processes to bribe or use other means to deter officials from effectively enforcing the rules). Third, the rules' wording may grant the role occupants or implementing officials broad discretion to decide how to behave, leaving them scope to respond to inappropriate subjective motivations. Finally, ambiguous or confusing language may leave polluters unclear as to requirements of the law's commands.

These four sets of potential causal factors, inherent in the rules themselves, tell lawmakers what to look at when they read a bill that purports to resolve a particular social problem, whether related to polluting or to other problematic behaviours.

Other non-legal objective factors in the role occupants' environments may also cause them to behave in problematic ways. One concerns *opportunity*. Do the circumstances enable the role occupants to behave as the law commands or, conversely, make it difficult or impossible for them to obey the law? For example, if government policy favours increased cash cropping among predominantly subsistence farmers, do feeder roads and a market for cash crops exist within easy reach of the farmers involved? If not, they may lack the opportunity to sell crops in the market even if the law requires them to do so. Or, despite laws forbidding corrupt behaviour, do the conditions in which government officials work nevertheless offer them opportunities to benefit from behaving corruptly? (For example, does an official make decisions alone, in secret, without having to give reasons or confront any form of effective supervision?)

Taking as given the existing environment, the category of *Capacity* focuses attention on the role occupants' characteristics, which may make it difficult or impossible for them to behave as the existing law prescribes. For example, even assuming a market exists, if subsistence farmers lack credit, tools and knowledge, they probably lack the Capacity to grow cash crops. In practice, Opportunity and Capacity overlap. As with all the interrelated ROCCIPI categories, it matters little which one inspires the formulation of an explanatory hypothesis as long as it helps to explain why the relevant actor behaves problematically.

One also has to ask whether the authorities have taken adequate steps to *Communicate* the existing rules to their addressees? If not, that may comprise a significant cause of those addressees' failure to behave as the law prescribes. A person cannot consciously obey (or disobey) a law unless he or she knows that it exists and what it prescribes. A country's channels for communicating information about laws may reflect, and in some cases foster, its social structure's skewed characteristics. Governments usually publish laws in some form of gazette, and the local media may report on the more important ones. Ministries usually make sure their officials know about the laws, especially when those officials should enforce them. Their lawyers or business associates usually inform urban elites, especially formal-sector entrepreneurs, about laws relevant to their affairs. Unless the responsible ministries make special efforts to inform the poor, especially the rural poor, however, those who have no access to the media seldom learn much about laws – even those laws designed to help them increase their productivity and incomes.

Finally, one must consider *Process*. By what processes – according to what criteria and procedures – do role occupants decide whether or not to obey the law? Usually, this Process category yields few useful hypotheses to explain the behaviours of individual role occupants; individuals usually decide by themselves whether or not to obey the rules. In contrast, for role occupants who participate in complex decision-making organizations – like corporations, non-government organizations (NGOs), trade unions and, in particular, implementing agencies – Process may constitute ROCCIPI's most fruitful category for explaining their problematic behaviours.

Decision-makers in complex organizations make significant choices in the context of three important processes: the first and second determine whose and what *inputs* and *feedbacks* of ideas and facts they consider? (Elites typically have (sometimes secret) channels for communicating with implementing agencies, but these usually remain blocked to the poor and vulnerable.) The third relates to how the decision-makers *convert* those inputs and feedbacks: do they make their decisions in a process that remains open to scrutiny? Accountable to anyone? In any sense participatory? (Experience in Africa, as well as everywhere else, demonstrates that when officials make implementing decisions in non-transparent, non-accountable and non-anticipatory ways, they frequently behave in ways that prove arbitrary and even corrupt.)

Consideration of each of the ROCCIPI categories helps to identify all the interrelated hypotheses that, together, seem to explain each set of people's problematic behaviours. These hypotheses guide the gathering and structuring of available evidence essential to warrant them. Once revised to prove consistent with available data, they logically lay a foundation for detailed legislative solutions that will likely alter or eliminate the causes identified. By weighing those measures' relative social and economic costs and benefits, lawmakers may decide which to include among the bill's detailed provisions.

Monitoring and evaluation are essential in a problem-solving method

Problem-solving's Step IV constitutes a central device for assessing whether, enacted into law, the legislative details prove effective in helping to resolve the targeted social problem. By monitoring and evaluating a law's social impact, lawmakers can determine whether or not, and how, to change its detailed prescriptions to achieve more desirable social consequences.

For purposes of overall quality control, legislative theory argues that drafters accompany important transformative laws with a research report that, using the problem-solving methodology, provides the facts and logic to justify that bill's detailed provisions.

Legislative theory's problem-solving methodology provides lawmakers with a guide to formulating laws based, not on intuition, 'visions' or appeals to authority, but on *reason informed by experience.* This undergirds the recommendation that drafters accompany important transformatory bills by a *research report.*

In the past, most African legislative drafters focused only on proposed bills' *form.* Instead, for three reasons, institutionalist legislative theory underscores that at least for transformatory laws, drafters must provide research reports that adequately demonstrate their bill's *substance:*

- to *justify* a bill, a competent research report must warrant the decision-making that led to the bill's substance;

- the report's problem-solving outline guides the drafters in gathering and structuring the available evidence; and
- the report provides the necessary facts logically structured in a way that enables lawmakers and, ultimately, the general public to assess whether the law will likely facilitate the essential institutional transformation.

In that sense, the research report comprises the bill's quality control.

Gathering the Facts

The requirement that drafters gather relevant evidence for their research reports does not constitute as formidable a task as it may appear at first blush. Social problems usually come to the stage of drafting legislation only after they have persisted for a long time. Line-ministry files and the heads of senior officials invariably contain vast quantities of information about them. In reality, in large part, drafters may canvass the available evidence by discussing the problem, its causes and possible solution with the responsible line-ministry officials.[6]

Structured by the problem-solving methodology, the research report's outline guides drafters in discovering and reporting in a logical sequence on the available evidence that seems to justify their bills' detailed provisions. In addition, legislative theory underscores the advantages of engaging all the stakeholders – especially the poor and vulnerable usually excluded from the halls of power – in gathering the relevant facts. Their lives impose on them invaluable experiences as to the nature of the difficulties they confront in their daily struggles for survival. Often, they can offer insights into whose and what behaviours comprise those difficulties, and into those behaviours' causes. Involving the stakeholders in the process of gathering relevant information not only ensures that lawmakers take those facts into consideration; it may also strengthen the stakeholders' own capacity to contribute to the design of legislative details likely to help improve their quality of life.

New initiatives in Africa

As the new century dawned, Africans joined in new global initiatives to take up that challenge. People in countries as different as China, Laos, Sri Lanka, Indonesia, Vietnam, Kazakhstan and Estonia took steps towards institutionalizing an ongoing legislative drafting learning process to strengthen their countries' lawmaking capacity. Unfortunately, in part because African polities had insufficient access to financial resources, they did not send abroad for training people who might effectively lead similar learning processes. Nevertheless, in recent years, people in several African countries, too, have begun to acquire and use the theor_ etical and practical tools to translate proposed social policies into effectively implemented transformatory legislation. This section briefly reviews some initial efforts in Mozambique, South Africa, Nigeria, Ghana and Zambia.

Mozambique

Shortly after civil war ended, members of Mozambique's new parliament, including FRELIMO, RENAMO and some smaller party's representatives, took part in the first of several workshops[7] to learn to use law to resolve the social problems which lay behind the years of armed conflict. The workshops aimed to equip them with the institutionalist legislative theory, methodology and techniques to assess and, when necessary, initiate the drafting of bills. The workshop participants, members of different parties, worked to draft bills accompanied by research reports that, using facts and logic, demonstrated the likelihood that they would 'work'. The teams' bills dealt with a range of social problems, from providing wheelchairs for the thousands of people disabled by anti-personnel mines to protecting the environment from mining's destructive impact, and providing farmers with security of land tenure. An organizer and translator for these workshops (a former Deputy Dean of Mondelane University), Theodosio Uate has completed his PhD dissertation research on ways to strengthen Mozambican capacity to draft transformatory legislation.

No thorough evaluation has fully assessed these workshops' results. Nevertheless, available evidence indicates that today a quarter or more of all the bills introduced in Mozambique parliament come from MPs – significantly more than in most developing countries. To the extent that MPs use facts and logic to assess proposed legislation, their debates and decisions hopefully reflect not simply their parties' relative power but a closer analysis, in Mozambique's unique circumstances, of the causes of relevant actors' problematic behaviours.

South Africa

About two years after the 1994 elections, the Gauteng Provincial Administration held a two-week workshop to help Provincial officials acquire tools to draft legislation designed to restructure Provincial institutions. Working in teams, the participants drafted bills, accompanied by research reports, to help resolve a number of problems relating to local government selection, training and upgrading personnel; and the use and improvement of subsidiary legislation under newly enacted Provincial laws.

A year later, selected members of Gauteng's Department of Social Welfare staff participated in a course on legislative theory, methodology and techniques at Wits University. In the process, they designed bills, accompanied by research reports, to transform the Department from that imposed under apartheid to one designed, within existing resource limits, to serve the historically disadvantaged majority's needs. Their bills focused on restructuring and strengthening the Department, and improving specific services to:

- ensure disabled persons' access to public buildings;
- restructure provincial health services to overcome the fragmentation imposed during apartheid;
- provide adequate homes for elderly persons excluded from apartheid facilities;

- improve relationships, especially in disadvantaged communities, between provincial and local welfare services;
- facilitate work of non-government welfare agencies with Provincial welfare offices to serve previously disadvantaged black communities. Unfortunately, we have received no evaluation of these measures' implementation or social impact.

A four-month legislative drafting distance course

In the year 2000, in part because relatively high costs hindered Africans from taking the four-month training-for-trainers' overseas residential course,[8] Boston University's School of Law initiated a Distance Course on Legislative Drafting for Democratic Social Change. That course aimed to enable would-be drafters (whether from government or non-government organizations; and whether or not they had had previous legal training) – without paying the residential programmes' high costs[9] – to use email to acquire the essential skills for assessing and drafting transformatory legislation. Along with participants from Asia and former socialist countries, the first four sessions of that course (2001–04) involved African participants from Nigeria, Ghana, Egypt, Ethiopia, Uganda, Rwanda, South Africa, Sierra Leone and Tanzania.[10]

Some working in groups, African distance-course participants have drafted bills, accompanied by reports, to resolve a variety of different kinds of social problems. These range from providing credit for small-scale enterprises (South Africa); and setting up a commission to prevent discrimination (Uganda); to registering Muslim marriages (Ghana), helping child street hawkers (Nigeria) and primary school age children (Rwanda) to attend school, protecting child labour (Egypt) and preventing discrimination against HIV/AIDS victims (Ethiopia). In the process, African participants have established contact and exchanged ideas directly and through the distance-course bulletin board with participants seeking to provide legislative solutions to similar problems in countries as widely different and far away as Kyrgyzstan, Indonesia, Vietnam, Estonia, Nepal, Sri Lanka, Laos, St Helena, East Timor, Cambodia and Canada.

In sum, the distance course created new, relatively low-cost opportunities for Africans interested in learning legislative theory and practical techniques for drafting effectively implemented transformatory legislation. For acquiring the skills essential to using facts and logic to assess and, when necessary, draft bills accompanied by well-designed research reports, those who took part in the 2001 and 2002 sessions evaluated the distance course as 'very good' to 'excellent'. The more recent emphasis on encouraging registered participants to work with a group of colleagues has begun to contribute towards accelerating a multiplier effect.

Proposed West Africa Institute for Legislative Drafting for Democratic Social Change (WAILDSC)

Two lawyers, Raymond Atuguba and Sam Amadi, have organized and for several years run legal aid clinics, respectively, in Ghana and Nigeria.[11] Atuguba's PhD thesis describes how the British-imposed law, interacting with pre-existing Ghanaian institutions, shaped Ghana's inherited policing system. Atuguba and his colleagues are preparing a bill, based on evidence he gathered for his doctoral thesis, to restructure the Ghanaian police from an oppressive instrument of the elite into one more attuned to assisting communities to attain effective development to fulfil the needs of all Ghanaians. As a University of Ghana law lecturer, Atuguba also led a group of students in taking the distance course. In it, they learned legislative theory, methodology and techniques by drafting a bill to change the inherited British 1907 marriage law to provide adequate protection for Muslim married women. Using the solving methodology to gather and organize the relevant evidence, they drafted a research report that demonstrated the likelihood that the bill's details would prove effectively implemented and improve the marriage status of Muslim women – Muslims now comprise about 25 per cent of Ghana's population.

In Nigeria, for some years, Sam Amadi (another recent PhD graduate from Harvard) and his colleagues have been building a legal aid clinic. Beginning with efforts to achieve justice for Ken Sarowiwa, they have recently undertaken efforts to work with national legislators to draft legislation to transform the full range of dysfunctional institutions that condemn a majority of rural Nigerians to live in poverty.

Together, Amadi and Atuguba have made plans to establish a West Africa Institute for Legislative Drafting for Democratic Social Change (WAILDSC) to strengthen the region's drafting capacity and regional cooperation for introducing transformatory regional legislation. Through the distance course, several members of their countries' civil society have learned legislative drafting theory and skills in preparing draft legislation for their own countries.

Already, Atuguba and Amadi have begun to organize workshops in their own countries. Each workshop involves some 30 participants, working in teams to draft six to eight bills to help resolve what they view as priority regional social problems; these may include:

- protecting the regional environment against industrial wastes;
- reducing corruption in government procurement;
- improving tax collection;
- providing technical and financial support for small enterprises; and
- democratizing lawmaking processes.

At those workshops, participants have begun to discuss the details for building an ongoing learning process to strengthen regional legislative drafting and law making institutions in their home countries:

- training of trainers to conduct workshops for national government officials and drafters, members of Parliament, and NGO personnel;
- conducting courses in West African universities to engage law and social science students in drafting programmes to learn legislative theory and practice by drafting bills, justified by research reports, to help local governments resolve local social problems; and

- establishing WAILDSC as a regional centre of excellence to provide training and guidance to West African countries and institutions interested in strengthening legislative drafting capacity; producing teaching materials, articles and books for use in government, university and non-government training programmes throughout the region; and developing research capacity to strengthen and improve the use of legislative theory, methodology and techniques as tools for helping to resolve social problems in the context of West African realities.

Zambia: A proposed Commission on Law and Integrated National Development

After half century of independent governance, Zambia's 11 million inhabitants, living in a land-locked area roughly the size of England, confronted a paradox: instead of the promised life of plenty, their economy, still hinged by powerful multinational corporations to the world's overcrowded copper market, had plunged downwards; formal sector unemployment mounted to about 40 per cent; their per capita incomes fell to among the continent's lowest. A group of Zambians, headed by Lucian N'gandwe, proposed to set up a Law and Integrated National Development Commission to begin a process of drafting legislation to implement an ongoing process of transforming the inherited institutions that perpetuated these gross resource misallocations. Using a problem-solving approach, Commission members would conduct research, design and submit bills for consideration by the Zambian parliament. They would accompany these bills with research reports that demonstrate the likelihood that the bills' detailed provisions would restructure the key sectors of Zambia's economy – agricultural and industrial production, domestic and international trade, and finance – to fulfil the basic needs of all Zambians (N'Gandwe, 2004).

N'gandwe prepared a draft bill to establish the Commission, accompanied by a research report on the available evidence, logically organized to justify that bill's details. Supported by Boston University's African Presidential Professors Archives and Research Center, he spent a month in 2004 discussing the proposal with government, university and civil society groups. On his return, the BU Presidential Center hosted a forum of concerned African scholars from the Boston area to comment on and suggest improvements in the drafts.

Summary and Conclusion

Africa stands at a crossroads. The half-century during which African nations attained independence witnessed a fatal race. Africa's first post-independence governments failed to exercise their newly won state power through law to restructure the institutions, which perpetuated most of their inhabitants' poverty and vulnerability. As a partial explanation, many people emphasize that those institutions themselves shaped bastions of power that blocked efforts to transform them. This chapter, however, has focused on another set of explanations, namely that – despite initial and even reopened windows of opportunity – the new lawmakers (including government officials, legislators and drafters) – had no theory or methodology to guide them in designing and implementing new laws to transform those institutions. Over time, unequipped to use state power to change their countries' inherited dysfunctional institutions, many African governors became cynical and corrupt. The vast majority of Africans, meanwhile, found themselves victims of deepening poverty and untreated (but curable) diseases, enmeshed in destructive ethnic conflicts, desperately struggling for bare survival.

Inhabiting a continent three times the size of the United States, with vast agricultural and mineral riches, Africans – as President Nkrumah proposed half a century ago – need to work together to transform the institutions that perpetuate and deepen their poverty and oppression. A few have begun to learn to exercise state power through governments' most effective tool for democratic social change: the formulation and implementation of transformatory law grounded on reason and experience.

This chapter describes the legislative theory and methodology that, in several African countries, has guided initial steps – in Mozambique, South Africa, Ghana, Nigeria and Zambia – to institutionalize an ongoing learning process to strengthen national legislative drafting capacities and law making institutions. Workshops and training programmes have already illustrated the potential benefits of equipping African government, university and NGO personnel with legislative tools to design legislation, grounded in the facts and logic of their country circumstances, to resolve potential conflicts not by superior power alone but by using reason informed by experience (Seidman and Seidman, 1994; Seidman et al, 1997; Seidman, Seidman and Uate, 1999; Seidman, Seidman and Walde, 1999; Seidman et al, 2001, p11, Box 1; Seidman et al, 2003). Working as individuals and members of groups in an international distance course, several Africans have begun using these tools to draft detailed laws to resolve their own countries' social problems.

Over time, tested through ongoing practice, these initiatives aim to introduce more transformatory legislation to improve governance and redirect the employment of Africa's' rich resources to meet the basic needs of all Africans. To the extent that new laws embody criteria and procedures that ensure transparency, accountability and participation, these efforts may empower new generations of African governors to use law to facilitate democratic social change, engaging their continent's vast human and physical resources to create increasingly productive employment and a better quality of life for all Africans.

Notes

1. For details for each country, see International Monetary Fund, International Financial Statistics, published annually; for a description of the way economic institutions perpetuate this distorted resource allocation pattern, see Seidman and Makgetla, 1980.
2. Legislative theory defines an 'institution' not as a building with a plaque on the door – like a bank, or a university – but as the repetitive patterns of behaviours of the many people who work together (Seidman et al, 2001).

3. The colonial rulers had perceived their government as a nightwatchman state, which did little more than to keep law and order and collect taxes (Adu, 1965). That colonialist perception seems disingenuous. In fact, the colonial state intervened substantially to make the colonies safe and profitable for investors from the imperial power. It did little to improve social welfare.

4. Here, we use the term 'law' in its broadest connotation to mean a norm promulgated by the government. So defined, it includes not only statutes but also implementing decrees, subordinate legislation, municipal regulations, administrative regulations and other state sponsored rules.

5. While language difficulties have hindered the authors from conducting research or teaching legislative drafting in the French African colonies, they have worked in former French (Vietnam and Lao PDR) and Dutch (Indonesian) colonies, as well as South Africa and Mozambique. Despite frequent claims that common law and European traditions differ, both traditions tend to foster drafting of general principles, leaving the detailed prescriptions (whether in the form of 'decrees,' 'regulations' or 'subordinate legislation') to implementing officials.

6. For the social science skills lawmakers need to assess the available information, see Seidman et al (2001).

7. Funded by USAID through the State University of New York (SUNY)-Albany.

8. The cost of tuition, living costs and transportation to Boston and return from most African countries exceeded many African government officials' annual income.

9. A registered course participant pays tuition of US$2000. In most cases, country offices of donor agencies, like the United Nations Development Programme, US Agency for International Development subcontractors (such as the State University of New York) and DANIDA, the Danish aid agency, have paid the tuition for registered participants. In 2004, Boston University (BU) distance course began to urge registered participants to work together with a group of two or more country nationals as a basis for institutionalizing an ongoing, self-reliant learning process for those interested in strengthening their countries' national drafting capacity and lawmaking institutions. In 2005, the International Consortium for Law and Development, which developed out of the BU Programme, assumed the task of administering the distance course (see its website, www.ICLAD-law.org).

10. The conduct of the course has encountered technological as well as substantive challenges. Because most Third World countries' internet access remains limited, the course relies primarily on email for communication between the participants, the instructors and their editors. This footnote briefly describes the course's global learning process.

   By airmail, each participant registered for the course receives the course manual 'Legislative Drafting for Democratic Social Change – a Manual for Drafters'; 28 hours of taped oral presentations; and two study guides which specify dates on which participants should submit to their editors the specified drafts of their bills and research reports. Each has a qualified editor who reads, edits and suggests improvements in those drafts.

   To make the distance course more useful, registered participants have organized groups of colleagues to work together in drafting bills and reports to help resolve social problems, which they have chosen as priorities in their country's unique circumstances. At no cost beyond the tuition (other than that of making copies), the registered participants copy all the course materials for the other group members. The registered participants email the group's drafts to their assigned editor.

The Distance Course 'bulletin board' facilitates interchange between course participants. The course instructors, editors, participants and auditors introduce themselves to each other by 'posting' the information (or sending an email) on the course bulletin board. In addition, each group may 'post' on the bulletin board their drafts of their bills and reports, and comments and suggestions about the course materials for all the participants to consider. For those who have internet access, the course administrator has recently established a course website on which she arranges all these exchanges by topic.

11. The Centre for Public Policy & Research (CPP&R) in Nigeria and the Legal Resources Centre (LRC) in Ghana have for some years been conducting research and helping to strengthen the rule of law in their countries (eg the Nigerian director served as a counsellor for Ken Sarowiwa).

References

Adu, A (1965) *The Civil Service in the New African States*, Praeger, New York

Dewey, J (1916) *Essays in Experimental Logic*, University of Chicago Press, Chicago

Dewey, J (1925) 'Logical Method and the Law', *Cornell Law Quarterly*, vol 10

Dewey, J (1939) *Theory of Valuation*, Chicago University Press, Chicago

N'Gandwe, L (2004) *Report to the Presidential Professors*, Archives and Research Center, Boston University, Boston

Seidman, A and Makgetla, N (1980) *Outposts of Monopoly Capital: Southern Africa in Transition*, CT Hill & Company and Zed Press, Westport and London

Seidman, A and Seidman, B (1994) *State and Law in the Development Process: Problem-Solving and Institutional Change in the Third World*, Macmillan, Houndsmills

Seidman, A, Seidman, R and Abeysekera, N (2001) *Legislative Theory, Methodology and Techniques: A Practical Manual for Drafters*, Kluwer Law, London

Seidman, A, Seidman, R and Abeysekera, N (2003) *Assessing Legislation: A Manual for Legislators*, downloadable at www.bu.edu/law/lawdrafting

Seidman, A, Seidman R and Payne, J (1997) *Legislative Drafting for Market Reform: Some Lessons from China*, Macmillan, Houndsmills

Seidman, A, Seidman, R and Uate, T (1999) 'Building Legislative Capacity to Assess Bills in Light of the Public Interest', *Statute Law Review*, Oxford University Press, Oxford

Seidman, A, Seidman, R and Walde T (eds) (1999) *Making Development Work: Legislative Reform for Institutional Transformation and Good Governance*, Kluwer Law, London

8

The Politics of Decentralization

Jesse C Ribot and Phil René Oyono

Introduction

Governments across Africa have undergone repeated decentralization reforms since the early colonial period.[1] Since the late 1980s, decentralization reforms are once again sweeping the continent, as well as the rest of the developing world (UNCDF, 2000, pp5–11).[2] Ethiopia, Ghana, Mali, Namibia, Nigeria, Senegal, South Africa and Uganda have constitutions that are pro-decentralization recognizing the existence of local government (Therkildsen, 1993, p83; UNCDF, 2000; Tötemeyer, 2000, p95). In this most recent wave of decentralizations, the language of reform has shifted from an emphasis on national cohesion and the management of local populations to a discourse more focused on democratization, governance, pluralism and rights. According to Oyugi (2000, p16) 'there is not a single country in Africa in which some form of local government is not in operation' and, he points out, the stated objective of virtually all decentralization reforms is to strengthen democratic governance and service provision.

Past decentralizations in Africa were designed to manage local populations either through administratively driven 'customary' rulers or administrative authorities of colonial and post-colonial governments. Local authorities were expected to carry out orders passed down the political-administrative hierarchy (Mawhood, 1983; Mamdani, 1996a; Crook and Manor, 1998). Local institutions were instruments of central authority. Current democratic decentralizations are ostensibly being designed to enfranchise local people through rights and representation in local public decision-making. Decentralized local institutions are now being cast as instruments of democratic decision-making, so that local people can make decisions based on their own needs and aspirations. For democratic decentralization to serve these ends, it requires transfer of discretionary powers into the hands of representative or at least downwardly accountable local authorities to replace administratively mandated managers (Agrawal and Ribot, 1999).

Like current community-based and decentralized approaches, colonial policies of 'indirect rule' under the British and '*association*' under the French were also justified in terms of local self-determination (Mair, 1936).[3] These policies were advocated by some idealists who believed they would lead to improved local well-being. But history has judged these institutions as oppressive instruments of central control (Mamdani, 1996a). The colonial governments used these ostensibly progressive policies as effective instruments of management and control. This should be taken as a cautionary note. Today's decentralizations also appear to be proceeding in ways that risk reproducing old patterns of indirect rule: administratively driven local authorities managing people in the name of self-determination (Ribot, 1999a). As decentralization policies are being formulated and implemented, they are running into resistance at multiple levels, mostly within government and among elites.

Decentralization is promoted on the assumption that greater participation in public decision-making is a positive good in itself or that it can improve efficiency, equity, development and resource management.[4] By bringing government decision-making closer to citizens, decentralization is widely believed to increase public-sector accountability and therefore effectiveness – better matching services to needs and better mobilizing local resources, labour and knowledge.[5] Democratic decentralization is its strong form because of the systematic mechanisms that hold local authorities accountable to the population. Administrative decentralization is its weak form, having proximity without democratic accountability (Ribot, 2001a). Many expectations of decentralization follow from the tenets of 'new institutionalism'. Among the adherents are development planners, international financial institutions and agencies, who advocate 'getting the institutions rights'. The effectiveness of reforms, however, is profoundly affected by 'the broad features of the political-economic context' in which these institutions and the reforms that would establish them are located (Boone, 2003, p356). The new institutional theory may be correct that *if* the right institutional arrangements are established certain outcomes will follow. But the theory fails to take into account the larger political economy that shapes the likelihood of establishing the required new arrangements.

This chapter is concerned with the multiple levels of resistance emerging against the current wave of democratic decentralization reforms. These reforms are in fetters. They promise enfranchisement and improvements, but are not able to deliver. This chapter first explores some of the ideological, structural, political and practical reasons decentralizations are in trouble and then looks at some of the actors that block decentralizations and the means they use for blocking them.

Fetters on Decentralization

Decentralization reforms have occurred in Africa under colonial rule, military regimes and democratic governments. Crook and Sverrisson (2001, p2) argue, however, that 'there is no evidence of a connection between regime type and either the presence of decentralized government itself or the broad type of decentralization system'. Decentralizations that have taken place to date have been explained as an outcome of pressure from economic crises (Therkildsen, 2001, p1; Olowu, 2001, p53); a means for central governments to shed fiscal and administrative burdens (Nsibambi, 1998, p2); failure of central administration (Wunsch and Olowu,

1995); emulation of reforms in other developing countries (Therkildsen, 2001, p1); a populist political success (Heller, 1996; Olowu, 2001, p53);[6] a result of donor pressures and conditions as part of structural adjustment and other programmes imposed from the outside (World Bank, 2000; Mutizwa-Mangiza, 2000, p24; Therkildsen, 2001, p1); a response to sub-national splinter groups and pressure to appease and incorporate local elite (Brock and Coulibaly, 1999, p30; World Bank, 2000, pp108–9; UNCDF, 2000, p3; Olowu, 2001, p53); and as the consequence of particular configurations of relations between central and local authorities (Crook and Sverrisson, 2001, p2). Of course, they are most likely a conjunctural result of these and other global, national and local forces.

Regardless of their origins, democratic decentralizations require the establishment of representative local actors who are downwardly accountable to the local population as a whole and who are entrusted with public powers (Manor, 1999; Ribot, 1999a). If a reform involves transfer of powers, but the actors receiving them are not representative or downwardly accountable, then perhaps it is privatization or deconcentration. If a reform creates representative actors with no public powers, then the institutional arrangement is not decentralization. Perhaps it is establishing advisory groups, or a 'privy council' as in colonial times. The choice by central government of the powers and structures to exercise authority are the defining aspects of decentralization. Unfortunately, many reforms now taking place in the name of democratic decentralization do not have these basic elements (for a detailed discussion, see Ribot, 2002a; 2000b). Resistance at many levels – from the discursive through policy-making and implementation – has prevented the transfer of sufficient powers and the creation or empowerment of appropriate institutions. This section discusses some of the obstacles to current decentralizations.

The leaning towards democratic forms of decentralization is confronting governments with the contradictions of a century of extractive and productivist policies towards the rural world. As democratic decentralization is legislated and applied, the procedural objectives of new democratic processes conflict with the instrumental objectives of central ministries (Shivaramakrishnan, 2000; Ribot, 2002a). Because local decisions are often inconsistent with central objectives, many ministries are approaching decentralization with an eye towards using the new ostensibly democratic institutions to pursue centrally defined infrastructure, health, education and environmental management objectives – by devolving obligations and creating requirements that diminish rather than enhance local discretion. Elected local authorities often turned into administrators of central mandates rather than executors of local interest. Such approaches undermine the core tenets of democratic decentralization.

Decentralization is also compromised when policies that require fiscal transfers coincide with austerity policies or fiscal crisis. Fiscal crisis or the weakening of the central state's fiscal leverage by structural adjustment programmes can weaken the central state's ability to support local action or to intervene to prevent the elite from overriding the needs and wishes of the poor (Crook and Sverrisson, 2001, pp26, 33). In Zimbabwe, new powers were officially transferred to local elected governments in 1993; however, the line ministries did not transfer any significant powers to them (Conyers, 2001, p4). 'The main obstacles were a general resistance to decentralization among line ministries and the dilemma of how to decentralize financial resources to local authorities while at the same time reducing public expenditure' which was required by structural adjustment programmes. Nevertheless, line ministries began to see decentralization as a means as extricating themselves from service delivery obligations that they could not meet as the economic situation worsened in Zimbabwe towards the end of 1999. Hence, obligations were transferred, but without adequate financial resources (Conyers, 2001, p4).

There are also ideological contradictions within the neo-liberal sphere that pit democratization against the fragmenting tendencies of what is being called 'pluralism' or 'stakeholder' approaches. In the name of pluralism, donor agencies and governments are empowering and creating a proliferation of non-state institutions – NGOs, PVOs, economic interest groups, corporations and traditional authorities – as if these authorities represent 'the people' or some vaguely defined notion of the public as 'civil society'. In doing so, they are taking powers that would otherwise be transferred to democratic local institutions and fragmenting them among multiple organizations, weakening democratic institutions and strengthening this alternative array of private actors. Its practitioners, although well-meaning, seem to forget that pluralism without representation sets a scene for elite capture – the most powerful interests dominate.

The uncritical inclusion of traditional authorities as part of this 'pluralism' is particularly troubling. It is often based on retrograde neo-traditionalist views of community that pit tradition against democracy – favouring identities bound to custom and those rights associated with being the first settlers in an area rather than residency-based citizenship (Mamdani, 1996a; Kassibo, 2004). When establishing a democratic decentralization the choice or construction of local institutions is as central as the devolution of discretionary powers. As in the colonial period, many international agencies and governments are appealing to 'traditional' leaders, claming they are representative and legitimate (van Rouveroy van Nieuwaal et al, 1999, p6).[7] But, this legitimacy may be based as easily on fear as on respect or habit, rather than the social good that such an authority performs (Ntsebeza, 2002). The inclusion of potentially unaccountable or autocratic customary authorities in a manner that displaces democratic authorities weakens the local institutional base for decentralization.

Much privatization is having a similar effect in undermining local democracy. Public and private are conflated by many practitioners who believe that democracy and decentralization are about letting anyone who is local make decisions and by believing that NGOs and other community groups represent the public. Much privatization of public goods, such as forests and pastures, to individuals takes place in the name of decentralization. Privatization also takes place in relation to NGOs – a kind of non-market privatization – since NGOs are ostensibly non-market, but are nonetheless private institutions. The process of privatization takes away public powers from local democratic institutions and undermines the local democratization processes.

There are also straightforward political problems that emerge in decentralization design and implementation. Heller (2001, p133) points out that states and those who control them have little interest in shaking up existing patterns of political control and patronage. Line ministries resist giving up their powers (Ribot, 1999a; 2002a; Smoke, 1999, 2000). Decentralization diminishes central-ministry control over important allocative patronage resources, such as agricultural extension, permitting processes, market regulation and natural resources (see Bates, 1981; Bazaara, 2002; Muhereza, 2003). They also threaten ruling parties by replacing local clients, such as party-appointed administrators or party-list councils, with more independent democratic institutions. In this manner democratic decentralization breaks up clientele networks through which central agents and parties can manipulate rural constituencies, threatening powerful interests. There is great institutional inertia to overcome in the context where the post-colonial states were born of 'developmentalism' and were anointed as the prime and central agents of development and change – top-down command-and-control systems persist.

Very concrete implementation problems also emerge to block decentralization. Principles of subsidiarity to guide central governments in deciding which powers can be devolved to local bodies have not been developed. Technical or managerial skills may be needed for local governments to act independently. Bureaucrats, administrators and technical agents often slow decentralization out of genuine fear that the public values they are responsible for will be undermined or that negative outcomes will be generated. Conflicts among local groups often emerge as local authorities and control over resources change. Decentralization is a large task involving development, passage and implementation of new laws, re-deployment of personnel, re-channelling of resources, development of new institutions and individual capacities etc (Heller, 2001; Ribot, 2002a). Further, new elected state authorities take time to adjust to a new structure after so long under a culture of administrative-managerial government (Sturgeon, 2003).

Democratic decentralization is also threatened when it is poorly or only partially implemented, thus not delivering the benefits it promises and losing the support of those it is meant to empower. Such failure to deliver also gives discursive fodder to other actors threatened by decentralization reforms, who can claim that the experiment (although it never took place) has failed. While democratic decentralization reforms around Africa have barely been implemented, there is already a growing backlash. Decentralizations that democratize and transfer powers threaten many actors. By and large, the decentralization experiment has only taken small steps, mostly in the direction of deconcentration, which may represent a new geography of state authority, but does not constitute a democratic reform. Many policy changes are taking place in the name of decentralization. Few, however, combine the essential elements *discretionary powers* and *democratic authority* in the local arena. In some cases, local democratic authorities are being created but given no powers. In others, powers are devolved to non-representative or upwardly accountable local authorities.

Means of Resistance: Powers Transfer and Institutional Choice

Decentralizations are often fettered by the tendency of central authorities to hang onto and concentrate powers (Ergas, 1987; Wunsch and Olowu, 1995;

Smoke and Lewis, 1996; Manor, 1999). 'Lack of political will' is often cited as an explanation for why decentralizations are poorly implemented if at all (Cheema and Rondinelli, 1983). But what does this term 'political will' mean? If all that it means is that 'the rich and powerful have failed to act against their interests', there is no surprise here (Chambers, 1983, p161, cited in Dove and Kammen, 2000). Some central political actors are certainly threatened by decentralizations. Some are simply reluctant to release powers. Others are threatened by the new local authorities who may change their political base. There is central political support to re-empower chiefs in Mozambique, South Africa and Zimbabwe. Is this a way for central authorities to maintain political allies in rural areas? Do chiefs support central government agendas better than local democracy would? These questions need to be posed to understand better why central governments resist democratic decentralization. It is not enough to know that decentralization is not always in the political interest of central actors (Conyers, 2000b, p22). Here we examine where and how it is being resisted – which may help to develop strategies for negotiating around this resistance. The examples in this section draw largely on experience in natural resource management as well as on the literature in other sectors.

Different actors use different mechanisms to block decentralizations. Central governments have their particular strategies. The two main areas in which blockage takes place are:

1. in the *transfer of insufficient powers;* and
2. in the *choice of non-democratic local institutions.*

In past – as in current – decentralizations, responsibilities have been devolved without devolving discretionary powers, effectively strengthening central authorities through burden shedding (Uphoff and Esman, 1974; Parker, 1995; Ribot, 1995a; Manor, 1999; Crook and Manor, 1998; Alcorn, 1999). Hesitancy in creating new, more democratic local authorities and transferring real powers are explained or justified by central authorities and enacted in many ways.

Discursive means of fettering decentralization are very common. Backlashes and subsequent recent realizations are spreading. Governments in Ghana and in Uganda have already began to argue that decentralization has gone too far and is causing over-exploitation of natural resources (Aaron DeGrasi, personal communication, February 2002; Bazaara, 2002; Resosudarmo, 2005). Justifying their backlashes, central authorities have argued that decentralization threatens national unity by weakening the central state. Central governments and their administrations often call on arguably specious scientific reasoning, asserting that decentralization is a threat to environmental sustainability.[8] Others, such as forest services and other line ministries, argue that local authorities lack the technical skills and 'capacity' to be given any real responsibilities. Yet others have argued that transfers of power and the creation of new local authorities will cause local conflict between customary and new state authorities or among multiple local groups.

When decentralizations are promoted or required by donors, resistance can take the form of obfuscation by officials and agents of the state. Often decentralization is talked of, designed and even implemented as a kind of theatrical performance for donors in which the image is produced but the power distributions do not change. For example, these performances can involve downward transfers through one new law and recentralization through another, as in the case of Mali where the transfer is well crafted, but new structures of oversight (*tutelle*) are being built that could return to central authorities control over approval of every decision (Ribot, 1998a; 1998b; 1999a). Donors pursuing decentralization and other programmes also often miss the mark by sidelining elected local authorities or local governments more generally because their charters oblige them to work directly with sovereign – that is central – governments (Sewell, 1996, p148).[9]

Two common fears are expressed by central government agencies involved in decentralization of natural resources. First is that the transfer will lead to the destruction of the resource. Second is that the transfers will lead to local conflict. These fears, which are often characterized as 'Risks to Manage' by technical agencies, are sometimes founded. Usually, however, they are unfounded or greatly exaggerated (Fairhead and Leach, 1996; Swift, 1996; Ribot, 1999c; Baviskar, 2005). Nevertheless, these fears are used to argue against the transfer of powers to local authorities. Arguments that there will be conflict with customary authorities are used in Burkina Faso, Senegal, Mali, South Africa, Zimbabwe, Niger and Mozambique (Ribot, 2001b). There is little evidence, however, that decentralization leads to environmental damage or conflict. Our Malian colleagues feel the conflict risk has been exaggerated. Continued central allocation practices, poorly crafted unregulated transfers or insecurities stemming from the newness of the laws are just as likely to be responsible if such effects are actually being observed.

Based on these expressed fears, arguments that local populations lack the capacity to manage resources and conflict are a very common affront against transferring resources. For example, a Malian Forest Service technical adviser working on the Malian decentralization recently argued, 'We cannot transfer responsibilities to the blind.' When asked who was blind, he said, 'the illiterate elected councillors and the villagers who elected them' (interview, Bamako, March 2002). These capacity arguments are backed by technical arguments concerning management requirements and by stories of conflicts and deaths from resource disputes since decentralization began. There is plenty of evidence, however, that there are management and use rights and powers that can be transferred without threatening the resource base or causing new conflicts (Ribot, 1999c; Latif, 2002). Further, we could find no evidence in any of the cases that conflicts represent an increase from the pre-decentralization period.

'Scientistical' arguments are another common means of retaining central control over natural resources. These include specious technical reasons to keep decisions central, even though we now know that there are many environmental use powers that can be transferred without threat to the resource base – and even without any need for enhanced capacities. But, forest services systematically refuse to acknowledge this. Further, these kinds of arguments have led to the establishment of overly complex management-planning requirements that have often made it impossible for local communities to use or manage surrounding resources with any degree of independence. These plans are so complex in Cameroon, Senegal and Mali that the only ways in which local communities can get permission to use the resources is if they have technical assistance from an international donor or NGO (Ribot, 1995a; Etoungou, 2002; Oyono, 2002b).

There are also a number of problems in the choice of powers being transferred: burdens are being transferred without or in place of positive powers, and non-commercially valuable uses are transferred in lieu of lucrative opportunities. Bazaara (2002) has described in Uganda the fusion of technical with political decisions. He argues that acting as if commercial allocation decisions are technical decisions for the forest service to make hides the fact that the central agencies are reserving for themselves what are ultimately political choices. Often there is also confusion between transferring the instrumental objectives of the state to local authorities rather than transferring discretionary powers. The language in Mali recently changed from transfer of 'competence' (meaning jurisdiction) to 'transfer of missions' (observation by author, Bamako, March 2002). The question is 'Whose mission?' By transferring central missions or responsibilities to local authorities, central governments are using elected local bodies to implement central agendas. This is not decentralization. This is a form of deconcentration that Resosudarmo has called 'Co-Administration', where decentralized bodies are treated as implementing bodies for central agendas.

Failure to create a local domain is another common problem. In Cameroon, there are progressive community-based management provisions in forestry law, but community forests can only be established in a very limited set of areas determined by a 'zoning plan'[10] and by the forest service (Ekoko, 2000; Oyono, 2002b). In Mali, the very strong decentralization laws that give local councils considerable powers over local forests are undermined because the central state has refused to establish a local domain in which to exercise them (Ribot, 1995a; Kassibo, 2002). A similar result is achieved through a different process in Uganda. In Masindi District, Uganda, the jurisdiction of local governments was severely restricted by re-classification of forests, placing central reserves under direct central government control and limiting district management to a few local forest reserves. The government reclassified 17 forests and designated 8 forests as local forest reserves. Only 2 of these 8 tiny reserves, Kirebe (49 hectares) and Masindi Port (18 hectares) remained under district council jurisdiction after the government returned the others to the Kingdom of Bunyoro-Kitara in May 2000. The local government was left with almost no decentralized domain (Muhereza, 2001a, pp17–19; Muhereza, 2003, pp22–3).

What Conyers (2001) calls 'means of transfer' mechanisms are commonly used to retain powers in the executive branch. Rather than transfers through legislation, laws include 'delays' that leave decisions to Ministerial or administrative decrees and orders. By this mechanism the transfer of powers is retained as a discretionary decision of the executive actors. When powers are transferred, they are allocated as privileges that can be withdrawn at executive will rather than as secure rights for local people to invest in. Further, under these conditions, local authorities must please the higher authorities to retain their privileges. This turns their accountability upward to the allocating authority, rather than downward to the populations they ostensibly represent and serve.

In Cameroon, the recentralization of tax revenues illustrates a backlash that took place at multiple levels, where transfers were not securely legislated. In 1994 10 per cent of forestry revenues were transferred to village communities. The villagers viewed the forestry tax revenues as a kind of repayment or compensation for generations of exclusion. One villager stated 'it is now our turn to drink and eat the money from the forests' (Oyono et al, 2005). But, in 1998, the Ministry of Economy and Finance and Ministry of Territorial Administration specified how the revenue must be spent and also relocated the revenues from the village to the local government level. All projects were to be planned jointly by the municipal authorities, the administrative authorities and the representatives of village forestry-fee management committees.

Under the new arrangements funds would be allocated to the regional level of local government and then handed down to local levels and projects. In this manner, the villages lost discretionary power over the revenues and hence government agencies gained power. Milol and Pierre (2000) and Bigombé Logo (2002) found that, at the regional level, funds are misappropriated by the municipal administrative authorities. Funding often goes to fictional projects. When it goes to real projects, the beneficiary communities are under the strict control of outside actors including the mayor, the sub-divisional officer and agents of the Ministry of Forestry. Djeukam and Nguiffo noted that:

> the downgrading of village development committees in the political process of managing the forestry fees, to benefit of the committees chaired by mayors who were appointed ... by the governor, is, to a certain extent, part of the logic of the patrimonialist and neo-patromonialist sharing of the revenue from forestry between the [central] authorities and the local political elite. (Djeukam and Nguiffo, 2002)

Further centralization of these funds for an inter-regional redistribution scheme is now being discussed at the national level.

Excessive oversight and overbearing approval processes are another means used almost universally to reduce local discretion. Examples include management-planning exercises (mentioned above) that are overly complex and restrictive, or that determine every move that anyone will make. In Cameroon, the path from demarcation of community forest boundaries through the signing of management agreements and final exploitation is long and slow. The forest service is omnipresent throughout the process. Over the past four years in Cameroon, 150 applications have been submitted to the Ministry of Forestry: 36 have been accepted, 14 have been rejected and 100 remain stuck in the system. Further, these agreements are signed for merely a five-year period. If the forest is poorly managed – in the judgment of the Ministry of Forestry – the agreement is withdrawn. The transfer then becomes a political allocation rather like a conditional loan – not a secure transfer of powers. This kind of transfer is open to abuse. Excessive oversight often includes conditionalities on capacity where transfers are not made unless certain capacity criteria are met (Ribot, 1999a). Communities are told that they will get powers when they demonstrate capacities defined by the technical services.

Front-line administrative authorities also often resist change towards more inclusive less-oversight-intensive approaches, and decentralization often threatens their roles. Elected local bodies may be given the power to take over decisions that civil servants have been used to making. In Cameroon, Etoungou (2002, pp40–7) and Bigombé Logo (2002, pp37–53) observed that state agents lack a 'participatory culture' and maintain old command reflexes. State agents at the provincial and regional levels deny village communities a mature political role and continue to use them as instruments for their own projects. In Burkina Faso, Mali, Senegal and Cameroon forestry services require elaborate and often unneeded forest-management plans that only the 'experts' of the forest services must design or approve (Ribot, 1999a; 2002a). These power-retaining strategies are partly explained by a survival reflex of agents whose livelihoods are based on the rents from their administrative positions. These all function to keep decision-making within the administrative branch.

In Mali, rural civil service agents were highly resentful of having lost their former role and anxious about what role they would play in the future (Ribot 1998b; see also Conyers, 1990, p30; Conyers, 2000b, p22; cf Sturgeon, 2003). In Ghana the Minister of Local Government lists 'uncertainty among civil service personnel' as a factor that sets back decentralizations. Therkildsen (2001, pp35–6), in Malawi, also describes bureaucrats' apathy, cynicism and feelings of being marginalized and resentful when faced with restrictive reforms that came down from external pressures from the Ministry of Finance and IMF (International Monetary Fund) as well as the political and bureaucratic elite. Therkildsen also points out that in South Africa and Uganda:

> One of the many reform paradoxes is that the same elite, whose past decisions and behaviors are being challenged by the present reform initiatives, are often deeply involved in their implementation. Some of them may not be committed to reforms for ideological reasons. Others may be outright against reforms when these aim to restrict former privileges and powers and diminish rent-seeking possibilities. (Therkildsen, 2001, p36)

He cites Oyugi (1990, p69) as pointing to class orientation of the bureaucracy as a barrier to changes that are not in their interest (Therkildsen, 2001, p37; see also Heller, 2001; Sturgeon, 2003).

Central control over local authorities is another attenuation. Although local governments may be elected, central governments often establish control over local elected representatives. In Cameroon, for example, Mawhood (1993) observed the whittling down of local elected authority through 'financial supervision of local governments by senior divisional officers'. Very recently, in Cameroon, the Ministry of Territorial Administration proposed the creation of a sub-ministry of decentralization. Local actors now fear an escalation of administrative and authoritarian control and a delayed transition to local democracy. In Senegal, while local government is elected, the state has given local governments too little power to have a meaningful relation with local populations. They have nothing to offer (Hesseling, undated). Further, the accountability of elected officials may be so circumscribed in the regulations as to render them accountable to central government rather than to the people who elected them. As in many francophone countries, local governments in Cameroon are under the supervision of the Ministry of Territorial Administration. Although the rural councils in Cameroon are elected and the council then elects a mayor from among its members, in practice the mayors are rarely accountable to the municipal council, and even more rarely to the local communities (Bigombé Logo, 2002, p4857).

Counter to their proclaimed backing of decentralization policies, donors and NGOs often avoid local government owing to their general lack of confidence in any form of government,[11] favouring non-state bodies (as in joint forest management, rural markets and *Gestion de Terroir* approaches) (Romeo, 1996) or, out of their concern to show sensitivity towards 'indigenous' claims, preferring to work with customary authorities. This is a long-standing mistrust for government – democratic or otherwise – in donor circles.[12] This has led many programmes to avoid local governments even when those local governments are ostensibly democratically elected. This is true, for example, in USAID's natural resource management programmes in Guinea[13] and has occurred in other programmes in Mali, Niger, Burkina Faso, The Gambia and elsewhere (Ribot, 1999a). Ironically, this mistrust can also be damaging to democratization processes by restricting the state's ability to do good and to therefore develop a positive role and legitimacy of its own (Evans, 1997). Clearly, this resistance to local democracy also constitutes a blockage for democratic decentralization. In notable exceptions, DANIDA has worked out an agreement to work with directly local government in Uganda, and the UN Capital Development Fund is supporting local government in Uganda, Mali and other countries in Africa (Saito, 2000, p6).

Customary authorities present a common excuse for not devolving powers and a common challenge to decentralization in practice. Central authorities evoke arguments of potential conflict with 'customary' or 'traditional' authorities (as in Zimbabwe, South Africa and Burkina Faso) as a reason not to empower local representative authorities (Ribot, 1995b; Ntsebeza, 1999; Mandondo, 2000).[14] This problematic set of arguments needs to be explored. Local chiefs are often as much administrative creations of the colonial state as local governments are creations of the post-colonial states, and further, they are not necessarily downwardly accountable or representative. Customary authorities are often promoted by donors and other outsiders who view them as a romantic category of legitimate popular local leader (CARE-Mali, 1993; World Bank cited in Porter and Young, 1998, p523).[15] This too diverts attention from the need for more democratic local institutions. As Geschiere (1993, p169) points out: 'In all areas discussed [in Cameroon], the position of chiefs is deeply affected by processes of (post)-colonial State formation. This makes it difficult to view the chiefs as a real alternative to State power.'

A related question that needs investigation is whether in privileging 'customary' local authorities projects undermine the establishment of more accountable replicable representative local governments. Does the privileging of customary and other non-governmental bodies ultimately help keep rural populations as the subjects of administrative managerial authorities, rather than enfranchising them and helping them become citizens (see Mamdani, 1996a)? Whether and when these arguments are just excuses by central governments to avoid devolving powers or whether customary authorities pose either a real threat or a positive alternative to rural democratization is an open question. The creation of elected, downwardly accountable local-government authorities in this contentious environment may be the Achilles heel of effective decentralization.

Other local elite can also block decentralization reforms. In Lesotho, Ferguson (1994, pp194–227) documented political resistance to a 'decentralized' integrated rural development project in the late 1970s and early 1980s. Ferguson (1994, p226) reports that 'the project, by its nature, was not equipped to play the political game it suddenly found itself in the midst of. Having taken on "decentralization", and with it the entrenched power of the governing classes in Maseru [District], the project had no teeth available to it to chew what it had bitten off.' In this classic example, ministers also systematically resisted relinquishing any power to local integrative or decentralized bodies (Ferguson, 1994, p203).

Elite capture of community management by civil servants and political elites is also an important attenuation of community involvement in natural resource management. In Cameroonian villages where community forests have been established, elites have begun to take interest in and join management committees (Oyono, 2002b). They also establish alliances with logging companies to whom they promise the village forests (Klein et al, 2001). Some elites have also invented methods to 'urbanize' management committees and take over the community forestry planning and management process.

These are among the most common ways in which decentralizations are restricted, stopped or undone. The result is that decentralizations are rarely creating the space of discretion that is critical for local democracy to be meaningful.

Conclusions

Decentralization is an institutional arrangement involving local authorities, relations of accountability and public powers. The central issues in democratic decentralizations concern the institutional form of local representation and responsiveness, and the kinds of powers local authorities hold. A review of the literature reflects surprisingly little empirical research on the institutional forms that decentralizations are actually taking (Ribot, 2002a). First indications are that there are almost no instances of strong or democratic decentralization – that combine accountable representation with discretionary powers – being created. Most reforms follow the contours of weak decentralization or deconcentration. The literature reflects extreme reluctance of governments to transfer meaningful powers to representative local authorities. Often various forms of delegation or privatization occur in the name of decentralization.

Powers and institutional choice matter in whether a decentralizaton is democratic or not, and whether it might have a chance of being efficient and equitable. But the cases in which *both* discretionary powers are being transferred *and* democratic institutions being chosen are very few. The clearest points that come from existing research are that:

- discretionary powers must be transferred for there to be meaningful decision-making in the local arena, but the powers now being transferred rarely establish such a domain of local discretion;
- discretionary powers must be transferred to democratic, as in downwardly accountable, local institutions, but the institutional choices now being made

do not support democratic decentralization – they frequently empower non-democratic institutions at the expense of democratic ones; and

- transfers are made more as insecure privileges than as rights, hence slowing the transformation of rural people from subjects to citizens.

At present democratic decentralizations are in fetters. These fetters take the form of arguments and actions that block the transfer of powers and the choice of appropriate democratic local institutions in so-called decentralization reforms. Peluso (1992) wrote that for each form of state control there is a corresponding form of peasant resistance. Here, if decentralizations are to advance, for each fetter being tied, we will need to envision and mobilize to create counter-actions. Resistance needs to be met with well thought out counter-resistance to un-fetter the process – to make decentralization emancipatory.[16]

While there is a current trend favouring democratic decentralization, the challenge before us is to assure that this trend moves from the realm of discourse into law and from law into practice. The primary challenge is to assess decentralizations to see whether legal reforms reflect the discourse in national political circles, and to ensure that the practice reflects the laws when they are indeed laws designed to establish real decentralization. The biggest challenge to decentralization on the horizon is the re-emergence or resuscitation of chieftaincy and custom to challenge the formation of local democracy. This trend is often supported by actors within the state and by international donors who favour customary authorities in choosing local actors with whom to interact. It constitutes a serious backlash against decentralization and local democracy, and may prove to block democratic change.

There are many other challenges on the path towards strong decentralization. This path will need to be paved by a multitude of local constituencies who believe they will benefit from decentralization – they need to constitute a counter-power to the centralizing tendencies of states. It will also need to be paved by grounded research[17] on decentralization, which is surprisingly scarce in Africa. In short, we need to map mechanisms of central retention of control. We need to find corresponding mechanisms of counter-power to leverage the transfer of power to local elected bodies. We need to get the experiment underway so that we can ask what the effects are of democratic decentralization on the environment, social well-being and justice.

Decentralization is about the transfer of powers among individuals and institutions. There will be winners and there will be losers; and both will fight. The losers, however, are now in power. They will resist and countering them will not be easy.

Notes

1. Decentralization in Africa is not new. Since 1917 there have been at least four waves of decentralization in francophone West Africa – after both world wars, shortly after independence and in the present decade (Hesseling, nd, p15; Buell, 1928, pp929–30; Cowan, 1958, p60; RDS, 1972; Schumacher, 1975,

pp89–90; RDM, 1977; Crook and Manor, 1994; Diallo, 1994; Ouali et al, 1994, p7; Gellar, 1995, p48; UNCDF, 2000). French Central Africa also decentralized just before independence (Weinstein, 1972, pp263–6), and in some countries after independence (Biya, 1986, p51; Therkildsen, 1993; Gellar, 1995). The anglophone and lusophone worlds have also seen multiple pre- and post-colonial decentralizations (Buell, 1928; Mawhood, 1983; Conyers, 1984; Rondinelli et al, 1989; de Valk and Wekwete, 1990; Therkildsen, 1993; Rothchild, 1994; Mbassi, 1995, p23; Mamdani, 1996; Ahwoi, 2000, p2; UNCDF, 2000).

2. Globally, all but 12 of the 75 developing and transitional countries with populations over 5 million claim to be transferring political powers to local units of government (see Dillinger, 1994, p8, cited in Crook and Manor, 1998; cf World Bank, 2000).

3. Before French and British colonization, German colonizers in Cameroon were concerned with getting indigenous people to 'manage their own affairs' (Mveng, 1985, pp23–40).

4. Arguments defending decentralization on the basis of greater participation of citizens in democratic governance, ie de Tocqueville (1945[1835]; Dahl, 1981, pp47–9; Green, 1993, p3). Webster (1992, p129), is the only one of the later figures to argue that decentralization is 'seen as a means by which the state can be more responsive, more adaptable, to regional and local needs than is the case with a concentration of administrative powers' (see also Bish and Ostrom, 1973; Weimer, 1996, pp49–50). For a counterview that does not see in decentralization any necessary benefits of responsiveness or freedom, see Riker (1964), who says, 'To one who believes in the majoritarian notion of freedom, it is impossible to interpret federalism as other than a device of minority tyranny' (p142). Schilder and Boeve, 1996, pp94–117 provide an argument favouring efficiency through decentralization. For efficiency arguments in the context of public choice see Oates, 1972, pp11–12; Tiebout, 1972.

5. Fox and Aranda, 1996, p1; World Bank, 1997.

6. For examples from the resistance to environmental-sector decentralizations see Ribot (2004) and Ribot and Larson (2005).

7. Van Rouveroy van Nieuwaal et al (1999) have argued that land and natural resource management are being renewed as arenas for chiefly power. NGOs 'appear to have turned chiefly office into an arena of brokerage, thus opening new perspectives and avenues for entrepreneurial activity'. Natural resources and land allocation are described as domains in which chiefs' 'nostalgic claims to authentic ritual power are effectuated in terms of real political power'. Chiefs use this discourse to their advantage in their relation with post-colonial African states. Chiefs use the domain of natural resource management and land allocation to manipulate this relation to their own advantage. 'In most cases chiefs succeed in invoking ritual rights from the "past", which they then translate into instruments for "hard" political brokerage. Chiefs negotiate their positions in the context of global discourse on sustainability, environmental awareness and national and international interest in ecological preservation' (van Rouveroy van Nieuwaal et al, 1999, p6).

8. Many authors have shown such specious scientific reasoning in Environmentalism (Guha, 1990; Beinart and Coates, 1995; Fairhead and Leach, 1996; Roe, 1996; Keeley and Scoones, 1999; Ribot, 2000).

9. As Sewell (1996, p148) notes, funding problems for local governments in decentralizations 'may pose difficulties for international financial institutions, but they should not be thought of as "Dangers of Decentralization"', as Prud'homme has called them.

10. Drawn up by the Ministry of Forest, the zoning plan is a plan of land use in the whole 'forested' Cameroon.

11. See Evans (1997) and Tendler (1997) who question the basis of this lack of confidence.

12. Images of the 'bad' state and the 'good' society in what Tendler calls 'mainstream development thinking' have deeply influenced the ways development practitioners give advice, orienting them towards policies that limit public-sector 'damages' by limiting government (Tendler, 1997, pp1–2). In the last decade the left and the right's attacks on the state have converged with the growth of a populist movement that sees everything local and indigenous as good and everything of the state as bad (Scott, 1976; Shiva, 1989; Western et al, 1994; Escobar, 1995; Singh and Titi, 1995). This negative view of the state seems to have erased the state, as powers were believed to be devolving downward towards NGOs and '*the people*' and upward towards the global arena (Rosenau, 1993). Further, channelling of international aid only through central governments or NGOs (as the alternative, anti-governmental route) has also conspired to blot out local government from the picture (Romeo, 1996, p4).

13. Based on interviews I conducted in Guinea in late 1998.

14. It should be noted that many of the powers to be devolved, however, have not been in the hands of chiefs or other local traditional authorities since the beginning of the colonial period. Hence, devolution of these powers to local government does not constitute a direct taking from customary authorities. This is particularly the case for commercial forest resources such as woodfuels and timber (Ribot, 1999b).

15. CARE-Mali (1993) is a good example of the privileging of customary authorities. Porter and Young (1998, pp523–4) also cite an example of the privileging of chiefs in natural resource management in Ghana, but they comment, 'While Chiefs clearly must not be ignored in environmental management, their representation as uncontentious "custodians" of natural resources seems unwise. In addition to the difficulties commonly associated with stool disputes (which occur not infrequently) there is ample evidence to indicate the extent of chieftaincy interests in – and wrangles over – natural resources such as salt in the coastal zone over this century and the dangers of undue dependence on chiefs representing the diverse interests of their subject populations.'

16. An extensive research agenda is outlined in Ribot (2002a).

17. To *ecological destruction arguments*, in the Hardenist school, we need to respond with good environmental analysis and propose a set of principles of environmental subsidiarity. As Bazaara (2002) observed, we need to use this kind of environmental analysis to separate technical (or ecological) from political

decisions, devolving those that are political. We must also question the need for complex management plans and ask whether a minimum environmental standards approach might not better match a decentralization strategy than does a planning approach that allows forestry and other environmental ministries to prescribe when, where and by whom every last branch that will be snipped. In reaction to *conflict arguments*, risks need to be assessed: are they reasons to be cautious or are they excuses? Which powers can be transferred without causing conflictual situations? Are there means to transfer powers along with mediation devices so that conflicts don't become violent? In reaction to *capacity arguments*, we need to present the multiple counter examples and to analyse carefully the ways in which this argument has been used in the environmental and other sectors throughout history (Ribot, 1998a). In reaction to *legitimacy and institutional efficiency arguments*, we need principles to guide institutional choice and we need to talk about the political nature and implications of this choice.

References

Agrawal, A and Ribot, J (1999) 'Accountability in Decentralization: A Framework with South Asian and African Cases', *Journal of Developing Areas*, vol 33, pp473–502

Ahwoi, K (2000) 'Challenges Facing Local Governments in Africa in the 21st Century: An Executive Summary', *Local Government Perspectives*, vol 7, no 3, pp1–7

Alcorn, J (1999) 'Community Governance of Biodiversity Resources: Policy Reforms that can Make a Difference', *The Good Society*, vol 9, no 2, pp42–6

Bates, R (1981) *Markets and States in Tropical Africa*, University of California Press, Berkeley

Baviskar, A. 'Between Micro-Politics and Administrative Imperatives: Decentralisation and the Watershed Mission in Madhya Pradesh, India', in J Ribot and A M Larson (eds) *Decentralization of Natural Resources: Experiences in Africa, Asia, and Latin America*, Routledge, London, pp26–40

Bazaara, N (2002) 'From Despotic to Democratic Decentralization in Uganda: A History of Control over Nature', *Draft report for the collaborative Center for Basic Research and World Resources Institute program 'Environmental Accountability in Decentralized Contexts'*, mimeo, Kampala

Beinart, W and Coates, P (1995) *Environment and History: The Taming of Nature in the USA and South Africa*, Routledge, London

Bigombé Logo, L (2002) 'The Decentralized Forestry Taxation System in Cameroon: Local Management and State Logic', Working Paper No 10, World Resource Institute, Washington, DC

Bish, R and Ostrom, V (1973) *Understanding Urban Government*, American Enterprise Institute for Public Policy Research, Washington, DC

Biya, P (1986) *Communal Liberalism,* Macmillan, London

Boone, C (2003) 'Decentralization as Political Strategy in West Africa', *Comparative Political Studies*, vol 36, no 4, pp355–80

Brock, K and Coulibaly, C (1999) 'Sustainable Rural Livelihoods in Mali', *Research Report 35*, Sustainable Livelihoods Programme, Institute for Development Studies, Brighton, Sussex

Buell, R (1928) *The Native Problem in Africa*, Vols 1 and 2, Macmillan, New York

CARE-Mali (1993) 'Ogokana', Agriculture and Natural Resources Technical Report Series, Projet d'Agro-Sylviculture Villageoise de Koro, December

Chambers, R (1983) *Rural Development: Putting the Last First*, Longman Scientific & Technical, Essex

Cheema, G and Rondinelli, A (eds) (1983) *Decentralization and Development: Polity Implementation in Developing Countries*, Sage Publications, Beverly Hills, CA

Conyers, D (1983) 'Decentralization: The Latest Fashion in Development Administration?', *Public Administration and Development*, vol 3, pp97–109

Conyers, D (1984) 'Decentralization and Development: A Review of the Literature', *Public Administration and Development*, vol 4, no 2, pp187–97

Conyers, D (1990) 'Decentralization and Development Planning: A Comparative Perspective', in P de Valk and K H Wekwete (eds) *Decentralizing for Participatory Planning: Comparing the Experiences of Zimbabwe and Other Anglophone Countries in Eastern and Southern Africa*, Avebury Press, Aldershot

Conyers, D (2000a) 'Decentralisation: A Conceptual Analysis', Part 1, *Local Government Perspectives: News and Views on Local Government in Sub-Saharan Africa*, vol 7, no 3, pp7–9, 13

Conyers, D (2000b) 'Decentralisation: A Conceptual Analysis', Part 2, *Local Government Perspectives: News and Views on Local Government in Sub-Saharan Africa*, vol 7, no 4, pp18–24

Conyers, D (2001) 'Whose Elephants Are They? Decentralization of Control over Wildlife Management through the CAMPFIRE Programme in Binga District, Zimbabwe', Draft Working Paper, submitted to World Resources Institute, May, mimeo

Cowan, R (1958) *Local Government in West Africa*, Columbia University Press, New York

Crook, R and Manor, J (1994) 'Enhancing Participation and Institutional Performance: Democratic Decentralization in South Asia and West Africa', *Report to the Overseas Development Administration, on Phase Two of a Two-Phase Research Project*, January

Crook, R and Manor, J (1998) *Democracy and Decentralization in South-East Asia and West Africa: Participation, Accountability, and Performance*, Cambridge University Press, Cambridge

Crook, R and Sverrisson, A (2001) 'Decentralization and Poverty-Alleviation in Developing Countries: A Comparative Analysis or, is West Bengal Unique?', IDS Working Paper 130, Institute for Development Studies, Brighton

Dahl, R (1981) 'The City in the Future of Democracy', in L Feldman (ed) *Politics and Government of Urban Canada*, Methuen, London

Diallo, M A (1994) 'Problématique de la décentralisation au Niger', preparatory document for the Praia Conference, CILSS, Republic of Niger (financed by the Netherlands and the US Agency for International Development, Niamy, Niger)

de Valk, P (1990) 'State, Decentralization and Participation', in P de Valk and K Wekwete (eds) *Decentralizing for Participatory Planning: Comparing the*

Experiences of Zimbabwe and Other Anglophone Countries in Eastern and Southern Africa, Avebury Press, Aldershot

de Valk, P and Wekwete, K (eds) (1990) *Decentralizing for Participatory Planning: Comparing the Experiences of Zimbabwe and Other Anglophone Countries in Eastern and Southern Africa*, Avebury Press, Aldershot

Djeukam, R and Nguiffo, S (2002) 'Guide juridique du contrôle forestier camerounais', Centre pour le Développement et l'Environnement, Yaoundé.

Dove, R and Kammen, D (2000) 'Vernacular Models of Development: An Analysis of Indonesia Under the "New Order"', *World Development*, vol 29, no 4, pp619–39

Ekoko, F (2000) 'Environmental Adjustment in Cameroon: Challenges and Opportunities for Policy Reform in the Forestry Sector', Draft paper for WRI, later published as *Bruner and Ekoko*, mimeo

Ergas, Z (ed) (1987) *The African State in Transition*, St Martin's Press, New York

Escobar, A (1995) *Encountering Development: The Making and Unmaking of the Third World*, Princeton University Press, Princeton

Etoungou, P (2002) 'L'Impensé des Forêts Communautaires: Décentralisation à l'Est Cameroun', Working Paper for the joint World Resources Institute/CIFOR-Cameroon Program on Decentralization and the Environment, June, Yaoundé

Evans, P (1997) 'The Eclipse of the State? Reflections on Stateness in an Era of Globalization', *World Politics*, vol 50, no 1, pp62–87

Fairhead, J and Leach, L (1996) *Misreading the African Landscape: Society and Ecology in a Forest-Savanna mosaic*, Cambridge University Press, Cambridge

Ferguson, J (1994) *The Anti-politics Machine: 'Development', Depoliticization and Bureaucratic Power in Lesotho*, University of Minnesota Press, Minneapolis

Fox, J and Aranda, J (1996) *Decentralization and Rural Development in Mexico: Community Participation in Oaxaca's Municipal Funds Program*, La Jolla, CA Center for US–Mexican Studies, University of California, San Diego

Gellar, S (1995) *Senegal: An African Nation Between Islam and the West*, Westview Press, Boulder

Geschiere, P (1993) 'Chiefs and Colonial Rule in Cameroon: Inventing Chieftaincy, French and British Style', *Africa*, vol 63, no 2, pp151–75

Goldman, M (2000) 'Partitioned Nature, Privileged Knowledge: Community Based Conservation in the Massai Ecosystem, Tanzania', Working paper for the World Resources Institute programme on Decentralization and the Environment, June 2001, Madison, WI

Green, P (ed) (1993) *Democracy: Key Concepts in Critical Theory*, Humanities Press, New Jersey

Guha, R (1990) 'An Early Environmental Debate: The Making of the 1878 Forest Act', *The Indian Economic and Social History Review*, vol 27, no 1, pp65–84

Heller, P (1996) 'Social Capital as a Product of Class Mobilization and State Intervention: Industrial Workers in Kerala, India', *World Development*, vol 24, no 6, pp1055–71

Heller, P (2001) 'Moving the State: The Politics of Democratic Decentralization in Kerala, South Africa, and Porto Alegre', *Politics & Society*, vol 29, no 1, pp129–62

Hesseling, G (1996) 'Legal and Institutional Incentives for Local Environmental Management', Occasional Paper No 17, H Marcussen (ed) International Development Studies, Roskilde University

Hesseling, G with Smit, M (undated, circa 1984) 'Le Droit Foncier au Sénégal: L'Impact de la Réforme Foncière en Basse Casamance', mimeo

Kassibo, B (ed) (1997) *La décentralisation au Mali: état des lieux,* APAD Bulletin No 14, Lit Verlag, Hamburg

Kassibo, B (2001) 'Résurgence des Autorités Coutumières au sein de l'Etat Moderne Africain: Le Cas des Chefferies Traditionnelles au Mali', Proposal for Joint Research with World Resources Institute, May, mimeo, Bamako and Washington, DC

Kassibo, B (2002) 'Décentralisation et responsabilité dans les modes de gestion des ressources naturelles et des redevances y afférentes. Les Bourgoutières Yallarbe de Youwarou', Draft working paper for the World Resources Institute programme on Decentralization and the Environment, mimeo, Washington, DC

Kassibo, B (2004) 'Historical and Political Foundations for Participative Management and Democratic Decentralization in Mali: A Synthesis of Two Case Studies', *Environmental Governance in Africa* series, working paper no 15, World Resources Institute, Washington, DC

Keeley, J and Scoones, I (1999) 'Understanding Environmental Policy Processes: A Review', IDS Working Paper 89, June, IDS, Sussex

Klein, M, Salla, B and Kok, J (2001) 'Forêts communautaires: les efforts de mise en oeuvre à Lomié', Réseau de foresterie pour le développement rural (Document 25f), ODI, London

Latif, M (2002) 'Minutes of the World Resources Institute Conference on Decentralization and the Environment', Bellagio, Italy, pp18–22

Mahwood, P (1993) 'Applying the French Model in Cameroon', in P Mahwood (ed) *Local Governments in the Third World: Experience of Decentralization in Tropical Africa*, 2nd edn, Africa Institute of South Africa, Johannesburg

Mair, L (1936) *Native Policies in Africa*, Negro University Press, New York

Mamdani, M (1996a), *Citizen and Subject: Contemporary Africa and the Legacy of Late Colonialism*, Princeton University Press, Princeton

Mamdani, M (1996b) 'Indirect Rule, Civil Society, and Ethnicity: The African Dilemma', *Social Justice,* vol 23, no 1–2 (Spring–Summer), pp145–6

Mamdani, M and Wamba-dia-Wamba, E (1995) *African Studies in Social Movements and Democracy,* CODESRIA, Dakar

Mandondo, A (2000) 'Situating Zimbabwe's Natural Resource Governance Systems in History', Occasional Paper No 31, December, CIFOR, Bogor

Mandondo, A (2000) 'Forging (Un) democratic Resource Governance Systems from the Relic of Zimbabwe's Colonial Past', Institute of Environmental Studies, University of Zimbabwe and Centre for International Forestry Research, mimeo

Manor, J (1999) *The Political Economy of Democratic Decentralization*, The World Bank, Washington

Manor, J (2000) 'Local Government in South Africa: Potential Disaster despite Genuine Promise', Paper prepared for the United Kingdom's Department for International Development, Institute for Development Studies, Sussex, mimeo

Mawhood, P (1983) *Local Government in the Third World*, John Wiley, Chichester

Mawhood, P (1993) 'Applying the French Model in Cameroon', in P Mawhood (ed), *Local Governments in the Third World: Experience of Decentralization in Tropical Africa*, 2nd edn, Africa Institute of South Africa, Johannesburg

Mbassi, J-P (ed) (1995) *La Décentralisation en Afrique de l'Ouest*, Conduite du processus dans les pays francophones et lusophones, Ouagadougou, 5–8 April 1994, PDM and CEDA, Cotonou, Bénin

Milol, A and Pierre, J (2000) 'Impact de la fiscalité décentralisée sur le développement local et les pratiques d'utilisation des ressources forestières au Cameroun', unpublished *rapport d'étude*, Banque Mondiale and DFID, Yaoundé

Muhereza, F (2001a) 'Concept Note on the Need to Re-think the Issue of Private Forests', February 2001, mimeo, Kampala, Uganda

Muhereza, F (2001b) 'Environmental Decentralization and the Management of Community Forests in Pakanyi Sub-county, Masindi District', Draft Report to the World Resources Institute/Centre for Basic Research Program on Decentralization and the Environment, February 2001, mimeo, Kampala

Muhereza, F (2003) 'Environmental Decentralization and the Management of Forest Resources in Masindi District, Uganda', Environmental Governance in Africa, Working Paper No 8, World Resources Institute, Mimeo, Washington, DC

Mutizwa-Mangiza, N (2000) 'Comment', *Regional Development Dialogue*, vol 21, no 1 (Spring), pp23–5

Mveng, E (1985) *Histoire du Cameroun*, Vol 2, CEPER, Yaoundé

Nsibambi, A (ed) (1998) *Decentralization and Civil Society in Uganda: The Quest for Good Governance*, Fountain Publishers, Kampala

Ntsebeza, L (1999) 'Land Tenure Reform in South Africa: An Example from the Eastern Cape Province', Issue Paper No 82, IIED, London

Ntsebeza, L (2002) 'Decentralization and Natural Resource Management in Rural South Africa: Problems and Prospects', paper submitted to the Conference on Decentralization and the Environment, Bellagio, Italy, 18–22 February

Oates, W (1972) *The Political Economy of Fiscal Federalism*, Mass Lexington Books, Lexington

Olowu, D (2001) 'Local Political and Institutional Structures and Processes', Draft Paper for the Participatory Symposium, Cape Town, South Africa, 26–30 March, in *Decentralization and Local Governance in Africa*, United Nations Capital Development Fund, New York

Ouali, F, Kiemdé, P and Yaméogo, D (1994) 'Etude de base sur l'état de la décentralisation au Burkina', summary report, Commission Nationale de la Décentralisation, Premier Ministère, Burkina Faso, June

Oyono, R (2002a) 'Forest Management, Systemic Crisis and Policy Change: Socio-Organizational Roots of Ecological Uncertainties in the Cameroon's Decentralization Model', paper presented at the Conference on *Decentralization and the Environment*, Bellagio, Italy

Oyono, R (2002b) 'Infrastructure organisationnelle de la gestion locale des forêts au Cameroun. Eléments de sociologie des ressources naturelles pour la théorie sociale et les politiques publiques', Working Paper Summary, World Resource Institute, CIFOR, Cameroun

Oyono, R, Kouna, C and Mala, W (2005) 'Benefits of Forests in Cameroon: Global Structure, Issues Involving Access and Decision Making Hiccoughs', *Forest Policy and Economics*, vol 7, no 3, pp357–68

Oyugi, W (1990) 'Civil Bureaucracy in East Africa: A Critical Analysis of Role Performance since Independence', in O P Dwiwedi and K M Henderson (eds) *Public Administration in World Perspective*, Iowa University Press, Ames

Oyugi, W (2000) 'Decentralization for Good Governance and Development', *Regional Development Dialogue*, vol 21, no 1, pp3–22

Parker, A (1995) 'Decentralization: The Way Forward for Rural Development?', Agriculture and Natural Resources Department, World Bank, Washington, DC

Peluso, N (1992) *Rich Forests, Poor People: Resource Control and Resistance in Java*, University of California Press, Berkeley

Porter, D and Onyach-Olaa, M (1999) 'Inclusive Planning and Allocation for Rural Services', *Development in Practice*, vol 9, nos 1–2, pp56–67

Porter, G and Young, E (1998) 'Decentralized Environmental Management and Popular Participation in Coastal Ghana', *Journal of International Development*, vol 10, pp515–26

RDM (1977) 'Ordonnance N77-44/CMLN du 12 juillet 1977 portant réorganisation territoriale et administrative de la République du Mali', RDM, Bamako, Mali

RDS (1972) 'Decret no 72–636 du 29 mai 1972 relatif aux attributions des chefs de circonscriptions administratives et chefs de village', *Journal Officiel de la République du Sénégal*, vol 17 (June)

Resosudarmo, I A P (2005) 'Closer to People and Trees: Will Decentralisation Work for the People and the Forests of Indonesia?', in J Ribot and A M Larson (eds) *Decentralization of Natural Resources: Experiences in Africa, Asia, and Latin America*, Routledge, London, pp110–32

Ribot, J (1993) 'Market-State Relations and Environmental Policy: Limits of State Capacity in Senegal', in R Lipschutz and K Conca (eds) *The State and Social Power in Global Environmental Politics*, Columbia University Press, New York

Ribot, J (1995a) 'From Exclusion to Participation: Turning Senegal's Forestry Policy Around', *World Development*. vol 23, no 9, pp1587–99

Ribot, J (1995b) 'Local Forest Control in Burkina Faso, Mali, Niger, Senegal and The Gambia: A Review and Critique of New Participatory Policies', Africa Region, World Bank, Washington, DC

Ribot, J (1996) 'Participation Without Representation: Chiefs, Councils and Rural Representation', *Cultural Survival Quarterly*, Fall. Special Issue on Participation, P Peters (ed)

Ribot, J (1998a) 'Theorizing Access: Forest Profits along Senegal's Charcoal Commodity Chain', *Development and Change*, vol 29, pp307–41

Ribot, J (1998b) 'A Political Economy of Cooperative Law Reform in Mali: The State is the Best Hen', Report to Management Systems International and US Agency for International Development, Mali

Ribot, J (1999a) 'Decentralization, Participation and Accountability in Sahelian Forestry: Legal Instruments of Political-Administrative Control', *Africa*, vol 69, no 1, pp23–65

Ribot, J (1999b) 'Integral Local Development: Authority, Accountability and Entrustment in Natural Resource Management', Working Paper prepared for the Regional Program for the Traditional Energy Sector (RPTES) in the Africa Technical Group (AFTG1 – Energy) of the World Bank, Washington, DC, April

Ribot, J (1999c) 'A History of Fear: Imagining Deforestation in the West African Dryland Forests', *Global Ecology and Biogeography*, no 8, pp291–300

Ribot, J (2000) 'Rebellion, Representation and Enfranchisement in the Forest Villages of Makacoulibantang, Eastern Senegal', in C Zerner (ed) *People, Plants and Justice: The Politics of Nature Conservation*, Columbia University Press, New York

Ribot, J (2001a) 'Integral Local Development: "Accommodating Multiple Interests" through Entrustment and Accountable Representation', *International Journal of Agriculture, Resources, Governance and Ecology*, vol 1, no 34, pp291–300

Ribot, J (2001b) Minutes to Re-emergence of Chieftaincy in Africa meeting, Program on Land and Agrarian Studies, University of Western Cape, Cape Town, South Africa, May

Ribot, J (2002a) 'African Decentralization: Local Actors, Powers and Accountability', Democracy, Governance and Human Rights, Working Paper No 8, UNRISD and IDRC, Geneva

Ribot, J (2002b) *Democratic Decentralization of Natural Resources: Institutionalizing Popular Participation*, World Resources Institute, Washington, DC

Ribot, J (2004) *Waiting for Democracy: The Politics of Choice in Natural Resource Decentralization*, World Resources Institute, Washington, DC

Ribot, J and Larson, A M (eds) *Decentralization of Natural Resources: Experiences in Africa, Asia, and Latin America*, Routledge, London

Riker, W (1964) *Federalism: Origin, Operation, Significance*, Little Brown, Boston

Roe, E (1995a) 'Except-Africa: Postscript to a Special Section on Development Narratives', *World Development*, vol 23, pp1064–9

Roe, E (1995b) 'More than the Politics of Decentralization: Local Government Reform, District Development and Public Administration in Zimbabwe', *World Development*, vol 23, no 5, pp833–43

Roe, E (1996) *Except-Africa: Remaking Development, Rethinking Power*, Transaction, New Brunswick

Romeo, L (1996) 'Local Development Funds: Promoting Decentralized Planning and Financing of Rural Development', United Nations Capital Development Fund, Policy Series, New York

Rondinelli, A, McCullough, J and Johnson, R (1989) 'Analysing Decentralization Politics in Developing Countries: A Political Economy Framework', *Development and Change*, vol 20, pp57–87

Rosenau, J (1993) 'Market-State Relations and Environmental Policy: Limits of State Capacity in Senegal', in R D Lipschutz and K Conca (eds) *The State and Social Power in Global Environmental Politics*, Columbia University Press, New York

Rothchild, D (1994) *Strengthening African Local Initiative: Local Self-Governance, Decentralisation and Accountability*, Institut für Afrika-Kunde, Hamburg

Saito, F (2000) 'Decentralisation in Uganda: Challenges for the 21st Century', paper delivered at the Centre for Basic Research Seminar Series, 25 May, presented at Workshop on Uganda, Institute of Commonwealth Studies, 7 April, University of London, mimeo

Schilder, A and Boeve, B (1996) 'An Institutional Approach to Local Economic Development: The Case of Sublocational Initiatives in Three Districts in Kenya', *Regional Development Dialog*, vol 17, no 2, pp94–117

Schumacher, J (1975) *Politics, Bureaucracy and Rural Development in Senegal*, University of California Press, Berkeley

Scott, J (1976) *The Moral Economy of the Peasant: Rebellion and Subsistence in Southeast Asia*, Yale University Press, New Haven

Sewell, D (1996) 'The Dangers of Decentralization According to Prud'Homme: Some Further Aspects', *World Bank Research Observer*, vol 11, no 1, pp143–50

Shiva, V (1989) *Staying Alive*, Zed Books. Atlantic Highlands, NJ

Shivaramakrishnan, K (2000) 'Crafting the Public Sphere in the Forests of West Bengal: Democracy, Development and Political Action', *American Ethnologist*, vol 27, no 2, pp431–61

Singh, N and Titi, V (1995) *Empowerment: Towards Sustainable Development*, Zed Books, Atlantic Highlands, NJ

Smoke, P (1999) 'Understanding Decentralization in Asia: An Overview of Key Issues and Challenges', *Regional Development Dialogue*, vol 20, no 2, pp 1–17

Smoke, P (2000) 'Fiscal Decentralization in Developing Countries: A Review of Current Concepts and Practice', paper prepared for the United Nations Research Institute for Social Development, Geneva, October 2000

Smoke, P and Lewis, B (1996) 'Fiscal Decentralization in Indonesia: A New Approach to an Old Idea', *World Development*, vol 24, no 8, pp1281–99

Stark, F (1980) 'Federalism in Cameroon: The Shadow and the Reality', in N Kofele-Kale (ed) *An African Experiment in Nation Building: The Bilingual Cameroon Republic Since Reunification*, Westview Press, Boulder

Sturgeon, J (2003) 'Socialist and Colonial Histories in the Global Present', paper presented for the conference *Articulating Development and Strengthening Local Practices*, Chiang Mai, Thailand, 11–14 July

Swift, J (1996) 'Desertification: Narratives, Winners and Losers', in M Leach and R Mearns (eds) *The Lie of the Land: Challenging Received Wisdom on the African Environment*, James Curry, Oxford, pp73–90

Tendler, J (1997) *Good Government in the Tropics*, Johns Hopkins University Press, Baltimore, MD

Therkildsen, O (1993) 'Legitimacy, Local Governments and Natural Resource Management in Sub-Saharan Africa', in H Marcussen (ed) *Institutional Issues in Natural Resources Management*, Occasional Paper No 9

Therkildsen, O (2001) 'Efficiency, Accountability and Implementation: Public Sector Reform in East and Southern Africa', Draft Copy of Democracy, Governance and Human Rights Programme, Paper No 3, United Nations Institute for Social Development, February, mimeo

Tiebout, C (1972) 'A Pure Theory of Local Expenditures', in M Edel and J Rothenberg (eds) *Readings in Urban Economics*, Macmillan, New York

Tocqueville, A de (1945[1835]), *Democracy in America*, Vintage, New York

Tötemeyer, G (2000) 'Decentralization for Empowerment of Local Units of Governance and Society: A Critical Analysis of the Namibian Case', *Regional Development Dialogue*, vol 21, no 1, pp95–118

UNCDF (2000) 'Africa: Decentralisation and Local Governance Conference Concept Paper', for *Decentralisation and Local Governance Conference*, Capetown, March 2001, United Nations Capital Development Fund, Draft

Uphoff, N and Esman, M (1974) 'Local Organization for Rural Development: Analysis of Asian Experience', RLG No 19, Rural Development Committee, Special Series on Rural Local Government, Ithaca, Cornell University, New York

Utting, P and Jaubert, R (eds) (1998) *Discours et réalités des politiques participatives de gestion de l'environnement: le cas du Sénégal*, UNRISD, Switzerland

van Rouveroy van Nieuwaal, E (1987) 'Chiefs and African States: Some Introductory Notes and an Extensive Bibliography on African Chieftaincy', *Journal of Legal Pluralism*, nos 25–26, pp1–46

van Rouveroy van Nieuwaal, E, Adriaan, B and van Dijk, R (1999) *African Chieftaincy in a New Socio-Political Landscape*, Lit Verlag, Hamburg

Veit, P and Faraday, G (2000) 'Beyond the Presidents' Men', paper prepared for the World Resources Institute, mimeo

Webster, N (1992) 'Panchayati Raj in West Bengal: Popular Participation for the People or the Party?', *Development and Change*, vol 23, no 4, pp129–63

Weimer, B (1996) 'Challenges for Democratization and Regional Development in Southern Africa: Focus on Mozambique', *Regional Development Dialogue*, vol 17, no 2, pp49–50

Weinstein, B (1972) *Éboué*, Oxford University Press, New York

Western, D and Wright, M (1994) 'Background to Community-based Conservation', in D Western, M Wright and S Strum (eds) *Natural Connections:Perspectives in Community-based Conservation*, Island Press, Washington

Western, D, Wright, M and Struml, S (eds) (1994) *Natural Connections: Perspectives in Community-based Conservation*, Island Press, Washington

World Bank (1996) *The World Bank Participation Sourcebook*, World Bank, Washington, DC

World Bank (1997) *World Development Report 1997: The State in a Changing World*, Oxford University Press, Oxford

World Bank (2000) *Entering the 21st Century: World Development Report 1999/2000*, Oxford University Press, Oxford

Wunsch, J and Olowu, D (1995) *The Failure of the Centralized State: Institutions and Self-Governance in Africa*, Institute for Contemporary Studies Press, San Francisco

9

National Institutions for Development: The Case of Botswana

Abdi Ismail Samatar

Introduction[1]

The fundamental secret of East Asia's economic success has been entrepreneurial states that governed and guided these societies' developmental agenda. In contrast, African states undermined their societies' vitality. African regimes' failure to induce sustained economies has immeasurably legitimated the last two decades' anti-statist policy agenda. Unfortunately, the minimalist state strategy of recent years has not enabled Africa to recover lost ground. The only exceptions to Africa's economic involution are the island states of Seychelles, Mauritius and the southern African nation of Botswana. Botswana maintained an annual growth rate comparable to East Asia's best performers during the years 1966–95. Botswana's performance for the last eight years has been modest but it has kept pace with its Asian rivals (Table 9.1).

The country's precipitous fall in the Human Development Index since 1994, from 87 to 125, is principally because of the ravages of HIV/AIDS and consequent decline in life expectancy. It seems that, in the early 1990s, Botswana's relatively alert and activist state underestimated the danger AIDS posed to its people's health and the country's economic well-being. The government's neglect of such a crucial public issue has been uncharacteristic of its modus operandi and it has embarked on a programme designed to short-circuit the calamity. The new policy mandates public health service to provide free standard medicines to all HIV victims. Investment in public health has increased from 1.9 per cent to 3.7 per cent of GDP between 1990 and 2003. (UNDP, 2001; 2003). These significant increases in health spending reflect the government's recognition of the seriousness of the disease. Fortunately, Botswana has the resources which other African states lack. However, the country needs to make fighting the disease its single most critical priority. This should be matched by substantial reallocation of resources and sustained political commitment to AIDS education in every corner of the country.

Table 9.1 *Trends in economic development: Botswana compared to select African and Asian countries*

	HDI 1994	HDI 2000	Annual GDP Growth 1980–91	Annual GDP Growth 1990–98	GNP 1991	GNP 1998
South Africa	93	103	3.3	1.7	102.0	136.0
Egypt	100	119	NA	4.6	33.5	79.2
Algeria	109	107	NA	1.4	52.3	46.4
Gabon	114	123	–0.9	3.2	4.7	4.9
Zimbabwe	122	130	3.6	1.8	6.9	7.2
Cameroon	124	134	2.1	0.5	10.4	8.7
Kenya	125	138	4.1	2.4	8.6	10.2
Ghana	134	129	3.1	4.3	6.4	7.3
Côte d'Ivoire	136	154	0.3	4.1	8.9	10.2
Nigeria	139	151	1.4	3.5	33.7	36.4
Zambia	138	153	0.7	1.4	3.4	3.2
Zaire	140	152	1.6	–5.3	8.1	5.4
Senegal	143	155	2.9	3.2	5.6	4.7
Ethiopia	161	171	1.5	3.3	6.4	6.2
Guinea	173	162	1.3	4.7	2.8	3.8
Botswana	**87**	**122**	**9.3**	**3.9**	**3.3**	**4.8**
Seychelles	83	53	3.2	2.9	0.4	0.4
Mauritius	60	71	7.2	5.2	2.6	4.3
Indonesia	105	109	5.8	4.1	116.6	130.6
Malaysia	57	61	5.6	6.4	47.3	81.3
Thailand	54	76	7.8	4.6	88.1	131.9
South Korea	32	31	10.0	5.1	297.1	398.8
Hong Kong	24	26	6.9	3.9	77.9	158.2

Source: United Nations Development Programme, *Human Development Report,* various years

While Botswana's fast-paced growth has slowed down, a few African states, such as Egypt, Ghana, Ivory Coast, Nigeria and Guinea, have shown signs of recovery. These countries still lack the necessary institutional capacity to maintain a transformative agenda.

Botswana is exceptional in Africa and in the Third World not only because of its superb and sustained economic performance, but also because that occurred in the context of a liberal democratic political order. The country has had free and fair elections every five years and held fewer political prisoners than its former colonial ruler, Britain. Moreover, Botswana built and steadily increased the institutional capacity of its public and private sectors. The story of this highly successful African state merits detailed narration.

In 1966 Botswana embarked on its post-colonial journey with severe natural, financial, strategic and social handicaps. The country was devastated by a long drought in the mid-1960s. Nearly one third of the population depended on government rations. The drought also killed nearly 50 per cent of the country's livestock and impoverished the population (Jacqz, 1967). The impact of this 'naturally' induced disaster was exacerbated by the dearth of a vibrant economy where the unskilled population could find employment.

One of Botswana's major handicaps was the shallowness of its financial base in 1966. Its per capita annual income was estimated between 40 and 60 rand (less than US$100). The local economy did not have the capacity to generate surplus income for investment and development. The government was also financially strapped, as it was not able to balance its budget. Consequently, it depended on annual budgetary subsidies from Britain, its former colonial master. These grants amounted to nearly 50 per cent of the government expenditure prior to independence (Republic of Botswana, 1966a, p8). These subsidies continued until the early 1970s. Finally, Botswana did not have its own currency and used the South African rand until 1976.

Strategically, the new Republic of Botswana was sandwiched between fascist and racist regimes. To Botswana's south and west were apartheid South Africa and Namibia, and to the north and east was Rhodesia. The only territorial link Botswana had with independent Africa was a short bridge over the Zambezi to Zambia. Botswana's geographical encirclement by racist-dominated countries was fortified by its total economic dependence on South Africa. The country's transport and communication links to the outside world were through its hostile southern neighbour. Moreover, nearly one half of Botswana's able-bodied adults worked as migrant labourers in the mines and fields of South Africa. Finally, as if to underscore Botswana's vulnerability, the capital of the Bechuanaland Protectorate was in the city of Mafeking in South Africa. Consequently, the independent republic had to start from scratch in establishing its capital in the village of Gaborone (population 6000 in 1966). Gaborone lacked rudimentary infrastructure such as office buildings for new government departments, electricity, running water and paved roads.

The financial, strategic and natural-resource constraints Botswana faced seemed insurmountable given the dearth of skilled labour and educated population (Luke, 1964). Most of the country's schools were single-room 'tribal' schools staffed by untrained teachers (Luke, 1964, p18). Botswana's secondary school produced 16 graduates capable of undertaking higher education in 1966. Moreover, over 80 years of British colonial rule produced 40 Batswana university graduates (Republic of Botswana, 1966a, p8). Batswana occupied non-skilled posts in colonial service while white South Africans were recruited even for clerical jobs until late in the colonial period (Gossett, 1986).

Finally, Batswana lacked some of the most basic skills in trade and commerce. British colonial authority barred native Batswana from even owning retail trade licences until after World War II. Europeans and Asians who had the support of the colonial state dominated commerce and capitalist enterprises, outside the cattle sector. Thus, Batswana had little presence in either the public or the private sector.

Experts and colonial authorities' prognosis of independent Botswana's future was bleak. They thought that Botswana's *survival* as a country would for a long time depend on the availability and generosity of Western aid.[2] Others imagined that Bechuanaland had little potential for political union because of its fragmented tribal structure dominated by strong and legitimate chiefs (Hailey, 1961). This opinion reflected many in the colonial circles and was certainly appreciated by the racist regime in South Africa, which wanted to absorb Bechuanaland. The pessimistic view of the colonial cadre was complemented by the dismissive attitudes of many new independent African governments who considered Botswana to be another South Africa Bantustan.

The gloom that shrouded Botswana's independence did not dismay the leaders of the new republic. They relentlessly but realistically pursued their project of state and nation building. Thirty-four years after independence Botswana is without doubt the continent's most successful and best managed economy, and enjoys the most developed liberal democratic culture. The relevant question, for the purpose of this chapter, is how was the institutional capacity of Africa's premier *interventionist* state built and how did it avoid the political economic maladies that bedevilled nearly all activists states in the Third World? This chapter maps out the making of the Botswana liberal democratic and developmentalist state and what lessons might be learned from its experience as African states are revamped and repositioned to play a more creative and democratic role.

The Botswana state plays a highly interventionist role, like many other African states, in fashioning the structure and dynamics of the Botswana political economy. However, unlike its counterparts, its interventions have not lead to economic involution, acute social alienation of the citizenry, ethnic fragmentation of the population or political decline. The Botswana State has been the principal *visible hand* that guided the country to its current status as the continent's high political economic performer. How did a South African labour reserve become a model of success? Given its humble beginnings in 1966, how has it been possible for the Botswana leaders to build such a capable and exceptional state, and what in the country social structure may have provided a basis for this accomplishment? I argue that the key to Botswana's success has been the combination of a united elite with legitimate, disciplined and conscious leadership, a weak civil society, and a professionally run and insulated public service.

Theorizing the Botswana State

G Gunderson, in a pioneering study, characterized Botswana as an 'administrative state' (Gunderson, 1970). He argued that an administrative elite made all the key decisions in this state without interference from the natives. Although the administrative state was colonial in origin, it retained its character after the establishment of the Republic of Botswana. Despite the democratization of the political process, the republic's bureaucrats were similarly insulated from direct societal pressures

(Gunderson, 1970, p7). Other studies confirmed Gunderson's findings (Picard, 1987, p13; Molutsi, 1989).

Gunderson's important contribution equated the leaders' conscious decision to protect the professional autonomy of the state bureaucracy with the former's marginalization in policy-making by senior and often expatriate civil servants (Gunderson, 1970, p434). The insulation of the policy-making process from particularistic societal influences was a deliberate strategy of the leadership. The nature of the relationship between political leaders and the bureaucracy was not examined for almost a decade (Parson, 1979). Parson and Isaksen's analysis of this relation were more conceptually oriented and dealt with the current *state autonomy* debate.[3] Isaksen's particular concern was not only the shape of this relationship but its effect on economic policy and management. Thus, his model is 'one in which the political elite, with little or no real influence from the grass roots, defines its policy in a very broad way thereby leaving wide policy areas open to the bureaucrats' (Isaksen, 1989, p18)[4]. He emphasized that the bureaucrats did not have free range but had to formulate the state's economic development strategy within a *particular* capitalist framework. After all, the first national development plan unequivocally announced that capitalism was the chosen economic order (Republic of Botswana, 1966).

The selection of capitalism as the broad economic development framework was reinforced by the historical conditions that bound Botswana fortunes to those of the South African economy. The choice of market economy was married to a public-sector management style left behind by the British. This style, managed with the help of senior expatriate bureaucrats, confounded conservative financial management with development.[5] In the absence of a vibrant local private market economy, political leaders and the bureaucrats shared a view of development where the state played a key role in jump-starting the economy. Such shared approach and the ability of the political leaders to hold the civil service accountable and intervene when necessary circumscribed the system. This political–bureaucratic relationship endured as R Charlton echoed Isaksen's findings a decade later:

> *Quite simply, the BDP [Botswana Democratic Party] has the power and the ability to intervene decisively and definitively if it wishes to do so, at any or all stages of the policy-making process, to secure and enforce its strategic policy priorities ... After two and a half decades of BDP rule the policy-making echelons of the civil service are* well aware *of what is expected of them both in general and, for the most part, in specific policy terms ...* (Charlton, 1991, pp273–4; emphasis added (upright type))

This political–bureaucratic relationship produced a relatively strong state system in Botswana 'where probity, relative autonomy and competency have been nurtured and sustained' (Raphaeli et al, 1984; Picard, 1987, p10).

Elite Unity, Underdevelopment and State Autonomy

State autonomy has been the subject of many debates in the literature. There are three identifiable positions in this debate. First, some scholars claim that autonomous African states have been unaccountable to the citizenry. Such state domination of economic, social and political life led to involution. The second thesis postulates that particularistic interest in civil society profoundly penetrated the state. Consequently, the state has been unable to nurture and professionally manage the national project. Third, recent contributions in the literature claim that the issue is not state autonomy versus its colonization by interest group, but the nature of the overlap between state agenda and key sectors of civil society. Despite the centrality of the state civil-society shared project, this thesis attaches critical importance to state leadership.

The arguments associated with any of these three positions unbundle the nature of state autonomy by examining the social constitution of the dominant class that manages the state and its relations to dominated classes. I feel such analysis will enable us to distinguish between different types of state autonomies. I also posit that differently constituted autonomies have contrasting effects on a state's *ability* to sustain a development agenda.

To understand the particularity of Botswana State autonomy, we need to assess this society's social geography and the dynamics of capitalist transformation in the region. Jack Parson's illuminating book on Botswana's liberal democracy and its labour reserve economy linked social and economic structure to modes of governance (Parson, 1984). His argument is that Botswana's liberal democracy is based on the partially transformed tributary social structure. The peasantry remains subservient to the cattle-owning class despite its becoming migrant labourers in South African mines. The peasant's continued loyalty to the dominant class was owing to:

- wages earned in South Africa were not enough to cover their household's reproductive needs;
- the 'flexible' nature of their employment compelled them to retain their bond in the countryside.

As such, they straddled two social categories: peasant and labour, hence Parson's apt term, *peasantariat*.

Botswana's traditional dominant class, the chiefs and other propertied groups, survived and flourished during the colonial period (Wylie, 1990). The colonial state ruled Bechuanaland through the chiefs who remained very strong until the end of British rule. The colonial state in Bechuanaland was thinly staffed and strapped for resources.[6] The protectorate economy stagnated without a vibrant private economy and an activist state. The limited commercialization of the economy disproportionately benefited the cattle-owning class.

The dearth of commercial and industrial development was accompanied by the underdevelopment of the public sector. As a consequence of these two processes, independent Botswana lacked a large and growing middle class. As noted earlier, South African whites staffed even the lowest rank of the colonial bureaucracy. The absence of a broad-based middle class enhanced the elite's autonomy. The dominant elite who claimed the mantle of the state was mainly large cattle owners who still maintained traditionally rooted patron–client relations with the peasantariat. The Botswana Democratic Party (BDP) under the able leadership of Seretse Khama and Quett Masire capitalized on this relationship and consequently won every national election since independence (Parson, 1990, p87).

Parson's thesis about the dominant class's unity and organic bonds to the peasantariat adds a critical element to our conceptual arsenal. However, assessing the nature of this group's unity can enhance the value of Parson's contribution. A simple and straightforward way to measure a class's unity is to examine the homogeneity of its resources base and its ideological orientation. For example, does the class consist only of large and medium-sized cattle owners? Or does it have a diverse resource base needing different and contradictory development programmes? Do class members share common political and economic strategies? The majority of the leaders who took over the state in 1966 were all large and medium-sized cattle owners. Table 9.2 lists the first three parliament's members and shows their educational and economic status. The educational achievements of these members were as follows: 13 went to school in Tiger Kloof, 2 attended Lovedale, 11 were schoolteachers, 5 had secondary school certificates, 1 had elementary education, 1 was a lawyer, 1 was a clerk, and the background of 6 are not known. In terms of wealth, 27 were large or medium cattle owners, 1 had a small herd, and we know little about the remaining 14 members. The small but growing middle class, largely in public service, owned some cattle or hoped to build their own herd.[7]

The emerging middle-class members planned to increase their cattle holdings in two ways: ensuring the growth of their salary and being promoted to higher posts in the bureaucracy which was dominated by expatriates. The third group was white settlers who owned large ranges or were in commerce. Their main concern was that the government left them free to run their enterprises and protect their private property.

The elite not only had a relatively homogenous resource base but also shared a common world-view. As one colleague at the University of Botswana told the author, 'We Batswana are more capitalistic than Americans. The only problem is that we have less capital than Americans.' This may be an exaggeration for the general population of the country, but it certainly applies to the elite:

> *The political system is dominated by (and policy is set in the interest of) a coalition of wealthy, well educated, cattle-owning political elites who are committed to rapid economic growth in the* framework of a largely free enterprise system. *This coalition of traditional leaders, teachers, junior state functionaries, and wealthy farmers was joined by more senior administrators beginning in the 1970s. Altogether, the members of this coalition represent educational and economic characteristics quite unlike the majority of the population.* (Picard, 1987, pp347–72; emphasis added)

The combination of shared world-view, a common resource base, and an organic relationship with the majority of the rural population clearly marked the unity and autonomy of the dominant class. The elite-dominated new state took on the characteristics of the former: autonomy. The autonomy of the state was sustained further by the absence of organized and mobilized social groups whose interests contradict the dominant class.

Table 9.2 *The economic and educational background of members of parliament*
(first three parliaments)

Number	Party	Education	Cattle ownership	Other business
1	BDP	Secondary	Large	NK
2	BDP	Tiger Kloof	Small	NK
3	BDP	NK	Large	Shop
4	BDP	Tiger Kloof	Large	Carpenter
5	BDP	Elementary	Large	Vet.rep
6	BDP	Secondary	NK	None
7	BDP	Tiger Kloof	NK	None
8	BDP	Little	Large	Retail
9	BIP	NK	NK	NK
10	BDP	Teacher	Large	Big
11	BDP	Teacher	Medium	Shop
12	BDP	Secondary	Large	Vast
13	BDP	Tiger Kloof	Large	Shop
14	BDP	Teacher	Medium	Shop
15	BDP	Teacher	Large	Shop
16	BDP	Clerk	Medium	Shop
17	BDP	Lawyer	Large	NK
18	BDP	Tiger Kloof	Large	NK
19	BDP	Tiger Kloof	Large	NK
20	BDP	Teacher	Large	NK
21	BDP	Lovedale	Medium	NK
22	BDP	NK	Large	Shops
23	BDP	Tiger Kloof	NK	NK
24	BPP	Teacher	NK	NK
25	BPP	BA (Tiger kloof)	NK	NK
26	BDP	Teacher	Large	NK
27	BDP	Tiger Kloof	NK	NK
28	BDP	Secondary	Medium	NK
29	BDP	Teacher	Medium	Shop
30	BDP	Lovedale	NK	NK
31	BDP	Teacher	Large	Farm
32	BDP	Little	Large	Farm
33	BDP	Teacher	Large	Farm
34	BDP	Tiger Kloof	NK	NK
35	BDP	Tiger Kloof	Large	Farm/shop
36	BDP	Teacher	NK	Big
37	BNF	Tiger Kloof	Large	NK
38	BDP	Secondary	NK	NK
39	BPP	NK	NK	NK
40	BDP	NK	Large	Farm
41	BPP	NK	NK	NK
42	BDP	Tiger Kloof	NK	NK

NK = Not known,   BDP = Botswana Democratic Party,   BIP = Botswana Independence Party,
BPP = Botswana People's Party,   BNF = Botswana National Front

The absence of motivated opposition with broad links to the population and elite unity did not spare the dominant classes elsewhere in the continent from internal strife and ultimately the subversion of a collective strategy. What saved the Botswana elite from trotting the beaten path?[8] Guaranteeing lasting cohesion of the elite and protection of the collective project required able and conscientious leaders. It also required leaders who possessed the discipline and foresight and who enjoyed dual popular legitimacy: from the elite and the public. The task of leading this group could not have rested on more appropriate people than Botswana's first President Khama and his vice-president and later President Masire. Khama enjoyed unchallenged leadership and legitimacy among the elite. As his biographers noted:

> *Seretse's Cabinet colleagues were men whose experience of life had been limited to the segregated lifestyles of southern Africa. They were beginning to gain wider experience, through attending international conferences and consultations,* but looked to Seretse as the cosmopolitan among them to take the lead in relations with the predominantly expatriate civil service and with foreign relations in general. (Parsons et al, 1995, p239; emphasis added)

Khama's social role and stature went beyond the cabinet as Parson so aptly and succinctly captured:

1. for the peasants, he is a chief;
2. for the small group of educated Africans, he is one of them;
3. for the large cattle-owners, he is one of them;
4. for the chiefs, he is one of them; and
5. for the Europeans, by dress, language, behaviour and experience, he has much in common with them (Parson, 1990, pp335–40).

Khama's political role was supported by the relentless and purposive effort of vice-president Masire to establish a development-oriented and professionally led state bureaucracy. The combination of Khama and Masire leadership cemented a national coalition, dominated by large cattle owners, European interests, and the small but growing bureaucratic middle class.

The coalition's stability, the discipline of the leadership, and the discovery of copper-nickel and, more critically, diamonds in the late 1960s and early 1970s further enhanced state autonomy. The nature of the coalition and its relations with the peasantariat enabled the state to pursue an economic strategy geared towards infrastructure, mining, cattle and commercial development. The peasantry benefited the least from this growth, and inequality increased (Government of Botswana, 1975; Bank of Botswana, 1987). The peasants, however, continued to support the BDP as the mineral-fuelled growth meant the state did not have to extract heavy taxes from the rural population.[9] Thus, the peasantry did not see the growth of the economy's other sectors coming at their expense.

Parson's study equates dominant class unity with state autonomy and implicitly with state institutional capacity. This is a questionable assumption. State autonomy from dominated classes does not mean that the dominant class's collective agenda will be pursued systematically by the state.[10] Moreover, the state's autonomy from the dominated classes does not mean that those directing state operations are conscious of the nature and the importance of the elite's collective project. And as such, political leaders may not use their freedom to build effective public institutions.

Patrick Molutsi re-examined the relationship between liberal democracy and inequality in Botswana. He noted how the state pursued the twin but contradictory objectives of economic injustice (accumulation by the dominant class) and liberal democracy (state's legitimacy with the poor majority) (Molutsi, 1986; Molutsi and Holm, 1990, pp323–40). He adds that an alliance between the local elite and international capital, such as mining, has jointly mapped the country's development contours. This strategy has intensified inequality without seriously eroding the ruling party's popular legitimacy. The manufacture and maintenance of such consent has been possible because of the state's intelligent use of foreign aid. This aid was effectively used to provide water, health and education for the rural masses (Molutsi and Holm, 1990, p374).

Molutsi's work builds on Parson's but does not explicitly deal with the cohesiveness of the dominant class. He also assumes the importance of group leadership and discipline to sustaining the collective project. Despite this oversight, Molutsi implicitly recognizes that mounting and maintaining accumulation, liberal democracy and social injustice entail conscious class agency.

A discussion of why and how BDP leadership translated the state's autonomy into effective action is missing from Molutsi's and Parson's work. Why did Botswana's public enterprises perform significantly better than their counterparts in Africa and elsewhere in the Third World? After all, many African states were relatively autonomous from domestic social classes at independence.

Translating autonomy into capacity requires the concurrence of three variables. First, a united dominant class must agree on the national interest. Second, those who command state power must be conscious of the nature of the collective project and what it requires from the state to take off. Third, a skilled and loyal technocratic class must exist or be created who can build institutions and plan and implement development programmes.

Molutsi and Parson note the dominant class unity, but they do not address the importance of conscious leadership and the art of creating autonomous and effective state institutions. Few African countries had as undeveloped an administration as Botswana at the time of independence. But unlike Botswana's leaders, their African counterparts did not see the need for effective public institutions capable of maintaining and reproducing state autonomy and implementing the state's development programme. Where individual leaders recognized the importance of such institutions, they lost political power to elite groups that attached little value to efficacious state apparatus.[11] Hence, the importance of the marriage between class unity and leadership. How then did Botswana's united elite and its conscious leadership go about creating effective state machinery for capitalist development?

Conscious Leadership and Class Unity:
The Foundation of State Capacity

Africanist analysis of the state has not successfully blended structural and contingency factors in explaining the performance of particular African states. Developmental states are products of the will of political leaders who use their mandate, democratic or otherwise, to build professionally managed institutions. How adept these leaders are in establishing the 'appropriate' institutions significantly depends on their understanding of the nature and the institutional requirements of the national product. The outcome of this effort is contingent on the leaders' willingness to experiment with different institutional mechanisms and learn from their mistakes and those of others. This analytical framework goes beyond an assessment of the interaction between agency and structure by *centring the analysis on the consciousness of that agency*. It goes without saying that the efforts of many well-intentioned leaders went awry because they misdiagnosed the problem and chose the wrong tools.

There is no magic formula for producing the leadership with the 'right' qualities. Such leadership arises both *accidentally* and *as result of particular historical conditions*. A long political tradition of autonomous leadership and struggles against domination by outside forces produced deliberative and often conservative leadership in Botswana. There were at least six elements to this tradition.

1. The traditional Botswana elite retained a significant degree of autonomy by resisting British colonial rule and Pretoria's attempts to incorporate Bechuanaland into South Africa.
2. This traditional leadership maintained its hegemony over the masses during the period of colonial transformation.
3. The destruction of African leaders in South Africa, and the enslavement and dispossession of their people, ingrained in the Botswana leaders a strong sense of themselves and their role as guardians of their society.
4. In Botswana the traditional, political and economic elite were almost one and the same, unlike many other African societies.
5. The Botswana leaders' long-term independent association with and support from a number of Europeans to fight against South African incorporation[12] meant that the leaders of the regime in power did not suspect those expatriates' intentions. The leaders 'freely' chose to associate with these expatriates, and hired them to do specific jobs.[13]
6. The dominant class was unchallenged by any other indigenous group. Large numbers of civil servants, major commercial/settler interests and mobilized peasantry, inherited from the colonial era, were absent (Molutsi and Holm, 1990, pp323–40; Holm et al, 1996, pp43–69). Mindful of these conditions, their hegemony and the absence of any meaningful challenge from other social groups, the leadership went about building efficacious institutions to spearhead the transformation of the economy.

The government's selection of *private enterprise* as its development framework was the first signal of the leaders' intentions.[14] This choice was made at the time when many governments in the continent were moving to the left of the political spectrum. The Botswana leadership, in tandem with the development thinking of the time, assumed that the state would play a vital role in guiding national development. In addition to endorsing this common assumption of the time, they felt that public institutions had to be run by skilled people in order to fulfil their development function. Their appreciation of the centrality of institutional autonomy and professional competency to the whole development project is clear from the debates over civil service reform and localization.

The remaining part of the chapter has two objectives. The discussion of civil service is meant to show the deliberative approach of the leaders with regard to civil service reform. I use the debate and the pace of localization as a proxy of how *conscious* the leaders were of creating an effective state apparatus. Secondly, it sketches how the Ministry of Finance and Development Planning (MFDP) developed into the nerve centre of the state apparatus. Finally, the section will show how the policy-making process at the strategy-setting level is insulated from the influences of civil society groups, while giving liberal democratic legitimacy to the process.

Localization debate

> *The stimulation of the private sector is an integral part of development policy in Bechuanaland. In this connection it is clear that Government can play a useful role in shaping attitudes favourable to economic growth....* My Government is deeply conscious of the dangers inherent in localizing the public service too quickly. Precipitate or reckless action in this field could have disastrous effects on the whole programme of services and development of the Government *... potential donor countries might be reluctant to provide aid as they would not wish to see such aid maladministered, and I must again emphasize that we need aid.*[15] (Parsons et al, 1995, p253; emphasis added)

In most African countries, the Africanization of the civil service was among the first acts of government immediately after independence. Africanizing public service entailed quick and massive promotions of indigenous bureaucrats in the military or civil service to positions previously earmarked for and occupied by white colonialists. Botswana was among the African states that, although eager to indigenize the service, were relatively slow and more deliberate in the speed with which the process unfolded in the senior professional and technical areas.

The government's slowness in this regard may have been owing to the fact that the ruling party was not a mass-based national liberation movement. Consequently, an immobilized but previously disfranchised population exerted little pressure to replace the colonialists quickly with Africans. The BDP was in fact part of the colonial administration since its formation in 1962. BDP leading members were 'trainee ministers' under the tutelage of Protectorate administrators whom they were expected to replace (Bechuanaland Protectorate, 1964). The BDP was the colonial state's party of choice. The colonial administration fully supported the BDP to ensure a smooth transition to an independent Botswana.[16]

The close relationship between the BDP and the colonial administration is not the sole explanation for the BDP's policies. Such an explanation is myopic and paternalistic for it presumes that the Botswana leaders were simply towing the colonial line rather than having their own ideas. The leaders' agenda may have dovetailed with the colonial administration's ideological orientation. When such confluence occurred, the BDP government used its contacts to maximum benefit. At other times, when BDP's ideas differed from those of the administration it went its own way.[17]

The BDP government's policy reflected the carefully thought-out agenda of the leaders of the class that dominated the new government. Their plan was to enhance accumulation and sustain their legitimacy with the public. The BDP preferred the term localization partly to retain the support of the small but economically important white population who contributed significantly to the party's coffers (Gossett, 1986, p257). Molutsi's argument that the post-colonial regime attempted to balance these twin, but contradictory, objectives helps us better understand the evolution of civil service policy in Botswana. Although the debate over localization began in 1958 in the African Advisory Council, its full development had to wait for independence. The first real hints of the BDP's localization strategy could be seen in both the 1960–64 and the 1963–68 development plans. These plans affirmed the centrality of a market economy for the Protectorate.

These early plans clearly articulated that the principal development strategy would be based on a market economy, and the government would play a crucial role in this agenda. To fulfil such a role, government institutions would stimulate and assist the market.[18] The BDP recognized that the government must be careful in orchestrating localization. The BDP manifesto for the pre-independence election in 1965 clearly showed that the leadership was aware of this dilemma:

> *Localization of the Service and In-Service Training: Briefly, while we must guard against* the lowering of standards reached so far *in the Civil Service, by unduly straining after replacing expatriates in the present government, the policy of the Bechuanaland Democratic Party will be to localize the service as fast as* suitably qualified *Bechuanaland citizens become available. We are not sure whether enough has been or is being done to prepare local officers for positions of responsibility in the service, but during the first period of self-government we would see to it that where local men with experience and ability can be found they will be appointed to any post in the Government for which they are qualified ... we would see to it that local men are appointed as understudies to serve in almost all positions of responsibility in Government service to prepare them for take over at the independence stage.* (Gossett, 1986, p260, emphasis added)

The manifesto recognized the need to localize at a 'reasonable' speed. Careful 'pacing' of localization showed that the BDP was the legitimate party of independence. It also ensured the maintenance of performance standards in the public service.

The BDP's landslide win in the 1965 election did not change the leadership's mind about their localization strategy. Nor did it change their minds about maintaining and improving the civil service's capacity for resource mobilization and development. The vice-president defiantly noted that well-run and efficient public institutions were necessary if resources- and budget-deficient Botswana was to mobilize overseas resources:

> *Even if we could afford to be irresponsible and just appoint people left and right, we must know that we are a poor country. We almost live on donations. Those countries which give us money if they think we put this money into good use, and therefore when we localize we must take account, I mean even if we meant to sacrifice the public good at least we must realize that unless we can use this money which we get externally, unless we can put it to good use, unless we can see that we use it properly we can not hope to continue to get it. It does not matter whether it comes from the United Kingdom … there is no country which would just throw its good money to another country and not be interested to know how the money is used, and money can only be properly used if it has* efficient people *to use it.*
> (Republic of Botswana, 1967, p189; emphasis added)

The small opposition made the civil service question an important political issue. The BDP government was confident although concerned about the consequence of a politicized civil service. To make the seriousness of this matter patently clear and put the weight of his presidency behind his government's 'go-slow' policy, the president convened a meeting for all public servants at the Gaborone national stadium in late 1967:

> *To begin with it is common knowledge that some local civil servants are dissatisfied with the rate at which my government is localizing the service, in spite of the fact that we have, in my opinion, carried out localization faster than we had hoped for. After all we had been quite unequivocal about the fact that we* would never sacrifice efficiency *on the altar of localization … no one can charge me with going back on promises to localize the service at a faster pace.* (Gossett, 1986, p273; emphasis added)[19]

President Khama and his party maintained their 'go-slow' agenda despite their losses in the 1969 elections and the vice-president's defeat by the President's strongest political opponent, former chief Bathoen S Gasetsiwe. The vice-president returned to parliament as one of the 'specially elected' members, and he retained his ministerial post.[20] After regaining the electoral momentum in 1974, the President reiterated his old position on localization (Gossett, 1986, p281). To eliminate any doubt about his commitment to the 'go-slow' policy, he retained Mr Phil Steenkamp, a former colonial officer of Afrikaner origin who became a naturalized Batswana, as the Permanent Secretary in the Office of the President. This post was one of the most sensitive in the administration. In addition, he also appointed Mr David Finlay, another naturalized Batswana and former Protectorate officer, as the Director of the newly created Directorate of Personnel.[21] These appointments raised the ire of Mr Matante and other leading opposition members of parliament.

Apart from such occasional criticism, the ship of state steamed ahead. The success of the government's team, all expatriates led by the vice-president, in renegotiating the Southern African Customs Unions Agreement in 1969 demonstrated the merits of their 'go-slow' strategy (Hermans, interview, 6 June 1994, Gaborone). If the government had hastily Africanized all civil service positions, the argument goes, it may have been forced to field a team which lacked the training and competency to negotiate successfully. This renegotiated Customs Agreement and the agreement with private firms and donors to finance and develop a copper/nickel complex, commonly known as the Shashe Project, in Selebe Phikwe, enabled Botswana to balance its annual budget for the first time in 1972, without grants from Britain. This was one of the government's major objectives. Its realization fortified the regime's convictions about its approach to development.

The discovery of diamonds[22] and the subsequent negotiations with De Beers and infrastructural development firms necessitated the employment of a large number of expatriates. The vice-president bluntly noted this in his budget speech in 1979/80:

> *The rapid expansion of Government activities has resulted in a rapid growth of demand for skilled manpower that exceeds the growth in domestic supply. Thus in spite of the rapid increase in resources allocated to education, the skilled manpower shortage will become worse. In order to bridge the gap, Government will continue to employ expatriates, but in the coming year, the housing shortage in Gaborone will allow only a small increase in the number of expatriates, recruited for service in Gaborone. More importantly, there is evidence that the increase of skilled manpower in Central Government has diverted manpower away from Local Government and the parastatal and private sectors thereby retarding development in these sectors.* (Gossett, 1986, p285)

The enormous wealth generated by exploiting the country's mineral wealth was final proof that the government's use of skilled expatriate labour, a fundamental tenet of its localization policy, had indeed paid off. Late Finance Minister and vice-president, Mr Peter Mmusi, succinctly stated the government's confidence in its strategy:

> *A purposeful government which acquires the expertise to deal with foreign companies on its own terms need not have a fear of domination by foreign companies, however large they may be. The important word is purposeful – and I believe our government has been able to put together strong negotiating teams, has backed them up with well-worked out negotiating mandates, and has then overseen the implementation of our major mining agreements with detailed care as well.* (Harvey and Lewis, 1990, p119)

Credit for Botswana's economic success and the vice president's subsequent and apparent confidence of its ministers goes to the republic's founding fathers, Khama and Masire. They saw the merit of institution building and advocated the 'go-slow' policy of localizing the civil service. Their 'leadership … was of unusually high quality' (Harvey and Lewis, 1990, p9). A crucial element of what Harvey and Lewis dub as 'high leadership quality' is the leaders' awareness of their goals and what was required to attain them. President Khama and his closest associates were unequivocal about the economy's capitalist nature that they wanted to develop. Other African leaders in the region, some of whom the President admired and respected (Presidents Nyerere and Kaunda), were planning economic strategies supposedly based on African Socialism or Humanism. Seretse Khama and his government unabashedly pursued capitalist development. He opposed communism and jokingly characterized himself as a capitalist. According to Henderson, Seretse 'often used to joke about being a capitalist among socialists, wryly commenting at one meeting that, although he was a capitalist, he was the only member of the front-line team to come to a meeting in a hired rather than private plane' (Henderson, 1990, p47).[23]

How did the leaders' consciousness of the need for effective institutions and their 'go-slow' localization strategy work in setting up the central agencies of the state? I will now turn to a discussion of the establishment of the government's pilot agency, MFDP, and the way it has managed the development agenda.

MFDP: institutional nerve centre

The Bechuanaland Protectorate had neither a dynamic private sector nor a state system capable of inducing economic growth and development. Despite this grid of inheritance, the state's capacity and the country's fortunes changed steadily after independence:

> *The country provided an outstanding example of the successful mobilization of aid resources and their deployment. At a time when the efforts of international agencies and developed country governments were under increasing attack for both the low level of transfers and the way in which these transfers were effected, Botswana provided an example of how aid could be made to work.* (Stevens, 1981, p159)

Michael Stevens's remarks are at the heart of the problem. How can the dominant class's unity and the leaders' consciousness translate into effective institutional capacity, catering to the collective accumulation project? And how did Botswana become a relatively efficient state model in such a short duration, especially given its history as an impoverished and economically backward British Protectorate? Like their counterparts elsewhere in Africa, the BDP leaders' principal long-term goal was economic development. However, the Botswana leadership also realized that establishing an effective and efficient administrative structure was a prerequisite for economic development. The bureaucracy the British left behind was hopelessly inadequate (Stevens, 1981, p160).

The Protectorate Administration's last two development plans (1960–64 and 1963–68) recognized the importance of planning for the country's development. These plans indicated the government needed to take responsibility for two tasks: developing the country's infrastructure and providing an appropriate social climate for private investment. However, the development plans did not specifically describe the state institutions necessary to carry out either this economic development programme or how to build these institutions. The last colonial report on Bechuanaland, however, fully recognized the centrality of such institutions for development. The Porter Report, commissioned by the Ministry of Overseas Development, was published after independence. It stressed the importance of an effective financial and planning mechanism:

> *While a certain amount of coordination of development activity can be achieved through interdepartmental consultation* ... there must be one place in the machinery of government where all departmental plans must be welded into a coherent whole which will enable the general development objectives of government to be achieved. *There will also be the problem of scaling down the finance, which is available to the programme which emerges in this fashion. The Economic Planning Unit has therefore two major functions. The first is to make clear to Ministers the economic implications of the general objectives which they would wish to adopt... [T]he second function ... is to analyze the implications of different allocations of investment programme as a whole, is likely to be more important in the foreseeable future...* It is clear that the Economic Planning Unit must, *if it is to be* effective, be placed in the centre of the administrative machine and headed by a civil servant of the top rank... *There are, therefore three possible locations for an Economic Planning Unit... There is, however, much to be said in favour of having the Economic Planning Unit report to a single Minister, whether it be the Minister of Finance or a Minister with a general responsibility for long-term economic development.* (Republic of Botswana, 1966b, pp110–11; emphasis added)

The new government shared the general development strategy prescribed in the previous plans. However, vice-president Masire took exception to the Porter Report regarding Botswana's economic prospects and the country's capacity to effectively absorb more external capital. Botswana's highest priorities were to establish a co-coordinated institutional capability and to attract sufficient public and overseas private funds. The government acted on the Porter Report's advice by further strengthening the Economic Planning Unit formed in 1965 as part of the Ministry of Finance. Botswana also established the Central Statistics Office (Hermans, interview, 6 June 1994, Gaborone). Expatriates or former colonial administrators, some of whom became Botswana citizens,[24] staffed all the critical ministry posts. The portfolio of this ministry was given to vice-president Masire, the President's closest political ally and confidant. This signalled that this ministry was the most powerful ministry in the cabinet, outside the Presidency. The President did not get involved in a detailed understanding of the economy.[25] Consequently, he relied heavily on his vice-president. As such, the vice-president was the cabinet's real economic authority.

The government split the Ministry of Finance into the Ministries of Development Planning and Finance a while later. The Ministry's subdivision was the result of internal turf struggles between those left from the colonial administration, who wanted to keep the books, and the vice-president and his young turks, who were eager to push an aggressive development agenda.[26] Then again the government recombined the two ministries into the Ministry of Finance and Development Planning (MFDP). This recombination signalled the victory of the developmental camp.

Botswana inherited and maintained the colonial civil service system with a high degree of autonomy. The government also established the Directorate of Personnel that reported to the President's office. The new establishment took over many of the old order's functions, but it also became responsible for developing the human resources skills necessary to develop the economy. This change was essential given the dire need for skilled Batswana to speed up the development process (Finlay, interview, 6 January 1994, Ramotswa).

Established in 1970, the Ministry of Finance and Development Planning was the institutional brain of the economic policy-making process. Once established, the Ministry took off. The activist Masire and his technocratic troops, headed by Hermans, consolidated the Ministry so that it dominated all other ministries. MFDP became responsible for planning, budgeting and coordinating all development activities. The line ministries were responsible for project implementation. MFDP also liaised and negotiated with all aid agencies. The MFDP carefully monitored the implementations of all development projects (Stevens, 1981, p167; Republic of Botswana, 1986). The Ministry had firm control over the state's financial affairs as it set the overall spending ceilings for the annual budgets and the multiyear development plans. Although the Ministry had the final say about government finance, its authority was not as firm as it had been in the early days (Isaksen, 1989, p35; MFDP, 1989; interview with Baledzi Gaolathe, Finance and Development Planning Minister, 15 December 1994, Gabarone).

The MFDP's centrality in agenda setting and management of development planning was the result of the government's experience in the Shashe Project. The Shashe project was a huge planning and coordination exercise. Its total annual expenditure exceeded Botswana's gross domestic product. As such, the government virtually devoted all of its resources and skilled people to establishing the copper-nickel complex. Given the project's economic dominance, nearly all sectors and ministries depended on the spin-off resources from it. Consequently, the government had to coordinate and balance Shashe developments with the rest of the economy. The project's success gave government leaders confidence that they could plan and manage the economy and play a lead role (Hermans, interview, 6 June 1994, Gaborone; see also Cobbe, 1979, Chapter 7). The government transferred the planning experience from the copper-nickel project to the Ministry of Finance and Development Planning. To ensure the MFDP's capacity to spearhead the development agenda, the government set up planning units, staffed by professional planners responsible to the Director of Economic Affairs of MFDP, in other ministries. These officers met weekly with the Director to discuss and report on progress and possible problems in 'their ministries' (Isaksen, 1989, p34).[27]

The scarcity of skilled professionals necessitated centralizing finance and development planning authority. However, even when skilled professionals became more available, the centralized structure appeared to be an effective and efficient way to manage the government's business. Institutions that often decried the inefficiencies of centralized public institution praised the Botswana model:

> *The centralization of the [system] permits a higher quality in estimating their costs and allows the government to take advantage of bulk purchasing and economies of standardization. Moreover, this centralization functions as a means of*

ensuring efficiency and control of operations while leaving line managers with adequate flexibility in carrying out their responsibilities. This efficiency is further encouraged ... without influence or political interference... The process of budgetary preparation and control is supported by sets of procedures which impose the discipline necessary for the production of a good budget and for its implementation. (Raphaeli et al, 1984, p3)

The severe underdevelopment of the educational system during the long colonial period meant that the technical and administrative skills necessary for development were not available in Botswana. Thus, the BDP government assumed that expatriates would play a crucial role in the near future (Nwako, interview, 22 March 1994, Gabarone; Hermans, interview, 6 June 1994, Gaborone; Republic of Botswana, 1966b), and the government was willing to bend over backwards to attract skilled young people.[28] Consequently, it retained a few expatriate administrators and technicians, some of whom became naturalized citizens; among the most illustrious were Hermans, Steenkamp and Finlay, who wanted to stay and serve the new regime.

The government's immediate needs forced employing expatriates in senior positions in a highly centralized system. The new government's first two major undertakings were renegotiating of the 1910 South African Customs Union and establishing the Shashe copper-nickel Project, culminating with the MFDP consolidation. A small staff from the Economic Planning Unit, particularly Pierre Landell-Mills and Steven Etinger, and Attorney-General Alan Tilbury worked on the negotiations (Hermans, interview, 6 June 1994, Gaborone). They had the President's and Vice-President's full backing. Initially, the old colonial guard opposed the renegotiation. They feared these negotiations might upset South Africa and create more problems for Botswana. The negotiations were successful, and the government's financial base improved dramatically.[29] While the renegotiation was in progress, the government was also bargaining with foreign donors and private capital to invest in the copper-nickel complex. In the copper-nickel and diamonds case, the government used consultants, given these projects' complexity.[30] The government knew that it needed first-class technical and negotiating teams to wrestle with giants like De Beers. These two major efforts' successes demonstrated that employing expatriates was wise, given the dearth of indigenous skilled labour. Consequently, the government made the employment of expatriates in the civil service and consultants a pillar of its institutions' building strategy.[31]

Aid agencies, particularly the British, were a major source of skilled expatriate labour for Botswana. These aid expatriates were often attached to specific projects and integrated into the civil service during their Botswana tenure. This strategy was so successful that the government pressed the United States to send Peace Corps to Botswana and change the Peace Corps regulations in such a way that these volunteers could be assigned to ministries or wherever Botswana needed them.[32] The US was reluctant to do this, but Botswana's persistence prevailed.

Given its need, Botswana made unconventional use of the Peace Corps. On one occasion, the government dispatched a young Peace Corp volunteer to

Table 9.3 *Professional officers in MFDP key departments*[a,b]

| | Mid-1972 | | Mid-1978 | | 1994* | |
	Total	Local	Total	Local	Total	Local
Department of Economic Affairs	23	5	25	10	65	59
Department of Financial Affairs	10	6	19	11	24	20

Notes: a Counting civil servants down to the rank of executive officer
b PS, Secretariat and consultants included under DEA
Source: Isaksen (1989, p51); and (for 1994) Modise D Modise, Director of Economic Affairs, Ministry of Finance and Development Planning, interview, 7 December 1994, Gaborone.

London to negotiate with the Britain's Overseas Development Administration (ODA) on Botswana's behalf. The ODA was surprised by the idea, but the process continued (Hermans, interview, 6 June 1994, Gaborone). As noted previously, the BDP government made serious efforts to localize the civil service, but it was not in a hurry to do so at the cost of effective and efficient administration. Consequently, expatriates held a large proportion of technical and professional posts in the service (Stevens, 1981, p172; Raphaeli et al, 1984; Isaksen, 1989, pp37, 51). For example, expatriates dominated the most important policy-making organs of the Ministry of Finance and Development Planning until recently as shown in Table 9.3 The relationship between the state's skilled expatriate employees and the political leaders was complementary. The BDP government sketched the broader outlines of its development plan, but the skilled technocrats crafted the details and then implemented the programmes. As an insider noted, the bureaucracy had wide leeway as long as its propositions were not

> *critically endangering the relationship with South Africa and to refrain from promoting interests which are seen as directly in competition with those of the cattle industry. Within these limits there exists an area of decision-making for the bureaucracy and bureaucratic politics. The formal political system, and the elite, seldom interfere in this area, but leave it to the bureaucracy and political elite. Even superficial observation shows contacts and social links bordering on camaraderie. The elite also takes definite interest in and supports plans and implementation. It is, however, the bureaucracy which is usually expected to perceive problems, come out with ideas, take initiative and gain administrative and political support for these initiatives. There is, however, an absence of political sifting of ideas and initiatives which makes the initiator … critically important for the direction of policies within the fixed limits.* (Isaksen, 1989)

These expatriates occupied critical bureaucratic positions; therefore they managed the operations of the state apparatus at the behest of the elite. The Batswana who joined their ranks, slowly but steadily, were trained in the same universities and schools of thought as the expatriates. These Batswana also served under these expatriates early on in their careers. Thus, little difference existed between the Batswana and the expatriates about management style and the nature of economic development.[33] The fact that the fundamental administrative procedures governing the Ministry's and others' operations were set in the years immediately after independence reinforced this fact. This administrative structure and culture valued effectiveness, orderliness and accountability.[34]

The BDP leaders laid the foundation for stable and relatively effective public institutions by:

- resisting the pressure to quickly localize technical and professional levels of the public service;
- insulating the public service from political intervention; and
- clearly demarcating the political and economic boundaries within which policy-making must operate. With the development and establishment of this administrative apparatus and with MFDP as its nerve centre, Botswana's economy kept growing.

The Ministry of Finance and Development Planning directs all economic activity and financial management of the state. The Ministry is the epicentre of the economic development process. That process has two phases: strategy setting and translating that strategy into plans and projects. The MFDP plays a central role in the latter process, while its part in the former is much less significant (Gaolathe, interview, 15 December 1994, Gaborone).[35] A sketch of these two processes illustrates the state's autonomy in strategy setting as well as MFDP's critical function in translating strategies into substance while guarding the state's purse.

Strategy setting

This phase of the development process is long-term in orientation and is less frequently tampered with by government. Capitalist economic growth, in which the state plays a leading role, has been Botswana's core strategy since independence. Setting the strategy entails the government producing 'white papers' on matters fundamental to the thrust of the economy, that is

- Financial Assistance Policy (1982);
- National Policy on Economic Opportunities (1982);
- Industrial Development Policy (1984);
- National Policy on Land Tenure (1985);
- Wildlife Conservation policy (1986);
- Revised National Policy on Incomes, Employment, Prices and Profits (1990);
- National Policy on Agricultural Development (1991); and the
- Revised National Policy on Education (1994).

Danevad's 1993 study of the Revised National Policy on Incomes, Employment, Prices and Profits vividly illustrates not only the autonomy of public policy formation from most sectors of civil society but also how the state attempts to legitimize its programme (Danevad, 1993).[36] The purpose here is not to address the income policy's substantive issues but to sketch:

- the general framework of strategy formulation;
- the relationship between the Commission responsible for the production of the paper and non-governmental organizations affected by the policy; and
- the role of the Ministry of Finance and Development Planning.

The government follows a standard format in producing a white paper:

> *The production of a white paper seems broadly to follow a uniform pattern: a point of departure is often a report by an appointed commission, academic schol-ars, or private consultants. The report and its recommendations are subsequently considered by the political executive, and a draft policy document is presented to the National Assembly, and finally a white paper is made public.* (Danevad, 1993, p106)

Botswana's incomes policy since the introduction of the first policy in 1972 has been to restrain wages to attract investment and nurture economic growth (Repub-lic of Botswana, 1972, p5). The country has gone through significant economic transformation since independence, and the government thought that the incomes policy, a central tenet of Botswana's development strategy, needed to be updated. A 1989 Presidential Commission revised and reviewed the Incomes Policy (Dane-vad, 1993, p108).

The Commission, chaired by the Minister for External Affairs, consisted of: two members of parliament; five representatives of state employees (one of whom was the Governor of the Bank of Botswana and who is a member of the Economic Committee of the Cabinet); a member of the civil service association; two repre-sentatives of the trade unions; two representatives of private employers; an indus-trial worker; two from the rural sector, and two scholars, one of whom worked for and advised the Bank of Botswana for many years. The Commission's composi-tion led Danevad to conclude that it was not independent from the government (1993, p108). Figure 9.1 depicts the process of reviewing the old incomes policy and producing a new one.

The Revised Income Policy Commission travelled to major population cen-tres to solicit information on incomes and wages. It invited and collected testimo-nies from anyone concerned about the issue. It received 250 oral testimonies, most of which came from 'public and parastatal employees, followed by private employers' (Danevad, 1993, p108). After soliciting inputs from the 'public', the government- and BDP-dominated Commission submitted their report to the government. Trade union and representatives of civil society organs did not sub-stantially affect the Commission's recommendations. Senior public employees who followed the commission with advice and who were well represented in the Commission effectively influenced it to recommend a significant increase in the salaries for their cohorts of civil servants. The trade union representative's sugges-tions, which argued against increased wages for senior bureaucrats and small increases for most public servants, were not included in the report.

Once the Commission submitted its report, the government 'consulted' with two bodies before drafting its white paper. These were the Economic Committee of the Cabinet (ECC) and the National Employment, Manpower and Income

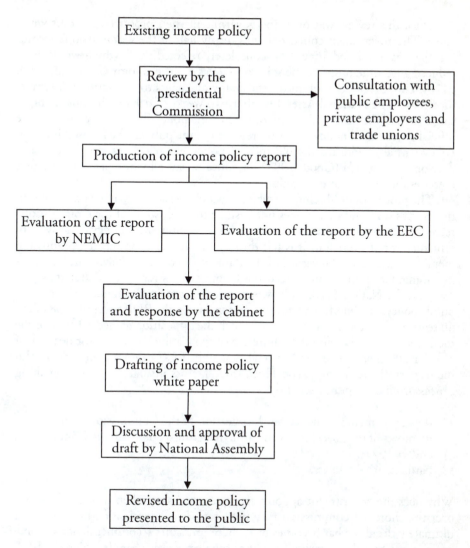

Figure 9.1 *White paper production process*

Council (NEMIC). The ECC includes all ministers, permanent secretaries, the Governor of the Bank of Botswana, the President and the commanders of the military and the police. The ECC secretariat is the Employment Policy Unit of MFDP. Thus, the MFDP influences the Committee through the presence of its Minister and Permanent Secretary, who are senior to their colleagues and through the use of the Secretariat (Danevad, 1993, pp111–13). The first two groups dominate NEMIC, which consists of representatives of the government, private employers and workers. Given that the ECC is in essence the government itself and that the NEMIC is dominated by government and private employers, who largely share the government's agenda of keeping wages low and competitive, the discussion of the report was an in-house review, not an examination by outsiders (Danevad, 1993, p113).

Once this review was over, the government then produced its draft white paper. The government concurred with nearly half of the Commission's recommendations, modified a few, and completely rejected those which would have reduced government involvement in some areas of the economy (Danevad, 1993, p110). The government submitted the draft white paper to the National Assembly for debate. The National Assembly, after two weeks of debate, did not change a single item in the proposed review of the income policy. The white paper became official government policy and was presented to the public. The Revised Incomes Policy partially modified the old income policy but reifies the dominant class's development agenda (Good, 1993). Needless to say, all white paper production exercises follow the same procedure.

The process of producing the white paper clearly shows that government is in the driver's seat, and that it does not hesitate to reject some of the Commission's recommendations that are contrary to its development strategy. The MFDP influence is not overt, but it is felt through the input of powerful Commission members, such as the Governor of the Bank of Botswana. Likewise, the cabinet's Economic Committee influenced the Commission's report at a later stage. By contrast, the National Assembly, which has the constitutional authority to alter public policy, was 'ineffective' for two reasons. First, the BDP controlled 38 of the 40 seats prior to the 1994 election in which the opposition gained 13 seats of the total. Second, the Economic Committee of the Cabinet accounts for nearly half of the BDP members of the National Assembly. ECC cabinet members are also the leaders of the ruling party. Thus, three factors insulate the policy-making process from close public scrutiny:

- the government's control over the selection of the Commission members;
- members of the government and affiliated groups dominate the Commission; and
- parliament's weakness.

Why does the government appoint such a commission when it has full control over the choice of commission members, sets the Commission's mandate, and ultimately decides what becomes of the Commission's recommendations? Some critics argue that this exercise is a part of the democratic charade which the BDP regime has been practising since independence. Others consider this as part of the regime's attempts to legitimate liberal capitalist economic strategy (Molutsi, 1986). Let us turn to how government strategy is translated into development programmes.

Development planning and implementation

The broad outlines of development strategy, spelled out in government white papers, have to be translated into plans and concrete projects. The Ministry of Finance and Development Planning spearheads, manages and controls this process. The MFDP initiates the production of a development plan by introducing a Keynote Policy Paper (KPP). This provides guidelines to all ministries regarding the government's development priorities and fiscal constraints:

The Keynote Policy Paper has deliberately confined itself to general themes for NDP7. It has not attempted to identify the crucial issues for each sector. This will be done by the sectoral ministries as they prepare Sectoral Keynote Issues Papers. Appropriate emphases will vary from sector to sector, but a number of the themes raised in the present paper should be followed through in each of the sectoral papers. In particular, the sectoral papers should address manpower and productivity within the sector; pricing and subsidy issues; employment creation and economic opportunities; sustainable development; the appropriate roles of Government, parastatals and private initiative; recurrent costs. (MFDP, 1989)

In response to the KPP, ministries develop sectoral keynote issue papers and submit them to MFDP on a specified date. Box 9.1 shows the process and stages of producing the National Development Plan 7.

The process of producing a development plan as depicted in Figure 9.1 seems participatory. Many actors at different levels of government, from local and district authorities, take part in the deliberations. Danevad's study indicated that the process's decentralized appearance does not reflect the actual critical hierarchical relations among the MFDP, the ministries and the district and local authorities (Danevad, 1993, Chapter 7). The public widely shares this assessment. The MFDP dominates and controls the process at every vital stage: from setting the broad priorities in KPP to producing the macro-economic forecasts through the Microeconomic Model of Botswana (MEMBOT) and establishing the expenditure ceiling with which every sector has to live. Other ministries dispute MFDP's ceiling and broader guidance, but MFDP is the undisputed process leader. The MFDP's central role in producing development plans has somewhat declined. The process has become relatively more participatory since Botswana's diamond-driven economic boom in the early 1980s (Gaolathe, interview, 15 December 1994, Gaborone).

Despite the MFDP's declining role in plan production, it continues to use two methods to dominate economic development (Gaolathe, interview). First, before any project can be included in a plan, sectoral ministries must carefully justify the project's economic viability.

Those projects which pass the economic viability test and become part of a plan do not get automatic funding unless they are included in the annual development budget.[37] The second way MFDP leads the development process is through its capacity to ensure that projects do not exceed expenditure ceilings and may even be reduced when necessary. For the MFDP to release funds a project must satisfy several conditions. First, the project must be in the national development plan and approved by parliament. Second, MFDP must evaluate and approve the project. Third, the funds must be in the development budget (Gaolathe, interview). If these conditions are met, a project is included into a ministry's annual budgetary warrant that the MFDP releases. MFDP release these warrants at the beginning of the financial year. If government revenue conditions have changed, however, the MFDP may warrant less than was budgeted for any ministry. This happened in 1982. Under adverse financial circumstances, the vice-president and Minister of Finance and Development Planning announced to parliament:

Box 9.1 *The key stages in the preparations of the plan*

1. Preparation by MFDP of economic projections for the plan period. These highlight important development issues such as the gap between labour force growth and likely job creations. The projections also provide an estimate of the resources that will be available to government and the country during the plan period.
2. Preparation by MFDP of a keynote policy paper. This summarizes the economic outlook, identifies the crucial policy issues that will determine the shape of the plan and proposes the themes to be stressed. The paper is submitted to the Economic Committee of the Cabinet for discussion and endorsement.
3. Preparation by line ministries of sectoral keynote papers that take up the themes proposed in MFDP's paper. These should be brief (not a 'first draft' of NDP chapter) and should concentrate on the new or more crucial issues to be resolved in the course of preparing the sector's plan. Ideally, a keynote policy paper is not more than 6–12 pages long and concentrates on *issues*, not a shopping list of projects.
4. Preparation by MFDP of initial resource guidelines (ceilings) for the plan period, allocated among sectors, ministries and departments in line with the priorities endorsed by ECC. Cabinet approves the ceilings as the basis for drafting of the plan, and MFDP then issues detailed drafting guidelines to ministries.
5. The first drafts of the plan proper are prepared. While sectoral ministries draft their chapters and prepare projects for part II, MFDP drafts the macro-economic and review chapters, continuously refining its economic and budgetary forecasts in the process.
6. Drafts are extensively circulated for comment – to all ministries and all local authorities and to various consultative bodies and committees. They form the subject of a National District Development Conference.
7. MFDP reviews and edits drafts, aiming to reconcile proposals with resources available and to ensure consistency. Contentious issues are resolved at ECC or cabinet level if necessary.
8. The complete draft is submitted to cabinet for approval. It is then tabled in the National Assembly and extensively debated. After any amendments have been agreed and parliament's approval given the new plan ceases to be a draft and becomes the blueprint for development policy until superseded by the next NDP.

Source: Republic of Botswana (1986, pp2–5)

This year we have seen a rapidly changing international situation affecting our budget. If we had known in August what we know now, I would be presenting different figures to this Honourable House. Because of the substantial deterioration in the international and our domestic situation, following approval of the budget, my ministry will only warrant authority to spend 80% of the amounts given in the estimates. (Raphaeli et al, 1984, p16)

This complex planning and budgetary process, centred in the Ministry of Finance and Development Planning, has enabled Botswana to remain in good fiscal health and ensure relatively successful implementation of its development plans.

Furthermore, the leadership demands accountable but autonomous and effective institutions that can plan and manage the state's affairs. This combination of conscious leadership and insulated bureaucracy has earned Botswana the status of a model state in Africa.

Finally, the government and MFDP have developed a monitoring and auditing system to ensure and enforce proper and legitimate use of public funds. This system has worked exceedingly well, sustaining the republic's reputation as a country free of systemic corruption and excessive rent-seeking. When individuals abuse their office, the system holds them accountable. Scandals in the early 1990s in the Botswana Housing Corporation, a government parastatal, and the peri-urban land speculation and corruption show that no one can escape the reach of the law. In the latter case, the government removed a minister and the vice-president and Minister of Finance and Development Planning from their posts for abusing their authority. More recently, many senior members of the ruling party, including the President of the Republic were forced to repay overdue loans that they owed to the National Development Bank.[38]

Conclusion

[Among the developing world] Botswana stands out in many respects. It has a functioning democratic system, the lines of authority are clearly defined, the civil servants are accountable ... control over financial management is enforced, plans and planning are taken seriously, technical assistance is utilized effectively, parastatals are managed on sound commercial principles and are not a drain on the national budget and, by and large, there are order, logic, efficiency, probity and rhythm in the conduct of government business. (Raphaeli et al, 1984, p10)

Independent Botswana inherited a colonial state not worth the name. It did not have an apparatus capable of promoting economic development. Nor did it have an agricultural and industrial resource base to marshal for future development. The state's new leadership recognized that it needed to establish sound and effective public institutions to carry out its development objectives. Building these institutions required skilled people who were scarce in Botswana. The government used a dual strategy to overcome such scarcity. First, it retained any skilled former Protectorate officers willing to stay. It also solicited donor agencies and countries to assist government by providing trained expatriates. Second, it embarked on training Batswana in significant numbers at home and abroad. The strategy worked well, and the government developed its institutional capacity.

How did Botswana's social history and structure assist the emergence of efficacious state? By the accounts of some current themes in social capital, Botswana's hierarchical social structure and its patron–client ties should have hobbled the state's liberal democratic and capitalist agenda. This society's social structure has had three major effects on democracy and development. First, traditional patron–client relations provided the glue that held together the elite and the vast majority of the rural population. The 'intelligent' deployment of these traditional ties sustained social cohesion among the elite and in the larger society in the face of significant economic inequality. Second, the small dominant class was united ideologically and economically. This coupled with the legitimacy of their leadership enabled the latter to build a state apparatus capable of professionally managing the state's affairs. Unlike many other African states, Botswana's disciplined political leaders ensured that sectarian agenda (among the elite) did not enter the political process and state institutional affairs through the back door. This political strategy guaranteed the bureaucracy's professional autonomy and safeguarded public resources from rent-seeking members of the elite. Third, the persistence of traditional patron–client relations, the government's provision of social services across the country, the insignificant tax burden on the rural population, and the absence of strong and stable opposition political parties to articulate the agenda of social justice and galvanize urban and rural poor left the elite's capitalist accumulation strategy unchallenged. This explains the endurance of 'radical' inequality in Botswana in spite of the government's enormous mineral wealth (its foreign exchange reserves are over US$6000 million dollars) and its technical capacity to effect change.[39]

Some critics will claim that the Botswana state has been able significantly to sustain a coherent development strategy because of the vast royalties from its diamond exports. There is no doubt that mineral revenue made matters easy for the state. However, if vast royalties were enough to explain Botswana's success, then other states that control similar resources such as Nigeria, Gabon, Democratic Republic of Congo and others elsewhere in the Third World should match this African miracle. Moreover, if the Botswana leadership and its bureaucracy were not alert to the need to negotiate with South Africa and De Beers on the basis of well-prepared plans, and if they did not severely contain rent-seekers, the diamond fortunes may have slipped into the pockets of criminals and De Beers and not the state. Such a mess would have led to political and economic turmoil similar to many in the continent. That the public owns Botswana's vast foreign exchange reserves significantly distinguishes it from other states. This also bodes well for the future if a new regime, whose orientation is social justice with equity, is elected. The key to this new project's success is the protection of the political, institutional, moral and economic gains of the last three decades and using them to advance both growth and equity.

The leadership's unity and legitimacy ensured that the policy-making process was managed so that even the National Assembly rarely, if ever, challenged or significantly amended government proposals. Two major factors contributed to Botswana becoming an autonomous state with capacity to effect planned change:

1. insulating the policy-making process from society-centred groups; and
2. protecting the MFDP technocratic cadre's ability to plan, budget and monitor programme implementation. It also enforced fiscal discipline while remaining free, for the most part, from 'political' influence.

This chapter's principal thesis has been that creating an autonomous state apparatus with significant capacity to effect change did not occur accidentally. Rather leading members of the dominant class assisted by expatriate technocratic cadre and later on by Batswana bureaucrats carefully crafted this autonomous and effective state apparatus. The relationship between conscious and wilful political authority and capable bureaucracy was brought together and institutionalized in the MFDP. The Ministry has the authority to manage the business of government and the nation. In a nutshell, MFDP played a role similar to that of Japan's 'pilot agency' (MITI – Ministry of International Trade and Industry) and Taiwan's Economic Bureaucracy. Thus contrary to the claims of those who advocate decentralization of state authority, the MFDP enabled Botswana to forge ahead in spite of the 'maladies' of centralization.

To understand fully the nature of the post-colonial African state, its role and (in)ability to transform the economy requires an appreciation of the motives and the agendas of two groups: those dominant class members who occupy strategic positions in the state apparatus and those bureaucrats who provide the leadership with technical advice. The MFDP's technical ability to plan, budget and judicially manage the public purse would not have been possible without a strong and united political leadership. This leadership recognized the importance of disciplined and technically competent public institutions for systemic capitalist development.

Notes

1. A different version of this chapter was published in A Samatar (1999) *An African Miracle*, Heinemann, Portsmouth. I thank Heinemann for permission to reproduce it.
2. Former President Masire recalled the pessimistic attitude that prevailed among colonial authorities at the time of independence: 'nothing happens here' (Obondo-Okoyo, 1986; Republic of Botswana, 1966b).
3. There were other important contributions such as Colclough and McCarthy (1980); Harvey (1981).
4. For a similar but recent expression of this view, see Gulhati, 1990, p1150.
5. There was a struggle between the old colonial guard led by Alfred Beebe and the young turks who shared the views of the vice-president. This 'conservative' financial management thesis glosses over significant differences between those led by the vice-president and old colonial boys. The vice-president championed the notion that Botswana had great capacity to absorb resources effectively in order to develop. The position of the vice-president and his young turks did not mean letting the purse strings loose.
6. Until the colonial development and welfare programme boosted the revenue base of the colonial state, it did little to improve the economy of the Protectorate; see the Pim Commission for indictment of British colonial policy in Bechuanaland. This is contrary to the claims of Steenkamp (1991, pp293–308).
7. The elite was a tightly knit group in which everyone knew everyone else: 'Old Tigers' educated at Tiger Kloof before the mid-1950s constituted the political elite in government and opposition. The next generation, now emerging as graduates from the University of Botswana, Lesotho and Swaziland (UBLS) had mostly been educated at Moeng College – the only large high school in

the late 1950s and early 1960s. It was civil servants of the Moeng generation who became permanent secretaries in ministries by 1970.

8. There was a widespread assumption in Botswana that individuals from the Kalanga community dominated the civil service and hence the government. It is reported that this notion turned into grist for some Tswana politicians and became an urgent political matter. President Khama considered this urgent enough that he had to intervene strongly in order to bring this speculation to an end. The late Peter Mmusi led the Tswana faction (Steenkamp, interview, 15 August 1994, Gaborone). Mr Philip Steenkamp was the Permanent Secretary of the Office of the President. He notes that many senior and very capable civil servants were from the Kalanga community because that community heavily agitated for and invested in schools during the colonial era. This paid off as many of the students from these schools completed their studies when Botswana became independent and were consequently well placed to take advantage of the professional opportunities. Mr Steenkamp attests to this as he was the District Commissioner in the northeast during the time this was taking place.

9. The development strategy of the BDP government had three phases (Parson, 1984, pp88–99): (a) 1966–74 was the period in which most of the major state institutions were created and the infrastructural boom began; (b) during 1975–80, the infrastructural development was consolidated and the initial tensions which began to appear as a result of the previous investment programme were managed, ie TGLP – partnership with MNCs. This period also saw the growth of a state-based middle class who were interested in maintaining existing patterns of growth; (c) Parson says that in 1980–83 the post-1980 era was one characterized by the appearance of fractures within the dominant coalition and the passing of Seretse; growth of a working class and its demand for better wages and working conditions; aspiration of the middle class to break into the private economy monopolized by Indians; and white South Africans; and the tension in the countryside created by the need for further commercialization of the range land via TGLP. Parson thought that during the last phase major cracks were appearing in the unity of the dominant class. Nearly a decade later, the fortress seems sufficiently strong although one sees cracks. See the Mmegi Newspaper for description of factional struggles among the BDP (Gaborone, various issues, 1994–95; see also Good, 1994, pp499–521).

10. Note that autonomy is only from the dominated classes but the distorting effect of dominant class on state autonomy and the choice of development policy is not fully developed.

11. For the struggle between national-institutionalists and their foes in Somalia, see Samatar, 1997, pp687–707.

12. A classic example of this was Tshekedi Khama who used missionaries, lawyers, and anti-colonial, anti-slavery voices to block the British and South African agenda for the Tswana. See Crowder,1987, pp25–42; 1988.

13. According to the former Governor of the Bank of Botswana, the government made brilliant use of qualified and knowledgeable expatriates after independence in the absence of a skilled citizen cadre (Hermans, interview, 6 June 1994, Gaborone).

14. There was an agreement between the leaders of the departing colonial regime and the Botswana elite regarding the centrality of capitalist economy in the development of independent Botswana. See the continuity between the last development plans of the colonial state and the *Transitional Plan of Independent Botswana* (Republic of Botswana, 1966b).

15. This statement was made by President Khama in his first presidential speech in 1966.

16. The leadership of BDP and the administration were very close and shared many ideas. The closeness of the relationship is verified by the words of Seretse Khama on the occasion of the departure of Sir Peter Fawcus: 'he will leave many devoted friends behind him and has made a home for himself here that will always be remembered. I, particularly, have had a long and valuable association with Sir Peter, and I wish both Sir Peter and Lady Fawcus a happy retirement' (Henderson, 1990, p36). This view is also supported by Governor Hermans and Mr David Finlay (interviews, 1994).

17. See the history of the relationship between Tshekedi Khama and the British colonial administration. Moreover, the Government of Botswana has had more autonomy from the policy dictates of others, ie the neo-liberal privatization bandwagon, by keeping its fiscal house in order. See Harvey, 1985, pp47, 51.

18. H C L Hermans, the former Governor of the Bank of Botswana, was the first Permanent Secretary of the Ministry of Finance and Development Planning. He notes, in hindsight, that his cadre of young turks acted and behaved like central planners to facilitate capitalist economic growth (Hermans, interview, 6 June 1994, Gaborone).

19. Many BDP members and expatriates fondly remember this lecture as 'when the President gave them hell'.

20. 'Specially elected' is a euphemism for appointed members of the National Assembly by the ruling party.

21. Directorate of Personnel is part of the Office of the President. It is an extremely important institution which is fully responsible for development and management of public employment.

22. The first discovery was made in 1967 in Orapa in north central Botswana. This mine was brought to production in 1971. A smaller mine was discovered in 1976 in Letlhakane. But the most important mine in Jwaneng, in the south, started producing diamonds in 1982. In the early 1990s another discovery was made in the Kalahari. This so-called Gope project in the Kalahari is being developed, making Botswana the world's largest producer of diamonds (*Financial Mail* (Johannesburg), 24 April 1998, p25).

23. At one point in the mid-1970s Vice-President Masire turned down President Khama's request for a presidential plane. The Vice President insisted that the country could not afford such expenditure. President Khama accepted the decision of his vice-president. Several years later the situation changed and Khama got his plane (Hermans, interview, 6 June 1994, Gaborone). Another source suggested that one of the reasons why a presidential plane was not an option for a while was security risks. Shortly after independence, the United States government gave a twin engine plane to Botswana. This plane became

a white elephant as Botswana could not afford to maintain it (Finlay, interview, 18 July 1995, Ramotswa).

24. The Economic Planning Unit was staffed by two young expatriates, Peter Landell-Mills and Steve Ettinger (Landell-Mills interview, October 1993, Gaborone).

25. Hermans notes that vice-president Masire was a keen listener: 'One of the most valuable institutions he had in those early days was an informal discussion group held fortnightly in the home of the Hermans. All young planning officers from the ministry, who were initially all expatriate (later joined by a few Batswana) will meet in an evening. The vice-president will come and sit on the floor … One of these youngesters will lead the discussion (10–15 minutes) on a planning matter and an intensive discussion will then ensue. The vice-president participated and there was a great deal of camaraderie. The seriousness of the vice-president impressed and enormously encouraged the young planning officers.'

26. The struggle between the old guard in the Ministry of Finance led by Alfred Bebe and the Developmentalists under the wing of the vice-president came to a showdown when Landell-Mills was dismissed by the Civil Service Commission for insubordination. This incident became known as the Landell-Mills Affair. The President sided with the civil Service Commission as that was the legal procedure. The President's action created a rift between him and his vice-president as Landell-Mills was the latter's principal economic adviser. 'Masire felt that Seretse had been got at by colonial rearguard and that Seretse had listened to their point of view before considering his' (Henderson, 1990, p41). I am also grateful to Governor Hermans for this information.

27. The weekly meeting had its origin in the fortnightly meeting the vice-president used to have in the Hermans home. To ensure effective compliance with the government's plans, President Khama received regular economic briefing from the vice-president and senior officers of the MFDP and then would quiz his ministers regarding the operations in their ministries. He often embarrassed them by seeming to know more about their jobs (Hermans, interview, 6 June 1994, Gaborone).

28. Hermans cites an incident which sums up this attitude. On one occasion, S McCarthy, an ODA fellow, was not happy with his government-provided housing. 'He kept storming into my office throwing tantrums. He kept saying his housing was not acceptable, and that he was not willing to live in type 4 housing any more. My instinct was to say here is your ticket, good bye. If that is your attitude you cannot really make a contribution here. Somehow vice-president Masire, who was my minister, heard about it and then called me in and said, "Wait a minute! You got to look at this problem in two ways. One is the short-term view which is these guys come to Botswana and go away and they have skills which we lack and they may not be perfect, but they are the best we have. The second is the long-term view. If these youngsters all have good experience here, they are going to fan out and stay in the development business and ultimately we are going to benefit, maybe not as a country, but the development business." My God he was right! There are 37 of these guys in the World Bank and they are some of

the best. These World Bank employees are now referred to as the "Botswana mafia".'

29. The lesson of the Customs renegotiations was the value of careful prior analysis and contingency planning if the worst scenario became the only option. Hermans notes that both in the case of Customs Union renegotiation as well as the negotiation with De Beers over the diamonds the Botswana team was prepared to walk away knowing that their fall-back scenario was not too bad an option.

30. The team which negotiated with De Beers on behalf of Botswana included Charles Lipton, a Canadian resource economist from UNDP, Martin Maryal, a former management trainee with De Beers who had fallen out with the diamond giant. The latter provided extremely valuable information to Botswana, such as what would happen if Botswana decided not to sell its diamonds through the Central Selling Organization As a result of the work of this group, led by Hermans as Permanent Secretary of MFDP, Botswana was ready to withdraw from the negotiation if the terms of the final agreement were not favourable. In fact, Oppenheimer was so furious about the role of Maryal that he threatened to break off the negotiations if Maryal remained a member of the Botswana team. (Hermans, interview, 6 June 1994, Gaborone).

31. Baledzi Gaolathe, the former Permanent Secretary of MFDP for 17 years and current Governor of the Bank of Botswana, noted that the government of Botswana determined the terms of reference and controlled the process and therefore was not worried that those it hired to do a job would not deliver. If there was a problem with an employee not meeting the terms of the contract, then it simply terminated the agreement. The contracting and consulting system worked very well and the government of Botswana took ownership of the products (Gaolathe, interview, 15 December 1994, Gaborone).

32. Botswana was not a Peace Corps recipient country, but it persisted in its request for such status. A United States Senator's administrative assistant, who was Hermans' brother-in-law, helped Botswana achieve this status. The assistant urged his Senator to speak in support of Botswana's request. The Senator agreed and the US administration was persuaded to offer Peace Corps assistance to Botswana (Hermans, interview, 6 June 1994, Gaborone).

33. Isaksen notes that one of the few differences between expatriates and Batswana bureaucrats is that the latter wanted to spend more on development while the former were financially more conservative.

34. Hermans reported one of the first administrative manuals was produced by Michael Stevens. Such manuals which govern the routine operations of ministries and employees became the bible of the Botswana bureaucracy.

35. He notes that the strength of the MFDP has declined relatively as more revenues have become available.

36. The discussion of the Revised Incomes Policy draws heavily from Danevad.

37. One of the hallmarks of Botswana's success is the integration of development plans with annual budgets.

38. This does not mean that more systematic ways of eluding the bite of the law are not available. For instance, the National Development Bank was made to write off loans to all farmers after a long and devastating drought. Many have

argued that this benefited the rich, mostly civil servants and politicians who had most of the loans. The write-off of these loans was done in the guise of helping poor and small farmers. See Government of Botswana (1991, 1992); see also *Mmegi* newspaper, various issues, 1994. Through public pressure the government has created the Directorate of Corruption in 1994 to monitor such misdeeds and bring the culprits to court.

39. A puzzle is why the government has not used its resources and capacity to deal more urgently with the AIDS epidemic!

References

Bank of Botswana (1987) *Report on the Rural Economic Survey 1986*, Gaborone

Bechuanaland Protectorate (1963–8) *Development Plan*, Gaborone

Bechuanaland Protectorate (1964) *Annual Report*, HMSO, London

Charlton, R (1991) 'Bureaucrats and Politicians in Botswana: A Re-interpretation', *Journal of Commonwealth & Comparative Politics*, vol 29, no 3, pp273–4

Cobbe, J (1979) 'Minerals in Botswana', in *Government and Mining in Developing Countries*, Westview Press, Boulder

Cohen, D (1979) 'The Botswana Political Elite: Evidence from the 1974 General Election', *Journal of Southern African Affairs*, vol 4, pp347–72

Colclough, C and McCarthy, S (1980) *The Political Economy of Botswana: A Study of Growth and Income Distribution*, Oxford University Press, Oxford

Crowder, M (1987) 'Tshekedi Khama, Smuts, and South West Africa', *Journal of Modern African Studies*, vol 25, no 1, pp25–42

Crowder, M (1988) *The Flogging of Phinehas McIntosh: a Tale of Colonial Folly, Bechuanaland 1933*, Yale University Press, New Haven

Danevad, A (1993) 'Development Planning and the Importance of Democratic Institutions in Botswana', Report 7, Chr. Michelsen Institute, Bergen

Good, K (1993) 'At the End of the Ladder: Radical Inequalities in Botswana', *Journal of Modern African Studies*, vol 31, no 2, pp203–30

Good, K (1994) 'Corruption and Mismanagement in Botswana: a Best-Case Example?', *Journal of Modern African Studies*, vol 32, no 3, pp499–521

Gossett, C (1986) *The Civil Service in Botswana: Personnel Policies in Comparative Perspective*, PhD dissertation, Stanford University

Government of Botswana (1975) *The Rural Income Distribution Survey in Botswana 1974–75*, Gaborone

Government of Botswana (1991) *Report of the Presidential Commission on the Inquiry into the Land Problems in Mogodishane and Other Peri-Urban Villages*, Gaborone

Government of Botswana (1992) *Report of the Presidential Commission of Inquiry into the Operation of the Botswana Housing Corporation*, Gaborone

Gulhati, R (1990) 'Who Makes Economic Policy in Africa and How?', *World Development*, vol 18, no 8, p1150

Gunderson, G (1970) *Nation Building and the Administrative State: The Case of Botswana*, PhD dissertation, University of California. Berkeley

Hailey, L (1961) *The Republic of South Africa and the High Commission Territories*, Oxford University Press, Oxford

Harvey, C (ed) (1981) *Papers on the Economy of Botswana*, Heinemann, London

Harvey, C (1985) 'Successful Adjustment in Botswana', *IDS Bulletin*, vol 16, no 3, pp47–51

Harvey, C and Lewis, S (1990) *Policy Choice and Development Performance in Botswana*, Macmillan, London

Henderson, W (1990) 'Seretse Khama: A Personal Appreciation', *African Affairs*, no 89

Holm, J, Molutsi, P and Somolekae, G (1996) 'The Development of Civil Society in a Democratic State: The Botswana Model', *African Studies Review*, vol 39, no 2, pp43–69

Isaksen, J (1989) *Macro-Economic Management*: 35; Ministry of Finance and Development Planning, Keynote Policy Paper, Gabarone

Jacqz, J W (1967) *Report of a Conference on United States Assistance to Botswana and Lesotho*, The African American Institute, New York

Luke, T (1964) *Report on Localization and Training*, Government of Bechuanaland, Gaborone

Ministry of Finance and Development Planning (1989) *Keynote Policy Paper*, Gaborone

Molutsi, P (1986) *Social Stratification and Inequality in Botswana: Issues in Development 1950–1985*, PhD dissertation, Oxford University

Molutsi, P (1989) 'The Ruling-Class and Democracy in Botswana', in J D Holm and P P Molutsi (eds) *Democracy in Botswana*, Macmillan, Gaborone

Molutsi, P and Holm, H (1990) 'Developing Democracy When Civil Society is Weak: The Botswana Case', *African Affairs*, vol 89, no 356, pp323–40

Obondo-Okoyo, T (ed) (1986) *Botswana 1966–1986: Twenty Years of Progress*, Department of Information and Broadcasting, Gaborone

Parson, J (1979) *The Political Economy of Botswana: A Case in the Study of Politics and Social Change in Post-Colonial Botswana*, PhD thesis, Sussex University, Brighton

Parson, J (1984) *Botswana: Liberal Democracy and the Labour Reserve in Southern Africa*, Westview Press, Boulder

Parson, J (ed) (1990) *Succession to High Office in Botswana: Three Case Studies*, University Center for International Studies, Athens, OH

Parsons, N, Henderson, W and Tlou, T (1995) *Seretse Khama 1921–1980*, Macmillan, Gaborone

Picard, L (1987) *The Politics of Development in Botswana: A Model of Success?*, Lynne Rienner, Boulder

Pim, A (1933) *Financial and Economic Position of the Bechuanaland Protectorate*, Command Paper 4368, HMSO, London

Raphaeli, N, Roumani, J and Makellar, A (1984) *Public Sector Management in Botswana: Lessons in Pragmatism*, World Bank Staff Working Paper No 709, Washington, DC

Republic of Botswana (1966a) *The Development of Bechuanaland Economy: Report of the Ministry of Overseas Development: Economic Survey Mission*, Gaborone

Republic of Botswana (1966b) *Transitional Plan for Social and Economic Development*, Gaborone

Republic of Botswana (1967) *National Assembly Official Report* (Hansard 22), Part II, Gaborone

Republic of Botswana (1972) *National Policy on Incomes, Employment, Prices and Profits*, Government Paper No 2, Gaborone

Republic of Botswana (1986) *Planning Officers Manual*, Gaborone

Samatar, A (1997) 'Leadership and Ethnicity in the Making of African State Models: Botswana Versus Somalia', *Third World Quarterly*, vol 18, no 4, pp687–707

Steenkamp, P (1991) 'Cinderella of Empire? Development Policy in Bechuanaland in the 1930s', *Journal of Southern African Studies*

Stevens, M (1981) 'Aid Management in Botswana: From One to Many Donors', in C Harvey, *Papers on the Economy of Botswana*, Macmillan, Gaborone

UNDP (United Nations Development Programme) (2001) *Human Development Report 2001: Making New Technologies Work for Human Development*, available at http://hdr.undp.org/reports/global/2001/en/

UNDP (2003) *Human Development Report 2003: Millennium Development Goals – A Compact Among Nations to End Human Poverty*, available at http://www.undp.org.np/publications/hdr2003/

Wylie, D (1990) *A Little God: The Twilight of Patriarchy in a Southern African Chiefdom*, Witwatersrand University Press, Johannesburg

10

Identity and National Governance

Mahmood Mamdani

My starting point is the generation that inherited Africa's colonial legacy. Our generation followed on the heels of nationalists. We went to school in the colonial period and to university after independence. We were Africa's first generation of post-colonial intellectuals. Our political consciousness was shaped by a central assumption: we were convinced that the impact of colonialism on our societies was mainly economic. In the decade that followed African political independence, militant nationalist intellectuals focused on the expropriation of the native as the great crime of colonialism. Walter Rodney wrote *How Europe Underdeveloped Africa* (Rodney, 1971). But no one wrote of how Europe *ruled* Africa.

We were convinced that the method of political economy was the way to come to analytical grips with the colonial legacy. The great contribution of underdevelopment theorists was to historicize the construction of colonial markets and thereby of market-based identities. The popularity of political economy spread like a forest fire in post-independence Africa precisely because it historicized colonial realities, even if in a narrowly economic way. Political economy provided a way of countering two kinds of colonial presumptions, embedded in various theories of modernization (Wallerstein, 2000). The first was that colonial cultures were not grounded in historical processes. The second was that colonial contact marked the beginning of a history for these societies, since colonialism was presumed to have animated them culturally, economically and politically.

The limits of political economy as a framework for political analysis began to surface in the face of post-colonial political violence. For political economy could only explain violence when it resulted from a clash between market-based identities – either class or division of labour. From this point of view, political violence had to be either revolutionary or counter-revolutionary. In the face of political violence that cut *across* social classes rather than between them – violence neither revolutionary nor counter-revolutionary but simply non-revolutionary, violence animated mainly by distinctions crafted in colonial law rather than sprouting from the soil of a commodity economy – explanations rooted in political economy offered less and less analytical clarity. This limit provided an opening for a second coming of cultural explanations of political conflict, most obviously those addressing the political resurgence of ethnicity.

My objective here is to try to understand the spread of non-revolutionary political violence by breaking from widely held culturalist assumptions in two ways. First, I will argue that the process of state formation generates political identities that are distinct not only from market-based identities but also from cultural identities. Second, faced with a growing tendency to root causes of violence in cultural difference – now ominously called a clash of civilizations (eg in Huntingdon, 1996) – I will differentiate between cultural and political identities.

To return to the time of Rodney, it strikes me that none of us – neither nationalists nor Marxists – historicized the political legacy of colonialism, of the colonial state as a legal/institutional complex that reproduced particular political identities. The tendency was to discuss agency in an institutional void, by focusing on how it was harnessed to the colonial project; Marxists called the agents 'compradors' and nationalists called them 'collaborators'. Both bemoaned 'tribe' and 'tribalism' as colonial concoctions, while assuming 'race' and 'racism' to exist as something real, in a positivist sense. It was said that ethnicity was cultural and race biological. Neither Marxists nor nationalists tried to historicize race and ethnicity as political identities under-girded and reproduced by colonial institutions – perhaps because neither had yet managed sufficient analytical distance from that legacy. Because our emphasis on agency was to the exclusion of institutions, we failed to historicize agency, to understand the extent to which colonial institutions did shape the agency of the colonized.

The question of institutions of rule has surfaced only recently, in the face of a breakdown of political institutions and an eruption of internal conflict. In the West, it has stimulated an entire genre of literature, generally called the literature on state collapse (see Zartman, 1995). When I first heard of the crisis of governance in post-colonial Africa being referred to as a state collapse, I was a bit suspicious. I remembered the tradition from Aristotle to Hegel that considered the capacity for state life as the peak of human historical achievement. I also remembered the Hamitic hypothesis, which took all evidence of state-building in Africa as the influence of Hamites, considered as black but not Negro. And I remembered that the rationale for colonialism was always the need for tutelage, given that Africans were said to lack the capacity to build stable states and a durable law and order.

On second thoughts, however, I realized that these Africanists do have a point. There is a state collapse. But the point they have is too general. It is not just any state that is collapsing; it is specifically what remains of the colonial state in Africa that is collapsing. True, Africa's political institutions are in crisis. But which institutions are these? If we look at the crisis closely, we will recognize at its heart the institutional legacy of colonial rule, particularly the political institutions of colonial rule.

There is also a second response to the crisis. It goes under the name of Pan-Africanism. This tendency even has an organization by that name, called the Pan-African Congress, with headquarters in Kampala patronized by the Yoweri Museveni government and, until recently, by the entire phalanx of what used to be referred to as the 'new generation' of Africa's leaders: those from Rwanda, Ethiopia, Eritrea and Libya. The Pan-Africanists believe that state crisis is a crisis of colonial boundaries, because these boundaries were and are artificial – in the African case more so, since they were drawn up with a pencil and a ruler on a map at a conference table in Berlin in the 1880s. Well, what would be genuine boundaries? From this point of view the answer would be that they would be 'natural', meaning they would not cut through ethnic boundaries. In other words, the political map of Africa should have followed its cultural map.

I find two problems with this kind of argument. All boundaries are artificial; none is natural. War and conquest have always been integral to state-building. This was particularly the case before the era of the extraordinary mobility of finance capital; then, shifting power relations often translated into shifting boundaries, with each new boundary being claimed more natural than the previous one. With the growing power of finance capital, however, all boundaries became porous.

The real problem with this point of view is the assumption that cultural and political boundaries should coincide, and that the state should be a nation-state – that the natural boundaries of a state are those of a common *cultural* community. Basil Davidson called this 'the curse of the nation state', but he was never able to define the institutional nature of that curse (Davidson, 1992). After arguing – rightly, I think – that the curse led to the politics of ethnic cleansing in the Balkans, he argued – wrongly, and illogically – that the problem in Africa was that Europe ignored the ethnic map of Africa. Thereby, Davidson thought, Europe ignored Africa's *real traditions* in drawing state boundaries. So he brought us right back to the question of colonial boundaries.

I will argue differently from both these schools. The solution does not lie in bringing back the Europeans to address 'state collapse', or even in 'recolonization' by presumably more benign Africans, as Ali Mazrui once suggested (Mazrui, 1994). Nor does the solution lie in redrawing Africa's boundaries. For no matter how much we redraw boundaries, the political crisis will remain incomprehensible until we address the institutional – political – legacy of colonial rule.

The Colonial State and Legally Inscribed Identities

There is a language particular to the modern state, including its colonial version. That is the language of law. Legal distinctions are different from all others in that they are enforced by the state, and are in turn reproduced by institutions that structure citizen participation within the state.

The colonial state made a distinction in law between 'race' and 'ethnicity'. This is the question with which I would like to begin. What is the difference in law between a race and an ethnicity? Is it the difference between biology and culture, between biological race and cultural ethnicity? Not really, if you take a closer look. In indirect-rule Africa, only natives were said to belong to ethnic groups; non-natives had no ethnicity. Non-natives were identified racially, not ethnically. There was in fact an entire racial hierarchy, with Europeans – meaning whites – at the top, followed by 'Coloureds', then Asians, then Arabs and then Hamites (the Tutsi). Races were considered a civilizing influence, even if in different degrees, while ethnicities were considered to be in dire need of being civilized.

The colonial state divided the population into two: races and ethnicities. Each lived in a different legal universe. Races were governed through civil law. They were considered as members, actually or potentially, of civil society. Civil society excluded ethnicities. If we understand civil society not as an idealized prescription but as a historical construct, we will recognize that the original sin of civil society under colonialism was racism.

Ethnicities were governed through customary laws. While civil law spoke the language of rights, customary law spoke the language of tradition, of authenticity. These were different languages with different effects, even opposite effects. The language of rights bounded law. It claimed to set limits to power. For civic power was bounded by the rule of law, and was supposed to observe the sanctity of the domain of rights. The language of custom, in contrast, did not circumscribe power, for custom was *enforced*. The language of custom *enabled* power instead of checking it by drawing boundaries around it. In such an arrangement, no rule of law was possible.

Let me return to my basic point. Colonial law made a fundamental distinction between two types of persons: those indigenous and those not indigenous; in a word, natives and non-natives. My *first* observation – I will have a second one later – is that rights belonged to non-natives, not to natives. Natives had to live according to custom. Nationalism was a struggle of natives to be recognized as a trans-ethnic identity, as a race, as 'Africans', and thus – as a race – to gain admission to the world of rights, to civil society, which was a short form for *civilized* society. Before going farther, I would like to take a closer look at the two worlds: the world of the native and the world of the settler (which we shall see was not always synonymous with 'non-native'), the world of the ethnicities and the world of races, the world of customary law and the world of civil law.

Customary law

In the indirect-rule state, there was never a single customary law for all natives. For customary law was not racially specific; it was ethnically specific. It made a horizontal distinction, a distinction in law, between different ethnic groups. This was not a cultural but a legal distinction. The point is that each ethnic group had to have its *own* law. If Europe had nations, Africa was said to have ethnicities, then called tribes. If every 'historical' nation in Europe had its own state, every tribe in Africa had to have its own native authority to enter history. If every nation-state in Europe promulgated its own civic law, every native authority in Africa had to enforce its own customary law. So went the logic of indirect rule.

The colonial state was from this point of view an ethnic federation, comprising so many Native Authorities, each defined ethnically. Each Native Authority was like a local state under central supervision. If decolonization meant getting rid of the colonial power from the central state, what should decolonization have meant in the local state? I wrote a book about this in 1996, called *Citizen and Subject* (Mamdani, 1996). Here, let me simply say that to answer the question one would need to take a closer look at what colonialism constructed as custom. I have three things in mind.

First, precolonial Africa did not have a single customary authority, but several. Each of these defined custom in its own domain. There were thus age groups, clans, women's groups, chiefs, religious groups and so on. It is worth noting that only one of these – chiefs – was sanctified as a native authority under indirect-rule colonialism and only its version of custom was declared 'genuine'. The rest were officially silenced. In constructing native custom as unchanging and singular, colonial power sought to sanctify the authoritarian version of custom as genuine.

Second, this single native authority was reorganized as despotic. If we contrast the mode of organization of civil and customary authority under colonial rule, the point will be clear. Civic authority was organized on the basis of functional specificity and the principle of a balance of power. Even if there were no elections, there was a clear distinction between the executive, the legislative, the judicial and the administrative moments of power. In contrast, the native authority was organized on the basis of a fusion of power.

I chaired a commission of inquiry on local government in Uganda the year after President Museveni came to power. We spent two years in different parts of the country. One thing stood out in all areas, no matter how different they were in other aspects: the relationship between the chief and the peasant. When the year began, the chief would enumerate the peasant's property and assess it for tax purposes. If the peasant was dissatisfied, he appealed to the chief. After the chief made a ruling, he would return to collect tax. If the peasant failed to pay the tax, the chief would arrest him, then decide where to put him to work during his prison term. At the end of the term, the chief would release him and require him to pay the unpaid portion of the original tax, as well as a fine on top of it for having failed to pay it in the first place. This same chief could also pass and enforce a bylaw, provided it did not contradict a national law. For example, the chief could decide that every peasant must donate a chicken for purposes of 'development'. So the cycle of life went on. The chief combined in his hands executive, legislative, judicial and administrative powers. When he faced the peasant, his fingers closed and the hand became a clenched fist.

When we returned to Kampala from our district tours, we began to meet officials at the Ministry of Local Government. The single most enduring impression I carried away with me was how different the Ministry of Local Government was from every other ministry that I knew of. Every line ministry – be it the ministry of education, finance, agriculture, industry or health – was functionally specific except for one, the Ministry of Local Government. Its concerns included primary – but not secondary – education; feeder – but not major – roads; primary – but not hospital – health; and so on. The Ministry of Local Government was like a state within the state. I realized that this was the ministry for peasants. It was the heart of the colonial state.

The *third* common thing about customary law was the great emphasis on corporal punishment. You could almost say that the very definition of a customary authority was an authority that had the customary right to use force to coerce subjects to follow custom. I wonder to what extent this may also apply to Sharia law in the colonial context. I think there is great need to historicize Sharia law, so as to understand the impact of colonialism on Sharia. Is it true, as some scholars suggest, that early Sharia – particularly when *ijtihad*, judicial interpretation, was a regular practice – functioned more like our understanding of common law?[1] Every legal principle was interpreted in light of changing circumstances. I think we need particularly to look at two aspects of Sharia law in the post-colonial context: the fusion between the executive and the judiciary, to the exclusion of judicial interpretation (*ijtihad*), and the growing emphasis on *hudud*, that is, corporal punishment.

Civic law

While ethnicities were demarcated horizontally and were said to represent a cultural diversity, races were differentiated vertically and were said to reflect a civilizational hierarchy. Some races were said to be more civilized than others, and therefore were said to have a claim to higher rights. While each ethnicity was said to have its own customary law, races were constituted within a single legal domain, that of civil law, except that civil law was full of discriminations; there were citizens of different categories, some real, others virtual.

My *second* observation is that the distinction between races and ethnicities was not the same as the distinction between colonizers and colonized. The hierarchy of races included both colonizers and colonized. Similarly, the colonized divided into those indigenous and those not; in other words, whereas all natives were colonized, not all non-natives were colonizers. The hierarchy of race included master races and subject races.[2] Who were the subject races of indirect-rule Africa? They were the Indians of east, central and southern Africa, the Arabs of Zanzibar, the Tutsi of Rwanda and Burundi, and the 'Coloureds' of southern Africa. The distinction between subject races and subject ethnicities is worth grasping. While both were colonized, the former were a fraction of the latter. Subject races were either non-indigenous immigrants, like the Indians of east, central and southern Africa, or they were constructed as non-indigenous by the colonial powers, such as, for example, the Tutsi of Rwanda and Burundi. In contrast, subject ethnicities were indigenous. Finally, subject races usually performed a middleman function, in either the state or the market, and their position was marked by petty privilege economically and preferential treatment legally.

The distinction between subject races and subject ethnicities recalls another distinction drawn in a different context by Malcolm X. This is the distinction between the 'Field Negro' and the 'House Negro', the former in the field and the latter in the mansion. This distinction too was marked by petty privilege and preferential treatment and, as a consequence, had its own ideological effects. As Malcolm X put it, when the master was sick, the House Negro would mimic the master – 'We sick' – and when the master was tired – 'We tired'.

Precisely because the legal category 'non-native' included both master races and subject races, it is important to distinguish 'non-native' as a legal identity from 'settler' as a political identity. To my knowledge, the law never spoke of settlers, only of non-natives. 'Settler' was rather a political libel hurled by natives at master races, not subject races. The notion of 'settler' distinguished conquerors from immigrants. It was an identity undergirded by a conquest state, a colonial state (see Mamdani, 1998). In the course of time, anti-colonial nationalism would splinter into two distinct, even contradictory tendencies. Radical nationalism would identify settlers with conquerors, whereas conservative nationalism would identify them with all immigrants. In this latter category would belong the 1959 Revolution in Rwanda and the 1963 Revolution in Zanzibar.

My main concern in this chapter is the following: how does this institutional inheritance, with its legally enforced distinctions between races and ethnicities, civil law and customary law, rights and customs, subject races and subject ethnicities, play out after colonialism?

Post-colonial Dilemmas

I will focus on three post-colonial dilemmas. The first dilemma arises from the growing tendency for indigeneity to become the litmus test for rights under the post-colonial state, as under the colonial state. The second dilemma arises from the fact we have built upon this foundation and turned indigeneity into a test for justice, and thus for entitlement under the post-colonial state. The third dilemma arises from the growing tendency to identify a colonially constructed regime of customary law with Africa's authentic tradition.

Indigeneity and rights

To understand why the link between indigeneity and rights continued to be reproduced after colonialism, we need to focus on the character of conservative – mainstream – nationalism. Mainstream nationalism shared with its radical counterpart a common effort to de-racialize civic rights. In contrast to militant nationalists who were determined to de-ethnicize the customary sphere, however, mainstream nationalists pledged to reproduce the customary as the authentic tradition of Africa. As a consequence, mainstream nationalists reproduced the dual legacy of colonialism. This time around, though, they hoped to privilege indigenous over non-indigenous citizens. In addition to civil rights for all citizens, the indigenous were given a bonus: customary rights.

In this context arose the question of defining who was indigenous and who was not, at both the central and local levels. Within the country as a whole, one had to decide which ethnic groups were indigenous and which ones were not, for only the former would have a right to a native authority of their own. Locally, each native authority would have to distinguish between those ethnically indigenous and those not, for only the former would belong to the native authority ethnically and thus have the right of custom.

Let us begin with the first type of indigenous person. How do you tell who is indigenous to the country and who is not? Given a history of migration, what is the dividing line between the indigenous and the non-indigenous? In 1997, a colleague and I undertook a mission for the Council for the Development of Social Research in Africa (CODESRIA) to Kivu Province in Congo. The particular focus of the mission was the citizenship dilemma of the Kinyarwanda-speaking population of Kivu. In North Kivu, there were two Kinyarwanda-speaking groups: Banyarutshuru and Banyamasisi. The former were considered indigenous, the latter were not. We wondered why. The answer was disarmingly simple: unlike the Banyarutshuru, whose presence predated Belgian colonization, the Banyamasisi had only moved to Congo in the colonial period, as labour migrants.

It is worth noting that whereas the Mobutist state wavered in its legal treatment of colonial migrants, in 1972 even going to the point of passing a decree that recognized as citizens all those who had been resident on Congolese soil since 1959, the democratic opposition to Mobutu showed little inclination to repudiate the colonial legacy on this question. Organized as the Congolese National Conference, a gathering of over 400 civil society organizations and nearly 100 political groups, the democratic opposition passed a law in 1991 defining a Congolese as anyone with an ancestor then living in the territory demarcated by Belgians as the colony of Congo. Let us ponder the meaning of this declaration. It means that the independent state of Congo accepts the establishment of the colonial state of Congo as its official date of birth, the date establishing the line of demarcation between those considered to be indigenous to the land and those considered to be immigrants. The Congo was not and is not an exception. If we look at the definition of citizenship in most African states, we will realize that the colonial state lives on, albeit with some reforms. My point is that in privileging the indigenous over the non-indigenous, we turned the colonial world upside down, but we did not change it. As a result, the native sat on the top of the political world designed by the settler. Indigeneity remained the test for rights.

The native–settler dialectic is also played out at the micro-level, the level of the native authority. Where neither customary law nor customary authority are de-ethnicized, the customary realm is uncritically reproduced as authentic tradition. The dilemma here is that while the population on the ground is multi-ethnic, the authority, the law and the definition of rights are mono- or uni-ethnic. The consequence is to divide the population ethnically, empowering those considered indigenous and disempowering others considered non-indigenous.

The irony is that this dialectic inevitably leads to an unravelling of the movement built up as nationalist in the colonial period, for the non-indigenous in the post-colonial period are less and less racial, more and more ethnic. The clashes about rights too are less and less racial, more and more ethnic. Put differently, ethnic clashes are more and more about rights, particularly the right to land and to a native authority that can empower those identified with it as ethnically indigenous. For evidence, look at Kivu in eastern Congo, the Rift Valley in Kenya, or contemporary Nigeria.

There was a time when a clash of this sort was a signal for an exodus: those branded non-indigenous would leave, their belongings on their head, and run in the direction of home. Now, the tendency is for them to fight it out. Faced with a native authority that divides the resident population into two, pitting the indigenous against the non-indigenous, the trend is for the non-indigenous to arm themselves in self-defence. Thus the proliferation of armed militia in the context of ethnically driven clashes about land and other rights.

At this point I suggest we pause and ask ourselves two questions. First, is not the shift from a homeward flight to a tendency to fight it out where one is resident proof enough that the definition of home has changed? That immigrants of yesterday have now become indigenous? That were it not for the form of the state and its definition of indigeneity, yesterday's immigrants would be today's citizens? Second, what is likely to be our future if these tendencies continue? For if they do, clashes will increase, not decrease. The dilemma is the following: the commodity economy moves people at the top and the bottom, traders and capitalists of all types at the top, land-poor peasants and jobless workers below. The more dynamic the economy, the greater the movement across native authorities; and the more the movement, the greater the number of non-indigenous residents inside each native authority. Here, then, is the structural dilemma: the commodity economy dynamizes, but the state penalizes those more dynamic by defining them as settlers. Even with the colonial power gone, we keep on defining every citizen as either a native or a settler!

Indigeneity and entitlements

The *second* post-colonial dilemma arises from the very struggle to decolonize. How do you address the past without reproducing it? Just as customary law made the distinction between indigenous and non-indigenous ethnicities a claim for group rights, civil law made a distinction between indigenous and non-indigenous races when it came to entitlements. From the time it faced militant nationalist opposition after World War II, the colonial state defined 'native' entitlements in response to the struggle for justice.

The history of entitlements has gone through two phases. In the first phase, entitlements were at the expense of *subject races*. Africa's worst internal violence in the post-colonial period has targeted those defined as subject races under colonialism. This was true both of the Tutsi of Rwanda in the 'social revolution' of 1959 and of the Arabs of Zanzibar in the Zanzibar Revolution of 1963. It was also true, though to a lesser extent, of the Asians of Uganda in 1972. The difference between these two types of cases lies in the following. Where the subject races made a bid for power, as in Zanzibar in 1963 and in Rwanda in 1959–63 and 1994, they were slaughtered. Where their demand was seen to be for the protection of privilege and not a quest for power, they met a response disenfranchising them, as in the case of the Ugandan Asians, which went as far as expulsion.

The response of the subject races has been diverse. During the constitutional discussions in Uganda in the early 1990s, the Ugandan Asians who had returned demanded that they be listed in the new constitution as one of Uganda's ethnic groups. Not surprisingly, this bid for indigeneity was seen by many as minimally an attempt to get legal protection against any future expropriation, and maximally to get access to land as an ethnic home. Not surprisingly, it was rejected. The returning Arabs of Zanzibar chose to secure the same objective a different way: they gave full support to liberalization and privatization, and thereby to narrowing the scope of citizenship-based action against them. The Boers of South Africa have taken both the Ugandan Asian and the Zanzibar Arab routes: the mainly Afrikaner poor have agitated for an ethnic homeland, complete with a customary home, and their own native authority that can enforce its own customary law, while the rich have pinned their hopes on liberalization and privatization as their salvation from majority demands for justice. Certainly the most tragic and troubling response comes from the Tutsi of Rwanda. Like the Israelis after the Holocaust, the Rwandan Tutsi seem to have reached a conclusion that is more of a cul-de-sac: there can be no survival without power; the only durable peace possible is an armed peace.

It is the second phase in the development of the culture of entitlement as a form of justice that shows the real dilemma of turning indigeneity into the basis for entitlement. In this phase, conservative African regimes – the bearers of mainstream nationalism – have succeeded in redividing yesterday's natives into post-colonial settlers and post-colonial natives. This dilemma is perhaps best illustrated by the Nigerian case. I am referring specifically to the ethnic character of the

Nigerian federation, as embodied in the constitutional provision, that key federal institutions – universities, civil service and, indeed, the army – must reflect the 'federal character' of Nigeria. This means that entrance to federal universities, to the civil service and to the army is quota driven. Where quotas are set for each state in the Nigerian federation, only those indigenous to the state may qualify for a quota. All Nigerians resident outside their ancestral home are considered non-indigenous in the state in which they reside. The effective elements of the Nigerian federation are neither territorial units called states nor ethnic groups but those ethnic groups that have their own states.

The ethnic character of the Nigerian federation has an outcome that reinforces two tendencies. First, given the way 'federal character' is defined, every ethnic group in Nigeria is compelled sooner or later to seek its own ethnic home, its own native authority, its own state in the Nigerian federation. Second, with each new state, the number of Nigerians defined as non-indigenous in all its states continues to grow. The cumulative outcome is to intensify the contradiction between economic and political processes. I return to my original hypothesis: the more the economy dynamizes, the more the polity disenfranchises. The irony and the tragedy are that our post-independence political arrangements disenfranchise those most energized by the commodity economy. Once the law makes cultural identity the basis for political identity, it inevitably turns ethnicity into a political identity.

The law thus penalizes those who try to fashion a future different from the past by mechanically translating cultural into political identities. We need to recognize that the past and the future overlap, as do culture and politics, but they are not the same thing. Cultural communities rooted in a common past do not necessarily have a common future. Some may have a diasporic future. Similarly, political communities may include immigrants and thus be characterized by cultural diversities, even if there is a dominant culture signifying a history shared by the majority. The point is that political communities are defined, in the final analysis, not by a common past but by a resolve to forge a common future under a single political roof, regardless of how different or similar their pasts may be.

Our challenge is to define political identities as distinct from cultural identities, without denying that there may be a significant overlap between the two. One way of doing so is to accent common residence over common descent – *indigeneity* – as the basis of rights. For initiatives that tried to make this shift, we would need to turn to the second, and militant, variant of nationalism. It is militant nationalism that tried to de-ethnicize the colonial political legacy and thereby repudiate the notion that indigeneity be the basis of rights. Militant nationalist initiatives were taken from both the seat of power and from oppositional standpoints. The key experiences, in my view, were those of Tanzania under the leadership of Julius Nyerere and the National Resistance Movement during its guerilla struggle in Uganda from 1981 to 1986.

Our final challenge is also to rethink our notion of custom, for the idea of 'custom' is closely tied to the idea of 'native.'

Rethinking the customary regime

Custom is not just the authoritarian version rescued and built upon by colonial power. It also includes emancipatory legacies officially silenced by the same power. Neither custom nor sources of custom are singular. Both are plural, multiple and diverse. If custom is to have any meaning, its reproduction has to be more through consent than coercion. Every living tradition grows; it has both a past and a future. Consensus can only be born of conflict. The idea of custom as some kind of geological fossil from the past, one that cannot be questioned or changed, is one point of view. This point of view has been key to identifying, buttressing and salvaging a domestic authoritarianism as an authentic tradition.

Colonially crafted customary authority had two big African homes in the colonial period. One was Nigeria; the other was South Africa. While the apartheid struggle tended to debunk customary authority as antidemocratic, the post-apartheid transition has kept custom intact, as 'customary' homes, 'customary' authorities and 'customary' rights. Having at first dismissed this legacy as 'anti-democratic', the African National Congress turned to embracing the regime of the customary as 'tradition'. As a result, post-apartheid South Africa has a dual legal structure – as did apartheid South Africa. While the new government has de-racialized civil law, civil society and civil rights, it still works with an ethnicized 'customary' law enforced by an ethnicized native authority. If the legal definition of non-natives was as citizens governed under civic law and of natives as tribespersons governed under customary law, would it be an exaggeration to say that the post-apartheid transition has given us a non-racial apartheid?

Political Identity: A Methodological Consideration

We are used to thinking of identities as either market-based or cultural. Left-wing intellectuals generally saw 'real' identities as market-based class identities, such as 'worker' and 'capitalist' or 'landlord' and 'tenant'. Those on the right had a habit of arguing that the 'real' identity was cultural. Both agreed that political identities were to be understood as expressions of pre-political identities – 'real' identities – in the political arena. The left had its verifying literature on class struggle and revolution, and the right had its version on tribalism and nationalism. Since the end of the Cold War, there has been a growing tendency on the left also to see political identities as expressions of cultural identities. The literature on class struggle is gradually giving way to that on social movements. Thus it is no longer the right-wing intelligentsia but also many on the left who now call for rights, even self-determination, for ethnicities.

I want to suggest the need to think of political identities as distinct from economic or cultural identities. If economic identities are a consequence of the history of development of markets, and cultural identities of the development of communities that share a common language and meaning, political identities need to be understood as specifically a consequence of the history of state formation. As such, political identities are inscribed in law. In the first instance, they are legally enforced.

Box 10.1 *Shared values and public institutions:*
Anchoring Somalia's reconstruction

Abdi Ismail Samatar

No one could have predicted Somalia's disintegration into 'clan' fiefdoms. The country was thought to be one of the most homogenous nation-states in Africa. Many observers stridently insist that clan structures are necessary for Somalia's rehabilitation. All international sponsored reconciliation conferences premised on the centrality of the clan failed. I argue that Somalia's shared cultural values were necessary, but *an insufficient basis* for national cohesion. Public institutions are key to sustaining shared values and forging an inclusive identity. Abusing public resources wrecked the sense of common belonging even in culturally united Somalia. Local initiatives like Amoud and Mogadishu Universities, community-owned institutions, could be forerunners of a new type of Somali institution that caters to common, rather than sectarian, interests. If initial steps are sustained, this local initiative could reverse sectarian trends and mark the birth of a new Somalia.

Attempts to rebuild the Somali State have floundered and conventional international strategies seem unlikely to produce meaningful results. Warlords' and faction leaders' machinations to create bantustan-like mini-states in the provinces have also failed to gain public respect and the international community's recognition. The alternative to these efforts has been civic-minded local initiatives to repair community infrastructure. These initiatives have made important contributions to reducing hardships in many communities. However, such efforts and others have not been able to do more than restore local services in particular localities.

Amoud and Mogadishu Universities are the only *known* exception to this locally oriented activity. These recently chartered, *community-owned* institutions are kindling new debate between localities about national concerns. The idea of establishing the two universities originated with a small group of Somali intellectuals living in Saudi Arabia, the Gulf Emirates, and in Somalia. Their intentions were to find an outlet for the many children in the regions who had no real prospect of productive employment other than joining the roaming militias, and to rekindle national reconstruction.

Mogadishu and Amoud universities were established in 1997 and 1998 respectively. Mogadishu University has over 700 students while Amoud has 300 students. Somali students from any region who pass each institution's entrance examination are admitted. However, the problem is that most students live in regions where the universities cannot conduct the entrance examination. Amoud's student population is predominately from the northwest region of northern Somalia while Mogadishu's students come from the ruined city vicinity. Security conditions in the city and region make it impossible for students from other regions of the south to study in Mogadishu. Mogadishu University has a Board of Trustees that oversees its affairs while Amoud has yet to establish such an organ.

Administrators of the two universities are also sensitive to the gender gap in their student population. Local activists have been urging authorities to develop urgently a strategy to narrow this gap. Both groups agree that a major factor in girls' low enrolment in high schools, and consequently the universities, is the heavy responsibilities girls bear in families. The girls' burden in the family has become more exacting since Somalia's disintegration. These conditions have decimated girls' enrolment in schools and negatively affected their classroom performance. The universities are working to increase girls' enrolments despite these obstacles.

The universities face many challenges that may in combination undermine their national mission and existence. There are four formidable risks. First, because of their shallow financial base, the projects may not be sustainable. Student fees cover nearly all operating costs, despite some support from the Diaspora and outside sources. Second, the influences of sectarian elements in Borama and in Mogadishu, and the universities' management, could become dominant and turn them into 'tribal' ghettos. Violence in Mogadishu and warlords' tyranny could make the project untenable. Third, divisive overseas groups, such as the so-called Amoud Foundation, may distort the inclusive reputation of Amoud. Fourth, it is conceivable that sectarian entrepreneurs in other regions may try to duplicate these efforts and therefore undermine their national appeal and civic scope.

Despite these dangers, Mogadishu and Amoud have already made their mark on the national map by pioneering reinvestment in public institutions that cater to the Somali community's common interest and enhance shared values. First, the two universities drove home the necessity of peace and stability for any development. Second, the organizers' appropriate use of public contributions to jumpstart the universities restored a measure of the sceptics' faith in the feasibility of collective projects. Third, the universities have given the population confidence that local resources can be effectively mobilized and honestly managed to address development needs. Further, the institutions underscored the benefits of investing in collective projects that strengthen common values and deepen peace. Fourth, the most potent lesson of the two universities is that well-managed community or public institutions are the best defence against sectarian fragmentation and national mayhem. Fifth, northern Somalis and many in Mogadishu have witnessed the birth of a new type of public institution that is answerable to the community.

Finally, the Somali calamity and the universities' establishment speak directly to the ways in which shared values are destroyed or formed. Instrumentalist uses of public institutions can easily demolish shared values built over centuries. This means that communities and states cannot take inclusive common traditions for granted. Somalia's story alerts us that national authority and the people should continuously reinvest in public institutions lest the nation's heritage is eroded and/or destroyed. Moreover, common heritage is insufficient to unite people purposively unless it is embodied in collective institutions that cater to the whole community.

Note: A different version of the text in this box was published in *Bildhaan: An International Journal of Somali Studies*, no 1 (2001).

If the law recognizes you as member of an ethnicity, and state institutions treat you as member of that particular ethnicity, then you become an ethnic being legally. By contrast, if the law recognizes you as a member of a racial group, then your legal identity is racial. You understand your relationship to the state, and your relationship to other legally defined groups through the mediation of the law and of the state, as a consequence of your legally inscribed identity. Similarly, you understand your inclusion or exclusion from rights or entitlements based on your legally defined and inscribed race or ethnicity. From this point of view, both race and ethnicity need to be understood as political – not cultural, or even biological – identities.

The tendency of the left has been to think of the law as individuating or dis-aggregating classes and thus creating false identities. But the law does not just indi-viduate, it also collates. It does not just treat each person as an abstract being – the owner of a commodity in the market, a potential party to a contract – it also cre-ates group identities. These identities are legally inscribed and legally enforced. They shape our relationship to the state and to one another through the state. In so doing, they also form the starting point of our struggles.

Democracy and Institutions: A Conclusion

Democracy is not just about who governs and how governors are chosen. More important, it is about how they govern, the institutions through which they gov-ern and the institutional identities by and through which they organize different categories of citizens. Colonialism was not just about the identity of governors, whether they were white or European; it concerned even more the institutions they created to enable a minority to rule over a majority. During indirect rule, these institutions unified the minority as rights-bearing citizens and fragmented the majority as so many custom-driven ethnicities. I have suggested that this is what the legal discourse on race and ethnicity was all about. Instead of racializing the colonized into a majority identity called 'natives', as 19th-century direct rule did, 20th-century indirect rule dismantled this racialized majority into so many ethnicized minorities. Thus it was said that there were no majorities, only minor-ities, in the African colonies.

This core colonial legacy is at the root of our dilemma; I defined it in the context of my discussion of the Nigerian federation. The dilemma is the form of the state: the economy dynamizes, and the state disenfranchises the most dynamic. In this context, what are we to do? How do we support those disenfran-chised? By demanding that each ethnicity also have its own state or native author-ity, as, for example, in the new Ethiopian constitution? If so, do we not risk multiplying the problem, since the number of minorities will grow as will the number of ethnically defined states or native authorities? To oppose that demand, however, would be seen to be joining forces with ethnic chauvinists. Is there a solution to this dilemma? The only solution, I have argued, is to rethink the insti-tutional legacy of colonialism, and thus to challenge the idea that we must define political identity, political rights and political justice first and foremost in relation to indigeneity. Let us reconsider the colonial legacy that each of us is either a native or a settler, and that it is with that compass in hand that we must fashion our political world.

In sum, I suggest we go beyond the conventional belief that the real crime of colonialism was to expropriate the indigenous, and consider that colonialism perpetrated an even greater crime: that of politicizing indigeneity, first as a settler libel against the native and then as a native self-assertion.

Notes

1. See, for example, the analysis of Shar'ia with reference to colonial rule in Yemen in Messick (1993).
2. I elaborate the dilemma of the Tutsi as a subject race in Mamdani (2001).

References

Davidson, B (1992) *The Black Man's Burden: Africa and the Curse of the Nation-State*, Times Books, New York

Huntington, S (1996) *The Clash of Civilizations and the Remaking of World Order*, Simon & Schuster, New York

Mamdani, M (1996) *Citizen and Subject: Contemporary Africa and the Legacy of Late Colonialism*, Princeton University Press, Princeton

Mamdani, M (1998) 'When Does a Settler Become a Native? Reflections on the Colonial Roots of Citizenship in Equatorial and South Africa', Inaugural Lecture, University of Cape Town, New Series No 208, 13 May

Mamdani, M (2001) *When Victims Become Killers: Colonialism, Nativism and Genocide in Rwanda*, Princeton University Press, Princeton

Mazrui, A (1994) 'Decaying Parts of Africa Need Benign Colonization', *International Herald Tribune*, 4 August, *Codesria* Bulletin, 2, *Codesria*, Dakar

Messick, B (1993) *The Calligraphic State: Textual Domination and History in a Muslim Society*, University of California Press, Berkeley and Los Angeles

Rodney, W (1971) *How Europe Underdeveloped Africa*, TPH, Dar-es-Salaam

Samatar, A I (2001) 'Shared values and public institutions: Anchoring Somalia's reconstruction', *Bildaan: An International Journal of Somali studies*, no1

Wallerstein, I (2000) 'The Uses of Racism', *London Review of Books*, vol 22, no 10, 18 May, pp11–14

Zartman, W (1995) *Collapsed States: The Disintegration and Restoration of Legitimate Authority*, Lynne Rienner, Boulder, CO

11

Regional Economic and Political Institutions

Edward Ramsamy

Introduction

The past two decades have witnessed significant changes in the political economy of international relations. The end of the Cold War, the increased globalization of trade and production, and new ideological currents have all generated new pressures and challenges for development theory and practice. One important concern among contemporary thinkers is the role of the nation-state. Indeed, many observers have grown pessimistic about the ability of nation-states to manage their traditional functions effectively in these times of great change. Ohmae (1995, p39), for example, argues that 'Power over economic activities will inevitably migrate from the central governments of nation states to the borderless network of countless individual market based decisions.' However, it is premature to relegate nation-states to 'the dustbins of history' (Glassman and Samatar, 1997, p165), as their role is becoming increasingly complicated in an era of globalization.

In this period of flux, regionalism and regional development are regaining prominence in international development discourse. For example, Swyngedouw (2000) argues that nation-states have, in some instances, responded to globalization with the 'up-scaling of governance', believing that this will enhance national competitive advantages. Klaus Schwab, President of the World Economic Forum, claimed that 'In the global economy, regional strength is paramount.' The expansion of the European Union, the formation of the North American Free Trade Agreement and the increasing prominence of the Association of South East Asian Nations are but a few examples of this trend.

In the African context, regional integration is increasingly being promoted by nations, development organizations and policy-makers as a way to address the multiple economic and political problems confronting the continent. Yet, in itself, regional integration is not a new phenomenon in Africa, where there is a long record of such initiatives. In 1963, heads of states of newly independent nations met in Addis Ababa to establish the Organization of African Unity (OAU), where the possibility and merit of regional integration were explored. The All African Peoples Conferences held in the late 1950s and early 1960s called for a common African market and economic community. 'Pan-African unity' and 'regional cooperation' were popular rally themes during the decades of anti-colonial struggle.

The fascination with regional integration in Africa is due, at least in part, to the geographic fragmentation of the continent. If, as Smith (1994, p492) notes, 'nation states are, by definition, geographic solutions to political problems', then national territorial boundaries represent the political compromises agreed upon by the European powers that scrambled for Africa's resources during the colonial era. Africa's colonial legacy imposed numerous challenges. For instance, ethnic groups are divided across different national territories; there are many small states with limited markets and resources; several states are landlocked. Furthermore, European-designed state structures, also inherited by the new governments after independence, do not take traditional territorial boundaries or modes of govern-ance into account. Given these issues, regional integration has always been an attractive idea that promises to reverse Africa's inherited geography.

However, in spite of these grim realities on the one hand and their rhetoric of radical restructuring on the other, post-independence leaders remained wedded to the colonial map; the OAU rejected, at its first meeting, the question of redraw-ing Africa's colonial borders, claiming that 'the sovereignty and territorial integrity of each state for its inalienable right to independent existence' (Kawango, 1998, p161). Thus, Africa's early experiments with regional cooperation in the post-independence period fell far short of expectations and soon became paper tigers (M'Buyinga, 1982).

A second wave of interest in regional integration arose in Africa in the 1980s and 1990s, concurring with trends elsewhere, as a possible response to the nega-tive effects of several worldwide phenomena loosely grouped together under the heading of 'globalization'. For example, Themba Masuku, a cabinet member in the Swaziland government, echoed the prevailing sentiment that 'The world is globalizing rapidly and regional cooperation is vital if we are to cope with increas-ing competition for trade and investment in the fast-improving world' (*Sunday Independent*, 1996).

SADC is frequently represented as one of the most viable and promising regional development institutions in Africa (Bischoff, 2004). This chapter aims to over-view critically the experience of the Southern African Development Community (SADC) in light of the issues discussed above. The first part of the chapter offers a brief summary of SADCC's formation and its achievements during its first decade of existence. The second part of the chapter outlines how SADC reconsti-tuted itself after the demise of apartheid rule in South Africa, paying particular attention to the asymmetrical relations between South Africa and other SADC member countries thereafter. This section also highlights some key issues pertain-ing to economic imbalances, bilateral regional development projects such as the Spatial Development Initiatives (SDIs) and Trans-frontier Conservation Areas (TFCAs), and migration between member countries. The chapter concludes with some observations on the problems and prospects for regional integration in southern Africa as well as Africa as a whole.

The Southern African Development Community (SADC): A Historical Overview

The Southern African Development Coordination Conference (SADCC), the forerunner to the present South African Development Community (SADC), was established in 1980 by southern African states in order to reduce their economic dependence on South Africa and achieve collective self-reliance. The organization initially consisted of 9 southern African states: Angola, Botswana, Lesotho, Malawi, Mozambique, Swaziland, Tanzania, Zambia and Zimbabwe (SADC now consists of 14 countries: the Democratic Republic of Congo, Mauritius, Namibia, the Seychelles and South Africa). The Lusaka Declaration of 1980 established four principal goals for the organization:

- the reduction of economic dependence, particularly but not only on the Republic of South Africa;
- the forging of links to create a genuine and equitable regional integration;
- the mobilization of resources to promote the implementation of national, interstate and regional policies;
- concerted action to secure international cooperation within the strategy for economic liberation.

The structure of SADCC was intended to promote a pragmatic, step-by-step approach to regional cooperation. No central authority was established to make plans for the entire region; SADCC operated for three years without a central governing body (the current SADC Secretariat is located in Gaborone, Botswana). Instead, decisions were made by the national state executives of the region, usually at the annual meeting of the nine heads of state. Furthermore, projects were neither carried out nor were funds disbursed through SADCC. Instead, various sectoral commissions developed project proposals which were presented directly to foreign donors and the projects themselves were primarily the responsibilities of the country in which they were to be implemented. Funding for joint projects was shared between the countries concerned (McDonald, 1990).

Such a pragmatic philosophy was adopted as a matter of necessity because SADCC member countries were politically and economically diverse and had conflicting interests (Blumenfeld, 1991, p38). Membership ranged from Botswana, whose economic and political system is based on free-market principles and liberal trade, to that of Angola and Mozambique, which initially espoused Marxist-Leninist ideologies and central planning methods based on Eastern European and Soviet models.

SADCC had some notable achievements. For example, its early concentration on the transportation sector met with some success. By early 1991, Mozambique's Beira corridor port was handling about 2 million tons of cargo annually. Sixty per cent of the transit traffic from the six landlocked states was moving through SADCC ports in 1991, as compared to 20 per cent in 1980. By the late 1980s, SADCC member states were able to improve telecommunications and were connected directly by satellite technology, whereas previously all international telecommunications had to be routed through apartheid South Africa. Furthermore, air travel between southern African countries required connections through Johannesburg until 1990, when SADCC was able to establish direct links between its capitals (Stoneman and Thompson, 1991).

SADCC member states also had some success in obtaining aid from international development institutions like the World Bank, as well as various government aid agencies. In 1988, the World Bank vice-president for Africa, Edward Jaycox, described SADCC as a 'functioning example of how regional cooperation in Africa might work', while former UK aid minister, Chris Patten, commented that to 'support SADCC is to support success' (quoted in Stoneman and Thompson, 1991, p6). The percentage of foreign funding varied between 66 and 100 per cent for SADCC's different initiatives. SADCC's Annual Progress Report (1989–90) indicated that external funding of over US$3000 million had been secured for a range of projects.

SADCC has been widely regarded as 'one of Africa's few successful attempts at regional cooperation' (Morna, 1990, p49). SADCC concentrated on specific projects, thereby steering it away from some of the problems encountered by other attempts at regional integration in Africa and elsewhere, such as the disproportionate burden placed on smaller and poorer states whose domestically produced goods are unable to compete with those of neighbouring, more developed, states. On one hand, in spite of broader structural limitations, SADCC countries were partly successful in attaining some of the goals of the Lusaka Declaration. On the other, while SADCC's success in achieving pragmatic cooperation among member states and securing foreign funding for projects is laudable at one level, it is possible that dependency may have been displaced rather than eliminated. Furthermore, the funding received was linked to specific foreign policy objectives of OECD countries to support SADCC as a way of voicing their protest against South Africa. During the 1990s, however, the end of apartheid and the democratization of South Africa brought about a number of changes that eventually led to the reconstitution of SADCC and its mission. The next section explores this issue.

Regional Transformations in the 1990s: Implications for SADC

A number of significant political changes in the southern African region after 1990 led to the transformation of SADCC. Of particular significance was Namibia's independence and the unbanning of the African National Congress (ANC) and other liberation movements in South Africa. The democratization of South Africa and the subsequent election of a black majority government led some to question the very raison d'être of SADCC. However, SADCC member states and others felt that the economic problems confronting the region, as well as the effects of global forces, still necessitated a regional structure albeit one that included the 'new' South Africa. In response to these dynamics, SADCC reconstituted itself as the Southern African Development Community (SADC) at the Summit meeting of August 1992, with the goal of 'reducing dependence on South Africa' omitted from the new agenda. The Summit also advanced broad proposals to move away from project-oriented cooperation toward closer political cooperation in order to facilitate equitable trade integration, institutionalize policy measures that would reduce tariff barriers for intra-SADCC trade, promote a less restricted movement of capital and people, create a regional infrastructure authority and possibly even establish a development bank (Maasdorp, 1992; SADC, 1992). South Africa officially joined SADC in November 1994.

However, despite SADC's broad ambition, the reality of effective regional integration in southern Africa is complicated by the gross economic imbalance between South Africa and other member countries. South Africa's economic output, about US$130,000 million, exceeds the others by far; in other words, the combined GDP of the other 13 members of SADC is only US$51,200 million, or 39.6 per cent of South Africa's GDP (Dieter et al, 2001, p55). Zimbabwe, the second largest economy in SADC, represents only 6.6 per cent of South Africa's GDP, but its economy is in serious decline because of the political turmoil within the country.

In South Africa, the ANC was aware of the serious disparities between South Africa and other SADC member countries before coming into power. In an article published in *Foreign Affairs*, Nelson Mandela observed that:

> *The regional economy that emerged under colonialism entrenched the domination of one country (South Africa) and incorporated other countries in subsidiary and dependent roles as labor reserves, markets for South African commodities, supplies of certain services (such as transport) or providers of cheap and convenient resources (like water, electricity and some raw materials). South Africa's visible exports to the rest of the region exceed imports by more than five to one. This is a reflection of not just a stronger productive base of the South African economy, but of barriers of various kinds that have kept goods produced in regional states out of the South African market... We are sensitive to the fact that any programme that promotes greater regional cooperation and integration in Southern Africa must be sensitive to the acute imbalances in existing economic relations... It is essential therefore that a programme to restructure regional economic relations after apartheid be carefully calibrated to avoid exacerbating inequalities.* (Mandela, 1993, p90)

During the transition to democratic rule in South Africa, the ANC made a number of rhetorical commitments to address these imbalances between South Africa and its neighbours. For instance, the ANC stated in a policy discussion paper that

> *A future democratic government should actively seek to promote greater regional cooperation along new lines which would not be exploitative and which would correct the imbalances in current relationships. The new state must be prepared to enter negotiations with its neighbors to promote a dynamic and mutually*

beneficial form of cooperation and development. While all of us stand to benefit from such an arrangement, it should be recognized that creating a new non-exploitative form of regional cooperation will require prioritizing the interests of the most impoverished of our neighbors, according to principles of affirmative action. (ANC, 1991, pp15–16)

The ANC emphasized three principles in order to achieve a more balanced regional order in southern Africa (ANC, 1991). First, it stressed that there should be a collective approach to regional development. Second, it called for a de-militarization campaign and a 'people-centered development paradigm'. Third, it called for a democratic South Africa to abandon all hegemonic ambitions in the region.

Yet some SADC member states remained unconvinced and were concerned about the added possibility of South Africa's potential domination of the organization itself. For example, Makoni wrote that

There is indeed a role for a free and democratic South Africa in SADC as an equal partner, not an overlord and domineer; to contribute positively to our joint endeavours toward a balanced and equitable regional integration. A free and democratic South Africa, accepting and respecting the norms and mores of international and regional partnership and interdependence, has a guaranteed place in the SADC family. (Makoni, 1990, p23)

A Zimbabwean economist insisted that the entry of South Africa would diminish the roles played by other states in SADCC:

When South Africa comes in, not only will the size of the pond increase dramatically, but it will be as though a whale – maybe even a shark – has been put into it. Although this is not a popular thing to say right now, it is not clear that the economic impact of a free South Africa will be less harmful than the economic impact of overt destabilization. (cited in Morna, 1990)

The August 1992 SADC Summit meeting stressed that regional cooperation in South Africa should be based on the principles of 'equity' and 'mutual benefit' (SADC, 1992, p5). This could be interpreted as a realization by SADC members that the economic legacies of apartheid for the region are likely to persist into the foreseeable future and that the regional policies of an ANC-led government may not deviate substantially from those of past governments, except perhaps for overt destabilization.

South Africa: An unequal partner

In spite of the ANC leadership's rhetoric of pursuing an equitable regional development plan, South Africa's regional dominance has continued into the post-apartheid period. South Africa's trading relationship with other SADC member countries continues to show gross imbalances, as if 'the mercantilist trade policy of South Africa has survived the end of apartheid' (Dieter et al, 2001, p56). South Africa's post-apartheid macro-economic policies have created difficulties for peripheral states like Namibia and Botswana to attract direct foreign investment, especially in the manufacturing sector (Simon, 1991, 1998). For example, during the 1990s, Hyundai and Volvo located motor assembly plants in Gaborone. In contrast to the spirit of Nelson Mandela's and the ANC's own statements on regional cooperation, the South African government, in concert with the South African trade union movement, opposed this development and went to great lengths to undermine these enterprises (Simon, 2003). South African authorities saw these plants as a threat to their status as the regional, if not continental, hub of the motor industry. Good and Hughes observe that:

> *South Africa's gains from the termination of car assembly in Gaborone were about as complete as Botswana's losses. The demise of car assembly in Gaborone was a profoundly serious blow to the Botswana economy. Quality foreign investment in manufacturing industry has come and gone from Botswana lock, stock and barrel. The government seriously underestimated South Africa's opposition to foreign investment and industrial development in its periphery, and how relentlessly the ANC government would pursue this.* (Good and Hughes, 2002, p58)

Furthermore, following the demise of apartheid, South African companies have made significant inroads into the region and beyond. South African mining corporations have expanded their networks into Zambia, the Democratic Republic of Congo and Tanzania. The South African supermarket chain Shoprite/Checkers has opened stores in neighbouring countries and regional markets are full of South African products. Between 1994 and 2002, South Africa's direct investment in SADC was 32 per cent (in US$ terms) of the total direct investment in the region. These trends have raised the spectre of 'South Africa becoming the continent's newest colonizer' (*Electronic Mail and Guardian*, 2004).

Spatial Development Initiatives (SDIs) and Trans-Frontier Conservation Areas (TFCAs)

While South Africa actively participates in SADC's forums, conferences and summits, it has undertaken a number of bilateral regional initiatives outside the SADC's organizational structures. Two of the most prominent of these are the cross-border Spatial Development Initiatives (SDIs) and Trans-Frontier Conservation Areas (TFCAs). The basic aim of the SDI strategy is twofold: first, to invigorate economically depressed areas and, second, to address the legacy of regional inequality in the southern African region from the apartheid era. The South African government's ministry for trade and industry undertook the research, planning and mobilization of resources for this initiative.

While the SDI concept evolved out of internal debates within South Africa to deal with the regional legacies of apartheid, South Africa's prominent position within SADC and the regional dimensions inherent in the SDI idea itself contributed to wider support for the concept among SADC member countries. These initiatives include transportation corridors that link industrial centres to ports across national borders, cross-national parks and conservation areas that are transnationally managed.

The Maputo Development Corridor (MDC) was launched in 1996 by the presidents of Mozambique and South Africa as the first SDI in the southern African region. The project connected the province of Gauteng (South Africa's industrial centre) with the Indian ocean port of Maputo. The MDC was based on four overarching objectives (Söderbaum and Taylor, 2003, p6):

- to rehabilitate the primary infrastructure network along the corridor, notably road, rail, port and dredging, and border posts, with the participation of the private sector in order to have the minimum impact on government expenditure;
- to maximize investment in both the inherent potential of the corridor area and the added opportunities which infrastructure rehabilitation will create, including the provision of access to global capital and facilitation of regional economic integration;
- to maximize social development, employment opportunities and increase the participation of historically disadvantaged communities; and
- to ensure sustainability by developing policy, strategies and frameworks that ensure a holistic, participatory and environmentally sustainable approach to development.

While MDC initiative is itself a product of the 1990s, economic and socio-political relations in the South Africa–Mozambique region existed for centuries (McGregor, 1994). In the modern period, white South African capital used black Mozambicans as a source of reserve labour for the mining industries, interlocking southern Mozambique and the mining industrial heartland of South Africa. Thus, the MDC and other regional development initiatives can be seen as a revitalization of past relationships (Sidaway, 1993).

The MDC initiative consists of two components: infrastructure and economic development. Infrastructure involved the upgrading/construction of a toll road linking Johannesburg to Maputo and the improvement of rail and port operations. A bi-national entity, the Maputo Corridor Company, was formed to coordinate and promote the project. Infrastructure upgrading was a central component of the MDC initiative. The project consisted of five core elements: the completion of the N4 toll highway parallel to the existing national road between Witbank and Maputo; the upgrading of the railway line; port-side facilities; telecommunications links; and the dredging of the harbour. The economic development component of the project consisted of the Mozal aluminum smelter and an iron and steel plant.

The MDC regional development plan does have some immediate, tangible benefits. By 2001 some 6200 jobs were generated of which 1000 were in Mozambique. Of the 9000 workers who were employed in the construction of the Mozal aluminium smelting plant, 70 per cent were Mozambican and some 8000 more jobs are expected when the plant is completed (Hentz, 2003). Increased tax revenue from the project is expected to benefit both the South African and Mozambican governments. However, the potential gains for underprivileged South Africans are limited (Baptista-Lundin and Taylor, 2003). While the project has contributed to job growth, many are temporary construction jobs. Additionally, historically disadvantaged black communities, especially in Mpumalanga, have not yet benefited from the programme. The MDC also has a strong urban bias and whites own the majority of the economic assets (de Beer and Arkwright, 2003). It threatens to polarize regions within Mozambique as 70 per cent of the industrial activity is confined to Biera and Maputo (Weimer, 1996).

One of the most controversial issues with regard to the MDC is the toll road and the privatization of transportation routes that previously had public access. The location of the toll road has created tensions between local communities and the project developers. Rural women vendors were particularly concerned when they were initially prevented from selling their produce along the roadside, something they had done for decades. Those women also walked along the road between Nelspruit and Maputo carrying bowls of fruit and other produce on their heads. After a few protests, a plan was devised to build two markets with 30 stalls, each equipped with electricity, water and sanitation facilities (Matlou, 2001). It remains to be seen how beneficial this arrangement will be for local traders, especially women. People were also concerned about the fact that the location of the toll road separated communities from schools, jobs and key shopping centres. The fact that the interests and needs of local communities were not part of the initial planning process betrays the MDC's top-down, elite-driven approach. Consultation with local communities was taken into consideration only after complaints were heard. Neither does the MDC address South Africa's hegemonic position in the region. Driver and De Barros (2000) point out that more than 90 per cent of revenue from tolls came from the South African side of the border. Furthermore, 90 per cent of the 29,000 tons of goods passing through the port was channelled to South Africa.

Paralleling the SDI concept, the Trans-frontier Conservation Areas (TFCAs), also referred to as SADC 'peace parks', represent another recent attempt at cross-border cooperation in southern Africa. TFCAs are premised on the conservation principle that fenced political boundaries do not consider ecological zones or the migration patterns of wildlife. In the late 1980s, the World Conservation Union promoted the idea that conservation areas that cross over international boundaries ought to be linked together. Anton Rupert, a South African industrialist and conservationist, emerged as a strong advocate for TFCAs in southern Africa.[1] Rupert met Mozambican President Joaquim Chissano in 1990 to discuss the possibility of establishing a permanent link between protected areas in southern Mozambique and adjacent areas in South Africa, Swaziland and Zimbabwe. As a consequence of this meeting, the World Wildlife Fund (South Africa) conducted a feasibility study which was submitted to the government of Mozambique in 1991. The Mozambican government then approached the World Bank and received full support (World Bank, 1996). This was followed by a TFCA initiative meeting on 8 August 1996 under the joint chairmanship of Mozambique's Minister of Transport and Communications, Paulo Muxango, and South Africa's Minister of Transportation, Mac Maharaj. At this meeting, the Mozambican and South African ministers, along with representatives from Swaziland and Zimbabwe, agreed to cooperate in establishing TFCAs across their respective territories.

On recommendation of the executive committee of the World Wildlife Fund of South Africa, a separate body known as the Peace Parks Foundation (PPF) was set up to coordinate the establishment of TFCAs in the region. The PPF was chaired by Rupert with seven southern African heads of state serving as honorary patrons. The concept was enthusiastically endorsed by then President Mandela and now enjoys the support of current President Mbeki. The PPF, headquartered in Cape Town, maintains that 'its initiative epitomize[s] the African Renaissance by ensuring peace, prosperity and stability for generations to come.' While TFCAs did not originate within SADC, the organization has endorsed the concept because the PPF's objectives coincide with SADC's mission of promoting conservation across the southern Africa region. At present, TFCAs are being implemented with much energy across the region. The Kgalagadi TFCA, linking South Africa's and Bostwana's existing national parks in the Kalahari desert, opened in May 2000 and placed 37,991 km^2 of land under a bi-national management team. A number of other Peace Park initiatives are in progress across the southern Africa region.[2]

The PPF programme is based on conservation ideas that seek to preserve the integrity of ecosystems, promote ecotourism, generate local economic development, and market southern Africa as a major tourist destination (Simon, 2003). One of the important benefits of the TFCA initiative for South Africa is the relocation of surplus animals from the Kruger National Park to Mozamibque, where herds were decimated during the civil war. Furthermore, revenue from the projects is expected to assist the cash-strapped Mozambican wildlife and conservation agencies (Simon, 2003; Wolmer, 2003).

The Peace Parks and SDI initiatives are seen by some as effective tools for sustainable and viable regional integration (Warburton-Lee, 1999). Griggs states that

> *Like the SDIs, the experience of setting up peace parks offers value for developing alternative geographic spaces... Both the Peace Parks and the SDIs offer opportunities for constructing democratic spaces – there is cooperation on customs and immigration, tourism and other forms of cross boundary integration through inclusive planning. The TFCs and SDIs offer examples of cross boundary development that are firmly in place in the landscape, offering models and foundations for reconstructing the African space economy that could be taken continent-wide.* (Griggs, 2003, p93)

SDIs and TFCAs are promoted by the participating countries as progressive, post-apartheid plans that promote the new spirit of cooperation in the southern African region. According to Ramutsindela (quoted in Simon, 2003, p85):

> *The schemes are presented as a decolonising strategy – breaking down the bondage imposed by colonial boundaries in order to free animals and people. It is claimed that the schemes contribute to the African Renaissance as they foster unity across colonial borders. This claim resonates with the on-going continental schemes toward the African Union.*

However, despite government officials' positive portrayals of SDIs and TFCAs, Simon (2003, p85) notes the glaring omission of environmental or social justice concerns and 'other concepts from a more radical or progressive lexicon' in these regional development programmes, which tend to be propelled by a powerful elite consensus of political and corporate interests. Farmers and local communities impacted by TFCAs in SADC member countries are concerned about exclusion from and dispossession of indigenous land (de Villiers, 1999). Furthermore, there is minimal community-based participatory engagement. Indeed, bilateral regional initiatives that exclude other SADC member states may ultimately fragment the organization and undermine long-term regional unity.

South Africa's commitment to the SDIs/TFCAs on one hand, and its under-mining of the very successful motor assembly ventures in Bostwana, on the other, clearly illustrate that its regional policies are driven by national interest rather than a genuine commitment to regional development and integration. South Africa supported the MDC initiative because Mozambique offers a favourable location, cheap labour, land and natural gas resources. Furthermore, Mozambique is one of the largest sources of legal and illegal immigration to South Africa. Policy-makers in South Africa hoped that the MDC programme would generate enough employ-ment within Mozambique itself to reduce the influx of migrants into South Africa. Botswana, on the other hand, is a relatively minor source of migration into South Africa, but the expansion of its industrial sector poses a direct threat to employ-ment and revenues in South Africa.

Asymmetry, trade and regional population movements

The asymmetrical relationship between South Africa and surrounding countries is one of the major problems confronting the region at present. For example, while South African exports to SADC countries have increased dramatically since the ANC came into power in 1994, there has not been a corresponding increase in the level of South African imports from SADC member countries; in fact, Gibb (2004) reports that SADC imports into South Africa have actually declined in recent years. In an attempt to confront this problem, SADC members signed a 'Protocol on Trade' in August 1996, committing member countries to establish a free trade area and to gradually eliminate all barriers to inter-regional trade. The objectives of the SADC Trade Protocol were set out as follows (SADC, 1996b):

- to liberalize intra-regional trade further in goods and services on the basis of fair, mutually equitable and beneficial trade arrangements, complemented by protocols in other areas;
- to ensure efficient production within the SADC reflecting the current and dynamic comparative advantages of its members;
- to contribute towards the improvement of the climate for domestic, cross-border and foreign investment;
- to enhance economic development, diversification and industrialization of the region;
- to establish a free-trade area in the SADC region.

Part of the problem is that while SADC continues to call for more equal regional development, the proposed free-trade area does not pay adequate attention to inequalities in the region. As Gibb (1998, p304) observes, 'Despite the calls for balanced growth, the creation of a regional market based upon trade liberalization and free market principles does not confront the problem of size disparities and the threat of de-industrialization in, for example, Zimbabwe and Zambia.'

One consequence of the economic disparities between South Africa and neighbouring countries is the exacerbation of immigration, both legal and illegal, into South Africa. This is part of a global trend in which the world's more developed areas (the wealthier states of western Europe, the United States and, to a lesser extent, the core countries of the Pacific Rim) are experiencing an increased influx of illegal migrants from declining regions and peripheralized countries (Sassen, 1996). Migrant labour from southern African states into South Africa has always been a thorny issue in South Africa's already troubled relationship with neighbouring countries, during the apartheid years and afterward. Some 700,000 citizens of independent states are legally registered as migrant workers in South Africa. Migrant workers from Lesotho, Mozambique, Swaziland and Malawi take foreign exchange back to their countries, which is a major source of income for some SADC member states. In addition to formal migrant labour, the South African Department of Labor estimates that there are some 5 million illegal migrants in South Africa. Others have estimated the figure to be as high as 8 million.[3]

SADC has had a number of discussions throughout the 1990s on how to deal with migration issues and facilitate cross-border population movement in the region. In the mid-1990s, the SADC Secretariat drafted a Protocol on the Free Movement of Persons among member states. The Protocol called for a radical departure from current policies and advocated unrestricted movement of capital, goods and people across the region. The main objective of the protocol was to 'confer, promote, and protect':

- the right of people to enter freely and without a visa the territory of another member state;
- the right to reside in the territory of a member state;
- the right to establish oneself and work in the territory of another member state.

The protocol proposed abolishing all controls of movements across member countries and recommended phased implementation:

- Phase 1 (within 12 months): visa-free entry from one state to another would be effective for visits of up to six months provided that the individual had valid travel documents and entered through an official border post.
- Phase 2 (within three years): any citizen would have the right to reside in another state in order to take up employment and to enter freely for the purpose of seeking employment.
- Phase 3 (within five years): states would abolish all restrictions on the freedom of establishment (permanent residence) of citizens of other member states in its territory.

South Africa reacted very negatively to the Free Movement Protocol, arguing that it compromised South Africa's own immigration policy:

For South Africa to compromise its immigration policy and control and allow free movement, will place the citizens in a [sic] more of an already precarious situation with disastrous consequences for the Reconstruction and Development Program and commitment to a better life. (Department of Home Affairs, 1996)

The South African government responded with a two-pronged strategy to thwart the implementation of the Free Movement Protocol. First, they voiced a number of concerns over how the protocol would adversely affect South Africa and began to court Botswana and Namibia as allies. Second, they commissioned the authors of the original protocol from the SADC Secretariat to rewrite the proposal in a manner that was acceptable to South Africa. The new proposal, entitled, 'The South African Draft Proposal on the Facilitation of Movement', was presented to the SADC Secretariat in 1997 for consideration. According to Oucho and Crush (2001, p149), the South African proposal 'aimed to assert the sovereignty of national interest over regional considerations, and place the emphasis back on policing and the control of national borders'. In contrast to the Free Movement Protocol, which had as its main objective the aim 'to confer, promote and protect the right to enter another state freely', the South African proposal aimed to:

- facilitate cross-border movement of citizens between states by gradually removing obstacles impeding such movement;
- expand bilateral agreements between states;
- cooperate in preventing the illegal movements of citizens of member states and the illegal movement of nationals of third states within and into the region.

The South African recommendations advanced no substantive proposals except for reciprocal visa-free admission through bilateral agreements. Proposals to facilitate the free movements of people across the region were abandoned. Even this watered-down version of the Migration Protocol was eventually rejected when South Africa, Namibia and Botswana expressed concern that the political conflict in Angola and the Democratic Republic of the Congo would lead to a major refugee crisis if border restrictions were relaxed. In light of these objections, the implementation of the Free Movement of People Protocol among SADC nations was abandoned. However, the massive movement of people from SADC member states into South Africa may be interpreted as a bottom-up vote for regional unity. In Basil Davidson's (1994, p280) words, 'It is perhaps the Pan-Africanism of ordinary people, a kind of "people's Pan-Africanism."'

Conclusion

This chapter discussed how SADC(C) was formed by southern African states to reduce dependence on apartheid South Africa. During its early years, the organization had some success in the areas of transportation and communication. After reconstituting itself from a loose regional coordinating committee into a regional development organization in 1992, SADC member states signed protocols on trade, shared water resources, transport, mining, a SADC tribunal, communications, education and vocational training. Griggs (2003, p86) characterizes SADC as one of the most powerful and economically advanced regional economic communities in Africa because it has:

- the highest level of internal trade among the regional economic communities;
- leadership capacity (eg the African Renaissance discourse originated here);
- advanced infrastructure including a common electricity grid for southern Africa that constitutes a free trade energy zone;
- strategically situated ports midway between Asia and the Americas;
- legendary mineral wealth including 99 per cent of the world's chrome reserves, 85 per cent of its platinum, 70 per cent of its tantalite, 68 per cent of its cobalt and 50 per cent of the world's vanadium, along with diamonds and gold;
- the world's richest fisheries; a large market, comprising a free trade area (in terms of agreement since September 2000) of 200 million people that with stability can attract larger capital flows and build a cooperative basis for industrial development and the construction of a stable middle class.

A major restructuring of the organization was announced at its March 2001 summit meeting in Windhoek. The 19 sectors formerly run by individual member states were merged into four clusters, comprising the following areas: trade, industry, finance and investment; infrastructure and services; food, agriculture and national resources; and social and human development.

It was hoped that this cluster approach would enhance regional integration and strengthen the weak Secretariat in Gaborone. In March 2004, the newly empowered Executive Secretariat announced ambitious plans for the following: the creation of a SADC regional development fund and self-financing mechanism by 2005; the elimination of exchange controls on intra-SADC transactions by 2006; the creation of a free-trade area by 2008; the establishment of a SADC customs union and implementation of a common external tariff by 2010; a common market pact by 2012; and the establishment of a SADC central bank and preparation for a single SADC currency by 2016.

This chapter highlights certain problems that SADC faces in spite of the organization's achievements and future potential. Particularly significant in this respect is South Africa's economic dominance in the region, and the resulting asymmetrical patterns of development. South Africa has proposed the SDI as one strategy to overcome the spatial imbalances in the region. However, there remains the question of whether bilateral agreements between South Africa and other SADC member states impede rather than promote effective regional integration.

A second, greater challenge for effective regional integration lies in defining the role and function of the state itself in southern Africa and Africa as a whole. At present, SADC functions through inter-governmental cooperation and coordination; the sovereignty of individual member states is not questioned. In addition to retaining inherited state structures, boundaries and modes of governance, SADC's approach to regional integration regards the state itself as a fixed entity, an all-powerful actor in the regional development process. This long-standing assumption continues to pose a significant obstacle to effective regional integration.

The third major challenge is the 'democratic deficit' in SADC at present (Shaw, 2002, p183). For instance, there are no elections, direct or indirect, in member states for representation in SADC. This raises some doubt about the democratic accountability of the organization as a whole (Sidaway and Gibb, 1998). States and other official bodies ought to be seen as only one set of actors among many others in the region; other entities, such as non-governmental organizations, civic groups and community development associations, hitherto excluded from meaningful participation, ought to be included in regional planning initiatives. A major roadblock in this regard is the reluctance of government leaders to transfer state sovereignty to transparent democratic structures at the regional level.

Finally, many of the current regional initiatives in Africa, including SADC and the continent-wide New Partnership for Africa's Development (NEPAD), are deeply influenced by the neo-liberal economic paradigm (Simon, 2003), a commitment to which is further reinforced by supranational institutions like the World Bank, International Monetary Fund, as well as Western bilateral development agencies. These organizations have enthusiastically promoted neo-liberal regional initiatives in Africa without paying adequate attention to global patterns of uneven economic development. The neo-liberal approach, according to Taylor and Nel (2002, p164), allows these institutions to 'avoid blaming particular policies or global trade structures for Africa's marginalization but rather, if pushed, simply pass[es] the blame on to the mystical notion that is known as globalization'.

Thus, if regionalism in southern Africa and Africa as a whole is to succeed, narrow state-centric paradigms as well as the neo-liberal economic models that generate inequality ought to be reconsidered. Social justice, democratic participation in planning and implementation, transparency and accountability must become integral to the development agenda.

Notes

1. See www.ecovisiononline.com
2. See www.peaceparks.org
3. See *Migration News*, www.migration.ucdavis.edu

References

ANC (1991) *Discussion Document: Economic Policy*, Department of Economic Policy, Johannesburg

Baptista-Lundin, I and Taylor, I (2003) 'A View of Maputo', in F Söderbaum and I Taylor (eds) *Regionalism and Uneven Development in Southern Africa: The Case of the Maputo Development Corridor*, Ashgate, Burlington, pp97–105

Bischoff, P (2004) 'Regionalism and Regional Cooperation in Africa: New Century Challenges and Prospects', in M Mbaku and S Saxena (eds) *Africa at the Crossroads: Between Regionalism and Globalization*, Praeger, Westport

Blumenfeld, J (1991) *Economic Independence in Southern Africa: From Conflict to Cooperation*, St Martin's Press, New York

Davidson, B (1994) *The Search for Africa: History, Culture, Politics*, Random House, New York

de Beer, G and Arkwright, D (2003) 'The Maputo Development Corridor: Progress Achieved and Lessons Learned', in F Söderbaum and I Taylor (eds) *Regionalism and Uneven Development in Southern Africa: The Case of the Maputo Development Corridor*, Ashgate, Burlington, T, pp 19–31

de Villiers, B (1999) *Peace Parks – the Way Ahead: International Experience and Indicators for South Africa*, Human Sciences Research Council, Pretoria

Department of Home Affairs (1996) *SADC Protocol and the Free Movement of People*, Department of Home Affairs, Pretoria

Dieter, H, Lamb, G and Melber, H (2001) 'Prospects for Regional Cooperation in Southern Africa', in *Regionalism and Regional Integration in Africa: A Debate of Current Aspects and Issues*, Nordiska Afrikainstitutet, Uppsala, pp54–74

Driver, A and De Barros, J (2000) 'The Impact of the Maputo Development Corridor on Freight Flows', DPRU Working Paper 00/38, Development Policy Unit, University of Cape Town, Cape Town

Electronic Mail and Gvardian (2004) 'South Africa: The New Colonial Power', www.mg.co.za, 8 March

Gibb, R (1998) 'South Africa in Transition: Prospects and Problems facing Regional Integration', *Journal of Modern African Studies*, vol 36, no 2, pp287–306

Gibb, R (2004) 'International and Regional Trade in Eastern and Southern Africa', in D Potts and T Bowyer-Bower (eds) *Eastern and Southern Africa: Development Challenges in a Volatile Region*, Prentice Hall, New York, pp295–327

Glassman, J and Samatar, A (1997) 'Development Geography and the Third World State', *Progress in Human Geography*, vol 22, no 1, pp164–98

Good, K and Hughes, S (2002) 'Globalization and Diversification: Two Cases in Southern Africa', *African Affairs*, vol 101, no 402, pp39–59

Griggs, R (2003) 'Geopolitical Discourse, Global Actors and the Spatial Construction of the African Union', *Geopolitics*, vol 8, no 2, pp69–98

Hentz, J (2003) 'The Mozambique Aluminium Smelter: Partnership for Exploitation or Development', in F Söderbaum and I Taylor (eds) *Regionalism and Uneven Development in Southern Africa: The Case of the Maputo Development Corridor*, Ashgate, Burlington, pp83–97

Kawango, A (1998) 'Vanishing Borders within Sub-Saharan African States: Achievements, Counter Forces and Prospects', in L Boon-Thong and T Shamsul Bahrin (eds) *Vanishing Borders: The International Order of the 21st Century*, Ashgate, Brookfield, VT, pp159–73

Maasdorp, G (1992) *Economic Cooperation in Southern Africa: Prospects for Regional Integration*, The Research Institute for the Study of Conflict and Terrorism, London

Makoni, S (1990) 'Blowing the SADCC Trupet', *Southern African Economist*, vol 2, no 3

McDonald, H (1990) Planning Reconstruction and Reform on a Regional Scale: the Efforts of the Southern African Development Coordination Conference, unpublished PhD thesis, Rutgers University, New Brunswick

McGregor, J (1994) 'People without Fathers: Mozambicans in Swaziland, 1988–1993', *Journal of Southern African Studies*, vol 24, no 1, pp37–60

Mandela, N (1993) 'South Africa's Future Foreign Policy', *Foreign Affairs*, vol 72, no 5 (November/December), pp86–97

Matlou, J (2001) 'Hawkers' Highway to Happiness', Electronic Mail and Guardian, 26 Oct, www.mg.co.za

M'Buyinga, E (1982) *Pan Africanism or Neo-Colonialism: The Bankruptcy of the O.A.U.*, Zed Press, London

Morna, C (1990) 'SADCC First Decade', *African Report*, May–June, pp49–52

Ohmae, K (1995) *The End of the Nation State: The Rise of Regional Economies*, Collins, London

Oucho, J and Crush, J (2001) 'Contra Free Movement: South Africa and the SADC Migration Protocols', *Africa Today*, vol 48, no 3, pp139–58

SADC (1992) Treaty of the Southern African Development Community, SADC, Gaborone

SADC (1996a) Communique: Summit of the Heads of State or Governments of SADC, June, SADC Gaborone

SADC (1996b) Protocol on Trade in SADC, SADC, Gaborone

Sassen, S (1996) *Losing Control, Sovereignty in an Age of Globalization*, Columbia University Press, New York

Shaw, T M (2002) 'New Regionalisms in Africa in the New Millennium', in S Breslin, C Hughes and N Philips (eds) *New Regionalisms in the Global Political Economy*, Routledge, London, pp177–89

Sidaway, J (1993) 'Urban and Regional Planning in Post-Independence Mozambique', *International Journal of Urban and Regional Research*, vol 17, no 2, pp241–59

Sidaway, J and Gibb, R (1998) 'SADC, COMESA, SACU: Contradictory Formats for Regional Integration', in D Simon (ed), *South Africa in Southern Africa: Reconfiguring the Region*, Ohio State University Press, Athens, Ohio, pp164–86

Simon, D (1991) 'Namibia in Southern Africa: The Regional Implications of Independence', *Tijdschrift voor Economische en Sociale Geografie*, vol 82, no 5, pp377–87

Simon, D (ed) (1998) *South Africa in Southern Africa: Reconfiguring the Region*, James Currey, Oxford

Simon, D (2003) 'Regional Development-Environment Discourses, Policies and Practices in Post-Apartheid Southern Africa', in J Grant and F Söderbaum (eds) *The New Regionalism in Africa*, Ashgate, Burlington, T, pp67–92

Smith, N (1994) 'Geography, Empire and Social Theory', *Progress in Human Geography*, vol 18, no 4, pp491–500

Söderbaum, F and Taylor, I (2003) 'Introduction: Understanding the Dynamics of Micro-regionalism in Southern Africa', in F Söderbaum and I Taylor (eds) *Regionalism and Uneven Development in Southern Africa: The Case of the Maputo Development Corridor*, Ashgate, Burlington, VT, pp1–18

Stoneman, D and Thompson, C B (1991) 'Southern Africa, after Apartheid: Economic Repercussions for a Free South Africa, New York', Africa Recovery Briefing Paper No 4, United Nations, Department of Public Information

Swyngedouw, E (2000) 'Authoritarian Governance, Power and the Politics of Rescaling', *Environment and Planning D: Space and Society*, 20

Sunday Independent (1996) Johannesburg newspaper, 6 November edition

Taylor, I and Nel, P (2002) 'New Africa: Globalization and the Confines of Elite Reformism: Getting the Rhetoric Right, Getting the Strategy Wrong', *Third World Quarterly*, vol 23, no 1, pp163–80

Warburton-Lee, J (1999) 'Breaking Down the Barricades', *International Boundary Research Unit Boundary and Security Bulletin*, vol 7, no 3, University of Durham, pp62–6

Weimer, B (1996) 'Challenges to Democratization and Regional Development: Focus on Mozambique', *Regional Development Dialogue*, vol 17, no 2, pp32–59

Wolmer, W (2003) 'Transboundary Natural Resource Management: Politics, Ecological Integrity and Economic Integration in the Gaza-Kruger-Gonarshous Trans-frontier Conservation Area', *Journal of Southern African Studies*, vol 29, no 1, pp46–63

World Bank (1996) *Mozambique: Trans-frontier Conservation Pilot and Institutional Strengthening Project*, World Bank, Washington, DC

12

Institutions for Conflict Resolution and Peacemaking

Michelle Parlevliet

Introduction

In various violent intra-state conflicts on the African continent, balancing peace and justice has been a regular dilemma. Reconciling the demands of justice and the enforcement of human rights with the political and strategic concerns of peacemaking is often difficult. Nevertheless, there is growing awareness among scholars, practitioners and policy-makers that peace and justice are inextricably linked. The absence of justice generally leads to an absence of peace. Those concerned with respect for human rights and pursuing justice, and those working towards peace in contexts of societal conflict, share a common goal of promoting sustainable peace with justice, even though they may view conflict from different perspectives and may use different strategies in addressing it. This chapter explores how human rights and conflict management play out in contemporary Africa. It argues that peace and justice are necessary components of one another and that insights and practices from both fields are needed in order to prevent and end civil wars on the continent.[1]

Human Rights and Conflict Management in Africa: Five Propositions

Human rights abuses are both symptoms and causes of violent conflict

Violent and destructive conflict can *lead to* gross human rights violations, but can also *result from* a sustained denial of rights. Human rights abuses can be a *cause* and consequence, or *symptom*, of violent conflict. Continuous reports on armed conflict around the world reflect the symptomatic nature of rights violations when recounting the consequences in terms of loss of life and mass movements of people escaping from violence and destruction. The 1994 genocide in Rwanda, in which some 800,000 people died in just 100 days, stands as a chilling illustration of the atrocities that violent conflict can generate. Protracted conflicts in Angola and Sudan demonstrate that this kind of abuse does not only occur in the short-term: the population in both countries has experienced decades of human rights violations resulting from the countries' civil wars. One could argue that a culture of abuse has become entrenched (Lamb, 2000, p35). At times, specific violations have deliberately been used as a strategy of war to intimidate opponents and terrorize civilians. The mutilation and amputation of people's hands and other body parts by the rebels of Foday Sankoh's Revolutionary United Front in Sierra Leone is a case in point.[2] Human rights may also be affected by violent conflict in more indirect ways, through, for example, the destruction of people's livelihoods or the refusal of belligerent parties to allow humanitarian relief activities in areas under their control.

On the other hand, numerous conflicts have been caused by human rights issues such as inadequate political participation, the quest for self-determination, limited access to resources, exploitation, forced acculturation and discrimination (Nherere and Ansah-Koi, 1990). For example, the conflict in the Delta Region in Nigeria is not only due to the oil-related pollution in the traditional living areas of the Ogoni people, but also to the fact that they seek a larger degree of autonomy and greater control of the oil production and profit (Douglas and Ola, 1999; Rubin and Asuni, 1999). Rights-related concerns also motivated the uprising of the Banyamulenge Tutsi minority in eastern Zaire in 1996 and their overthrow of Mobutu. These included, among other things, discrimination at the hands of Mobutu's regime over three decades, the decision of a provincial governor to expel this minority from Zaire where they had lived for 200 years, and Mobutu's support for Hutu *Interahamwe* (militia) who had been involved in the Rwandan genocide (Nathan, 2000, p192). In the case of South Africa under the apartheid regime, a sustained denial of human rights gave rise to high-intensity conflict. The state's systemic oppression of the civil and political liberties of the majority of the population, and its restraints on their social, economic and cultural rights, resulted in a long-lasting armed liberation struggle.

The denial of human rights may not only occur through active repression, but can also come about through the inability of the state to realize the rights of its citizens, especially in the socio-economic domain. Such 'passive violation' also deepens social cleavages and rivalries, thus enhancing the potential for destructive conflict. In several African countries, this is reflected in the way in which access to the political system is highly contested: in societies marked by abject poverty, control of the state is often the only way to achieve economic security. Political polarization in countries like Malawi, Zambia and Mozambique reflects this dynamic.

In terms of peacemaking and conflict resolution, it matters whether gross human rights violations resulting from conflict are the main concern, or whether the focus is on conflict resulting from a denial of human rights. The problems to be addressed are different and so are the desired outcomes. If one is concerned with human rights violations as a symptom of conflict, one's primary objective is to protect people from further abuses. Activities of intermediaries are then aimed at mitigating, alleviating and containing the destructive manifestation of conflict. They include peacekeeping, peacemaking, peace-enforcement, humanitarian intervention, human rights monitoring, negotiating ceasefires and the settlement of displaced persons.[3] When, however, human rights violations are causing violent conflict, the main objective of activities by human rights and conflict management actors is to reduce the level of structural violence through the transformation of the structural, systemic conditions that give rise to violent conflict in a society. Activities can include peacemaking, peace-building, reconciliation, development and reconstruction, institution building, and accommodation of diversity by protecting minorities.

Thus, whereas direct, physical violence is the main concern when one focuses on human rights violations as symptoms of destructive conflict, considering rights violations as a cause relates to structural violence. The desired outcome of the former is peace in the sense of an absence of direct violence – so-called negative *peace*. In the case of the latter the goal is to achieve *positive peace*, meaning the absence of structural violence, or, framed differently, the presence of social justice, including harmonious relationships between parties that are conducive to mutual development, growth and the attainment of goals (Galtung, 1969; Webb, 1986; Yarn, 1999: pp347–8).[4] It should be noted that both aspects of the human rights/ conflict relationship can be present in the same situation – that is generally the case in civil wars. The distinction between human rights violations as a symptom and cause of destructive conflict relates specifically to the *focus* and the *aim* of interventions, not to different scenarios.

A sustained denial of human rights is a structural cause of high-intensity conflict

One conflict management perspective on human rights, by Galtung and Wirak (1977), helps explain *why* a sustained denial of rights can be a cause of rebellion and civil strife by focusing on the relationship between human rights and human needs. It is based on human needs theory as propounded by Burton (1990) and applied by Azar (1986) in his analysis of protracted social conflict. Needs, defined by Burton as universal motivations that are an integral part of human beings, relate in this perspective to both material and non-material concerns. They include goods such as food and shelter, and aspects like identity, recognition and personal growth (Burton, 1990, pp37–8; Miall et al, 1999, pp47–8). Burton posits that needs are generally non-negotiable in that they cannot be traded or bargained away. They are so fundamental to human survival, subsistence and development that people will consistently seek ways of meeting them, even if they are frustrated or oppressed. In other words, when individuals or groups find that their needs and values are denied, they may behave in ways that express their frustration, or may refuse to submit to practices and policies that are unacceptable to them.[5]

This concept of needs is broader than the way in which needs are usually understood from a human rights perspective, which considers them primarily in terms of material and social goods such as food, shelter, clothing, medical care and schooling (Claude and Weston, 1992, pp137–211). Galtung and Wirak (1977) suggest that needs fall into four categories, namely welfare, freedom, security and identity. *Security*-related needs pertain to protection against attack and destruction, as well as physical and mental preservation. Needs involving *welfare* fall within the physiological, ecological and socio-cultural domain (eg food, shelter, clean environment, education, cultural preservation), whereas *freedom*-related needs are concerned with mobility, exchange, politics and work. *Identity*-related needs are concerned with self-expression, self-actualization, affection, association, support and recognition. This understanding of needs largely corresponds with Max-Neef's view (1991, p17): he identifies nine fundamental human needs in the context of human development: subsistence, protection, affection, understanding, participation, leisure, creation, identity and freedom. Wisner (1988) distinguishes between 'strong' and 'weak' basic needs approaches. The 'strong' approach emphasizes participatory definition of people's own needs and obstacles to satisfying them. The 'weak' approach merely tries to 'deliver' need satisfiers such as food or water from the top down.

The relevance of this conceptualization of human needs is that it sheds light on the relationship between rights and needs, and between rights and conflict. From this perspective, all needs give rise to certain rights, which help secure the goods or services necessary to meet these needs. As Galtung and Wirak (1977, p254) put it, '[human rights are] instrumental to the satisfaction of ... needs'. A comparison of the needs listed above with rights contained in the Universal Declaration of Human Rights and the African Charter on Human and Peoples' Rights shows that all rights relate to several needs (UNGA, 1948; OAU, 1981). Implementation of rights helps to address fundamental human needs. For example, self-determination, usually conceived of in terms of rights, is a collective need for identity, freedom and security (Claude and Weston, 1992, p142). In the words of Nigerian scholar Osaghae (1996, p172), 'human rights are ... an instrument of individual and collective struggle to protect core interests'. The South African Constitutional Court recognized this connection between rights and needs when it ruled that 'the right of access to adequate housing is entrenched because we value human beings and want to ensure that they are afforded their basic human needs. A society must seek to ensure that the basic necessities of life are provided to all if it is to be a society based on human dignity, freedom and equality' (Chaskalson, 2000a).[6]

The direct relationship between rights and needs explains why a sustained denial of rights may cause violent conflict in a society because it entails long-term frustration of needs, and people will tend to persist in seeking ways to address their needs if these are not met. If this is possible through peaceful, constructive avenues, individuals or groups will generally engage in conventional forms of political action in order to bring about change. If, however, they are marginalized or excluded, they may eventually resort to armed resistance in the belief that this is the only way to bring about the transformation of society. The uprising of the Banyamulenge Tutsi minority in eastern Zaire in 1996 mentioned earlier is relevant here in that violence became a way to act out deep resentment and frustration in the absence of non-violent, legitimate avenues to address concerns. It is important to note that such exclusion or victimization can be either real or perceived as such by groups. The latter is often the case when groups experience frustration in realizing their political and economic *expectations*. Such perceived deprivation can also make groups more disposed to violence as a way of achieving their goals (Azar, 1986; Gurr, 1970, p23).

Deprivation of needs through the sustained denial of rights is a *structural* cause of violent conflict because it is generally embedded in structures of governance, in terms of how the state is organized, institutions operate and society functions. For example, a particular social group may, on the basis of its identity, be systematically barred from participating in the political process through certain laws or policies. Or a state may be characterized by a consistent lack of development in those regions where the majority of inhabitants are members of a social group other than the politically dominant group. Long-standing grievances over land and other resource allocations can also constitute structural causes of destructive conflict.

Nathan (2000, pp188–92) identifies four critical structural conditions that predispose to violent conditions in Africa: authoritarian rule; exclusion of minorities from governance; socio-economic deprivation combined with inequity; and weak states that lack the institutional capacity to manage conflicts constructively (see also Azar, 1986, p30.) UN Secretary-General Kofi Annan (2001, p24, para 100) lists the following as 'key structural risk factors that fuel violent conflict' in Africa: inequity (disparities among identity groups), inequality (policies and practices that institutionalize discrimination), injustice (lack of the rule of law, ineffective and unfair law enforcement, inequitable representation in institutions serving the rule of law) and insecurity (lack of accountable and transparent governance and human security). Each of the causes mentioned here can be traced back to human rights concerns related to security, identity, well-being and freedom as discussed by Galtung and Wirak. Osaghae (1996, p172) thus argues that 'the human rights approach to conflict management [recognizes] that conflicts arise from inequalities, discrimination, domination, exclusion and injustices which attend the competition among people and groups for scarce political, social, and economic resources and benefits.' Issues of governance are essential in this regard as the way the state is organized determines whether needs are frustrated or satisfied: groups are allowed or denied access to the resources or processes necessary to address their needs.

According to Nathan, these structural conditions create tensions in society that provide fertile ground for violent conflict. He suggests that they give rise to a *societal propensity* to violence, and as such pose a fundamental threat to human security and the stability of the state (2000, pp192–4, original emphasis). This propensity stems from the non-negotiable character of needs and is enhanced if several structural problems are present simultaneously; for example, when discrimination in one area coincides with marginalization in another. A pattern of negative interaction between social groups – manifested in hostility, fear, prejudices and violent skirmishes occurring over a period of time – can exacerbate a propensity to violence. The outbreak of destructive conflict in the form of direct, physical violence is thus generally a *symptom* of deeper-lying structural problems. For example, violent protests in Mauritius in February 1999 following the death of a popular singer in a police cell were largely related to a sense of exclusion and socio-economic discrimination felt by certain communities on the island (Republic of Mauritius, 2000). The Commission of Inquiry established to look into these events concluded in its report that:

> *they are symptoms of latent social problems in the country; they represent the smouldering flames underneath the ashes that may spark off any time. One year after the situation the country is still potentially explosive. The country is sitting on a powder keg. Any minor incident can provide the spark.* (Republic of Mauritius, 2000, Chapter 9)

In short, the absence of justice is often the primary reason for the absence of peace. The presence of justice, on the other hand, can lead to both positive and negative peace (Galtung, 1969; Nathan, 2000; pp190–1). A sustained denial of human rights can thus be a structural cause of high-intensity conflict. Violence manifested in such conflict often reflects that needs are frustrated, legitimate aspirations are denied, and obvious injustices are present.

Towards conflict prevention

Institutionalized respect for human rights and the structural accommodation of diversity is a primary form of conflict prevention. As the above discussion highlights, it is more important to focus on the structural causes of violence than on violence itself if we are to *prevent* violent conflict in any effective way. Violence, however significant from a humanitarian point of view, is the outward manifestation of a structural crisis. As long as destructive structural conditions remain in place in a society, the potential for violence remains (Nathan, 2000, pp193–5). Monitoring events that may have a destabilizing impact on particular societies (such as a crop failure, influx of weapons or a significant currency devaluation), as is often done for 'early warning purposes', may be of limited value in this regard. After all, a single event may have very different consequences in different contexts, depending on the structural conditions present. A crop failure or the arrest of a political opponent may 'trigger' the outbreak of violence in some states but go largely unnoticed in others, because they intensify structural tensions in the former but not in the latter (Nathan, 2000, pp193–5; Annan, 2001, p7, para 7). Thus, focusing on emergencies or crises where violence has started to occur is insufficient to prevent violent conflict.

A distinction made by the Carnegie Commission for the Prevention of Deadly Conflict between operational and structural prevention is relevant in this regard (1997, pp39–102). Operational prevention aims to prevent latent conflicts with the potential for violence from degenerating into serious armed conflicts, whereas structural prevention is meant to address 'deep-rooted socio-economic, cultural, environmental, institutional and other structural causes that underlie the immediate political symptoms' of violent conflicts (Annan, 2001, p2).[7] In the case of the former, prevention amounts to fire-fighting; in the latter, it means removing the logs that catch fire.

The protection and promotion of human rights addresses structural causes of violent conflict by working towards the satisfaction of basic human needs.

Institutionalizing respect for human rights – through, for example, constitutional endorsement of fundamental human rights, independence of the judiciary, an independent human rights commission – may ensure that such protection is sustained over a period of time and becomes a matter of state policy. It helps prevent high-intensity conflict by limiting the power of the state, affording citizens protection against abuse of rights, and allowing them a large measure of freedom and participation. Noteworthy in this respect is that the introduction of a Bill of Rights was specifically recommended in Nigeria in the 1950s in order to reduce tensions between regions and ethnic groups (Osaghae, 1996, pp180–1).

Institutionalizing respect for human rights also means that mechanisms are developed within state structures that provide consensual ways for dealing with discontent, thus limiting the need to resort to violence. It enhances the state's capacity to engage in constructive conflict management by facilitating dialogue and participatory decision-making. This is particularly relevant in situations where the state has limited resources at its disposal to implement human rights, which result in a limited alleviation of structural tensions. In South Africa, for example, continuing socio-economic deprivation and poverty is an important factor undermining societal stability. The extent to which a state has effective coping mechanisms for dealing with such tensions is then important, which makes societal norms for dealing with dissatisfaction and dissent relevant. Where a transparent and representative system of governance exists with legitimate institutions, there is a greater capacity to manage such tensions in a constructive way (Webb 1986, p431; Annan, 2001, p7, para 7).

Specific attention must be devoted to the structural accommodation of diversity, which means formally entrenching inclusiveness and respect for diversity in the political system, state institutions and the law (Nathan 2000, pp200–1). This is particularly important because identity groups are often the primary actors in intra-state conflict and governance tends to be a central problem in that context. A strong sense of identity is often the core around which social groups are mobilized in order to raise grievances related to needs deprivation. Yet, as Amoo and Odendaal (2002) point out, ethnic conflict does not stem so much from an inherent inability of different identities to co-exist within one state as from the marginalization or exclusion of groups; formalizing inclusiveness in governance is thus pivotal. Burundi is a case in point. Mthembu-Salter (2002, pp1–4) observes that, while Burundi's ethnic cleavage today may manifest itself as primordial and the root of all political division, this was not the case during precolonial and colonial times. In his view, Burundi's conflict revolves around intense competition between rival political elites for state power, who mobilize their constituencies around ethnicity. Others support this, with Leatherman et al (1999, p131) pointing to a long-standing strategy by the minority leadership to exclude, intimidate and repress the majority. They speak of 'generations of abuse of power at the hands of a military oligarchy defined by region and ethnicity which maintained its position only through massive intimidation and systematic repression'.

In light of the crucial role of governance in matters of ethnicity, Amoo and Odendaal (2002) argue that a primary way of pre-empting (violent) ethnic conflict is the adoption of appropriate political and legal structures that allow for meaningful participation of identity groups in a state's political, economic, social and cultural affairs. The former High Commissioner for National Minorities of the Organisation for Co-operation and Security in Europe, Max van der Stoel, concurs:

> *the protection of persons belonging to national minorities has to be seen as essentially in the interests of the state and of the majority. As a rule, peace and stability are best served by ensuring that persons belonging to national minorities can effectively enjoy their rights.* (van der Stoel, 1999, p73)

Accommodating diversity is not simply a matter of recognizing formal equality between various groups in society. Efforts to treat people from different groups equally can amount to precluding members systematically from disadvantaged groups. Writing on Nigeria, Osaghae (1996, pp184–6) suggests that that the principle of non-discrimination is most applicable when all groups are similar in size and have reasonably identical levels of development. If, on the other hand, political parties are organized along ethnic lines and the political system is based on a 'winner-takes-all' approach, minorities will be completely and permanently excluded from governance in a formal democracy. In such situations of democratic majoritarianism, minorities may come to believe that political institutions and processes do not sufficiently meet their needs and interests, making them more inclined to violence as a means of expression and objection (Eide, 1995, pp97–100; Nathan, 2000, pp200–1).

Various mechanisms exist for the accommodation of diversity. These include constitutional rights regarding language, religion and culture, forms of power-sharing (such as federalism, proportional representation, decentralization in which the local or regional units have a large degree of autonomy) and so on. Realizing the aspirations of identity groups can be realized through legislation providing for the preservation of identity in the areas of culture, education and language, or through guarantees of effective participation in public decision-making processes, and carefully constructed electoral processes (van der Stoel, 1999, pp73–5). At the very least, respect for diversity must be ensured through the formal acknowledgement that identity groups have a right to exist, to protect their language and culture, and to participate in public affairs on an equal basis with others. The process of institutionalizing respect for human rights is thus not only concerned with individual rights but also with group rights.

Effective and sustainable resolution of intra-state conflict

The prescriptive approach of human rights actors must be combined with the facilitative approach of conflict management practitioners for the effective and sustainable resolution of intra-state conflict.

The previous discussion emphasized that the human rights perspective is deeply concerned with substantive issues related to the distribution of political power and economic resources, security and identity. In the context of negotiation processes aimed at ending a long-term violent conflict in a society, this generally translates into a prescriptive approach towards the outcome or product of negotiations. The outcome must be in line with human rights standards and must embrace constitutionalism and the legal protection of rights. While these are also concerns of conflict management practitioners, the latter generally adopt a more facilitative approach towards the outcome. Their emphasis is more on a particular kind of process – one that is aimed at establishing dialogue, developing relationships and building trust between the parties. They are aware that the quality of the outcome depends on the process used to achieve it. A process that is flawed in the eyes of the parties involved contaminates the product by making its legitimacy questionable, hence undermining its sustainability. This has been, for example, one of the main challenges to peace in Sudan as per the Machakos Protocol signed in July 2002: the agreement involved only the two main parties to the conflict, the Sudanese People's Liberation Movement from the South and the Khartoum-based Government of Sudan. Several political parties in the North and ethnic groups in the South did not take part in the Protocol negotiations. Commentators in the South and North soon emphasized the importance of bringing these parties into the process if the peace is to last (Nyaba, 2002; Taban, 2002).

The process used in resolving issues between parties is especially significant in the context of intra-state conflict where many groups, all with different needs, values and interests, co-exist within the same territory. The conflictual nature of their relationships may originally stem from their different access to political and economic resources, but it is deepened by feelings of hostility, mistrust and fear that have become entrenched over long periods of time. In some cases, such polarization and enemy images become a driving dynamic in fuelling continuous conflict, with violence countering violence, leading Sisk to speak of the 'self-perpetuating nature of civil wars' (Sisk, 1997, p187). Tracing what they call 'indigenous patterns of perception and action' in Burundi, Leatherman et al observe that

> the circulation of stories, songs and other expressive forms related to tragic events or touching on selectively recalled incidents of ethnic animosity, has tended to flow in separate channels within each community thereby contributing to increased cohesion and exclusivity of both, while at the same time … providing fertile ground for 'political leaders using symbolism associated with these events to transform division and separation into antagonism and violence'. (Leatherman et al, 1999, p138, including quotation from Kadende-Kaiser and Kaiser, 1997)

Others have also recognized the significant role of perceptions, emotions and relationships in contemporary conflicts. Nathan (1999, p1) stresses that high-intensity conflict evokes and is fuelled by a range of strong emotions, including fear, insecurity, anger, a sense of grievance and suspicion. These emotions make the parties resistant to negotiations and inhibit progress once talks are underway because parties view their differences as irreconcilable and fear that a settlement will entail unacceptable compromises. They lack confidence in negotiations as a means of achieving a satisfactory outcome, even if they are unlikely to gain an outright victory on the battlefield. He therefore speaks of the 'psycho-political dynamics' of civil conflict, a term that reflects that the subjective dynamics of conflict originate from objective conditions related to power and political relationships, such as exclusion, marginalization and persecution (Nathan, 1999, pp19–20; see also Lederach, 1997, pp12–15).

Because the negative character of relationships between groups is both a product and a further cause of conflict, attention needs to be devoted simultaneously to addressing root causes *and* building positive relationships between parties (Parlevliet, 2001). As long as relationships remain fiercely adversarial, parties – being locked in positions of fear and suspicion – will be reluctant to engage in negotiations towards a settlement. The development of trust between parties in the course of negotiations is therefore essential, since 'negotiations tend to focus on issues, but their success depends on people' (Bloomfield et al, 1998, p63). In the negotiations to end Mozambique's civil war, for example, a high level of mistrust between the parties was a major obstacle to a swift settlement. Neither of the negotiation teams could afford to be seen as being sympathetic to the concerns of 'the enemy' or keen to reach a compromise with 'them'. The mediators had to help the parties gain confidence in the negotiation process itself and to build trust in each other (Honwana and Lalá, 2002, pp23–5). This enabled the parties to move 'from mutual perceptions of enmity and threat to mutual acknowledgement and respect as political adversaries and inevitable partners in the search for peace' (p26).

Whether intervention by a third party is required is an important process consideration. This raises questions of whether such an intervenor should be of a governmental, intergovernmental or non-governmental nature and what facilitation techniques will be used. For example, many interventions in African civil wars have been conducted by intergovernmental organizations, both regional and global. These have often relied on a top-down approach where the leaders of parties are coaxed and bullied into negotiations through the use of 'carrots and sticks'. Nathan has argued, however, that the use of power and coercion by external intervenors in civil wars is problematic. It may well increase the intransigence of parties by heightening their insecurity and causing resentment towards solutions that are imposed on them. A confidence-building approach, non-coercive in nature and oriented towards joint problem-solving and raising the parties' confidence – in each other, in negotiations and in the mediator – is likely to yield a more positive result, also with a view to the psycho-political dynamics of conflict referred to above (Nathan, 1999).

This view is borne out by a recent case study of previous mediation efforts in Burundi, which relied heavily on power brokerage by regional heads of state and the two intervenors (first, former President Nyerere of Tanzania and, from December 1999, former President Mandela of South Africa). Mthembu-Salter asserts that the leverage used polarized their relations with Burundian actors and that Nyerere's support for a trade embargo imposed by regional heads of state ended one party's confidence in him as a neutral mediator (2002, p13). He observes that intense pressure on the parties did produce a peace agreement, but one that so lacked Burundian ownership that 'those who must implement it in Burundi give only qualified support' (p23). Important issues were also left unresolved, including a ceasefire. Consequently, the agreement did not deliver an end to the war, making it a failure in the eyes of most Burundians (p3) and requiring further mediation.

Examples of the confidence-building style of mediation advocated by Nathan include the mediation by the Santo Egidio Community in Mozambique, and the 1972 mediation by the All African Council of Churches with the World Council of Churches and the Sudanese Council of Churches in the first Sudanese civil war.[8] In his analysis of the latter, Assefa (2002, pp10–18) points to the characteristics and approach of the mediators as critical factors in the mediation's successful outcome. He highlights strategies such as trust-building; development of consensus of what the issues were; careful structuring of the agenda so that the less difficult issues were handled first; creation of a 'safe space' by a media policy that ensured that only the chairperson would speak to the media, thus avoiding a politicization of the process; separate consultations with the parties when the negotiations got emotionally charged; careful control of the communication process; utilization of other third parties who had the parties' confidence and could influence them; creation of small technical committees involving people from both parties with common professional backgrounds, thus forming alliances across delegation loyalties; appeals to shared values among the parties and reminders of the consequences of failure etc. A process that takes place on a confidence-building basis builds norms of dialogue, accommodation and cooperation among political actors, thus laying the foundation for future political relations between groups and individuals. In other words, if the process by which the product is agreed upon embodies the values that are to be contained in the settlement, this can enhance its sustainability.

The emphasis on addressing root causes *and* building relationships here implies that the resolution of intra-state conflict is a lengthy process. The reality of civil wars defies 'quick-fixes', as the issues involved are manifold, complex and deep-rooted, and situations have degenerated over long periods of time. It also means that local actors must play central roles in devising both the product and the process, so as to secure the local ownership necessary for the willingness of parties to implement an agreement and to pre-empt the build-up of resentment against solutions imposed by outsiders. Combining the prescriptive focus from the human rights field with the facilitative emphasis from the conflict management field thus will ensure that peacemaking and peace-building processes, both in form and content, are in line with universal human rights standards and will develop relationships between parties that provide a basis for future co-existence.

Interpretation and application of rights

Whereas human rights and justice per se are non-negotiable, the interpretation and application of rights and justice are negotiable in the context of a negotiated settlement. Rights and freedoms, as enshrined in the Universal Declaration of Human Rights and the African Charter on Human and Peoples' Rights, reflect internationally and/or nationally agreed-upon norms of behaviour between individuals, groups of people and between the state and its citizens. As such, they are not negotiable, which is also underlined by the close relationship between rights and needs explained above. Rights set the parameters for the management of conflict. However, *within* this framework, there is great scope for variation in how rights are realized in terms of, for example, the electoral system, form of government, degree of autonomy of regional units, constitutional arrangements and the precise formulation of a Bill of Rights. Despite the non-negotiable character of fundamental rights and freedoms, the manner in which they are recognized is negotiable and will vary depending on the context. There are many different ways in which rights relating to participation, equality, freedom, identity, well-being and security can be realized without undermining the substance and significance of those rights.

The political structure of the state (ie federalism, decentralization), the form of the state's legislature and executive and the electoral system are three broad areas of constitutional design that warrant examination in this regard. This entails considering different forms of power-sharing arrangements, federalism and autonomy, parliamentary versus presidential government, electoral system design and the structure and procedures of legislative bodies among others (Harris et al, 1998, pp133–259). The details of such structural arrangements should be worked out by local actors through inclusive negotiations so as to enhance the suitability and sustainability of the mechanisms adopted. Institutions that are transplanted from other contexts or imposed by external intervenors, however democratic they may be, tend to have little staying power, because they may be inappropriate or considered illegitimate by the local population. The importance of local actors in shaping the institutions that regulate their society also suggests that the implementation of rights is negotiable and depends on the context, even though the rights themselves are not negotiable.

A similar argument can be applied to the concept of justice. Justice is as nonnegotiable as human rights are; it is without doubt the foundation for sustainable peace. Yet the interpretation of 'justice' is invariably disputed and the form in which justice is shaped in a particular case is negotiable. Within the human rights field there has been extensive debate on the forms justice can take in a transitional situation with regard to accountability for violations committed during the conflict. In exploring the legal, ethical and political aspects of the quest for justice in transitional situations, questions of punishment and/or pardon, and of establishing the truth and/or establishing criminal responsibility, have received much attention. Much research has focused on various mechanisms for transitional justice – such as truth commissions, war crimes tribunals, purges – and their respective virtues and drawbacks.[9] (See Hayner, 1994; Bronkhorst, 1995; Roht-Arriaza, 1995; Kritz, 1995; Baehr, 1996; McAdam, 1997; Mendez, 1997; Hayner, 2001.)

Nevertheless, whether the discussion emphasizes retributive or restorative justice, in both cases the 'justice' concerned is mainly backward-looking. This preoccupation with the past is flawed in several respects. First, it hinges in part on the assumption that holding perpetrators accountable will end a culture of impunity. There is insufficient, if any, evidence to support this thesis. Second, the threat of prosecution and accountability can inhibit the resolution of the conflict because it can be 'a clear disincentive for actors in an armed conflict to give up their resort to violence' as Mendez puts it (1997, p273). This is not to argue that a blanket amnesty is appropriate or necessary, but rather to acknowledge that the process of addressing past abuses must take into consideration the need to consolidate a young and volatile democracy and the need to end hostilities between parties. Third, it creates the impression that justice is dependent on dealing with past atrocities, whereas justice is concerned with both the past *and* the future. It relates to both human rights violations committed during a violent conflict, and to transforming unjust structures and entrenching respect for human rights in state institutions and the societal infrastructure. In South Africa, for example, human rights organizations worked hard for the development of an appropriate Bill of Rights and for the establishment of a range of independent bodies charged with supporting constitutional democracy.

Thus, while the attainment of justice is related to the pursuit of accountability for past abuses, it is also dependent on wider processes of transformation, redistribution and reform. A 1997 conference focusing on the integration of human rights in peace processes indeed found that the scope and definition of human rights should be expanded to include at least four components: transitional justice (in the sense of prosecutions and/or truth-telling); mechanisms to ensure the personal freedom and security of civilians and identity groups during the transition; mechanisms to prevent the outbreak of future hostilities (including constitutional reforms, restructuring of the government, security forces, and judicial system); and mechanisms aimed at broader social, political and economic reform (targeting inequities, redistribution, discrimination etc) (Kunder, 1998, pp4–5).

This is not to deny that accountability for past abuses is important and should be given serious consideration in the context of negotiating a settlement. Rather, the point here is that this is only *one* aspect of implementing justice, and that justice has multiple components that should be taken into account. In South Africa, much of the recent criticism of the Truth and Reconciliation Commission has centred on the lack of reparations to victims, many of whom are in dire financial circumstances, following the handing over of the TRC's Final Report in October 1998. This criticism is especially poignant when considering that policy initiatives of the government towards socio-economic redistribution and reform have either been aborted (as was the case with its Redistribution and Development Programme) or are progressing at a very slow pace (in the case of land reform). The lack of justice in the form of tangible reform in the socio-economic sphere threatens to undo or contaminate progress made towards achieving justice for past human rights violations through the TRC process.[10]

In sum, even if rights and justice are non-negotiable, there is no single, absolute way in which they should be applied or implemented in each context. The human rights priorities of local actors should inform their interpretation and application in each case. This approach does not diminish the critical and universal value of human rights and justice, but ensures that these are implemented in line with the needs and circumstances of particular contexts – within the internationally accepted framework of human rights. It also encourages paying more attention to the question of how justice can be built into settlements in a prospective way (ensuring the protection of rights in a structural, institutional manner) rather than overemphasizing its retrospective aspects.

The five propositions laid out above have many implications for a variety of actors, including governmental bodies and intergovernmental agencies. There is a need for dialogue between the fields of human rights and conflict management in order to gain an understanding of one another's mission, guiding principles and methods, and to strengthen efforts towards peace, justice and reconciliation. Closely related is the need to pursue an integrated approach in dealing with conflicts involving issues of rights. Many conflicts cannot be addressed solely from either a human rights or a conflict management resolution perspective. The two fields should be considered in conjunction with one another because of the close relationship between human rights and conflict management. For example, the high level of xenophobia in South Africa necessitates an integrated approach on the part of the various bodies that deal with migrants, asylum-seekers and refugees. Considering xenophobia only from a human rights point of view fails to engage the needs and interests that make South Africans so reluctant to accept foreigners in their midst. At the same time, focusing exclusively on such concerns with a view to resolving specific disputes between locals and foreigners may give insufficient consideration to the rights of the latter. Only a combination of the two perspectives can ensure that strategies are developed for resolving xenophobia-related conflicts in ways that uphold the rights of various parties, while taking their needs and interests into account as well.

Box 12.1 *The role of NGOs*

Firoze Manji

NGOs: a mission to depoliticize poverty

Development NGOs operating in Africa have, inadvertently or otherwise, become part of the neo-liberal global agenda, serving to undermine the battle for social justice and human rights in much the same way as their missionary predecessors. The contribution of NGOs to relieving poverty is minimal, while they play a significant role in undermining the struggle of African people to emancipate themselves from economic, social and political oppression. In this compromised position, NGOs face a stark choice: they can move into the political domain and support social movements that seek to challenge a social system that benefits a few and impoverishes the majority; or they can continue unchanged and thus become complicit in a system that leaves the majority in misery.

Development NGOs have evolved in Africa from their precursors, the missionary societies. In colonial Africa, missionary organizations played a key role in winning the ideological war that supported the colonial apparatus. While colonial philanthropy may have been motivated by religious conviction, status, compassion or guilt, it was also motivated by fear. In Britain and the colonies alike, politicians frequently alluded to the threat of revolution and actively encouraged greater interest in works of benevolence as a solution to social unrest. In short, charity was not only designed to help the poor, it also served to protect the rich. In some cases, charitable organizations actively helped to suppress anti-colonial struggles, as was the case in Kenya, where the Women's Association, Maendeleo Ya Wanawake Organization (MYWO) and the Christian Council of Kenya (CCK) were both involved in government-funded schemes designed to subvert black resistance during the 'Mau Mau' uprising.

The period following the Second World War witnessed an unprecedented level of popular mobilizations and the formation of numerous popular organizations throughout the continent. Such developments were informed at the grassroots not so much (at least, not initially) by desires for abstract concepts of self-determination, but more around struggles for basic rights that were part of everyday experiences of the majority. The initial spark for most people was provided by the desire to organize around the right to food, shelter, water, land, education and health care; around the right to freedom of association, freedom of speech, freedom of movement, freedom from harassment and other forms of human rights abuses. Different groups within society organized around issues with which they were themselves most preoccupied – aspiring local capitalists organizing around restraints on their freedom to accumulate, while squatters organized around their rights of access to land.

It was these numerous civil agitations (urban and rural) that provided the impetus to the liberation movements. Political independence was achieved through the ability of the leadership of the nationalist movements to capture the imagination of these formations, uniting them in the promise that only through self-determination and independence could all their aspirations be achieved.

But independence created a crisis for these organizations because they had in many cases opposed nationalistic tendencies. However, instead of dying a natural death they were in fact able to prosper because of the emergence of the 'development NGO' on the national and international stage. Independence forced missionary societies and charitable organizations to reinvent their attitude of 'trusteeship' associated with colonial oppression. They did this by replacing white staff with black and revamping their ideological outlook by appropriating the new discourse on 'development' in place of overt racism. The difference was in name only. Development discourse was flawed from the beginning because non-Western people were defined by their divergence from Western cultural standards. While the vision of 'development' appeared to offer a more inclusive path to 'progress' than had previously been the case, in fact the discourse was little more than a superficial reformulation of old colonial prejudices. During this period NGOs were regarded by development agencies as playing a peripheral role in development, with the state assuming overarching responsibility for this role. This meant that the role of NGOs in the post-independence period remained marginal.

This was set to change with a new set of political circumstances that led to a boom in NGOs on the continent. The late 1970s saw the rise to power of Margaret Thatcher in the UK and Ronald Reagan in the US, with both leaders championing the concept of the minimalist state. According to this outlook the state had to take a backseat in development and create the economic conditions for the accumulation of wealth by a minority. The rest of society would begin to benefit when growth 'trickled down' from the wealthy. This neo-liberal agenda 'radically' altered the landscape of development practice. African countries were at this time heavily in debt and this gave the multilateral lending agencies the leverage they needed to impose their neo-liberal policy demands, something that was not always popular with African people. Unhappiness with economic adjustment and its polices was often widespread and led to demonstrations that were sometimes violently suppressed. The protests in turn led to an attempt by lending agencies to present a 'human face' to their policies. What emerged was the 'good governance' agenda of the 1990s and the decision to coopt NGOs and other civil society organizations to a repackaged programme of welfare provision.

NGOs suddenly found themselves in the situation where they usurped the state as provider of social services to the 'vulnerable' and became the beneficiaries of funds intended to mitigate the inequalities of adjustment policies. This had a profound impact on the sector and together with an increase in their function as a conduit for government aid led to dramatic growth in the number of NGOs in Africa. Globalization has led to a 'loss of authority' by African states over social development and policy. At the same time, social conditions worsened because of external controls over areas such as health, education and welfare measures and social programmes, tax concessions on profits, liberalization of price controls and dismantling of state-owned enterprises.

Development appears to have failed, with real per capita GDP falling and welfare gains achieved after independence reversed. Per capita incomes in sub-Saharan Africa fell by 21 per cent in real terms between 1981 and 1989. In 16 other sub-Saharan countries per capita incomes were lower in 1999 than in 1975.

If the development process has become 'who gets access to what', then civil war is but a continuation of that process by other, albeit more destructive, means. Civil war has frequently become the inexorable outcome of the development process itself. In Sierra Leone both the army and the 'rebels' are the main actors in the mining industry. The war in Liberia has become a lucrative venture for illegal mining, drug trafficking and money laundering. Angola's protracted war has helped Savimbi and some multinational corporations to extract diamonds from the country: in 1993 alone, Savimbi's rebel group pocketed $250 million from the mining towns that it controls. The South African mining conglomerate De Beers has admitted to buying illegally diamonds mined in Angola worth some $500 million. In 1992 alone, money laundered from drugs in war-torn countries amounted to about $856 million. The conflict which took place in Rwanda in 1994, resulting in the massacre of a million people in less than nine months, was a human catastrophe of immense proportions. But its underlying causes are a tragic example of the consequences of the combination of the factors referred to above.

The situation in which NGOs thrived was therefore one of continued poverty and an increase in armed conflict. As African governments are increasingly pushed into becoming caretakers of what might be described as the peripheral Bantustans of globalization, are we seeing a return to the colonial paradigm in which social services are delivered on the basis of favour or charity and their power to placate?

Development NGOs have come to be preferred to the state as providers of services. They have become an integral, and necessary part of a system that sacrifices respect for justice and rights. They have taken the 'missionary position' – service delivery, running projects that are motivated by charity, pity and doing things for people (implicitly who can't do it for themselves), albeit with the verbiage of 'participatory approaches'. Whether willingly or otherwise, development NGOs became the means by which poverty has been depoliticized.

The challenge that both local and Western NGOs face in making this choice will be that funding – at least from the bilateral and multilateral agencies – will not necessarily be forthcoming to support the struggle for emancipation. But then, one would hardly have expected the apartheid regime in South Africa to have funded the movement that brought about its downfall.

Enhancing Understanding

This chapter has argued for the need for human rights actors and conflict management practitioners to be more familiar with each other's principal concerns and methods. In this section, training is discussed as a strategy to enhance both the mutual understanding between and the effectiveness of both sets of actors.

Training conflict management practitioners in human rights awareness and instruments

As argued above, there are strong reasons why actors in the conflict management field should acquire greater understanding of human rights and be more knowledgeable about human rights instruments. Conflict management must take place within a framework in which human rights are non-negotiable. While there is much scope for dialogue, negotiation and accommodation within that framework, practitioners must be aware of its parameters in order to ensure that their interventions are in line with fundamental rights and freedoms. Moreover, instruments such as the Universal Declaration or the African Charter provide internationally accepted principles of freedom, fairness and respect. Actors within the conflict management field can use such standards to gain a different perspective on possible solutions, assess different options or lay the foundation for agreements. Human rights standards thus provide practitioners and parties to a conflict with objective measures for understanding the moral and legal consequences of their actions. Individual parties may not always realize that certain activities or practices are violating the rights of other parties. Practitioners with human rights knowledge can assist such parties in making them aware of their obligations and how respect for rights can help to resolve conflictual issues (Arnold, 1998, pp3–4). Moreover, human rights serve to protect all parties, which means that respect for human rights is pragmatically in everyone's interests (groups, individuals and political parties). It has also been suggested that, in the context of a peace process, conflict management actors can help conflicting parties understand that supporting human rights may enhance their domestic and international stature, legitimacy and negotiation position, thus prompting their cooperation with the process (Kunder, 1998, p6).

A primary reason for enhancing the understanding of conflict management actors on human rights is that they need to understand the relationship between rights and conflict, and in particular the conflict-causing potential of rights denial, or they will not act effectively; conflict analysis helps practitioners to determine an intervention strategy. If they are insufficiently aware of the conflict's human rights aspects they may focus more on the manifest, visible issues that trigger conflict rather than on the structural causes that underlie violent conflict. They can also help parties understand the long-term ramifications of agreements that do not abide by human rights standards. In some situations, parties may be reluctant to accept that their conflict relates to issues of rights. The relevance of human rights knowledge for conflict resolution practitioners applies to situations where a denial of human rights is a cause of high-intensity conflict and to instances where gross human rights violations are a consequence of violent conflict. In the latter cases, intervenors must be aware of the rules and instruments that can help to regulate or mitigate conflict.

Knowledge of human rights and an understanding of rights language is also important for conflict management practitioners because they need to liaise with human rights organizations in situations where both sets of actors are involved. Human rights actors can alert conflict management practitioners if a situation seems to be deteriorating; mounting human rights violations are widely acknowledged as an early warning sign of imminent conflict. Serving as indicators of communities or states in distress, the occurrence and frequency of human rights violations signal the need for timely intervention and constructive methods to address social, political and economic inequities. Conflict management practitioners also need to assure human rights actors that their concerns will be addressed during a peace process, and how this will be undertaken. If they fail to do so, they risk critical, public statements by human rights actors that may affect the process negatively. Moreover, human rights actors are often aware of solutions used in other countries to manage certain rights issues or they can provide 'lessons learned' from elsewhere that may assist the process. Finally, conflict management practitioners need to be able to explain to human rights actors how and why a certain agreement came about if it is 'less than ideal', as Arnold (1998, pp3–4) puts it.

Training human rights actors and humanitarian agencies in conflict management skills

As much as conflict management practitioners must learn about human rights, human rights actors can also benefit from training in conflict management. They often work in volatile environments characterized by tension, polarization and violence. They frequently deal with people who are coming to terms with loss, anger and fear, and who may be so distressed, anxious or afraid that facilitated communication is essential to ensure that substantive dialogue can take place about what happened. Human rights activists also often have to deal with conflict in the course of implementing their mandate. For example, gaining access to prisoners, to potential witnesses, or to sites where gross human violations have allegedly occurred, often involves some degree of negotiation. Human rights actors may also encounter officials or non-state actors who try to impede or thwart their work for fear of outside scrutiny, or because human rights activities are seen as 'subversive'. In addition, human rights actors may be called upon to intervene in conflicts or facilitate meetings with several parties, especially if they enjoy respect in communities because of their principled and independent stance (Arnold, 1998, pp2–3). This may apply to non-governmental actors, but also to governmental or constitutional bodies. For example, the legislation governing the South African Human Rights Commission provides for the use of mediation to resolve human rights complaints received by the Commission (Republic of South Africa, Act 54 of 1994, section 8).

Techniques for crisis intervention, negotiation and facilitation, problem-solving skills and communication skills are useful for human rights actors. Communication skills are particularly relevant, as these can help defuse tension and prevent confrontation. Conflict management training also enables human rights actors to frame rights issues in terms of interests, meaning that they can explain to others why it is in their interests to respect rights. This enables human rights actors to convey the importance of upholding rights without resorting to bland and categorical statements along the lines that rights must be protected. People are generally more willing and capable of understanding rights issues if these are explained in relation to their own needs and interests, than if they encounter a prescriptive or adversarial stance about what rules apply and what action should or should not be undertaken. For example, insisting to the police that they have to respect human rights may get them to comply but does not necessarily build their understanding of why this is necessary and important. On the contrary, it may cause resentment if rights are perceived as impeding their work and benefiting suspects. However, when it is explained exactly how they can benefit from rights protection, they are more likely to make a genuine effort to comply with an instruction to uphold rights.

In this sense, arguments in favour of a confidence-building approach to mediation rather than a power-based one can be extended to the realm of human rights work. Because it relies on coercion to obtain the 'cooperation' of parties, power-based mediation often hardens the resistance of parties and leads to resentment against solutions imposed upon them. In contrast, a confidence-building approach seeks to obtain the cooperation of parties through dialogue, relationship building and the development of trust. As such, it is more likely to secure a lasting agreement (Nathan, 1999). Similarly, a confidence-building approach to the protection and promotion of rights tends to make parties less defensive. This approach involves raising human rights concerns in a constructive and non-confrontational way, and developing relationships between parties. For example, the United Nations High Commissioner for Refugees and the Centre for Common Ground (CCG) in Angola are training internally displaced persons in human rights and negotiation skills. The combination of human rights education with conflict resolution stems from the realization that

> teaching people about their rights without building a capacity to talk about, defend and present those rights in a non-adversarial way is like giving a fisherman a net with gaping holes. Rights have to be respected and if they are not, individuals must be able to demand respect in an appropriate way, i.e. non-violent and strategic. (Utterwulghe, 2001, pp3–4)[11]

In cases of mediation, such a confidence-building approach is generally preferable. In a human rights context, on the other hand, the most appropriate communication style should probably be assessed on a case-by-case basis in light of the specific situation and the objectives pursued. There may be situations in which human rights actors have to take a strong, confrontational stance in order to emphasize that certain practices are illegal and wholly unacceptable, and that universal standards have to be upheld. Training in conflict management theory and practice helps human rights actors reflect on how their attitude, behaviour and communication style can escalate or defuse conflictual situations. Based on this awareness, they can then determine how best to address certain rights concerns.

The skills mentioned above are as relevant for humanitarian agencies as they are for human rights actors. The humanitarian context is pre-eminently one where the fields of human rights and conflict management intersect. Whether their mandate is to protect refugees, internally displaced people and children or provide immediate relief or restore essential services, humanitarian agencies are constantly dealing with conflict. For example, extensive assistance to displaced people often provokes tension among local populations because of scarce resources. Aid to civilians in areas under the control of insurgents can feed suspicions of supporting the enemy or pursuing a political agenda, which need to be managed. Mass movements of people require negotiation around issues of settlement, integration and repatriation. Conflict is also highly likely to erupt in situations where many people of different cultural, ethnic, religious and political backgrounds are thrown together in a confined area, such as a refugee camp. Many acknowledge that humanitarian intervention in war zones is inevitably politicized and that the organizations involved play a number of conflict management roles (Anderson, 1996; Miall et al, 1999, pp145–7).

Bodies like the United Nations High Commissioner for Refugees (UNHCR) and the International Committee of the Red Cross (ICRC) may not be conflict-management organizations, but they have to manage conflict continuously in the implementation of their humanitarian mandates (see eg Nathan, 2000). For example, the ICRC has had to negotiate ceasefires with belligerent parties at times in order to reach populations affected by the fighting. In 1998, a group of Namibians from the Caprivi region fled to Botswana following violent clashes with government forces, after the group had allegedly called for secession of the region. The group applied for asylum in Botswana on grounds of political persecution, but the Namibian government demanded their extradition to face charges of treason. The regional office of the UNHCR was then asked to intervene in order to resolve the situation (*Africa Confidential*, 1999). Similarly, the UNHCR office in northern Kenya facilitated an agreement in 1997 between Oromo refugees and local communities after conflicts over livestock had led to fighting and loss of life. In other words, an organization such as the UNHCR must address certain types of conflict in order to fulfil its mandate. Thus, training in conflict management skills enhances the capacity of humanitarian bodies to perform their mandated functions and allows them to develop appropriate strategies for conflict situations that they regularly encounter in the execution of their primary humanitarian duties in complex and volatile environments.

Conclusion

The above has highlighted the close relationship between human rights and conflict management. Human rights are relevant in the generation, manifestation, resolution and prevention of violent conflict, and must therefore be taken into account throughout the whole conflict management process. Failure to recognize the human rights dimension of conflict is likely to impact negatively on conflict management efforts since the analysis used to determine an intervention strategy is flawed. At the same time, conflict management can contribute to endeavours to assert and realize rights in various ways. Approaches and techniques from the conflict management field – for crisis intervention, negotiation, mediation, joint problem-solving and communication – assist human rights actors in effectively working towards the protection and promotion of human rights. Thus, there is a clear need for dialogue between the fields of human rights and conflict management in order to gain understanding of the objectives, guiding principles and methods in both fields, and to strengthen efforts towards peace, justice and reconciliation. Closely related is the need to pursue an integrated approach in dealing with conflicts involving rights issues; these cannot be addressed solely from either a human rights or a conflict management perspective.

Fortunately, actors in Africa have become more and more aware of this important relationship. Since the beginning of the 1990s, human rights concerns have increasingly been considered in peacemaking and peace-building processes, as is reflected in a stronger emphasis on power-sharing arrangements, institution-building, socio-economic reform, and mechanisms to uphold accountability. Moreover, bodies or institutions that once considered themselves as firmly lodged in either the human rights or the conflict resolution field, are now exploring how insights and practices from the other field can strengthen their efforts. Conflict resolution organizations embark on human rights programmes to integrate a human rights dimension in their interventions and capacity-building with governmental, inter-governmental, non-governmental and community-based actors; national human rights institutions are examining alternative dispute resolution for addressing rights-related disputes in constructive, non-adversarial ways.

Of course, the reality of Africa today indicates that we have nowhere near reached the end of this journey and that much remains to be done. Building the capacity of those working towards human rights and the constructive management of conflict is an important priority in this regard, as is developing legitimate, inclusive systems of governance, strong independent judiciaries, vibrant civil societies and equitable distributions of resources and opportunities. Acknowledging the relationship between human rights and conflict management highlights the road ahead when it comes to pursuing peace with justice in Africa.

Notes

1. This chapter is an edited version of a paper originally published as 'Bridging the Divide: Exploring the Relationship between Human Rights and Conflict Management', Track Two, Occasional Paper, vol 11, no 1 (March 2002), Centre for Conflict Resolution, available at http://ccrweb.ccr.uct.ac.za. See this paper for a detailed discussion of the differences between the human rights and conflict management field and an assessment of whether the fields are contradictory or complementary. The term 'conflict management' is used here in recognition of the fact that conflict is a natural, normal and inevitable part of life. As such, it is a social and political phenomenon that cannot be eliminated, prevented or resolved; the challenge is to manage it in a constructive way that allows for the expression of discord and legitimate struggle without violence. One can, however, speak of the resolution and prevention of a

specific conflict regarding a particular issue or set of issues. A distinction is thus made here between the management of conflict as a general phenomenon and the resolution of a specific conflict. Another distinction made here is between 'normal' conflict and 'violent' or 'destructive' conflict. Considering conflict as natural and inevitable means that conflict in itself is not inherently violent; this chapter will thus refer to 'violent' or 'destructive' conflict if direct, physical violence is involved.

2. On Sierra Leone, see Human Rights Watch (1999) and International Crisis Group (1999).

3. Two notes of caution are warranted when considering interventions such as peacekeeping and peace-enforcement in order to put an end to abuses resulting from violent conflict. First, the introduction of peacekeeping forces should not *automatically* be seen as the appropriate mechanism for intervention in these scenarios, as in some instances such forces may incite panic and trigger further killings rather than reducing bloodshed. This fear, for example, lay at the basis of the reluctance of Ahmedou Ould Abdallah, the Secretary-General's Special Representative to Burundi, to endorse the sending of foreign troops to Burundi when this was discussed in the UN Security Council in February 1996. In his view, foreign troops were perceived in Rwanda and Burundi as favouring one ethnic group over another, and their arrival could hence provoke massacres (Abdallah, as quoted in Leatherman et al, 1999, p128). Second, it presupposes that peacekeeping forces refrain from committing human rights violations, which has not always been the case in practice. For example, serious abuses have been attributed to the regional intervention force of the Economic Community of West African States in Sierra Leone, ECOMOG (International Crisis Group, 1999; 'UN Monitors Accuse Sierra Leone Peacekeepers of Killings', *New York Times*, 12 February 1999).

4. The term *structural violence* refers to situations where injustice, repression and exploitation are built into the fundamental structures in society and where individuals or groups are damaged by differential access to social resources built into a social system (Galtung, 1969, pp168–70). Yarn (1999, pp347–8) defines positive peace as a situation where states or non-state groups continually engage in the non-violent, constructive management of their differences with the goal of mutually satisfying relations. Yarn also argues that the notion is closely linked to 'security' (lack of threats of violence or civil disorder and stable relations among stable societies) and 'justice' (the stability is fair, equitable and cognizant of fundamental human rights).

5. It must be acknowledged that human needs theory has been criticized in the conflict management field. The criticism relates to, among other things, the 'testability' of basic human needs (their existence cannot be proven). It has also been questioned whether needs are truly universal and fundamental in the sense of not changing over time and in different contexts; and whether a needs hierarchy exists. For critical commentaries on needs theory, see for example Mitchell (1990); Roy (1990).

6. Constitutional Court of South Africa, judgement in *Grootboom* case, CT 11/00 – as quoted in Chaskalson (2000b). The nexus between rights and needs has been criticized by some. Manji (1998) argues that the struggle for

rights and justice in Africa became transformed and demobilized in post-colonial states as it was increasingly subsumed in the pursuit of 'development' by the new nationalist leadership. The focus on development in newly independent states (with its emphasis on attending to the 'basic needs' of the population) replaced the earlier popular mobilization for accountability, democracy and justice. He asserts that this has led to the depoliticization of poverty, which was no longer seen as a consequence of unjust and illegitimate structures of governance, but as something politically neutral that simply warrants technical expertise to help people cope with impoverishment. This justifies even less political pluralism and popular participation in public affairs. Manji also questions the concept of needs, arguing that they imply a degree of dependency and portray people as 'victims' of lack of development or as 'beneficiaries' of aid, rather than as active social and political agents. In this chapter, I use the concept of needs as related to security, welfare, freedom and identity, thus locating them in the political, social, economic and cultural domain.

7. This Carnegie distinction was adopted by the UN Secretary-General in his report on the prevention of armed conflict (Annan, 2001). Operational prevention entails actions that can be employed when violence is imminent and includes diplomatic interventions, fact-finding missions, preventive deployment of military and civil contingents.

8. It is perhaps no coincidence that in both cases, non-governmental actors took the lead in the mediation. They are less inclined to utilize power-brokerage for the simple reason that they do not have power or coercion at their disposal in the way state bodies or intergovernmental institutions do. Their 'power' resides more in their relationships with the parties, their credibility and moral standing. Consequently, they may be more geared to a confidence-building approach to mediation. For a discussion of the role of civil society organizations in conflict prevention, see Parlevliet (2001).

9. See Hayner, 1994; Bronkhorst, 1995; Roht-Arriaza, 1995; Kritz, 1995; Baehr, 1996; McAdam, 1997; Mendez, 1997; Hayner, 2001.

10. See Parlevliet (1998) for a more detailed discussion of the background, operations, merits and flaws of the South African Truth and Reconciliation Commission.

11. Utterwulghe is the Director of the Centre for Common Ground, Angola.

References

Africa Confidential (1999) Vol 40, no 1 (8 January) of the fortnightly bulletin

Amoo, S and Odendaal, A (2002) 'The Political Management of Ethnic Conflict in Africa: A Human Needs Approach', *Track Two*, vol 11, no 4 (October)

Anderson, M B (1996) 'Humanitarian NGOs in Conflict Intervention', in C Crocker and F Hampson (eds) *Managing Global Chaos: Sources of and Responses to International Conflict*, United States Institute of Peace, Washington, DC, pp342–54

Annan, K (2001) *Prevention of Armed Conflict. Report of the Secretary-General to the United Nations General Assembly and Security Council*, Document A/55/985-S/2001/574, United Nations, New York

Arnold, K (1998) 'Exploring the Relationship Between Human Rights and Conflict Resolution', *FORUM* (National Institute for Dispute Resolution), pp1–5

Assefa, H (2002) *Mediation in the Sudan Civil War of 1955–72*, paper prepared for seminar 'International Mediation in African Civil Wars', Centre for Conflict Resolution, Cape Town, 29–31 July

Azar, E (1986) 'Protracted International Conflicts: Ten Propositions', in E Azar and J Burton, *International Conflict Resolution: Theory and Practice*, Wheatsheaf, Sussex, pp28–39

Baehr, P (1996) 'Afrekenen met het verleden', in C Brants, C Kelk and M Moerings (eds) *Er is Meer: Opstellen over Mensenrechten in Internationaal en Nationaal Perspectief*, Deventer, Gouda Quint,: pp37–50.

Bloomfield, D, Nupen, C and Harris, P (1998) 'Negotiation Processes', in Harris and Reilly (eds) *Democracy and Deep-Rooted Conflict: Options for Negotiators*, International Institute for Democracy and Electoral Assistance (IDEA), Stockholm, pp59–120

Bronkhorst, D (1995) *Truth and Reconciliation: Obstacles and Opportunities for Human Rights*, Amnesty International, Dutch Section, Amsterdam

Burton, J (1990) *Conflict: Resolution and Prevention*, Macmillan, London

Carnegie Commission for the Prevention of Deadly Conflict (1997) *Preventing Deadly Conflict: Final Report*, Washington, DC

Chaskalson, A (2000a) 'The Third Bram Fischer Lecture. Human Dignity as a Foundational Value of Our Constitutional Order', *South African Journal of Human Rights*, vol 16, pp193–205, originally delivered on 18 May at an event hosted by the Legal Resources Centre in the Johannesburg Civic Theatre

Chaskalson, A (2000b) *Equality as a Founding Value of the South African Constitution*, Oliver Schreiner Memorial Lecture, 22 February 2001, Johannesburg, available through the Constitutional Court of South Africa

Claude, R and Weston, B (eds) (1992) *Human Rights in the World Community. Issues and Action*, 2nd edn, University of Pennsylvania Press, Philadelphia

Douglas, O and Ola, D (1999) 'Defending Nature, Protecting Human Dignity – Conflicts in the Niger Delta', in European Platform for Conflict Prevention and Transformation, *Searching for Peace in Africa: An Overview of Conflict Prevention and Management Activities*, Utrecht, pp334–8

Eide, A (1995) *Peaceful and Constructive Resolution of Situations Involving Minorities*, United Nations University, Tokyo

Galtung, J (1969) 'Violence, Peace, and Peace Research', *Journal of Peace Research*, vol. 6, pp167–91

Galtung, J and Wirak, A (1977) 'Human Needs and Human Rights: A Theoretical Approach', *Bulletin of Peace Proposals*, vol 8, pp251–8

Gurr, T (1970) *Why Men Rebel*, Princeton University Press, Princeton, NJ

Harris, P and Reilly, B (eds) (1998) *Democracy and Deep-Rooted Conflict: Options for Negotiators*, International Institute for Democracy and Electoral Assistance (IDEA), Stockholm

Hayner, P (1994) 'Fifteen Truth Commissions – 1974 to 1994: A Comparative Study', *Human Rights Quarterly*, vol 16, pp597–655

Hayner, P (2001) *Unspeakable Truths. Confronting State Terror and Atrocity*, Routledge, New York and London

Honwana, J and Lalá, A (2002) *The Case of Mozambique*, paper prepared for seminar 'International Mediation in African Civil Wars', Centre for Conflict Resolution, Cape Town, 29–31 July

Human Rights Watch (1999) *Sierra Leone. Getting Away with Murder, Mutilation, Rape*, July (HRW: A1103/6/99) Washington, DC

International Crisis Group (1999) *Sierra Leone: A New Beginning? Situation Analysis*, 18 March

Kadende-Kaiser, R M and Kaiser, P (1997) 'Modern Folklore, Identity and Political Change In Burundi', *African Studies Review*, vol 40, no 3, pp29–54

Kritz, N (ed) (1995) *Transitional Justice: How Emerging Democracies Reckon with Former Regimes, Vol. I–III*, United States Institute of Peace, Washington, DC

Kunder, J (1998) *How Can Human Rights Be Better Integrated into Peace Processes?* Conference Report, Fund for Peace, Washington, DC

Lamb, G (2000) 'Putting Belligerents in Context: The Cases of Namibia and Angola', in S Chesterman (ed) *Civilians in War*, Lynne Rienner, CO, pp25–43

Leatherman, J, DeMars, W, Gaffney, P and Väyrynen, R (1999) *Breaking Cycles of Violence: Conflict Prevention in Intrastate Crises*, Kumarian Press, Connecticut

Lederach, J (1997) *Building Peace: Sustainable Reconciliation in Divided Societies*, United States Institute of Peace, Washington, DC

Lederach, J (1999) 'Justpeace – the Challenge of the 21st Century,' in European Centre for Conflict Prevention, *People Building Peace. 35 Inspiring Stories from Around the World*, European Centre for Conflict Prevention, Utrecht, pp27–36

McAdam, J (ed) (1997) *Transitional Justice and the Rule of Law in New Democracies*, University of Notre Dame Press, Notre Dame

Manji, F (1998) 'Depoliticization of Poverty', in *Development and Rights Development in Practice Reader*, Oxfam UK, Oxford, pp12–33

Manji, F and O'Coill, C (2002) 'The Missionary Position: NGOs and Development in Africa', *International Affairs*, vol 78, no 3, pp567–83

Max-Neef, M (1991) *Human Scale Development: Conception, Application and Further Reflections*, Apex Press, New York and London

Mendez, J (1997) 'Accountability for Past Abuses', *Human Rights Quarterly*, vol 19, pp255–82

Miall, H, Ramsbotham, O and Woodhouse, T (1999) *Contemporary Conflict Resolution*, Polity Press, Cambridge

Mitchell, C (1990) 'Necessitous Man and Conflict Resolution: More Basic Questions about Basic Human Needs Theory', in J Burton (ed) *Conflict: Human Needs Theory*, St Martin's Press, New York, pp149–76

Mthembu-Salter, G (2002) 'A Peace Agreement without Peace: The Case of Burundi', paper prepared for seminar *International Mediation in African Civil Wars*, Centre for Conflict Resolution, Cape Town, 29–31 July 2002 (publication forthcoming)

Nathan, L (1999) '"When Push Comes to Shove", The Failure of International Mediation in African Civil Wars', Occasional Paper, *Track Two*, vol 8, no 2, November, pp1–27

Nathan, L (2000) '"The Four Horsemen of the Apocalypse": The Structural Causes of Conflict in Africa', *Peace & Change*, vol 25, no 2, April, pp188–207

Nherere, P and Ansah-Koi, K (1990) 'Human Rights and Conflict Resolution', in G Lindgren, P Wallensteen and K Nordquist, *Issues in Third World Conflict Resolution*, Department of Peace and Conflict Research, Uppsala University, Uppsala, pp3–42

Nyaba, P (2002) 'State of Disunity', *BBC Focus on Africa*, vol 13, no 4 (October–December), pp28–9

OAU (Organisation of African Unity) (1981) *African Charter on Human and Peoples' Rights*, available at www1.umn.edu/humanrts/instree/z1afchar.htm

Osaghae, E (1996) 'Human Rights and Ethnic Conflict Management: The Case of Nigeria', *Journal of Peace Research*, vol 33, no 2, pp171–88

Parlevliet, M (1998) 'Between Facilitator and Advocate: The South African Truth and Reconciliation Commission', *Forum,* National Institute for Dispute Resolution, December, no 36, pp6–15

Parlevliet, M (2001) 'Conflict Prevention in Africa: A Matter of Containment or Change? The Role of Civil Society in Preventing Deadly Conflict in Africa', in E Sidiropoulos (ed) *A Continent Apart. Kosovo, Africa and Humanitarian Intervention*, South African Institute of International Affairs, Johannesburg, pp61–88

Parlevliet, M (2002) 'Bridging the Divide: Exploring the Relationship between Human Rights and Conflict Management,' *Track Two* Occasional Paper, vol 11, no 1 (March), pp8–43

Republic of Mauritius (2000) *Matadeen Report: Commission of Inquiry into the Riots and Disturbances that Occurred in Different Areas in Mauritius after 21 February 1999,* Republic of Mauritius, Port Louis

Roht-Arriaza, N (ed) (1995) *Impunity and Human Rights in International Law and Practice*, Oxford University Press, New York and Oxford

Roy, R (1990) 'Social Conflicts and Needs Theories: Some Observations', in J Burton (ed) *Conflict: Human Needs Theory*, St Martin's Press, New York, pp125–48

Rubin, B and Asuni, J (1999) 'Transition, a New Opportunity to Transform Nigeria's Numerous Conflicts', in European Platform for Conflict Prevention and Transformation, *Searching for Peace in Africa: An Overview of Conflict Prevention and Management Activities*, European Platform for Conflict Prevention and Transformation, Utrecht, pp332–3

Sisk, T (1997) 'Mediating Africa's Civil Conflicts: A User's Guide', in G M Sørbø and P Vale (eds) *Out of Conflict: From War to Peace in Africa*, Nordiska Afrikainstitutet, Uppsala, pp179–98

Taban, A (2002) 'Northern Divisions', *BBC Focus on Africa*, vol 13, no 4 (October–December), p30

UNGA (United Nations General Assembly) (1948) *Universal Declaration of Human Rights*, GA Res. 217 A (III), 3(1) UN GAOR Res. 71, UN Doc A/810 (1948)

Utterwulghe, S (2001) *This Also Happens in Angola: Internally Displaced People Resolving Conflicts* (unpublished paper)

van der Stoel, M (1999) 'The Role of the OSCE High Commissioner in Conflict Prevention', in A Crocker, F O Hampson and P Aall (eds) *Herding Cats: Multiparty Mediation in a Complex World*, United States Institute of Peace, Washington, DC, pp67–83

Webb, K (1986) 'Structural Violence and the Definition of Conflict', in L Pauling, E Laszlo and J Youl Yoo, *World Encyclopedia of Peace, Vol 2*, Pergamon Press, Oxford, New York, Beijing, Frankfurt, pp431–4

Wisner, B (1988) *Power and Need in Africa: Basic Human Needs and Development Policy*, Earthscan, London

Yarn, D (1999) *Dictionary of Conflict Resolution*, Jossey-Bass, San Francisco

Part III
CONCLUSIONS

13
Agenda for Action

Abdi Samatar, Ben Wisner, Rutendo Chitiga, Thomas A. Smucker, Edna Wangui and Camilla Toulmin

Introduction

When Julius Nyerere stepped down as Tanzania's first president, he took up – among many duties of an elder statesman – the chair of the South–South Commission. In preface to its report, he wrote:

> *[T]he South does not know the South – what goes on in its countries, what are the ideas of its peoples, what its potential is, and the manner in which South–South co-operation can widen development options for all countries. Instead each country is forced to make its own mistakes, without being able to learn from the experience of their successes.* (Nyerere, 1990, pv)

The same may be said of Africa, as part of the global South. Although many African leaders meet and interact with African intellectuals, still the lessons of mistakes and successes are not widely enough known on the continent. The 'new map' of Africa must sketch out these mistakes and successes clearly. In this volume we have begun the task of gathering up that experience of the African past and present marked by mistakes and successes. Historian Basil Davidson began his book, *The African Genius* (Davidson, 1969), with a story about Ananse, 'the great spider of venerable memory' who gathered all of the world's wisdom into a gourd and tried to keep it safe for future generations high in a tree. He failed. The gourd fell and broke, and wisdom was scattered far and wide. We draw a lesson from this allegory. We are acutely aware of the dangers and pitfalls of trying to gather all wisdom about Africa into a single book, and generalize about a broad, hugely diverse continent, whether in social, historical, political or ecological terms. Nevertheless, even a crude sketch map with a few landmarks makes a good beginning.

Looking back over the chapters in this book, we think it is possible to identify some of those landmarks. *Towards a New Map of Africa* tells us that we must, for a start, negotiate considerable difficulties.

The difficult dozen: Major challenges to sustainable human development in Africa

The major challenges to sustainable human development in Africa are:

- peripheral position within the global economy, principally as a zone of extraction;
- abundant natural resources not used to satisfy ordinary African needs and aspirations;
- heavy and growing disease burden – HIV/AIDS and malaria (especially affecting women and children) and tuberculosis;
- low investment in health care and education, with particularly poor achievement in women's health care and education of girls;
- lack of political accountability and accumulation of political and economic power by a small elite;
- persistence of regional, ethnic and gender dimensions to socio-economic inequality;
- regional tensions and perceived injustices leading to violence;
- rapid, unplanned and under-served urbanization, with increasing numbers of street children;
- land degradation, destruction of coastal wetlands, biodiversity erosion and deforestation;
- high vulnerability to negative impacts of global climate change;
- devaluation of local knowledge, traditional culture and language;
- loss of skilled people through out-migration.

Towards a New Map of Africa also has landmarks that reveal strengths and resources. These are the strengths and resources evoked in a poem written by Angola's first president, Augustinho Neto, when he was a young man. The protagonist redefines 'hope' as activism and 'the hope of life recovered' (Neto, 1984, p27):

> *My mother*
> *(oh black mothers whose children have departed)*
> *you taught me to wait and to hope*
> *as you have done through disastrous hours*
>
> *But in me*
> *life has killed that mysterious hope*
>
> *I wait no more*
> *it is I who am awaited*
>
> *Hope is ourselves*
> *your children*
> *traveling toward a faith that feeds life ...*

The durable dozen: Major strengths and resources Africa can draw on

The major strengths and resources Africa can draw on are:

- complex and resilient agro-pastoral systems, rich in indigenous knowledge;
- rich biotic water and land resources, fisheries and mineral wealth;
- very diverse linguistic and cultural assets;
- long history of resistance to slave trading, colonialism and the struggle for independence;
- continued strength of collective structures at family and village levels;
- vigorous entrepreneurship in the 'informal' sector;
- increasingly militant and effective civil society;
- vocal and active women and women's groups;
- solidarity among African governments and with other LDCs in relation to global processes, such as the WTO;
- new initiatives in intra-African regional economic cooperation;
- new impetus behind African peacemaking and peacekeeping roles;
- growing democratization, though patchy.

In developing an Agenda for Action, we have simply asked what various groups of stakeholders can do in the face of such a list of challenges when such strengths and resources are available. This is what we came up with. Each bulleted action is highly condensed and simplified. Much in the preceding chapters helps to flesh this out. We are only sketching out the roughest of 'new maps', a starting point for human exploration.

This agenda may seem to some too radical and to others not radical enough. Clearly we have here a diverse set of ideas that encompass the pragmatic, adaptive, reformist and more radical. We are not concerned here with bringing all items into ideological alignment. On the other hand, we are broadly critical of past and present policy toward Africa. We view the larger issues of Africa's economic and political marginality and the advance of a neo-liberal order in Africa as placing severe constraints on the more pragmatic aspects of the agenda. This is particularly true of those actions to be carried out by civil society and NGOs where, in general, we see some of the most hopeful and exciting innovations taking place.

What African Civil Society can Do

The concept of civil society has gained much popularity among social scientists and development professionals in the past twenty years. Yet, the meaning of the concept is vague and in need of clearer definition. The concept has been used to include NGOs and many other organizations, some of which have been created as a result of pressure from the outside. In our discussion, we will separate NGOs from CSOs and only include as civil society organizations (CSOs) those that have developed through local initiative. These may be both formal and informal community groups, women's groups, artisan networks and groups focused on environmental justice. NGOs are treated separately below. We also include environmental and political movements that engage with major environment-development issues. Like NGOs, the scale of operation for CSOs ranges from local (grassroots environmental organizations and local women's groups) to national and international (trade unions and professional associations). In the rest of this section, we discuss the role of CSOs in addressing issues of marginalization, gender inequity and funding for grassroots development projects.

Addressing marginalization issues

Environmental marginalization

CSOs can play an important role in addressing major livelihood issues in the most marginalized areas of society. This would include issues of environmental, economic and political marginalization. CSO efforts to address environmental marginalization have been widely recognized in the international arena. Women's and youth movements all over the continent are actively engaged in a variety of conservation efforts in their immediate localities. One such is the Green Belt Movement in Kenya, headed by Nobel Peace Prize laureate Professor Wangari Mathaai. Activities of this movement and others like it show clearly the need to understand poverty and environmental degradation in the broader context of Africa's position in the world economy. Grassroots CSOs have unique opportunities to design and implement multipronged solutions to environmental degradation, which also improve people's economic situation.

Economic marginalization

Associations of merchants, artisans, farmers, and other producers can provide their members with benefits of scale economies, in purchasing inputs and marketing produce. They can also build on each others' skills in the production and marketing of their goods. Artisan and farmer associations have been particularly successful in promoting economic diversification using local resources. For example, beekeepers and wood carvers of Cameroon forests have found profitable outlets for their products because they formed strong producer cooperatives. Horizontal linkages can also be formed between two or more different kinds of CSOs, providing members with opportunities to form complementary and symbiotic relationships. These relations are especially important when CSOs negotiate for resource use and resource access, particularly land and credit facilities.

Political marginalization

CSOs have the potential to play a significant role in increasing popular participation in the political process. This potential has been largely overlooked by institutions working towards multiparty democracy. Through CSO consciousness-raising activities, political participation should help people to understand the linkages between government policies and their own livelihoods. CSOs can play a leading role in promoting civil liberties. In Zimbabwe, for example, the cause of the rural poor, the landless, women and the illiterate are represented by different grass roots groups. ZALA (the Zimbabwean Adult Learners Association), which operates in remote areas, has started a literacy campaign that is ultimately geared to prepare non-literate farmers for the 2005 elections.

Through more active participation in the political process, civil society can do much to put greater pressure on states to use their scarce ministerial budgets wisely. CSOs can demand accountability and transparency from local and national governments by finding ways to hold their political representatives accountable to the people. Ultimately, African civil society must also recognize the limits of the state in the present neo-liberal order and develop an alternative political vision that can provide a more democratic shape to African politics and a fairer place for Africa in the world.

CSOs also play a role in helping youth find their place in the new map of Africa. According to the Commission for Africa's consultation document, 'Africa's shifting demography means that half of the population on the continent are now under the age of fifteen.' Such youth represents tomorrow's leaders, in whom investment needs to be made. CSOs can help fill the gaps in current educational systems, for example by starting clubs that teach youth to be proud of their African heritage and culture. The curriculum has to be geared at instilling national values in the children, teaching self-reliance and encouraging alternative visions of development. Wisner and Toulmin (this volume) discuss the proliferation of Western popular culture in Africa through music, magazines, movies and even the news. CSOs could help interest children and youth in their own past, their own philosophical and religious ideas.

Addressing gender issues

Economic inequality

CSOs can play an important role in reducing social and economic inequality between men and women. CSOs involved in trying to mainstream gender into a range of government policies can review the implications for women of current allocations in national and local government budgets. Uganda's Forum for Women in Democracy is an example of a CSO that has gender budgeting at the heart of its agenda. Gender-balanced budgets would address the needs of men, women, boys and girls equally. As has happened in Kenya and Uganda, CSOs can provide governments with constructive criticisms on existing budget allocations and offer more gender-balanced budgets as alternatives.

Gender violence

CSOs can also contribute to gender equity by explicitly addressing issues of gender and child violence. CSOs in the legal profession can educate the general public on the legal rights of men, women, boys and girls and when necessary provide affordable legal representation for victims of domestic violence. CSOs can educate the general public on the serious psychological trauma resulting from violence against women and children, and help train health and law enforcement officials on effective ways of dealing with domestic violence. CSOs also need to highlight for national governments and the international community the extent of violence against women and children in war and post-war situations. Tragically, there are millions of African women currently living in such situations. CSOs can take an active role in reducing gender-based violence in post-war situations once the majority of aid institutions have left the scene.

Reproductive rights

CSOs can help persuade public and private institutions of the need to provide reproductive health services for women and girls, and institutionalize women's rights to safe and affordable contraception. They can also speak out against female genital mutilation, childhood and forced marriages, rape and unsafe abortions among other things.

Making peace and managing conflict

CSOs can build upon local and indigenous methods for managing conflict. They can also play a role in rebuilding societies after civil wars through providing support for elections, by demanding accountability from the government and ensuring that all eligible voters have a chance to vote. CSOs in places like Sierra Leone, Angola and the Democratic Republic of Congo have played a role in highlighting human rights abuses and in the re-establishment of legitimate, democratic governments.

Seeking funding for grassroots projects

Grassroots CSOs face a dilemma when it comes to seeking funds for their activities. They can seek to form vertical linkages with national or regional CSOs, NGOs, bilateral agencies or government ministries. Vertical linkages allow for exchange of knowledge between the community and higher-level structures. The link between external agents and grassroots organizations can also provide opportunities for the integration of technical know-how and indigenous knowledge in the development process. However, vertical linkages present grassroots organizations with the risk of being coopted by those that fund them and they therefore need to exercise caution when selecting from whom they take money. Support may depend on following the donor's approach, which may hold few opportunities for participation by grassroots organizations. While initial funding may be necessary, local groups should focus on developing initiatives that can be sustained by them in the long term. Local development, whether rural or urban, will not occur unless it can be sustained through local initiative.

When looking at CSOs we often neglect the role that the African diaspora can play. There needs to be greater collaboration between local CSOs and the diaspora. For example, African organizations based in the diaspora can also play a role in nation building, through providing financial and technological support and human resources. The World Bank estimates that remittances sent by migrants account for at least US$100,000 million every year, 60 per cent of which flow into developing countries, a figure which is twice the size of current aid flows. Such resource flows partly counteract the adverse impacts on African social, political and economic development generated by the 'brain drain'.

What African Governments can Do

In the economic sphere

Increasing regional cooperation

All agree that greater regional cooperation is essential for Africa, but how best to move towards that goal? Although regional associations such as SADC and IGAD are important political fora, they have not functioned as serious political-economic organizations. Rather than seek the establishment of new fora, it might be more productive to strengthen existing tangible initiatives that exploit the complementarities between countries. Examples include projects such as:

- range management, environmental protection and livestock development in neighbouring areas of Somalia and Ethiopia;
- fishery stocks management and development of processing linking Namibia and Angola;
- watershed protection along major rivers, such as the Niger basin in West Africa;
- conservation and management of cross-border wildlife areas, as with South African, Mozambique and Zimbabwe.

Other facets of cooperation which governments could help facilitate but not organize or control are a network of eminent civic leaders from the region's respective countries. In the case of the Horn of Africa, such a group will have a regional forum that will discuss peace and conflict issues within and between countries. One of the network's objectives could be to act as a respected and independent critic of governance, seeking transparency in the management of public affairs.

Vigorously supporting the development of national scientific and technological capacity

Dr Calestous Juma, who chairs the Task Force on Science, Technology and Innovation of the UN Millennium Project commissioned by Kofi Annan, 'fear[s] that without a strong focus on technological and institutional innovation, taking into account key social issues, Africa's map will remain the same or degenerate'.[1] The Task Force's report was launched on 17 January 2005 and it makes clear that, among other things, implementation of the Millennium Development Goals will depend on rapidly developing Africa's own scientific and technological capacity.[2]

Developing Pan-African strategies for success in the global economy

African economies have for long been heavily engaged in world trade, but with limited benefits for economic growth and diversification. Governments across the continent need to work together to build support for trade adjustment assistance and northern reciprocity in reducing trade barriers. A good example is the joint position adopted by many African countries for reducing rich country farm subsidies, within the WTO negotiations. Equally, their solidarity on the West African cotton case has been a valuable asset in strengthening their case at global level.

In the political sphere

Developing regional peacemaking within the AU and UN

As Parlevliet argues in Chapter 12, it is very important that peacemaking and advocacy of human rights be closely linked, and offer a range of actions to be taken forward, from national policy measures to specific training courses. Over the past few years there has been positive experience with regional peacekeeping in Lesotho, Burundi and Liberia. African states need to build on this experience and develop their capacity to address the great challenges presented by cases such as Darfur.

Regulating production and trade of small arms/light weapons

Africa is still awash with small arms, despite commitments such as the Bamako Convention signed in 2000 by African Ministers of State,[3] and regional initiatives of SADC and ECOWAS. The unchecked flood of weapons makes it much more difficult to negotiate and maintain peace. African governments can do much more to enforce the regulation of the production and trade in small arms and light weapons by continuing to develop and implement regional agreements.

Promoting international initiatives on transparency.

National governments can support attempts by civil society and NGOs to raise awareness and develop means of addressing persistent problems of corruption, such as carried out by Transparency International (TI)[4] and Extractive Industries Transparency Initiative (EITI).[5] Transparency International's annual corruption survey in 2004 found that one in three people in Cameroon, Kenya and Nigeria had paid a bribe that year. Among institutions in Africa, political parties and police forces ranked as the most corrupt in this survey (Hodess and Wolkers, 2004). However, there may be clear limits to government interest in support for organizations that by their very nature and mandate are seeking to investigate and expose wrongdoing in government and amongst the elite. The harassment and intimidation of advocacy groups, as well as the press and other media, bear tribute to the unwillingness of many governments to have their weaknesses exposed.

Ensure civil society voices will be heard within NEPAD

Numerous non-governmental organizations and trade unions in Africa have expressed concern with the emphasis given by the New Plan for African Development (NEPAD) on top-down, 'business-as-usual' investment in mega-projects and privatized infrastructure development.[6] Governments participating in NEPAD could provide better channels thorough which ordinary people can have a role in shaping the priorities and activities of NEPAD.

Exercising state power through law to transform inherited institutions

Many institutions in Africa are still inherited from the colonial period. These perpetuate the external dependence and poverty of people and continent. The transformation of such institutions requires an understanding of the potential and limits of the law. To date, many governments have not generally demonstrated an interest in transforming the institutions of government, and have rather preferred to strengthen central government control, rather than opening up to more democratic processes. A greater grasp of legislative theory, methodology and techniques would help bring about a questioning of how institutions might better be transformed to achieve the ends espoused (see Chapter 7 by Seidman and Seidman).

In the political ecological sphere

Addressing land tenure issues

The resolution of many outstanding land-tenure and land-access issues will remain central to addressing long-term questions of social and economic justice, conflict resolution and land degradation. For example, Kenya made an important step in this direction through the work of the Commission of Inquiry into the Land Law Systems of Kenya and the mobilization of civil society that has accompanied the release of its inquiry into land tenure problems in Kenya in 2003. The Commission held public fora throughout the country at which citizens provided testimony on the problems of current land policy and administration of land law. In addition to documenting the problem of illegal allocation of public land to political elites, the Commission's work has sparked a broader national discussion on inequitable access to land and the insecurity of customary tenure. The ensuing debates have called into question some of the assumptions of Kenya's long-standing land policy and the need to redress historical grievances. It also suggested new land policies that might curb ongoing abuses and be more supportive of rural livelihoods and customary institutions, particularly for communities in arid and semi-arid areas whose resource rights have long been tenuous.

Supporting community-based conservation initiatives

The last twenty years have seen many promising innovations in community-based conservation, including Communal Areas Management Programme for Indigenous Resources (CAMPFIRE) in Zimbabwe and many local initiatives throughout Africa ranging from forest management to ecotourism. An overarching lesson of the last three decades is that communities are likely to resist restrictions on resource use that have been imposed in a top-down fashion. On the other hand, many successes have been achieved where there is sharing of the economic benefits of wildlife conservation and tourism with local people, and where local environmental knowledge and needs are incorporated into the conservation objectives. Considerable challenges exist among communities bordering national parks that have historically had little participation in the setting of conservation objectives. Such communities bear the burden of wildlife conservation plans drawn up by government and conservationists, but share very little in the substantial tourism revenues of several African countries. Policy reform is urgently needed to reject the 'fortress national park' approach to conservation and take into account the grievances and needs of neighbouring communities.

What Donors and International Organizations can Do

In the economic sphere

Committing to cutting farm and export subsidies and providing support for trade adjustment assistance

There are still huge obstacles to African participation in world trade. One of the biggest is the more than US$300,000 million in rich country farm subsidies paid to farmers in the US, the European Union and Japan. These subsidies make it impossible for African farmers to compete in Northern markets and those of third countries. Additionally, the large agricultural surplus generated by subsidies is frequently dumped at very low prices on African markets, making it even more difficult for farmers to sell their produce. Donors and international organizations can follow the lead of the World Commission on Social Dimension of Globalization, in its blueprint for *A Fair Globalization: Creating Opportunities for All* (ILO, 2004); it calls for an 'urgent rethink' of current policies and institutions of global governance.

Considering linkages between relief, rehabilitation and development

A minimum threshold of 10 per cent of all humanitarian assistance provided for victims of natural hazards in Africa should be set aside for investment in mitigation and preparedness for the next extreme natural event. There is a huge gap between the work done by donor countries and international organizations in response to relief following a major disaster and work focused on prevention and risk reduction. This gap should be closed.[7]

Supporting national and civil society efforts to promote sustainable livelihoods

All donor country members of the OECD's Development Assistance Committee (DAC) should increase their aid to Africa so that a minimum of 0.7 per cent of gross national product is provided for development assistance. Firm deadlines for meeting this target are needed by mid-2005. In the meantime, the scale and approach to development assistance must be re-assessed so that Africa has the US$20–25,000 million per year channelled in the most appropriate way to meet the Millennium Development Goals (see below) (Oxfam, 2005, p11).

Taking seriously implementation of the MDGs in Africa

The Millennium Development Goals will not be achieved unless more effort is made to prioritize this task. The multiple frameworks imposed on recipient governments havè not helped, although there is now growing harmonization between donor approaches and common adoption of the PRSP as the single national level framework within which to operate. Recent reviews and progress reports summarized by Oxfam towards the end of 2004 show that intermediate targets for the MDGs are not being met in most parts of Africa. Each year US$20–25,000 million is needed to meet the eight goals of halving the number of people in Africa living on less than US$1 a day by 2015, as well as tackling maternal and child health, increased access to education, gender equality, HIV/AIDS, water and sanitation, and environmental sustainability. MDG8, which aims to promote a 'global partnership' between all nations in favour of a fairer and more sustainable planet is far adrift in the current global context. When looking at the apparent size of the funding needs, Oxfam reminds us that annual global spending on cosmetics and perfume is US$33,000 million (Oxfam, 2005, pp13–14, 41).

Listening more carefully to Pan-African, South–South and North–South solidarity in arguments on debt relief

The Oxfam report rightly recommends that all members of the OECD's Development Assistance Committee should cancel 100 per cent of the debt of the poorest countries, many of which are in Africa, whether bilateral or debts owed to the World Bank and African Development Bank. These enormous debts constrain the ability of African countries to achieve the MDGs. (Oxfam, 2005, p11)

In the political sphere

Supporting regional peacemaking and peacekeeping within the AU and UN

The year 2004 saw a major increase in the willingness of African governments to engage in collective peacemaking and peacekeeping operations, but the political and financial support of many donors lags behind. The situation in Darfur highlights the impasse that the world community has encountered, and the mix of political and economic interests which constrain collective action to protect the weak. Political support is as important as financial and logistical assistance.

*Supporting economic as well as political democracy through civil
society organizations such as trade unions and farmers unions*

The International Labor Organisation (ILO) holds a 'tripartite' mandate to work
together with workers, employers and UN member governments. This approach
should provide further encouragement to other international organizations, UN
agencies and donors, to work directly with trade unions, farmers' unions and
other organs of civil society as well as with governments. In the body of our book
we have documented some progress in the sphere of political democracy in Africa.
However, this advance means little in the long run if not accompanied by economic democracy. While gross inequities persist in access to incomes and assets
for the majority of Africa's population, political stability, peace and human development will remain in question.

Developing enforceable codes of conduct for foreign corporations

'Mega-projects' are much discussed in Africa as a way of boosting economic growth.
Large-scale mines, smelters, petroleum exploration, oil pipelines and hydroelectric projects are seen as the new way forward. Governments are actively promoting
increased foreign investment in forestry, large-scale farming and livestock production. This kind of investment, together with infrastructure development, is at the
heart of the New Plan for African Development (NEPAD). Yet such investment
is negotiated behind closed doors, with no oversight by civil society groups of the
terms. Thus, there are serious fears of Africa's land and other assets being sold off
to outside interests, especially those involved in privatization of public utilities
such as water and electricity, as well as those in energy, mining and agri-business.
At a minimum, corporations that win contracts to implement these mega-projects
should agree to a specific African code of conduct as regards the social and environmental impacts of their activities. Donor countries and international organizations, especially the IFIs, can help to encourage the development of such a code,
as a means to ensure scrutiny and its enforcement.

In the political ecological sphere

Strengthening participatory agricultural research

Local farmers represent an invaluable asset for achieving future agricultural growth.
Experience shows the unparalleled success obtained when researchers work closely
with farmers on practical problems they face, whether within the CGIAR system
or at national or local level. A focus on vulnerability and poverty would help assist
in the targeting of research and services, especially towards the small-scale farm
sector. Some greater emphasis is being given now to small-scale, resource-poor
farmers than in the past, but it is still not enough. Women's food production is
largely ignored, and urban agriculture is little understood, because it does not fit
accepted categories. Debate among donors and international organizations is currently at a crossroads, with some donors arguing for the transformation of the
smallholder sector, and support for large-scale commercial farms. Others remain
convinced that smallholders will remain for the foreseeable future at the heart of

economic growth and prospects for poverty reduction in most parts of Africa. Donors need to listen to voices from the African farming community in drawing up their own 'strategies', instead of designing these in the North based on economic theory rather than local priorities.

Recognizing that Africa's biodiversity and land-preservation efforts will depend fundamentally on inclusive and sustainable social systems

Some donors and international organizations still have a mistaken, overly simple view that poverty causes land degradation and loss of biodiversity. By not acknowledging and addressing the root causes of rural poverty and marginality, they end up 'blaming the victims'. Reality is more complex reality. The politics of exclusion and the vulnerability of social and economic systems undermine the sustainability of rural livelihoods. The institutional vacuum over local rights and responsibilities within which many rural people make their living, forces some people to over-exploit local ecosystems. This, in turn, eventually puts yet further stress on these rural households. At the same time, outsiders exploit the power vacuum to grab land, forest resources and wildlife in an unsustainable fashion.

Fully funding the UN Global Fund to combat HIV/AIDS, tuberculosis and malaria

By December 2004 the Global Fund had disbursed US$3000 million in 128 countries (www.theglobalfund.org/en/). This sounds impressive only until one realizes the size of the HIV/AIDS challenge and the fact that in 2001 Secretary General Kofi Annan estimated that the HIV/AIDS effort would need an additional US$7–10,000 million a year.[8] Chapter 4 of this volume makes it clear that HIV/AIDS is not only ruining the lives of individual Africans today, but also dangerously undermining the basis of food production and social stability for future generations. Full financing of the Global Fund is absolutely necessary, along with support to the necessary health delivery systems.

What Non-governmental Organizations can Do

Understanding the limitations of the 'NGO revolution'

Earlier we made the distinction between NGOs often created and funded by outside support and 'civil society organizations (CSOs) that have developed through local initiative, including both formal and informal community groups, women's groups, artisan networks, and groups focused on environmental justice'. While this distinction is somewhat fuzzy, it is important. There has been a proliferation of foreign-funded NGOs in Africa, seen by some as a panacea for development. This view has now been tempered by an understanding of the limitations of NGO-led development in addressing the major issues of underdevelopment facing African societies. The proliferation of NGOs in the past 20 years has stemmed from an international agenda of neo-liberal reform that sought alternatives to support for African states. Underlying these trends was an over-optimistic view that sustainable development would spring from the combination of a diverse civil society and 'free' markets. But as can be seen, NGOs alone cannot address the basic needs left unfulfilled in the wake of the debt crisis and the decline of state power and authority. There seems little doubt that NGOs will continue to play a central role in the delivery of overseas development assistance in Africa; however, NGOs must assess their limitations and also their complicity in reproducing a neo-liberal approach in Africa that has failed. There is also scepticism of some international NGOs and their willingness to establish true partnerships with African NGOs and civil society groups.

Helping create and maintain democratic spaces within African countries

The growing influence of human rights organizations and those advocating the rights of women has been an important aspect of recent democratization movements in many African countries. A major challenge for NGOs promoting human rights will be to expand their impact geographically, to cover rural areas and conflict zones where access is difficult. Decentralization and local governance reforms are occurring in many parts of Africa, with risks of abuse of power by these newly established governance structures. Working to strengthen local civil society as a check and balance on such structures will be important. The protection of the political rights of ethnic minorities, women and the marginalized is particularly important in rural areas, where questions of access to land and other resources are often based on social status and ethnic origin. Promoting inclusive systems of management and decision-making as regards rural assets needs support. NGOs can and should work with broader civil society to address issues of transparency both in government and in terms of their own structures and decision-making.

Developing innovative processes of conflict resolution in issues of resource tenure in both rural and urban areas

Given the declining role in many areas of traditional institutions as mediators of conflicts over water and land rights, NGOs can support representative, grassroots organizations in their efforts to resolve emerging conflicts. In rural areas, developing processes of community collaboration in conflict resolution can assist in preempting the political manipulation of overlapping claims to resources and settlement rights. In urban and peri-urban areas, the growth of informal settlements and the development of complex tenure and rental arrangements have resulted in greatly increased social tension which local governments have had little success in defusing. In both cases, NGOs can play a valuable role in helping to strengthen local processes for conflict mediation, with the assistance of local community organizations.

Addressing major environmental challenges facing African societies

In their close interactions with donors, NGOs can articulate the crucial connection between political economy and resource use that is central to support of more sustainable livelihoods. In many instances, African and international NGOs have worked successfully with community organizations on pilot projects that develop appropriate institutions and technologies to check land degradation and biodiversity loss. NGOs can and should mobilize indigenous knowledge and community partnerships for protection of land, natural resources and biodiversity. NGOs can partner with communities to support community-based wildlife conservation as a means of sharing in the revenues of wildlife tourism. In this regard, NGOs can help mediate the demands generated by the top-down approach of some conservationist groups and the priorities of local communities.

Expanding participation and deepening partnerships to address accountability

As advocates of a diverse and democratic civil society, NGOs must work towards greater transparency in setting development objectives and implementing interventions. Too often, the line between 'community participation' and manipulation has blurred, as the rhetoric is invoked to justify incorporation of local people into predetermined plans. NGOs must keep in mind their essential role as a bridge between those driving the development agenda and the communities for whom 'development' is designed but whose voices are too often forgotten. The issue of participation strikes at the heart of NGO accountability. One means of improving NGO accountability is to deepen cooperative relationships between international, national and local NGOs. Such partnerships require that local NGOs and their constituents take full part in deciding what will be done and the allocation of funds between purposes. Mechanisms for grassroots organizations to participate more actively in the monitoring and evaluation of development interventions are crucial.

Advocating reform of development assistance and North–South relations

Many NGOs have been forced to come to terms with the broader political context within which they work and inherent limitations on the NGO sector in delivering broad-based development. International NGOs have potential to contribute to policy change in rich countries, by mobilizing the population of wealthy societies to demand change, such as was seen with the work of Jubilee 2000 and debt relief. Additionally, through recognition of the limits to their own work, NGOs can articulate alternative visions of state–civil society relations that would emphasize the importance of a re-invigorated public life. NGOs also should advocate for reform of IFIs and development priorities in the North, based on discussion and consultation with partners in the South.

Conclusion

The year 2005 provides many openings for global policy to move forward with this ambitious agenda. The report of the Blair Commission for Africa in March and meeting of G8 nations in July combine with the mid-term review of the MDGs in September to bring about an alignment of events which should focus the world's attention on the urgent need for change. The heart-rending loss of human life and damage to livelihoods following the tsunami in Asia offer a sober lesson in the terrifying power of natural forces, which should remind us of our vulnerability and need to husband the gifts and resources of our planet. The response to suffering following the tsunami also shows us the innate decency, solidarity and care which humans can show to their fellows. On this we must build.

Notes

1. Personal communication with Calestous Juma, Harvard University, 20 December 2004.
2. On the Task Force, see www.cid.harvard.edu/cidtech/TF-Advance.pdf
3. Bamako Declaration (www.smallarmssurvey.org/source_documents/Regional %20fora/Africa/Bamakodecl011201.pdf).
4. Transparency International (www.transparency.org/)
5. Extractive Industries Transparency Initiative (www2.dfid.gov.uk/pubs/files/ eitidraftreporttransparency.pdf)
6. For example, Patrick Bond, '"Nepad, No Thanks" Say African Progressives', ZNET, www.aidc.org.za, 20 June 2002.
7. Hopefully the World Conference on Disaster Reduction in Kobe, January 2005, will address this gap and begin measures to bridge it. See WCDR (www. unisdr.org/wcdr/).
8. United Nations, 'Secretary-General Proposes Global Fund for Fight against HIV/AIDS and Other Infectious Diseases at African Leaders Summit' (www. un.org/News/Press/docs/2001/SGSM7779R1.doc.htm).

References

Davidson, B (1969) *The African Genius: An Introduction to African Social and Cultural History,* Atlantic Monthly Press, Boston

Hodess, R and Wolkers, M (2004) *Report on the Transparency International Global Corruption Barometer*, Transparency International, Berlin

International Labor Organization (ILO) (2004) *A Fair Globalization: Report of the World Commission on Social Dimension of Globalization,* ILO, Geneva, www. ilo.org/public/english/fairglobalization/

Neto, A (1984) 'Farewell to the Moment of Parting', in G Moore and U Beier (eds) *The Penguin Book of Modern African Poetry*, 3rd edn, Penguin, Hammonds- worth, Middlesex, p27

Nyerere, J (1990) 'Chairman's Preface', in *The Challenge to the South: Report of the South–South Commission*, ppv–viii, Oxford University Press, Oxford
Oxfam (2005) *Paying the Price: Why Rich Countries Must Invest Now in a War on Poverty*, Oxfam UK, Oxford, www.oxfam.org.uk/what_we_do/issues/debt_aid/mdgs_price.htm

Index